MACROECONOMICS

THE MEASUREMENT, ANALYSIS, AND CONTROL
OF AGGREGATE ECONOMIC ACTIVITY

THOMAS F. DERNBURG
PROFESSOR OF ECONOMICS
OBERLIN COLLEGE

DUNCAN M. McDOUGALL
PROFESSOR OF ECONOMICS
UNIVERSITY OF KANSAS

THIRD EDITION

McGRAW-HILL BOOK COMPANY
New York   St. Louis   San Francisco   Toronto   London   Sydney

PREFACE

We are exceedingly pleased that the reception accorded the earlier versions of our book has warranted the preparation of a third edition. Our purpose remains unchanged. First, we attempt in these pages to provide a fairly comprehensive survey of the subject matter normally included in a first course in macroeconomics. Second, we attempt to span the gap between the elementary and the advanced level, providing a framework and a point of departure for more advanced study.

Extensive changes are in evidence throughout the book. Really drastic revision has, however, been confined to the chapters on fiscal policy and international finance of Part 2 and to Part 4 in its entirety. The algebraic analysis of taxation and expenditures of Chapter 6 has been replaced by numerical examples and graphic illustrations to emphasize the common sense of the equilibrium solutions and the logic behind the calculations rather than their algebraic aspects. However, the algebraic models may be found in a new appendix. Chapter 14, on international aspects of macroeconomic theory, has been redone with the aim of emphasizing the continuing importance for domestic stabilization policy of balance of payments considerations and of showing how different forms of international monetary organization influence the effectiveness of monetary and fiscal policies.

The policy discussion of Part 4 has been completely revamped and reorganized, and a new perspective has been introduced. Policy is viewed as the process of so manipulating a set of instruments as to attain a set of predetermined targets. Chapter 19 sets forth the general principles of economic policy. Chapter 20 is devoted to a discussion of the targets and includes such problems as the measurement of the GNP gap, the manpower gap, and the price level. Chapter 21 is devoted to the instruments of economic policy. Is the impact of the budget expansionary? What is the appropriate way to minimize the effect of lags in monetary and fiscal policy? Should monetary policy be conducted on a discretionary basis or should "rules" replace "authority?"

Since the appearance of the first edition in 1959 we have benefited from the comments and suggestions of innumerable teachers and students, and it is now practically impossible to single out particular persons for special thanks. We must, however, express our appreciation to Professors Case Sprenkle of the University of Illinois, W. H. Locke Anderson of the University of Michigan, and Arvid M. Zarley of the University of Kansas for their careful reviews and helpful suggestions. Judith Dukler Dernburg read the manuscript and was instrumental in effecting many improvements. Vera Alferio and Leigh Riker provided invaluable clerical assistance. Of course, no one but ourselves is to blame for any errors or shortcomings.

Thomas F. Dernburg
Duncan M. McDougall

CONTENTS

1
THE
FRAMEWORK

1–1 INTRODUCTION

The businessman faced with incessant demands for higher wages to "keep up with the cost of living," the retired person trying to live on a fixed income, and the housewife who struggles to put food on the family dinner table in a period of rising food prices need hardly be told that inflation is a serious economic problem. Similarly, the worker who is laid off from an assembly line, the graduating senior who despite his qualifications has difficulty finding a job, and the businessman who finds profits shrinking and orders declining are all too familiar with the evils of recession. Economic ailments affect us all. Allowed to become too severe, they create great physical and psychological hardships and strain the sinews of the social and political structure. The purpose of this book is to promote a better understanding of these ailments, to provide the tools with which to analyze them, and to suggest possible cures.

It may seem curious that an understanding of what is perfectly obvious to those suffering the consequences of an economic disease should require the complex analysis of economic theory. But personal experience is often a poor guide to generalization. For example, the housewife may feel that inflation is reducing her family's well-being when in fact the rise in the cost of living which she observes results from a temporary phenomenon such as a crop failure. While such a crop failure is an unfortunate occurrence, it would be quite erroneous to suppose that the increase in food prices is the result of a general inflationary trend. Similarly, the graduating senior may not find work in his chosen field because consumers no longer choose to buy the product manufactured by the particular industry in which he attempts to gain employment. A similar fate may befall a production worker. When automobile sales lag because of increasing public concern with automobile safety, it is not an indication that the economy as a whole is in a slump. It is, rather, an indication that resources should be shifted from the production of bigger and faster cars to the production of safer cars and to the construction of safer highways. Such shifts in resources are the very essence of economic progress. If we commit the fatal error of bringing policy weapons designed to affect the sum total of economic activity to bear on the particular problem of a declining industry, under the illusion that general economic activity is less than it should be, we not only obstruct the shift of resources but, as we shall soon see, give rise to inflationary pressures as well. Conversely, we may be so paralyzed by the fear of inflation that we are prevented from taking effective antirecessionary action.

It is clear then that a method of obtaining an overall picture of economic activity is essential. This is the function of the national income accounts which we shall study in the first part of the book. In addition, we need a theoretical superstructure within which to analyze this picture. On the theoretical level, it is again true that what is valid in a specific instance may not be true of the sum total. If we could simply analyze the operation of a single firm and assume that the economy as a whole is really only one big firm, there would be no need to study macroeconomics or to develop theories of macroeconomic behavior. But macroeconomics is set apart as a separate discipline with its own rules because aggregate economic behavior does not correspond to the summation of individual activities. We may, for example, find that if wages, and therefore production costs, fall, a single firm will find it profitable to expand output and therefore hire more workers. For the economy as a whole it does not follow that a wage cut will lead to a general expansion of employment. Similarly, one individual, in borrowing from another, borrows a claim over real resources which he must pay back at some future date by giving up a claim over real resources. The community as a whole cannot borrow real resources from itself in one year and pay these resources back in another year. Yet despite this obvious truth the fiction persists that World War II remains to be paid for and that the economic product of future generations is mortgaged to the follies of the past.[1] Similarly, if one individual plans to increase his saving by consuming less, he will, given the necessary self-control, be successful. But if the community as a whole makes such an effort, the reduction in total consumption expenditures may lead to such a shrinkage in income that aggregate saving may be less than before.

Many similar examples could be given. Most of these cases, which seem paradoxical at first, stem from the fact that what is true for an individual is true only if other things remain equal. This is an assumption which is legitimate in microeconomic (partial equilibrium) analysis. But in macroeconomics this so-called *ceteris paribus* assumption is not justified; therefore an entirely different approach to the analysis of macroeconomic problems must be developed.

1–2 THE RECORD OF THE AMERICAN ECONOMY

In order to introduce some of the concepts which will be used throughout the book, the remainder of this orientation chapter is devoted to a statistical description of the behavior of the American economy since 1929. Although the precise definition and measurement of the descriptive aggregates are complicated matters, for the time being little harm is done if we content ourselves with a fairly loose notion of the meanings of the terms.

A concept which has become practically a household word is that of gross national product, or GNP. GNP is the market value of the newly produced goods and services that are not resold in any form during the year. The national income statistician divides the goods produced into those purchased by consumers, by government, by business (investment goods), and by foreigners. In addition to producers' durable equipment and new construction, investment goods include net changes in inventory, i.e., changes in the stock of unsold production. Net changes in

---

[1] There is some truth to the notion that our grandchildren will be less well off because of our extravagances. Insofar as the resources that went into the war effort could have been utilized to build up the productive capacity of the nation, the product of the future will be reduced.

inventory are included because GNP is a measure of production. Failure to include changes in the stock of unsold goods would make GNP a measure of sales rather than production. Similarly, because foreigners sell goods to us, GNP includes what is called the "net export of goods and services," i.e., total exports minus total imports. This is a necessary inclusion because sales to Americans include goods produced in foreign countries. The value of these goods must be subtracted if a measure of American production only is to be derived.

It is useful to divide the purchases of the various sectors into different groups according to commodity classes. Personal consumption expenditures, for example, may be divided into expenditures on non-durable goods (food, clothing, etc.), services (medical attention, laundry, etc.), and durable goods (TV sets, automobiles, etc.). Gross private domestic investment may similarly be broken down into purchases of producers' durable equipment (machines, trucks, etc.), construction activity (both residential and nonresidential), and the change in inventories. Finally, government purchases of goods and services may be broken down into expenditures by the Federal government and by state and local governments.

From the economist's point of view, a more interesting though more difficult-to-estimate statistic than gross national product is net national product (NNP). Since a portion of annual output is used to replace equipment that has been worn out during the production of the year's output, a deduction known as "capital consumption allowance" (familiarly known as "depreciation") is made from GNP. The resulting figure is net national product, which may be defined as the net creation of new goods and services resulting from the productive activity of the economy during the accounting period.

Any economy produces a great variety of goods and services during a year. The diversity of output dictates that some common measure be used to aggregate it. The most convenient measure is the price of the various things produced. Thus, GNP and its components are given in terms of dollars, the sum of the market values of the goods and services produced. The difficulty with using prices is that they fluctuate over time. Because of this, an increase in GNP need not reflect an increase

Figure 1–1   Gross national product and the expenditure components, 1929–1965 (1958 prices) (Source: The data for this chart and the succeeding charts in this chapter were obtained from U.S. Department of Commerce, Survey of Current Business, July, 1966, U.S. Government Printing Office, Washington, 1966.)

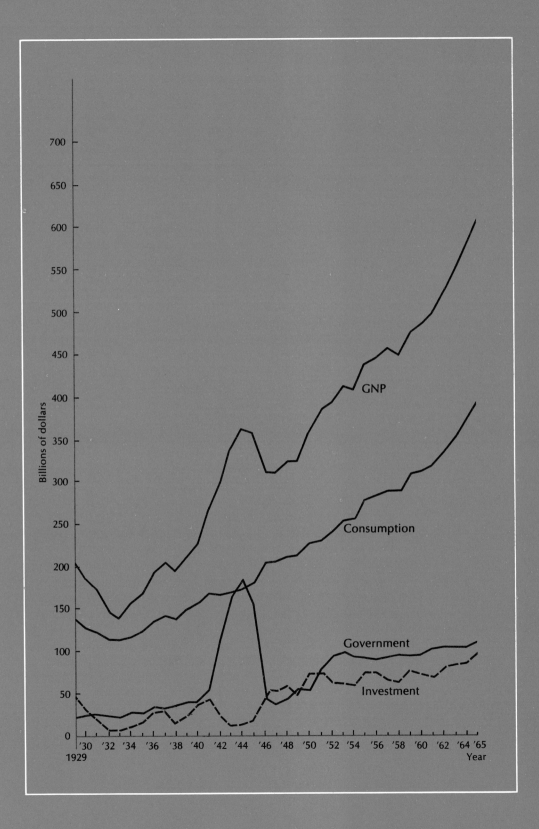

in output; it can, instead, result from an increase in prices. To avoid this difficulty, a measure of "real" GNP and its components is frequently given by valuing the output of any year in terms of the prices of a selected year. Therefore changes in GNP measured in terms of the prices of a given year reflect only changes in the physical output of the economy.

What do these "real" magnitudes look like over a period of time? In Figure 1–1 we plot GNP and its major components—personal consumption expenditures, gross private domestic investment, and government expenditures on goods and services—all in terms of 1958 prices. The net export of goods and services, which fluctuates rather closely about zero, is omitted. The first thing to notice about GNP is that it grows. During 1929, regarded as a full-employment year, GNP was $203.6 billion. By 1961 it had grown to $614.4 billion. The second thing to notice is that this growth process does not take place steadily. Thus GNP declined after 1929, falling to a low of $141.5 billion in 1933, the worst year of the great depression. Recovery began in 1934 and continued until 1938, when a mild slump again took place. With the coming of the war, GNP jumped precipitously and continued to climb until 1946, when a drastic reduction in government expenditures produced a decline. The following decade was marked by fairly even advance. A mild slump developed in 1949 but was soon followed by recovery and, subsequently, the Korean War. Another moderate slump occurred in 1953 from which the economy recovered with little difficulty. Between 1957 and 1964, however, the economy was once more beset by stagnation. The year 1958 was the worst of the postwar years, and the subsequent recovery was disappointing. It was not until the effects of the tax cut of 1964 were felt that GNP returned to full-employment levels.

Notice next how the components of GNP behave over time. Consumption expenditures rise as GNP rises and generally (but not always) fall as GNP falls. In terms of relative changes, consumption is far more stable than GNP, which in turn reflects the extreme volatility of investment expenditures.

Although it is true that consumption expenditures as a whole are fairly stable, the same cannot be said of all its components. The three components of aggregate consumption—durables, nondurables, and services—are plotted in Figure 1–2. Observe the remarkable stability of expenditures for consumer services over time. Expenditures on non-

Figure 1–2 Components of personal consumption expenditures, 1929–1965 (1958 prices) (Source: See Figure 1–1.)

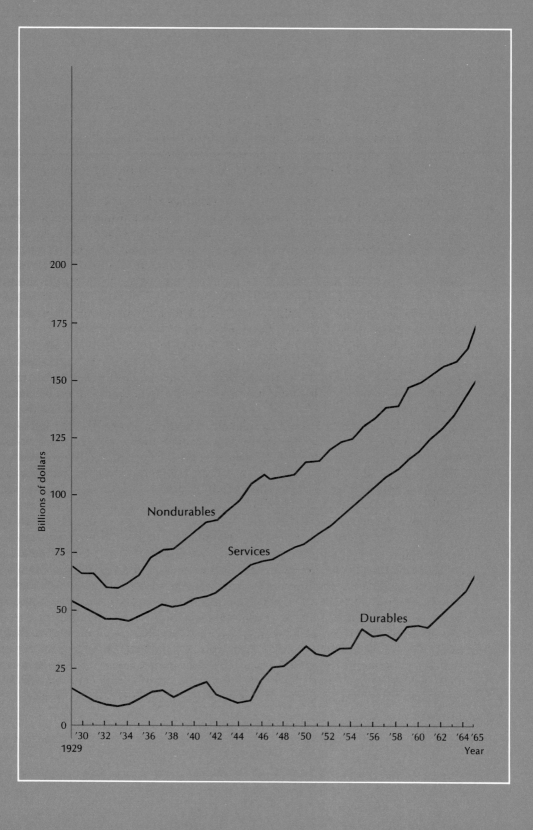

durables are similarly not subject to significant fluctuations. The same, however, is not true of durable goods expenditures. Since durables include postponable household items, a fall in family income is apt to cut into such expenditures to a greater degree than into nondurables and services, which tend instead to be unpostponable necessities. While, therefore, expenditures on nondurables fell by about 30 percent between 1929 and 1933, expenditures on durables fell by about 48 percent. Expenditures on services fell by only 15 percent. During the 1938 slump a more pronounced fluctuation is noticeable in durable goods than in the other components of consumption expenditures. The war years were, of course, exceptions. The manufacture of major durable consumer goods all but ceased. We therefore observe a decline from 1941 on, and a rapid upsurge in the immediate postwar period when consumers attempted to replace their obsolete and worn-out automobiles, refrigerators, and other durable goods.

Notice the upsurge in durable goods buying in 1950. That was the Korean War period, at which time the war scare apparently gave rise to the expectation of durable goods shortages, with the result that consumers rushed out to stock up on household appliances and other durable goods.

Figure 1–1 suggests that the explanation of fluctuations in GNP is largely a matter of explaining fluctuation in investment expenditures. When investment falls, GNP falls; when investment rises, GNP rises. This is true for all periods except the war years, when investment spending was suppressed by direct control. GNP, however, rose sharply during the war years as a result of the vast increase in government expenditures.

It is interesting, though somewhat bewildering, to observe the movement of the components of investment expenditures over time. The components are plotted in Figure 1–3. New construction and the purchase of producers' durable equipment seem to move together fairly closely. During the 1929–1933 period both all but collapsed. The period, moreover, was marked by a considerable reduction in inventories. Again, during the slump of 1938 all components of investment expenditures fell off, though new construction was least affected. The principal change, as frequently happens, was a reduction in inventories. Again in 1947 inventories declined drastically, but in this case the decline was due to the reduction of stocks of war materials and the acceleration of

Figure 1–3 Components of gross private domestic investment, 1929–1965 (1958 prices) (Source: See Figure 1–1.)

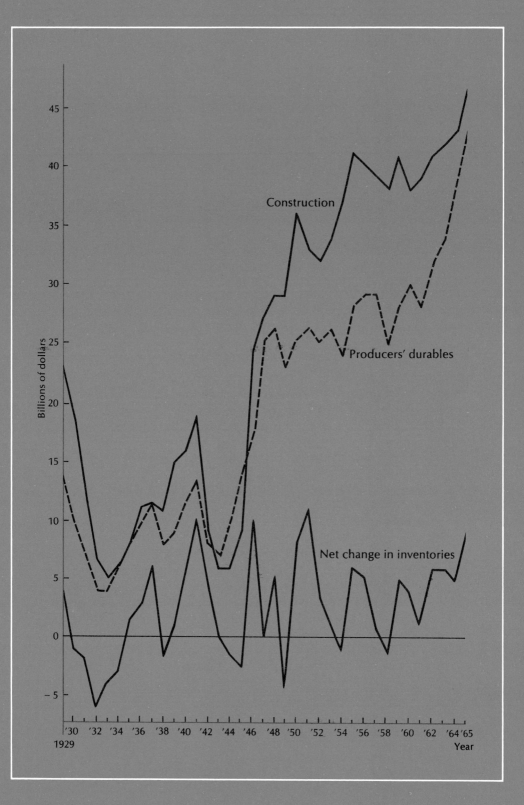

consumer purchases that took place immediately after the war. Subsequent recessions also showed a reduction in inventories.

A reduction of inventories is a typical manifestation of a recession. Such reductions, moreover, may be a key to the cumulative nature of business contraction and expansion. If entrepreneurs merely reduced their orders by the amount of the decline in sales, there would be no net change in inventories. But typically orders are reduced by more than this, which indicates that production and income payments will also decline by more than the initial fall in sales. This, in turn, causes a further reduction in sales.

During the postwar period new construction and producers' durable equipment expenditures advanced steadily until 1949, at which time the economy entered its first postwar decline. Recovery was, however, bolstered by a high level of consumer buying and by the coming of the Korean War. Until 1955 or 1956 construction and producers' durables expanded fairly evenly, but in 1958 both declined, and by 1961 producers' durables were only slightly above the level of 1957. In fact, investment expenditure as a whole was the same amount in 1961 as in 1957. This stagnation of investment continued into 1964, when an investment boom that has not yet abated began.

The so-called vast expansion of government during the 1930s seems, at first glance, to be a figment of the imagination of the more rabid anti-New Dealers. From a level of $22.0 billion in 1929, government purchases of goods and services rose to only $35.2 billion by 1939. Though the relative change is considerable, in absolute terms the increase might legitimately be termed a drop in the bucket. However, a closer look reveals that the increase was nearly all in the form of increases at the Federal level. In Figure 1–4 government purchases of goods and services are divided into Federal on the one hand and state and local on the other. From a low of $3.5 billion in 1929, spending by the Federal government rose throughout the decade of the 1930s to a 1939 level of $12.5 billion, at which time Federal spending was still less than spending by state and local governments. The big increase in Federal purchases, of course, came with the war, when they climbed to a 1944 peak of $165.4 billion. With the close of the war, Federal spending again fell to near prewar levels. But with the postwar foreign-aid programs, the Korean military buildup, the drain of the cold war, the space program, and conflict in Asia, Federal government purchases of goods and services continued to rise, reaching a 1966 level of $64.1 billion in real terms.

Figure 1–4 Components of government expenditures, 1929–1965 (1958 prices) (*Source: See Figure 1–1.*)

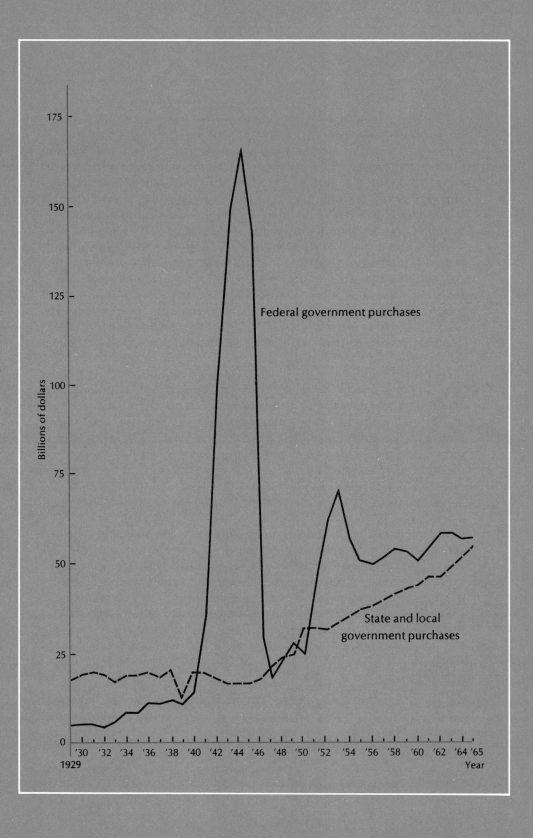

State and local spending remains among the most stable components of GNP. Between 1931 and 1933 state and local governments, behaving like most businesses, tightened their belts and, at a time when some felt they should be expanding activities reduced their expenditures. However, with the exception of this period and the contraction imposed by the war effort, state and local spending has been extremely stable, though rising at a rate that reflects the increases necessitated by population growth and the rising demand for state and local services.

Although it is impossible, at this early stage of the investigation, to answer a number of questions that are raised by even a superficial survey of the data, we can nevertheless begin to examine some of the fundamental changes that have taken place in the economy. One of the most interesting phenomena is the changing role of consumption. Notice in Figure 1–1 that the fall in GNP between 1929 and 1933 was accompanied by a fall in consumption expenditures. However, GNP fell in 1949, and again in 1958, and yet consumption expenditures continued to rise. Here, clearly, is a fundamental change which has taken place in the economy. To see how this has come about, let us introduce some additional national income concepts.

For each dollar spent by consumers, business, and the government, there must be a receipt of $1 of income by someone. This dollar will be reflected in an increase in wages, interest, rent, corporate profits, and the incomes of unincorporated enterprises. A portion of the gross receipts of business will be kept as depreciation, and a portion may be kept in the form of retained earnings. The sum of retained earnings and depreciation is called "gross business savings." The remainder, which is not retained by business, is then split between the public, which receives "disposable income," and the government, which receives "net taxes." While the government collects taxes, it also returns negative taxes, or "transfer payments." Such transfers include social security payments, unemployment insurance, and interest on the public debt.

In line with distinctions made in the last paragraph, we may look at the income pie as follows: Dividing the economy into a consuming sector, a business sector, and a government sector and ignoring foreign trade, we have:

	Receives	Spends
The consuming sector	Disposable income Y_d	Consumption C
The business sector	Retained earnings S_b	Net investment I_r
The government sector	Taxes net of transfers T	Purchases G
All sectors	Net national product NNP Depreciation D	Net national product NNP Depreciation D
	Gross national product GNP	Gross national product GNP

This table represents the model which will be used throughout the analysis in this book. Symbolically, we find that real NNP (which we shall agree to call Y) equals

$$Y = C + I_r + G \qquad (1-1)$$

and

$$Y = Y_d + S_b + T \qquad (1-2)$$

Since consumers may either spend their disposable income on consumption or save it, we may further write

$$Y = C + S_p + S_b + T \qquad (1-3)$$

where S_p stands for personal savings. Writing $S_p + S_b$ as S, where S stands for net private savings, and combining Eq. (1–3) with Eq. (1–1) yield the fundamental accounting identity

$$I_r + G = S + T \qquad (1-4)$$

or

$$I_r = S + (T - G) \qquad (1-5)$$

which indicates that the national income accountant must always find that net investment equals net private savings plus the government surplus.

In Figure 1–5, series relating to the disposition of income are plotted in current-price values. Note that GNP and NNP follow each other rather closely. Note also that consumption and disposable income, except for the war years, are fairly closely related. The notion that consumption is largely dependent on disposable income is one of the fundamental hypotheses of the theory of income determination. Observe finally that during the 1930s disposable income and NNP fluctuate together but that after World War II the correspondence is far less close. While NNP fell in 1949 below the 1948 level, and in 1954 below 1953, the same was not true of disposable income. In 1958, NNP rose by only $4 billion over the level of 1957, but disposable income rose by $10 billion. If disposable income now fluctuates less than NNP and there is a close relationship between disposable income and consumption, it follows that consumption now also fluctuates less than NNP. In both 1949 and 1954, when NNP fell below the level of the previous year, consumption expenditures actually increased. In 1958, when NNP rose by only $4 billion, consumption expenditure rose by $9 billion.

To what set of circumstances can this remarkable change be attributed? Notice that the chief item separating NNP from disposable income is net taxes. During the 1930s taxes remained fairly stable. But

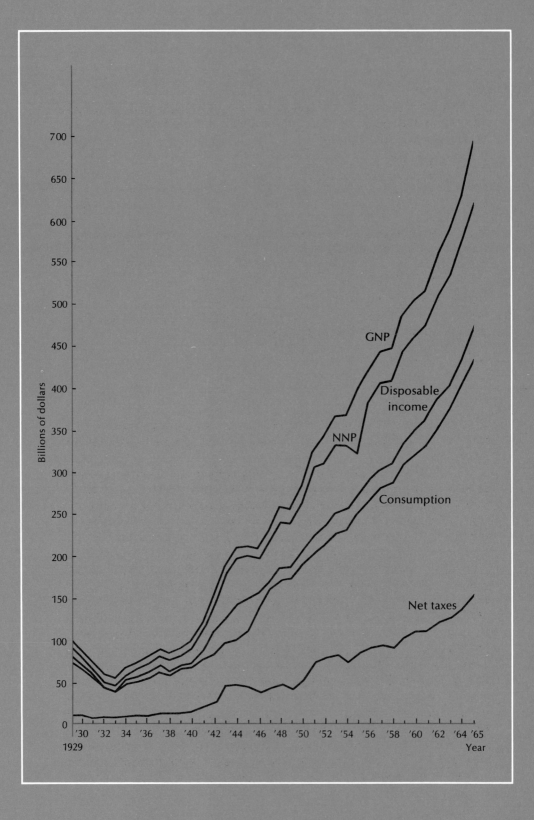

in the postwar period, instead of remaining stable, taxes seem to depend on the level of NNP. Because of wartime changes in tax laws, income taxes are now progressively graduated so that when NNP falls, income tax collections fall proportionately more than NNP. Corporate income taxes, moreover, are proportional to the level of corporate profits. Tax collections can therefore be seen to be quite closely linked to NNP. Add to this the fact that there are many ways in which negative taxes (transfer payments) automatically increase as NNP falls, and it becomes clear why disposable income, and therefore consumption, fluctuates less than NNP. Transfer payments and some government expenditures increase automatically because, as NNP falls and workers are laid off, unemployment compensations increase; when farm prices fall, price support expenditures increase via governmental purchases of farm commodities.

As a result of the progressive tax structure and the automatic increases in transfer payments resulting from falls in NNP, disposable income (and therefore consumption) tends to be stabilized, or, if you will, sheltered from fluctuations in NNP. These automatic or "built-in" stabilizers are a tremendous source of strength to the American economy since they protect the economy from the cumulative effects of a fall in one of the components of aggregate expenditure.

Retained earnings are the portion of NNP not received by the public as disposable income or by the government as taxes. Before 1950 these were so small that they have not been plotted in Figure 1–5. It is interesting to point out, however, that during the depression years retained earnings were typically negative. American business apparently made strong efforts to maintain dividend payments even when this involved dipping into accumulated surpluses of previous years.

1–3 DEFLATION AND INFLATION IN THE AMERICAN ECONOMY

Some idea of the tremendous waste resulting from depression can be gained from looking at Figure 1–1. A society that can more than double its output in the decade 1933–1943 must have had a vast amount of idle resources at its disposal at the beginning of the period. An even more remarkable conclusion can be drawn from an analysis of per capita real consumption. These data are plotted in Figure 1–6, where it appears that, despite the wartime suppression of consumption, the average

Figure 1–5 Disposition of income, 1929–1965
(current prices) (Source: See Figure 1–1.)

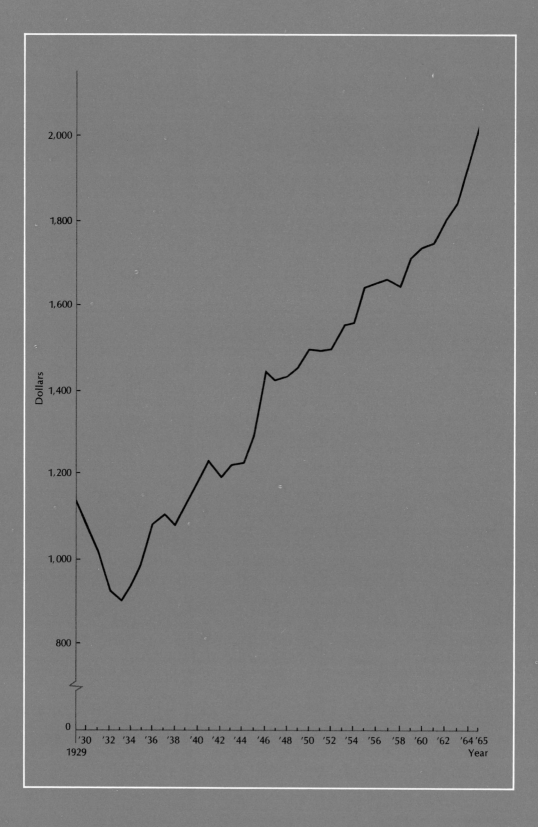

American family was better clothed and better fed during the war than prior to it. This is true despite the fact that in 1942, 1943, and 1944, respectively, 36, 45, and 47 percent of our total output went into the war effort.

Figure 1–7 records the movement of prices for the United States in conjunction with the movement of real and money GNP. The constant-price series of Figure 1–1 and the current-price GNP series of Figure 1–5 are included so that the behavior of the price index can be compared with changes in the level of economic activity.

From 1929 to 1933 both real and money GNP fell; but the fall in the price level during the same period indicates that real GNP fell by a greater percentage than money GNP. On the other hand, when the economy moved out of the trough of 1933, the percentage increase was greater in money GNP than in real GNP, as indicated by the rise in the price level.

Both real and money GNP marched steadily upward during the war years. The fantastic increase in real output which took place was made possible by the existence of a vast pool of unemployed resources at the start of the war and by the willingness of most Americans to work overtime to make up for the manpower drain to the armed forces. The fact that the price level did not increase as rapidly as might be expected was due to a combination of circumstances: the unemployed resources available at the start of the war; wartime price, credit, and production controls; and the willingness of consumers to save a larger proportion of their disposable income than they normally would.

After 1945 we observe a drastic fall in real GNP accompanied by an equally drastic rise in money GNP. The conversion from war to peacetime production resulted in a temporary fall in output. There was, however, no fall in the demand for goods and services. At a time when consumers were using wartime savings to replenish their stocks of worn and obsolete durable goods, Congress was busy dismembering the system of wartime price and wage controls. The consequence was a terrific inflationary push during the immediate postwar years; this is clearly shown by the movement of the price index.

The behavior of the three series since 1950 is extremely interesting.

Figure 1–6 Per capita consumption, 1929–1965 (1958 prices) (Source: For consumption expenditures, see Figure 1–1. Population refers to total population as of July 1 and is taken from U.S. Department of Commerce, Statistical Abstract of the United States, 1966, Table 2, U.S. Government Printing Office, Washington, 1966, p. 5.)

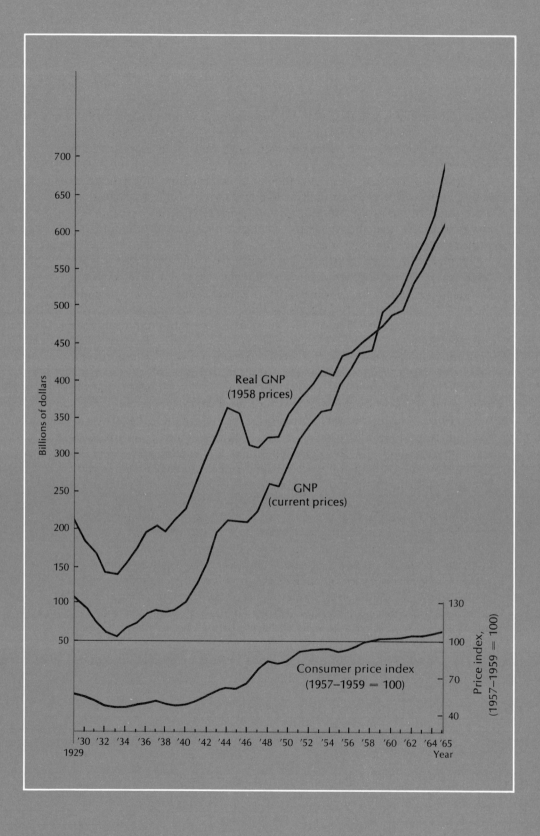

Notice their behavior in the recessions of 1954 and 1958. While there was a fall in the level of real GNP, the price index increased. When output and employment fall, one would expect, as in the 1930s, an accompanying fall in the price level. The behavior of the series in 1954 and 1958 probably can be attributed to three factors. First, there is developing in the American economy strong resistance to wage and price declines in the face of falling demand. Second, the increasing use of governmental policy tools to maintain full employment has probably accelerated the upward creep of the price level. Third, as will be shown in Chapter 20, the consumer price index is not necessarily a good indicator of the degree of inflation.

1–4 THE PROGRAM

This chapter has presented a picture of the United States economy since 1929 by using a simplified statistical framework. In Part 1 this framework will be analyzed more fully; in Part 2 the theory of the determination of net national product and its components will be studied. Part 3 is concerned with the determinants of the time path of both real and money net national product, and Part 4 is devoted to some of the policy problems of maintaining full employment, steady growth, and a stable price level.

Figure 1–7   Real and money gross national product and the consumer price index, 1929–1965 (Source: For GNP, see Figure 1–1. The price index is prepared by the U.S. Department of Labor and appears in U.S. Department of Commerce, Statistical Abstract of the United States, 1966, U.S. Government Printing Office, Washington, 1966, p. 356.)

ONE

THE MEASUREMENT OF ECONOMIC ACTIVITY

2

THE GROSS
NATIONAL
PRODUCT
ACCOUNT

2–1 INTRODUCTION

The national product account for the United States is presented by the
Department of Commerce in a form very similar to the income statement of an individual business enterprise. This is not surprising because
the two accounting statements are formulated for very similar reasons.
In fact, much of the statistical material used in constructing the national
product account is derived from business records. These business
records are taken as our starting point.

2–2   INCOME AND PRODUCTION STATEMENT FOR A HYPOTHETICAL FIRM

At the end of an accounting period a firm will have a summary statement drawn up from its accumulated records showing its progress over the period. This summary statement, which condenses the multitude of daily transactions into manageable form, is called the "income statement." It is a record of the flows of product and income involving the firm over a period of time.

Table 2–1 presents an example of such an income statement for a hypothetical business firm which we shall call the X Corporation. The right side of the income statement shows the source of all the receipts of the firm during the year. In this example the X Corporation is assumed to have sold $2 million worth of goods. Of this total, all but $125,000 was derived from the sale of goods to other business firms. The remaining $125,000 was derived from the sale of goods to other than business units, i.e., to nonbusiness sectors of the economy.

The left side of the income statement shows the allocation of these receipts among the various costs incurred in production and to profit. For the X Corporation these costs include, first, materials purchased from other firms of $780,000.[1] Second, they include the factor costs, wages and salaries of $800,000, social security contributions of the corporation of $25,000, and net interest payments by the corporation of

[1] This total will appear on the right side of the income statements of the other firms in the economy.

Table 2–1   Simplified income statement for the X Corporation for the period January 1, 1968 to December 31, 1968   (Thousands of dollars)

Expenditures			Receipts	
Purchases from other firms		$ 780	Sales to:	
Wages and salaries		800	Company A	$ 810
Social security contributions		25	Company B	240
Net interest		20	Company C	650
Depreciation		60	Company D	175
Indirect business taxes		30	Other sales	125
Corporate profits before tax		285		
Corporate profits tax	$148			
Dividends paid	100			
Undistributed profits	37			
Total current expenses		$2,000	Total current receipts	$2,000

$20,000.[1] The final element of cost is the nonfactor payments. The corporation charged $60,000 of its current receipts as an allowance for the depreciation or wear, tear, and obsolescence of its capital equipment. This depreciation allowance is the estimated reduction in the value of the capital equipment over the accounting period. Indirect taxes, such as excise and property taxes, added $30,000 to total cost.

The deduction of these costs from current receipts leaves a profit residual, the return to the factor entrepreneurship, of $285,000. From this profit residual the corporation paid profits tax of $148,000 and $100,000 to stockholders in the form of dividends. The remaining $37,000 represents retained earnings which may be used for working capital, future expansion, and the like.

The two sides of the income statement for the firm must balance. The right side gives the total receipts, and the left side shows the way these receipts were allocated among the various items of cost and to profit. Profit is the balancing item, which may be positive, negative, or zero depending upon the relative magnitudes of receipts and costs.

Although the income statements of the individual producing units within the economy are the basis of the national accounts, they do not give all the information necessary to construct the accounts. This is because an income statement does not show total production, but only current sales. A firm may sell more than it produces by drawing down its inventory of finished products, or it may sell less than it produces. Only when the physical change in inventory is zero does the right side of the income statement equal the value of current production.[2] Consequently the net change in inventories must be known if current production, as opposed to current sales, is to be determined.

In Table 2–2 the income statement of Table 2–1 has been revised into a production statement. The differences between the two tables result from the fact that a different bundle of goods is under consideration. The right side of Table 2–2 includes the value of an inventory increase, while the factor costs on the left side have been adjusted to include the production costs of the goods added to inventory. Because in this example the net change in inventory is positive, the value of total production as shown in Table 2–2 is greater than the total receipts shown in Table 2–1. Had the corporation sold more than it produced during the accounting period, the opposite would have been the case.

---

[1] This total is the net sum of interest paid minus interest received. Interest received is not treated as a current income receipt as is income derived from the sale of product.

[2] Inventories of other than finished goods are ignored in the problem.

**Table 2–2 Production statement for the X Corporation for the period
January 1, 1968 to December 31, 1968 (Thousands of dollars)**

Allocations			Receipts	
Purchases from other firms		$ 820	Sales to:	
Wages and salaries		846	Company A	$ 810
Social security contributions		27	Company B	240
Net interest		20	Company C	650
Depreciation		60	Company D	175
Indirect business taxes		30	Other sales	125
Corporate profits before tax		297	Inventory increase	100
Corporate profits tax	$155			
Dividends paid	100			
Undistributed profits	42			
Allocation of the total value of production				
		$2,100	Total value of production	$2,100

The right side of Table 2–2 would have shown a total value of production of less than $2 million. Costs and profit on the left side would also have been smaller, being only those amounts attributable to the actual current production.

Although the total value of production of the X Corporation was $2.1 million, the corporation's contribution to final output was somewhat less than this. The X Corporation purchased raw materials and partly finished goods from other firms, increased their value by further processing, and either sold the finished product to others or added it to inventory. The amount by which the corporation increased the value of the materials received from other firms is shown by the difference between the total value of production and the cost of materials purchased (intermediate product). This difference is called the "net value added" or the "value of final product." It is this net value added that is the contribution of the X Corporation to the final national product. To include the total value of production for each productive unit would be to count the value of some goods over and over again as they moved through the economy.

A simplified illustration will help to make this point clear. Take for example a loaf of bread purchased by a consumer. Assume that four productive units contributed to making and distributing the bread. Suppose that the value of the grain produced by the farmer was 5 cents, that the total value of production (for the loaf of bread) for the miller was 12 cents and for the baker was 20 cents, and that the grocer sold the loaf of bread for 25 cents. To add together the total values of production shown in the several production statements gives a total value of 62 cents. But the final consumer paid only 25 cents for the loaf of bread. The correct answer of 25 cents is derived by adding together the net value added of each productive unit. The net value added by the farmer (assuming he purchased no goods or materials from others) is 5 cents. The net value added by the miller is 7 cents (12 − 5). Similarly, the net value added for the baker is 8 cents, and for the grocer 5 cents. The sum of the net-value-added figures is 25 cents, or the cost of the loaf to the ultimate consumer. The 62-cent figure resulted from counting the 5 cents of value added by the farmer four times, the 7 cents of value added by the miller three times, the 8 cents of value added by the baker twice, and the 5 cents of value added by the grocer once.

There would be no need to consider this problem if the economy were so integrated that some firms produced only final product, and the other firms produced none. In that case the sum of the output of the former firms would represent total final product. In fact, of course, most firms produce both final and intermediate goods, so that the two must be distinguished for each firm before total national product can be derived.

Returning to Table 2–2, note that the net value added of the X Corporation will be exactly equal to the costs other than for intermediate product incurred by the corporation in production. That is, if the value of intermediate product is deducted from both sides of the production statement, the balance is not altered. This illustrates the fact that the net value added can be estimated either by adding together the factor and nonfactor costs incurred by an enterprise or by deducting the value of intermediate product from the total value of production. The national income accountant adds the net-value-added figure of a business unit to the flow of product (right side of the national accounts) and adds the equivalent total of costs incurred to the flow of income (left side of the national accounts).

2–3   THE NATIONAL ACCOUNTS

In presenting its national income estimates, the Department of Commerce begins from a basic division of the economy into business, personal (household and institution), government, and foreign (rest of the world) sectors. This is only one of many different schemes that could be used, and estimates are presented for different industries, levels of government, financial institutions, and nonfinancial corporations. However, as will be clear later, there are sound reasons based on different attitudes toward economic decisions that make the four-sector approach the most useful for our purposes.

Business sector   In addition to corporate enterprises, the business sector is defined to include all organizations producing goods and services sold at a price intended to cover at least the cost of production. This definition is broad enough to include such government business enterprises as the Tennessee Valley Authority. Also included are unincorporated business enterprises such as family businesses, farm operators, independent professional practitioners, and lessors of real property. Finally it includes financial intermediaries such as banks, insurance companies, and other financial institutions.

A consolidated income and product account for the business sector of the American economy based on figures for 1965 is shown in Table 2–3. Most of the items are familiar from the discussion of the production statement of the X Corporation given in Table 2–2; however, the

Table 2–3   Consolidated business income and product account, 1965   (Billions of dollars)

1. Employees' compensation		$307	*Sales by business to:*		
2. Wages and salaries	$279		17. Personal, government,		
3. Supplements	28		and foreign sectors		$484
4. Proprietor's income		56	18. Business on capital		
5. Rental income of persons		18	account		98
6. Net interest		17	19. Net change in inventory		9
7. Corporate profits and inventory valuation adjustment		71			
8. Profits tax liability	31				
9. Dividends (domestic)	18				
10. Undistributed profits	24				
11. Inventory valuation adjustment	−2				
12. Income originating		469			
13. Indirect business taxes		62			
14. Charges against business net product		531			
15. Depreciation		60			
16. Charges against business gross product		$591	20. Business gross product		$591

Source: This table and subsequent tables in Part 1 are based upon the national accounts of the United States for 1965 published in U.S. Department of Commerce, *Survey of Current Business, July 1966,* U.S. Government Printing Office, Washington, 1965.

presentation of certain items is somewhat different. For example, the right side of the account, which includes only the figures for the sale of final product, is divided between sales to the personal, government, and foreign sectors and sales to the "business sector on capital account."[1] In discussing the production statement of the X Corporation, we noted that sales to other firms represented intermediate and not final product. However, the sale of capital goods between businesses is treated as final product, and more will be said about this in the next chapter. The item "net change in inventory" is the current value of the total physical change in all inventories held by the business sector. Although this represents goods not sold, it is part of current production and is therefore included in the flow of product.

On the left side, proprietor's income is an unfamiliar item. This item includes the net income of various unincorporated business enterprises such as professional persons, farmers, and various small businesses that are not legally incorporated. If these enterprises were treated like corporations, their profit, salaries of proprietors, and interest on capital invested by proprietors would be included under the appropriate items in the accounts. However, these various items of return are customarily not calculated separately by the majority of unincorporated enterprises, and so an aggregate net income that includes some of all components (plus an inventory valuation adjustment) is entered as a separate item.

The subtotal "income originating" on the left side of Table 2–3 of $469 billion is the total factor payments by business. This total includes wages and salaries, rental income (including imputed rent), the net interest payments by business (interest paid minus interest received), and the profit of incorporated and unincorporated businesses. In each case the profit item includes an inventory valuation adjustment to take out of profits any element of inventory "gain" or "loss" resulting from price changes. This ensures that the two sides will balance because the net change in inventory on the right side is valued at current prices.

The item "rental income of persons" did not appear in Tables 2–1 or 2–2 because this category includes only certain rent payments. The Department of Commerce considers the ownership of a residential house as a business activity. Thus the homeowner is assumed to own the house as a "business" and to rent it to himself. The difficulty is that the rent does not take a monetary form, so it cannot be estimated directly. This means that the Department of Commerce must make an estimate of what the rent would be if it did take a monetary form. This imputed rent is added to the flow of income side of the accounts as "rental in-

[1] This item also includes the construction of residential houses.

come of persons," and the taxes and depreciation on the house are added to the appropriate items. An equivalent total is added to the flow of product side of the account. "Rental income of persons" also includes the earnings of those lessors of property who are not primarily engaged in the real estate business. Real estate businesses are treated as any other business, and their rental income is treated as part of the income of the business sector.

The treatment of taxes is one of the most troublesome problems in separating factor from nonfactor income in the consolidated business income and product account. The income-originating figure of $469 billion shown in Table 2–3 includes personal and corporate income taxes and social security contributions by employers,[1] but excludes indirect business taxes. Social security contributions can be easily justified as a factor cost on the ground that they represent a cost to the employer in hiring labor. The inclusion of income taxes as a part of factor costs and the exclusion of indirect business taxes are more difficult to justify. If the factor cost component of business product is to be a useful one, it should change in magnitude only if there is a change in factor employment or prices. It is on this basis that the Department of Commerce excludes from the factor cost total indirect business taxes, which include excise taxes, real property taxes, etc. A change in such a tax would cause a change in the factor income total without any corresponding change in employment or factor prices. On the other hand, there are grounds for assuming that a change in income taxes will not change the factor income total. An increase in the profits tax rate, for example, would probably not change total profits, or therefore the factor income total.

The addition of indirect business taxes to income originating gives the total charges against business net product shown as $531 billion in Table 2–3. If to this total is added depreciation allowance, the resulting total of $591 billion represents all the charges against the business gross product total shown on the right side of the account. The depreciation allowance of $60 billion is the sum of the estimates by the various business firms of the loss in value of their capital equipment resulting from wear and tear and obsolescence.

Personal sector   Consider next the income and product originating in the personal sector which is defined to include institutions of a non-business character such as universities, charitable organizations, and the like, as well as households. The first problem is that there is no twofold measurement of output, in terms of both product and cost, as

---

[1] Employee contributions are included with wages and salaries.

there is for the business sector. Because there is no transaction representing the sale of the product of a domestic servant, for example, as distinct from the purchase of the servant's services, the factor cost of the servant must be used also as a measure of the product he or she produces.[1] Similarly, the product of a university professor or the employee of a charitable foundation is assumed to be measured by the compensation he receives.

Prior to 1965, the Department of Commerce included as a part of factor cost or income originating in the personal sector the interest payments by households and nonprofit institutions to nonpersonal lenders. Interest paid on installment purchases is an example. Mortgage interest has always been excluded from the personal sector and instead appears as part of the income and product of the business sector as a result of treating homeownership as a business. Interest payments resulting from loan transactions between households have always been excluded also because such payments cancel out in the consolidation of all households.

The rationale for including personal sector interest payments to nonpersonal (business) lenders is similar to that which justifies the inclusion of business interest payments to nonbusiness lenders—such interest payments represent a measure of the productivity of real capital financed with borrowed funds. The interest payments on a corporate bond held by a household represent a charge against the output produced by the real capital financed by the borrowed funds. In 1965 it was decided that this procedure was no longer appropriate for the personal sector because much of the capital of the personal sector is not financed with borrowed money and much of the borrowing of the personal sector is not to purchase capital goods but instead to finance living expenses.[2] The result of this change in definition has been to reduce the level of GNP by the amount of the now excluded interest payments. It should be noted that numerous other statistical and definitional changes were made at the same time, none of which were quantitatively as important as the change in the treatment of personal interest payments but which in aggregate offset its impact. The result of all the changes made in 1965 was to increase slightly GNP estimates for recent years.

[1] To be strictly correct, supplies and materials used by the servant should be deducted as intermediate product. However, no attempt is made to do so; all such purchases are considered final product. The servant who "lives in" receives income in kind, and this is imputed as part of factor cost.

[2] See U.S. Department of Commerce, *Survey of Current Business,* U.S. Government Printing Office, Washington, August, 1965, p. 10.

Table 2–4 shows the income and product account for the household and institutional sector for the United States based on the figures for the year 1965. The wages and salary total of $18 billion includes, in addition to money payments to factors, employer contributions to social security and the imputed value of payments in kind. Notice that because the value of output is measured by income received, total, final, net, and gross outputs of this sector are all equal.

Table 2–4   Income and product account for the personal sector, 1965   (Billions of dollars)

1. Wages and salaries	$17		
2. Supplements	1	4. Net and gross product	
3. Income originating	$18	originating	$18

Source: See Table 2–3.

Government sector   The net and gross product originating in the government sector of the economy is measured, as in the personal sector, by the value of factor services purchased. In the case of government also, interest payments on public debt are excluded on the ground that such payments are not for a currently used productive service, as are wage payments.

The alternative would be to value the output of the government sector by the taxes paid by the community. In this case taxes would be treated as analogous to the prices paid for the output of the business sector. However, the use of such an approach is open to criticism. In the first place, taxes are obligatory payments, unlike prices paid for goods and services on the market. In addition, what meaning does this approach have during a period of government deficits or surpluses? During a period of deficit financing by government the community would presumably be undervaluing the services of government, and during a period of surplus it would tend to overvalue these services. It was just such problems of interpretation that persuaded the Department of Commerce to value government output by the cost of the labor services hired.

Given the above decisions, the actual formulation of an account for the government sector is a simple matter. Table 2–5 presents the account for the United States based on the figures for 1965. The income-originating figure of $68 billion is the sum of wages and salaries paid to government employees including the armed forces, plus government contributions to social security. The total also includes an imputed value

Table 2–5 Income and product account for the government sector, 1965 (Billions of dollars)

1. Wages and salaries	$66		
2. Supplements	2	4. Net and gross product	
3. Income originating	$68	originating	$68

Source: See Table 2–3.

of food and personal issue of the armed forces, as well as wages and salary payments of government employees (including armed forces) in positions requiring them to live abroad, who nevertheless are considered American residents. The same total of $68 billion appears on the right side of the account as net and gross product originating in government.

Rest-of-the-world sector Some of the income and product originating in the United States accrues to foreigners who control factors of production situated in this country. On the other hand, some of the income originating in foreign countries accrues to American residents who own factors of production located abroad. Income and product originating in the rest-of-the-world sector is defined as the net movement of such factor payments to American residents. Thus the total can be negative if American residents pay more factor income to foreigners than vice versa. The use of factor income payments to measure output originating in the rest-of-the-world sector is identical to the procedure followed in estimating the product originating in the personal and government sectors. Table 2–6 presents the account for the rest of the world. The left side itemizes the net factor payments under four headings, and the right side gives the same total as the measure of net and gross product.

Table 2–6 Income and product account for the rest of the world, 1965 (Billions of dollars)

1. Wages and salaries (net)	*		
2. Interest (net)	$1		
3. Dividends (net)	1		
4. Branch profits (net)	2		
5. Income originating	$4	6. Net and gross product originating	$4

* Less than $0.5 billion.

Source: See Table 2–3.

There is no necessity for a rest-of-the-world sector at all. The profits of an American branch plant located abroad could be entered directly with the consolidated business income and product account. Similar consolidations could be made for the other items of net factor payments shown in Table 2–6. But particular interest attaches to these net flows originating in the rest of the world, and for this reason the Department of Commerce includes a separate account for such transactions.

National income and product account   Having derived the income and the net and gross product originating in the four sectors, it becomes a simple matter to combine them into a national total. Table 2–7 presents such a total using the income and product figures of Tables 2–3 through 2–6. The right side of Table 2–7 lists the product originating, and the left side gives the factor and nonfactor costs incurred in the production of that total output. Every item in the table is followed by numbers in parentheses. These numbers indicate where the item appears in the tables given previously. The item "indirect business taxes," for example, is shown in Table 2–7 with the code (3.13). This indicates that indirect business taxes appeared previously as item 13 in Table 2–3.

The sum of the factor costs, $559 billion, is known as national income—the total income of factors from participation in the current productive process. The addition of indirect business taxes to national income yields $621 billion, the total charges against net national product.

Table 2–7 National income and product account by sector of origin, 1965   (Billions of dollars)

Income originating in:			Net and gross product originating in:		
Personal sector	$ 18	(4.3)	Personal sector	$ 18	(4.4)
Government sector	68	(5.3)	Government sector	68	(5.4)
Rest of the world	4	(6.5)	Rest of the world	4	(6.6)
Business sector	469	(3.12)	Gross product originating in business sector	591	(3.20)
National income	559				
Indirect business taxes	62	(3.13)			
Charges against net national product	621				
Depreciation	60	(3.15)			
Charges against gross national product	$681		Gross national product	$681	

Source: Tables 2–3 to 2–6. The code numbers used in this table refer to entries in Tables 2–3 to 2–6. See text.

Finally, the addition of depreciation charges yields $681 billion, the total charges against gross national product.

Although Table 2–7 is a perfectly correct presentation of the gross national product account, considerably more light can be thrown on the anatomy of the total by a slightly different presentation. This alternative formulation is the one used by the Department of Commerce in its published accounts. This method presents the flow of product classified by the sector purchasing it rather than by the sector of origin. Also, the flow of income is classified by type of factor payment rather than by sector of origin. Of course, either presentation is based on the fundamental accounting principle that the value of the flow of final output must be balanced by the flow of factor and nonfactor costs incurred in producing that output.

Because we are interested in the sector purchasing the nation's output rather than the sector producing it, the rest-of-the-world account must be reformulated to show, in addition to net factor payments, the net flow of goods between the United States and other countries. Table 2–8 is such an extension of Table 2–6. Again it is presented in net terms. Table 2–8 shows that foreign countries purchased from the United

Table 2–8   Foreign transactions account, 1965   (Billions of dollars)

1. Income originating and net and gross product	$4		4. Transfer payments to foreigners (net)	$3
2. Net purchases of goods from United States	3		5. Net foreign investment	4
3. Net export of goods and services	$7		6. Net payments abroad	$7

Source: See Table 2–3.

States merchandise with a value $3 billion in excess of United States purchases from other countries. This $3 billion surplus on merchandise trade plus the $4 billion net income flows into the United States meant that the United States accumulated during 1965 a total of $7 billion of credits against foreign countries. These credits, or increase in debts owed by foreign countries to the United States, were financed by foreign countries through transfer payments by the United States government (plus a small transfer from persons) of $3 billion and by investment abroad by American residents of $4 billion. This investment abroad by Americans took the form of both the extension of short-term commer-

Table 2–9   National income and product account, 1965   (Billions of dollars)

Wages, salaries, supplements		$393	
Proprietor's income		56	(3.4)
Rental income of persons		18	(3.5)
Net interest		18	(3.6, 6.2)
Corporate profits and inventory valuation adjustment		74	
Profits tax liability	$31 (3.8)		
Dividends (domestic)	18 (3.9)		
Dividends (foreign)	1 (6.3)		
Undistributed profits	24 (3.10)		
Foreign branch profits	2 (6.4)		
Inventory valuation adjustment	−2 (3.11)		
National income		$559	
Indirect business taxes		62	(3.13)
Charges against net national product		621	
Depreciation		60	(3.15)
Charges against gross national product		$681	

Source: Tables 2–3 to 2–6.

cial credits to finance trade flows and long-term investments by American business and individuals in foreign countries.

Table 2–9 presents the customary formulation of the gross national product account. All the figures used have been taken from previous tables in this chapter. The wages and salaries total of Table 2–9 does not carry a code number because it is made up of five items, which would be too clumsy to include in the table. The derivation of the total is shown in Table 2–10.

Table 2–10   Wages, salaries, and supplements, 1965   (Billions of dollars)

Business:	wages and salaries	$279	(3.2)
	supplements	28	(3.3)
Personal:	wages and salaries	17	(4.1)
	supplements	1	(4.2)
Government:	wages and salaries	66	(5.1)
	supplements	2	(5.2)
Rest of the world: wages and salaries		*	(6.1)
Total		$393	

* Less than $0.5 billion.

Source: Tables 2–3 to 2–6.

Personal consumption expenditures		$431
Gross private domestic investment		107
Business purchases on		
capital account	$98 (3.18)	
Net change in inventory	9 (3.19)	
Net export of goods and services		7
Government expenditures		136
		___
Gross national product		$681

Gross national expenditure A final method of presenting the data appearing in the gross national product account is presented in Table 2–11. This statement, in which items are listed by type of expenditure, corresponds to the form used in Chapter 1. Only the product flow side of the account is presented; the income side is the same as shown in Table 2–9.

Table 2–11 Gross national expenditures by type of commodity, 1965 (Billions of dollars)

Consumer expenditure		$431
Durables	$ 66	
Nondurables	190	
Services	175	
Gross private domestic investment		107
Construction	53	
Producers' durables	45	
Net change in inventory	9	
Net export of goods and services		7
Government expenditure		136
Federal	67	
State and local	69	___
Gross national product		$681

Source: See Table 2–3.

The Department of Commerce groups all consumer expenditures into three categories on the basis of durability. Goods consumed at the moment of purchase are classified as services; those consumed within a year are classified as nondurable commodities; and those lasting more than a year are classified as durable commodities. Gross private domestic investment is divided into three categories: construction, producers' durables, and net changes in inventory. Finally, government expenditures are divided between Federal expenditures and state and local expenditures.

2–4   SUMMARY

The gross national product total is a measure of the flow of final goods and services resulting from current production by Americans during a year. For each sector of the economy, an acccount is constructed showing the final, or unduplicated, output for all the units within the sector. Transactions between units within a sector are, in general, netted out in deriving final output. With the exception of business purchases of capital goods, which are clearly a part of final output, transactions between firms are netted out. Transactions between units in the personal sector, such as employment of domestic servants, are included as part of final product.

For the purpose of the accounts the consumer is considered to be at the center of the economic process. Anything which contributes to his present or future well-being is considered final product and is included in the account.

The actual structure of the accounts follows closely the accounting practices developed in business. Each transaction is recorded twice, representing the two sides of economic activity—a flow of product and a flow of income. The accounts therefore show who purchased the final output and how the income resulting from this productive activity was divided between the various elements of factor and nonfactor cost.

3

CONCEPTUAL PROBLEMS IN THE ESTIMATION OF GROSS NATIONAL PRODUCT

3–1 INTRODUCTION

Although the national product account for the economy as a whole is a combination of the consolidated current income and product accounts for the various sectors of the economy, the derivation of a national account is more than just a matter of simple addition. At every turn the income accountant is faced with fuzzy boundary areas that must be sharply delimited before he can proceed. At all such ambiguous points someone must make a decision about the procedure to be followed by the accountant. This chapter is concerned with these conceptual issues of national accounting.

As a general rule, we shall follow the conceptual judgments of the Department of Commerce accounts because these accounts are the most widely known, are the most up-to-date, and, because of the detail they present, have found the widest acceptance of any system of accounts. From time to time, however, alternative judgments will be presented for purposes of comparison.[1]

3–2 THE PRODUCT TO BE INCLUDED

The definition of economic activity A gross national product account measures the value of the current output of economic activity. Economic activity involves the use of scarce resources (including time) in the provision of goods to satisfy unlimited wants. An economic good provides satisfaction, is relatively scarce, and is disposable. It may take the form of a tangible good such as an automobile or a loaf of bread, or it may take an intangible form such as the service furnished to a patient by his doctor or to a student by his teacher. But to include any activity providing a good or service meeting these three conditions is far too wide a task for the income accountant. To do so would mean that the national product total would include the activity of shaving oneself, because it does not differ from the same activity when carried on by a barber. It is obviously impossible to include the value of such personally rendered services in the national product accounts.

A line must therefore be drawn between goods that can be called "economic" because they result from economic activity and those goods and services which, although they provide satisfaction, result from the general activity of life. Fortunately, a convenient means of separating the two types of activity is readily available. Economic goods include goods appearing on markets, and economic activity includes only activities producing marketable goods.[2] All such goods or services will render satisfaction, will be scarce, and will be disposable. This general rule can be applied to any particular country at any point in time, but its usefulness is obviously restricted to highly developed countries at recent

---

[1] The conceptual framework of the official national accounts is contained in U.S. Department of Commerce, *National Income Supplement, 1954,* U.S. Government Printing Office, Washington, 1954. See also Simon Kuznets, *National Income and Its Composition, 1919–1938,* Vol. I, Chap. 1, National Bureau of Economic Research, Inc., New York, 1941; Simon Kuznets, "National Income: A New Version," *Review of Economics and Statistics,* 30:151–179, 1948; G. Jaszi, E. F. Denison, M. Gilbert, and C. F. Schwartz, "Objectives of National Income Measurement: A Reply to Professor Kuznets," *Review of Economics and Statistics,* 30:179–195, 1948; and M. Gilbert and I. B. Kravis, *An International Comparison of National Products and the Purchasing Power of Currencies,* Chap. 6, Organization for European Economic Co-operation, Paris, 1954 (?).

[2] Some exceptions to the generality of this rule will be given later.

points in time. The farther one gets from a highly developed market economy, the less useful is the rule for distinguishing economic activity from the general activity of life.

It is important to realize the implications of this rule. For one thing, it means that many of the activities carried on within the household are excluded from the measurement of a nation's product. The most obvious example is the product of the activity of the housewife. The value of the meal cooked by the housewife and her effort in cooking it are excluded from economic activity, while the same activity carried on in a restaurant is considered to be economic activity. If housewives cooked each other's meals and received payment for their efforts, cooking the meals would be economic activity and the gross national product would be increased tremendously.[1]

The classification of activity carried on within the household as noneconomic is a generally accepted principle in income accounting. But it is accepted for practical rather than theoretical reasons. The difficulty of valuing the output of such activity is so great as to preclude its measurement entirely. Note that acceptance of the classification makes both intercountry comparisons and intertemporal comparisons within the same country of doubtful validity. Consider for a moment a comparison of national product estimates made for India and the United States. It is obvious that much activity considered economic in the United States because it takes place through markets is considered noneconomic in India because it takes place within the household. For example, when an Indian housewife bakes bread for her family, the value of the bread is excluded from Indian national product. The value of a loaf of bread purchased at a supermarket by an American housewife is included in American national product. Similarly, when comparing the national product of the United States in 1870 with that in 1968, there is the problem of an upward bias in the estimates due to the decrease in family activity.

There is no doubt that the degree of comparability between the national products of the United States and India, or of the United States at different times, is affected by the exclusion of some family activity. But there is a real question whether the value of such activity can be quantified, and whether or not, even if quantifiable, it should be included in national product. If the concept of national product is to have any meaning at all, it must be restricted to the output of economic activity defined as the use of scarce resources which have alternative

[1] The cost of intermediate production would have to be deducted from the selling price of the meals to arrive at the addition to national product.

productive uses. It is not clear that the labor of the Indian housewife is a scarce resource; even if it is, there is the problem of valuing her output, which means assigning a value to the production lost because she decided to bake bread. Her time spent baking bread is quite possibly leisure time from an economic point of view because the labor service is not taken from the total supply of scarce factors of production. The bread is therefore no more a product than the coffee table produced in a home workshop by an American in his leisure time.

Excluded market transactions   In the discussion thus far the assumption has been made that all market transactions involve goods or services that should be included in the national product total. But not all payments made represent exchanges of goods and services, and not all changes in the value of goods result from economic activity. The market transactions excluded from the national product total can be classified into three categories: transfer payments, capital gains, and illegal activities.

Transfer payments   Transfer payments are those payments of income that do not result from current productive activity. If a business firm distributes $100,000 in prize money for a contest held to publicize its product, the prize money, while representing a current expense to the firm, is a payment that differs fundamentally from a factor payment. The prize money is not a payment for a productive service currently used in producing a final good or service.[1] A transfer payment, unlike a factor payment, constitutes a redistribution of income and is excluded from national product.[2]

   The three levels of government are the largest source of transfer payments in the American economy. The recent growth in nondefense expenditures of American government has resulted from the increased duties imposed on government involving the redistribution of income. This redistribution of income by government takes a wide variety of forms, but in each case the payments are transfers of income and hence

[1] The cost to the firm of administering the contest represents an intermediate product and is therefore excluded from national product.

[2] It should be noted in passing that no attempt is made by the Department of Commerce to distinguish between wage payments on the basis of some definition of "productiveness." Some countries exclude pay and allowances of armed forces personnel from their national product total on the ground that these are not payments for a currently produced good or service and hence are really transfer payments. The American accounts make no such distinction. Wages include any compensation for current performance of work. Nonmoney income payments will be discussed later.

are excluded from the national product total. Examples of government transfer payments include the great variety of payments under the social insurance program, payments to veterans under the GI bills, and direct relief payments.

One further type of government payment which is excluded from the national product total is interest on the public debt. The rationale for exclusion rests on the ground that the size of the debt is not closely related to the value of the physical assets of government because it has arisen largely as a result of deficit financing during wartime. If the debt were closely related to the value of government physical assets, interest payments would be included as an estimate of the current return on these assets. Some countries do indeed include interest on the debt of the lower levels of government on the ground that this debt was incurred to finance existing real assets. Other countries go further and include an interest charge measured by applying the current rate of interest on long-term government debt to the current value of the physical assets of all levels of government as carried on the government's balance sheets.

Transfer payments of other kinds are excluded for similar reasons. Gifts, inheritances, and charity payments are examples of excluded income payments.[1] Furthermore, a payment made for a tangible good is excluded if the good is not produced currently. The purchase price of a medieval painting is excluded from the accounts because the transaction represents a transfer of assets rather than a payment for current productive activity. If, however, the art dealer has restored the painting, the value of the restoration, estimated by its cost (minus the cost of materials used), would be entered in the national total of productive activity. Thus the factor costs incurred by the art dealer, including profits on current activity, are entered on the income side of the account, and the corresponding value of the current activity of the art dealer is entered on the product side of the account. In the case of charitable institutions where there is no sale of product, factor payments must be used as the estimate of both income and product originating.

Capital gains and losses   Capital gains and losses are examples of changes in value resulting from market forces that nevertheless are excluded from the national product total. Suppose, for example, that the value of an existing capital asset, perhaps a house, increases as a

---

[1] Net international gifts by persons and government are included in personal and government expenditure but are canceled out in the accounts by the inclusion of the same total with opposite sign in the net foreign balance.

result of monetary inflation. In this case the increase in market value is excluded from the national product total because the increase was not a result of current productive activity. It differs in this fundamental respect from the increase in the value of a house resulting from additions, say a new wing, made to it currently. The increase in the value of this second house (minus the cost of materials used in the addition) would be included in the measure of national productive activity. While it is true that realized capital gains are considered income by the tax authorities, these gains are excluded from national product because they do not result from current economic activity. Thus if a house is sold for a gain, all the net return would be taxed even if part of the appreciation in the value of the house resulted from monetary inflation. The same argument applies to capital gains on common stocks which are taxed by the Internal Revenue Service but which are excluded from the national product.

Another example of capital gains and losses is the change in asset valuation resulting from exogenous shifts in consumer demand. When consumers suddenly shift from 78-r.p.m. to LP records, it is obvious that gains and losses for various firms will result. But the gains and losses did not result from current economic activity, and hence they are excluded from national product. For similar reasons a sudden increase in the value of a tract of Western grazing land because of the discovery of oil or of desolate land in Colorado because of the discovery of uranium is excluded. The increase in the value of the land over the previous investment in it is the result of an exogenous shift in demand.[1]

In general, those changes in the values of goods that result from ungovernable or unpredictable causes are treated as accidental shifts in the conditions of production outside economic activity proper. Those changes in value that can be anticipated and insured against, such as fire and flood, are also excluded because the adjustments for such shifts, i.e., insurance premiums, have been charged against the operations of previous years. Changes in asset valuation resulting from depreciation are subject to special treatment, which will be considered later.

Illegal activities The final category of market transactions excluded from national product is illegal activities. This is a category of market activity excluded by all national income accountants. It is true that such transactions involve satisfactions for which a price is paid, and if this were the only basis for inclusion, such activities could not be omitted.

[1] If discoveries of new natural resources are not included, the depletion (depreciation) of natural resources cannot be included as a charge against national product.

But the national accounts attempt, as far as possible, to be a measure of socially useful economic activity. Although those who participate in illegal markets might be willing to defend their social usefulness, the fact that such activities are outlawed by society is taken to be sufficient ground for their exclusion.

This question of an individual versus a social judgment of productivity raises a wider issue. The implicit assumption behind a national product total is that the products of all economic activity, not excluded on other grounds, have a positive satisfaction for all members of society. The product of the distillery is included on the same basis as the product of the Bible publishing house. Longer and higher fins on automobiles are included as product, though they may be anathema to some. In general, it is not always true that the product of economic activity provides satisfaction to everybody. The old adage that "one man's meat is another man's poison" expresses the point adequately. But the problem goes deeper than that. Suppose a paper mill dumps its waste into a stream and pollutes the water. The product of the paper mill is included in national product, but so are the expenses of the communities that must purify the water before it can be used. There is a real question, therefore, whether the product of the paper mill should not be reduced by the expenses incurred by others as a result of its operation.

The best answer to the problem would be to devise a calculus by which the satisfaction to each individual, and to society as a whole, from possession of a good or service could be measured. The national product total would then measure the net additions to social satisfaction of the flow of output from current economic activity. An account constructed on this basis would be truly a social account.

Such a calculus is completely out of the question, and any approximation to it would involve unnecessary arbitrariness. For society has already indicated in the legal code the activities that are not considered socially productive, and the national accountant includes all legal activity without distinction. Note that the acceptance of this criterion by the Department of Commerce is a departure from the production concept that is the general basis for the inclusion of the output of economic activity. Furthermore, such a criterion is a changing one, for social mores differ between countries at any point in time and in the same country at different times. The prohibition era in the United States is a good example of the latter.

Nonmarket activities   We have already seen that not all money income flows are included in national product. At the other extreme, the national product total includes an imputed value of some goods and services that do not appear on markets. As a general rule, an imputed value is assigned to nonmarket activities if this makes the accounts internally comparable, if the nonmarket good is clearly separable from its source, and if an imputed value can be clearly and easily assigned.

Some workers receive part of their pay in the form of room and board rather than in the form of money wages.[1] To assure conformity with other workers who receive their total remuneration in the form of money wages, a value is imputed to the payment in kind received and added to money wages. This procedure is followed although the cost to the employer of the food used to provide the meals would under ordinary circumstances be excluded, as are other intermediate products.

Another example of imputed valuation arises in the case of output retained by a producer in order to consume it himself. This arises primarily in agriculture where the farmer frequently retains part of the produce of the farm for his own consumption. An imputed value is assigned to this retained production and included in total national output. This is a case where the nonmarket activity can be estimated with a fairly high degree of certainty and where the assignment of a value is relatively easy because there are market equivalents.

The third example of imputed valuation arises in the field of residential housing. If a family rents a house or an apartment, the rent payments (minus the cost of upkeep and repair) are a measure of the value of the output of the real estate industry. In the case of owner-occupied houses, however, no rent is paid explicitly, even though a house is a substantial source of satisfaction to the homeowner. It is also true that an automobile is a substantial source of satisfaction, although no imputed value is given to the services of the automobile owned by an individual. A house differs in that the service rendered is easily separable from the house itself, and an imputed value can be readily assigned by using rent payments as a guide.

The final example of imputation arises in the case of financial institutions such as commercial banks, insurance companies, and mutual trust funds. Such institutions provide a service, and they pay costs that cancel one another out. The example of an indiivdual who has a checking account will illustrate this. The individual receives no interest on his deposit, although he could earn interest on the money were he to invest it. At the same time the bank makes only a nominal charge (perhaps with the requirement that a minimum balance be held) for safeguarding the money and processing the checks drawn against the account. In-

---

[1] This category includes also food and personal issue of armed forces personnel.

stead of paying interest on the money and then charging for services rendered, the bank cancels the one against the other. For the purposes of estimating national product, however, an imputed value must be given to these transactions if the total output of economic activity is to be evaluated. The other financial intermediaries have similar non-monetary flows that must be allotted an imputed value.

3–3   FINAL AND INTERMEDIATE PRODUCT

Final product   Thus far the discussion has been concerned with the distinction between economic and noneconomic activity. But as was pointed out in Chapter 2 with the example of a loaf of bread, what is wanted is an unduplicated total that measures only the flow of goods to the ultimate consumer. The Department of Commerce defines such a final good as one produced and/or purchased but not resold during the current accounting period. Goods purchased for resale, with or without further processing in the physical sense, are termed "intermediate goods," and all such goods are excluded from the national product total.

Some additional examples will help to clarify the distinction. If a steel mill purchases a million tons of coal and uses nine-tenths of it during the accounting period, that much coal is considered intermediate product. The one-tenth that is not used currently is considered final product and is entered in the accounts as a net change in inventory. On the other hand, all coal purchased by a householder for home heating is final product. To take another example, suppose the steel mill purchases a machine. This machine is a final product, but that part of it used during the current accounting period is intermediate product and should be excluded from the accounts.[1]

The distinction between final and intermediate products obviously depends upon the definition of a productive enterprise. The example above of coal purchased for home heating would not hold if the household were considered a productive enterprise selling its labor services as its product. In this case the coal purchased by the householder would be considered intermediate product—product necessary for the further production of the firm. For the same reason the clothing, food, recreation, and shelter purchased by households would be considered intermediate product and therefore would be excluded from the national product total. Also, the cost of raising and educating children would

---

[1] This intermediate product, the depreciation of capital equipment, is subject to particular difficulties, which will be discussed later.

be analogous to the costs of repair and maintenance of the capital stock of a business enterprise. To extend the definition of the productive enterprise to include the family unit is unthinkable, given the philosophies of most countries. Human beings are fundamentally different from machines. At the same time it means that the national product total is internally inconsistent when a distinction is made between the gross and net return on capital,[1] while no distinction is made between the gross and net return of wage earners.

Another result of treating households as final consumers is worth considering. A businessman traveling on an expense account can deduct such expenses from his income as a cost of operation, and the national income accountant will similarly deduct the expenses as intermediate product. The wage earner who must commute to his job cannot, however, treat such costs as an expense, and the national income investigator will count commuting costs as purchases of final product. Similarly, when a business buys water to use in its operations, the water is assumed to be intermediate product. When a householder buys water, it is assumed to be final product.

As the United States has become more and more an urbanized nation, the expenditures connected with urban living such as commuting, garbage collection, sewerage, and water supply have increased. Some investigators have contended that these expenditures by consumers should not be considered as expenditures for final products but rather as costs or offsets to urban living. Such products should, they contend, be treated as intermediate rather than as final. The argument is essentially that products should be counted as final if the consumer purchases them for the independent contribution they make to his welfare. Such investigators would exclude commuting costs, for example, because they are an expenditure resulting from urban living, i.e., an expense the consumer would not have if he did not live in the city. In other words, final product should be limited to those purchases the consumer would desire to make if he were not engaged in economic activity.

The answer given by the Department of Commerce is that this argument is fundamentally wrong and would lead to arbitrary measures of national product. Any attempt, for example, to divide the purchase price of a car by a wage earner into a production expense and a real consumption expense would of necessity be so arbitrary as to be worthless. In general, it is impossible to separate on any objective basis the ends

[1] See the discussion on depreciation at the end of this chapter.

and means involved in every consumer expenditure. Even if it were possible to make such a division, the Department of Commerce would contend that it was unnecessary. The wage earner who drives to work has a number of alternatives. He can walk, ride a bicycle, or take a bus. It is only reasonable to assume that if he drives his car he enjoys a product by so doing, and the value of the product he receives is equal to the expenses he incurs. All expenditure by the consumer is assumed by the Department of Commerce to be expenditure for final product.

In answer to the contention that the concept of intermediate product should be expanded to include substantial portions of consumer expenditure, the Department of Commerce argues that, even if it were possible to separate from each expenditure that amount representing real consumption, it would be a mistake to do so. Why should an increase in production resulting from increased urbanization be excluded if an increase in food production resulting from larger appetites is included? If Americans were not better off because of the existence of cities, they could always devote the resources to some other use. The fact that they do live in cities means that their product is greater, and the national product statistician must take account of this.

Net and gross investment   The distinction between net and gross national product hinges upon the fact that gross real capital formation includes the production of goods to replace elements of the capital stock worn out during the current period. Although the depreciation of a physical asset represents an intermediate product in the same way that coal used by a steel mill is intermediate product, the national product total given by the Department of Commerce includes depreciation. For that reason, the accounts are internally inconsistent; they include the net flow of goods and services to consumers, but the gross flow of capital goods. The inclusion of depreciation is necessary because it is almost impossible to estimate it on a basis comparable to that for other items in the product.[1]

Capital goods are divided into two general categories: the net change in inventory and the production of physical capital assets. Because depreciation does not enter into the net change in inventory, our concern in this section is only with real capital formation.

A real capital good is any good ordinarily consumed in a period greater than a year, generally as a result of its use in production. Real capital formation includes, in addition to producers' durables, construc-

---

[1] The valuation of depreciation will be discussed later.

tion activity of all kinds undertaken by business enterprises and residential construction.[1] The latter is considered capital formation rather than an ordinary consumption expenditure because home ownership is considered a business by the Department of Commerce.[2]

In calculating its depreciation allowance, a firm must take into account both the wear and tear on a piece of capital equipment and the decline in its relative efficiency as a result of obsolescence. The output attributable to the piece of equipment does not therefore represent a net addition to the flow of product.

Suppose, for example, that a lathe is used to produce a second exactly similar lathe; that this process takes the whole of the accounting period; and that the first lathe depreciates to zero in the process. Gross capital formation during the period is equal to one lathe. Net capital formation—the change in the stock of capital—is zero.[3] The number of lathes produced is exactly equal to the number of lathes consumed. If the original lathe is used to produce two of its kind during the accounting period, while itself depreciating to zero, gross capital formation will be equal to two lathes, while net capital formation will be equal to one. It is obvious that while net real capital formation can be positive, zero, or negative, it is never possible for gross real capital formation to be less than zero.

For the economy as a whole, if that part of the capital stock worn out during the process of production is exactly replaced by the current production of capital goods, then net real capital formation for the economy is zero. If current capital formation is greater than the depreciation of the existing capital stock, the capital stock has been increased and net capital formation is positive. On the other hand, if the capital stock is reduced during the accounting period, net capital formation is negative.

As has been suggested, the problem of estimating the depreciation of the capital stock is a difficult one. If a machine is used more intensively in one year than in another, the actual depreciation of the ma-

---

[1] Public construction (construction by government) is included by the Department of Commerce with other purchases of goods and services by government.

[2] Residential construction is the only expenditure by households that is not considered a consumption expenditure; any other good is assumed to be consumed by the household when purchased. This is obviously not the case with respect to automobiles and other durables. But because there is no practical way of estimating that part of the value of a durable consumed in any period of time, these goods are assumed to depreciate to zero within the accounting period.

[3] This assumes that prices do not change. Price changes will be discussed in the next section of this chapter.

chine would differ between the two years. But the business firm, having chosen a particular method of depreciation, is obliged to adhere to that method, irrespective of the actual intensity of use.[1] Moreover, the actual depreciation of identical machines will differ between business firms. Whereas one firm may wear out a machine in two years, another firm may be able to utilize the same machine for six years. If both machines are depreciated by the firms over a two-year period, both net national product and the size of the capital stock will be underestimated over the six-year period. If, on the other hand, the machines are depreciated over a six-year period, the reverse will be the case.

An additional difficulty is that a large part of the annual depreciation charges recorded for the economy represent obsolescence rather than the physical wearing out of capital equipment. In the American economy, in which rapid technological advances are continually being made, no business enterprise could afford to depreciate its capital equipment at a rate measuring only physical wear and tear. To do so would mean a continual loss of competitive position in favor of those firms depreciating at a more rapid rate and replacing their capital equipment as more efficient ones come on the market. Depreciation allowances recorded by business firms may therefore differ considerably from the actual depreciation of capital equipment.

Considerations such as the above are almost impossible to allow for in constructing a net national product total. Consequently, the Department of Commerce presents a gross national product total which, as we have seen, involves the inclusion of some intermediate product. In other words, gross investment is entered on the product flow side of the account instead of the difficult-to-estimate net investment. As a consequence an estimate of depreciation must be added to the income flow side to ensure that the two sides balance. Notice that if a correct estimate of depreciation could be derived, there would be no change in the gross national product total; only the relative size of the depreciation and profit items would change.

In summary, the gross national product total as estimated by the Department of Commerce includes the final output of the business, government, and foreign sectors of the economy plus a small product originating in the household. Of those goods not appearing on markets, only the imputed value of payments in kind to employees, retained output of producers, rental values of owner-occupied houses, and the nonmonetary income and product flows of financial intermediaries are included. Excluded are the money payments representing transfers of

---

[1] The Internal Revenue Service sets maximum permissible depreciation rates.

income, capital gains and losses (whether realized or not), and gains resulting from illegal activities.

Up to this point the product to be included in the gross national product total has been decided. Still to be determined is the way this product is combined into a comprehensive total.

3–4 VALUATION OF THE PRODUCT

The use of market prices The diversity of the goods and services produced within the economy dictates that a common unit of measurement be used to combine them into a meaningful total. The only reasonable common unit is the dollar value of each good and service produced, although this does create certain problems. The Department of Commerce views its measure of national product as a measure of productivity and uses market prices to arrive at the total because no more convenient substitute is available.

There is, however, an alternative interpretation, which views the gross national product total as a measure of welfare. This interpretation is based on the contention that prices, as determined by the dollar votes of consumers, represent the social value of goods. In this view, an increase in national product per capita represents an increase in welfare, and intercountry welfare differences can be measured by differences in national product per capita.

But each consumer does not have the same number of dollar votes. The distribution of income is such that there are families at one end of the income scale that can do no more than provide for the necessities of life, while at the other end there are families that have no difficulty in living lavishly. Market prices therefore are an imperfect measure of the satisfaction derived from a good, when such prices reflect only those demands that can be backed by purchasing power.

Furthermore, consider a comparison of American gross national product between 1929 and 1968. Can it be stated that all the increase in gross national product measures an increase in welfare, when nearly $70 billion is spent in 1968 for defense? Does air travel, which is a new addition to national product, represent a net addition when people are subjected to the noise associated with airports?

Finally, the welfare view is untenable in the case of intercountry comparisons. Canadian gross national product, for example, contains a large element of product associated with the relatively severe climate, but this item would not be included in the product of countries with more temperate climates. This does not mean, however, that Canadians are necessarily better off in a welfare sense. To appreciate this point, one has but to consider that in Elysium, where there is no economic activity, gross national product is zero.

Imputations The general problem of imputing value to nonmarket goods and services is solved by the Department of Commerce by assigning to them the value of identical or similar goods and services that do pass through markets. The trouble with this approach is that if the goods or services did appear on markets, market prices might change. A further problem arises from the fact that retained production or payments in kind may be of an inferior quality. To the extent that they are inferior, valuation by the prices of the nearest market equivalent will overstate the value of total production. A difficulty of a somewhat similar nature arises if those receiving payments in kind value such payments at less than market price. If such is the case, the factor cost as entered in the accounts overstates the true opportunity cost of the factors of production. Fortunately the actual magnitudes involved are relatively small, and erroneous imputations create only minor errors in the totals.

When the decision is made to include such goods at the value of their market equivalents, the adjustment of the accounts is a simple matter. In the case of retained farm production, the imputed gross value is added to consumption expenditure on the product side of the account, and an imputed net profit from farming is added on the income side. The difference between the gross and net figures is added to the appropriate expense items on the income flow side. In the case of payments in kind, the imputed value of these payments is added to consumption expenditure on the product side, and wages are increased by the same value on the income side.

The imputed rental value of owner-occupied houses is handled in a similar way. In effect, owning a house is conceptually separated into two transactions. The homeowner is assumed to own the house as a business and to rent the house to himself as a consumer. Thus the value of the output of the business sector of the economy is increased by the imputed gross rental payments, in the same way that rent payments to a real estate company are included in the value of output of the real estate industry. A net rental figure is entered on the income side of the account under net rent payments of persons. The difference between gross and net rent consists principally of depreciation and indirect business taxes that are included under the appropriate items on the income side. Materials purchased for the maintenance of an owner-occupied house are intermediate products of the business sector and hence do not enter the accounts.

Financial intermediaries such as commercial banks, investment funds, and life insurance companies raise another problem of imputation. A commercial bank, for example, holds customers' deposits in return for service charges collected on the number of checks drawn against the account. The value of the bank's final output is represented by the revenue received from the sale of its services minus its purchases from other firms. But the service charges actually assessed by the bank are such a small part of the value of the services rendered to depositors that the product of the bank will appear to be very small or even negative. The reason for this apparently nonsensical situation is that depositors pay for services received in a nonmonetary form. If a meaningful output figure for the bank is to be derived, a value must be imputed to these nonmonetary flows. The imputed money interest on checking accounts is assumed to be equal to the interest received by the bank from its loans minus the interest it actually pays on savings accounts. This total is entered on the income side of the gross national product account. The same total is entered on the product side of the account as the market value of the services provided by the bank. The imputed interest total is allocated between the three sectors on the basis of relative sizes of accounts held by each. Only the interest payments to individuals and to government actually enter the gross national product account; imputed interest to business representing an intermediate product is netted out of the total.

Inventory valuation   If the gross national product is to include a measure of the total output of the nation, it must take account of changes in inventories. Thus if a steel mill adds to its inventory of finished steel products during the year, it is clear that this increase represents current output and must be included in the gross national product. Also, if finished steel inventories are reduced during the year, total sales must have exceeded total production, and the inventory change will have to be deducted from the flow of product side of gross national product. At the same time, an increase in the inventory of iron ore held by the steel company represents current production not consumed as intermediate product; hence the increase must be included in the total of the nation's output.

It would appear to be a relatively simple matter to take figures of the net change in the physical volume of inventory (positive or negative), multiply by current prices, and add the resulting figure to total output. Not all business units, however, keep track of changing inventories, and those that do, keep records not in terms of physical units but in terms of value. This in itself is not a difficulty. The problem arises because items of inventory may be carried over more than one accounting period, because prices frequently change in the interim, and because the firm's record of inventory is generally kept in terms of original cost.

Suppose, for example, that over an accounting period the steel company sells some of its finished product inventory carried over from a previous period and adds to the inventory out of current production, so that there was a net increase in the physical volume of inventory. Suppose further that the whole period was one of rising steel prices. Because the units of inventory are carried on the books of the firm at their original cost, the units withdrawn will reduce the value of inventory held less than the added, currently produced units will increase it. The change in the book value of inventories will therefore overstate the actual physical change that occurred.

The similarity between this type of monetary gain (or loss) and capital gains and losses is obvious. Just as capital gains and losses are excluded from gross national product, so an inventory valuation adjustment is made to correct for gains and losses in inventory valuation resulting from price changes or other reasons. A negative inventory valuation adjustment means that "gains" were made in the book value of inventories as a result of rising prices. That is, the changes in the book value of inventories overstate the physical changes. A positive inventory valuation adjustment means that "losses" were made as a result of falling prices. The adjustment is added algebraically to the net change in inventories on the product side of the account and to business profits on the income side. The adjustment ensures that the actual physical change in inventories is measured in current prices—a necessary condition because all other current production is valued at current market prices.

Depreciation   The problem of valuing the depreciation of the capital stock is one of the most troublesome in the field of national income accounting. The problem is basically twofold. When the economist says that net investment is zero, he means that the nation's capital stock has been maintained unchanged. But what is the meaning of "keeping capital intact" in an economy in which the efficiency of capital equipment is constantly being improved? A further difficulty is that, as in the case of inventory, capital equipment is generally carried on a company's books at original cost rather than at current value or current replacement cost. In the case of inventory which has a relatively short life, the problem of estimating current value is not too difficult. But in the case of capital equipment, with a life of up to fifty years and more, the problem becomes in practice insurmountable.

The practical answer has been to accept business records as a measure of depreciation without attempting to rework the estimates in terms of current replacement cost. This means that depreciation is the only item in the accounts not on a current cost basis. For these reasons the Department of Commerce gives no estimate of net national product or net capital formation, but gives instead the gross total, even though it includes an admittedly intermediate product not valued at current prices.

3-5 SUMMARY

The gross national product total published by the Department of Commerce is a measure, at current market prices, of the flow of final output resulting from the economic activity of American residents during a selected accounting period.

Economic activity is defined as the use of scarce resources to produce goods and services yielding satisfaction. The use of market prices to value the output produced is a practical matter and does not imply any concept of social welfare.

The total output includes some goods and services that do not appear on markets valued at their market equivalents. On the other hand, some market activities are excluded because they do not represent current socially productive activity or because they merely represent redistribution of income.

The national product total is generally an unduplicated one, including only additions to the flow of goods and services to consumers and the flow of capital goods. Any good purchased for resale in the current period is an intermediate good and is excluded from the final product total. The flow of capital goods raises serious problems for the accountant because of the difficulty of measuring the depreciation item. Here the Department of Commerce does include an intermediate product, depreciation, and moreover values it at other than current prices.

4

SECTOR
ACCOUNTS

4–1   SECTOR ACCOUNTS

As was shown in the last chapter, the national product estimates omit various flows, such as transfer payments, that have a useful economic meaning. Consequently the Department of Commerce supplements the national income and product accounts with complete current accounts for the personal and government sectors. We have then added current accounts for the business and foreign sectors. These accounts detail the interrelated transactions between sectors and thus provide a clearer picture of the economic structure of the nation than could be gained from the product account alone. In addition, the Department of Commerce publishes a consolidated saving and investment account for the economy as a whole. The purpose of this chapter is to examine these so-called sector accounts.

The sectors discussed in this chapter are the same as those introduced previously—business, personal, government, and rest-of-the-world. It should be understood that there is nothing sacred about this particular sectoring of the economy. For some purposes it would be useful to sector the economy geographically; for others, to sector on an industrial basis. The sectoring used here has proved most useful for the type of analysis that follows in later chapters.

The business sector   The current account for the business sector is the same as that of Table 2–3. All current activity of the business sector is considered to be economic activity and is therefore included in gross national product. The account is shown here as Table 4–1.

The procedure used in Chapter 2 in which items in a table carry a two-part code is followed here. Thus item 1 of Table 4–1, "wages, salaries, supplements," is followed by the code (2.10) to indicate that it appears as item 10 of Table 4–2. Similarly, when it appears in Table 4–2, it carries the code (1.1).

Table 4–1   Consolidated business income and product account, 1965   (Billions of dollars)

1. Wages, salaries, supplements	$293	(2.10)	16. Sales to consumers,		
2. Social security payments	14	(3.15)	government, and		
3. Proprietor's income	56	(2.14)	abroad	$484	
4. Rental income of persons	18	(2.15)	17. Sales to business		
5. Net interest	17	(2.20)	on capital		
6. Corporate profits and inventory			account	98	(5.2)
valuation adjustment	71		18. Net change in		
7. Profits tax liability $31 (3.12)			inventory	9	(5.3)
8. Dividends (domestic) 18 (2.17)					
9. Undistributed profits 24 (5.8)					
10. Inventory valuation					
adjustment −2 (5.10)					
11. Income originating	469				
12. Indirect business taxes	62	(3.13)			
13. Charges against business					
net profit	531				
14. Depreciation	60	(5.11)			
15. Charges against business			19. Business gross		
gross product	$591		product	$591	

Source: See Table 2–3. The code numbers used in this table refer to entries in Tables 4–2 to 4–5.

The personal sector   The income and expenditure account of the personal sector is shown in Table 4–2. This table shows the transactions between the personal sector and the other sectors of the economy and in addition shows the wages, salaries, and supplements of employees of households and institutions as both an expense and a receipt of the sector (items 3 and 12). Because these sector accounts show income and expenditures, the income (left) side shows receipts of transfer payments and the expenditure (right) side shows payments of interest by consumers, neither of which are part of gross national product.

The largest source of receipts of the personal sector is wages, salaries, and supplements, which appear with the sector of origin. As the table indicates, the business sector is by far the largest source of labor income. Proprietor's income (plus inventory valuation adjustment) is also included as part of the receipts of the personal sector and represents the net income of unincorporated businesses, including in addition to profit other unallocated parts of income such as salaries and interest. In the case of corporate income where a proper allocation of costs is made, only dividends accrue to persons, and therefore dividends are the only part of corporate profits included among the receipts of the personal sector.

Personal interest income represents total interest receipts of persons and therefore includes, in addition to interest receipts from the business and foreign sectors which are part of GNP, interest received from other households (shown also as an expense of persons) and from government. The interest figure of $38 billion (item 19) is $20 billion greater than the interest component of the gross national product account, which is the sum of interest paid by consumers ($11 billion) and net interest payments of the government sector ($9 billion). The remaining item of personal receipts includes all other government transfer payments except, of course, those made to foreign countries. Personal social security contributions, which are a personal expense, are nevertheless shown on the receipts side of the sector accounts but with a negative sign. This procedure is followed because these contributions represent a deduction from wage and salary receipts as far as the personal sector is concerned.

The first expense shown for the personal sector is taxes paid to all levels of government. This total includes not only income taxes, but all forms of direct and indirect taxes (such as sales and property taxes), although it excludes social security contributions by wage and salary earners which, as explained above, are listed as a negative receipt. The second expense category is shown as personal outlays. Outlays include wage, salary, and supplement payments to employees of the households

Table 4–2   Personal income and outlay account, 1965 (Billions of dollars)

1. Personal taxes			$ 66 (3.11)	
2. Personal outlays			442	
3. Wages, salaries, supplements	$ 18	(2.12)		
4. Social security payments	*	(3.17)		
5. To business and foreign sectors	413			
6. Interest paid by consumers	11	(2.22)		
7. Personal saving			24 (5.6)	
8. Personal taxes, outlays, and saving			$532	

* Less than $0.5 billion.

Source: See Table 2–3. The code numbers used in this table refer to entries in Tables 4–1 to 4–5.

and institutions that compose the sector, and this sum of $18 billion will be recognized as the income originating and net and gross product of the sector. The employer social security contributions that are also part of the cost of direct services are relatively small, and no figure is given for them. The next outlay is by far the largest and is the total value of the purchases of goods and services from the business and foreign sectors. The final outlay is the interest payments made by consumers. This intrasectoral payment appears as both an expense and a receipt of the personal sector and therefore represents a transfer among units within the sector.

The saving of the personal sector is shown as $24 billion. This is a balancing item, the difference between receipts and expenditures. Thus saving is the total left over after the personal sector has covered its expenses; like the balancing item in other accounts, it can be positive, negative, or zero.

The government sector   The government receipts and expenditure account shown in Table 4–3, like the personal sector account, records

9. Wages, salaries, supplements				$377	
10.	Business	$293	(1.1)		
11.	Government	66	(3.2)		
12.	Personal	18	(2.3)		
13.	Abroad	*	(4.2)		
14. Proprietor's income				56	(1.3)
15. Rental income of persons				18	(1.4)
16. Dividends				19	
17.	Domestic	18	(1.8)		
18.	Foreign	1	(4.4)		
19. Personal interest income				38	
20.	Business	17	(1.5)		
21.	Government	9	(3.8)		
22.	Personal	11	(2.6)		
23.	Abroad	1	(4.3)		
24. Transfer payments				37	(3.6)
25. Minus: employee social security payments				−13	(3.18)
26. Personal income				$532	

total receipts and expenditures including transactions that do not appear as part of gross national product. In addition to the flows resulting from general government activity, Table 4–3 includes receipts and disbursements of social insurance funds administered by all levels of government.

The major share of the receipts of the government comes from taxes. The personal taxes of all kinds totaling $66 billion are expenses of the personal sector; the business sector contributes a total of $93 billion in the form of corporate income and indirect business taxes. The remaining receipt items are employer and employee contributions to social insurance funds. The employer contributions are shown in Table 4–3 by sector of origin.

On the expenditure side of the accounts, the first two items of government outlays are the cost of direct services, that is, the cost of purchasing labor services. This total of $68 billion is also the measure of income originating and net and gross product of the government sector. In the personal sector, income originating appears as both an expense and a receipt. This does not occur in the government sector, where only

**Table 4–3   Government receipts and expenditures account, 1965
(Billions of dollars)**

1. Government outlays		$136
2. Wages, salaries, supplements	$66 (2.11)	
3. Social security payments	2 (3.16)	
4. Net purchases from business and abroad	68	
5. Transfer payments		40
6. To persons	37 (2.24)	
7. To foreigners	3 (4.8)	
8. Net interest paid		9 (2.21)
9. Surplus or deficit (−)		3 (5.12)
10. Government expenditure and surplus		$188

* Less than $0.5 billion.

Source: See Table 2–3. The code numbers used in this table refer to entries in Tables 4–1 to 4–5.

social security contributions by government to employees appear directly on both sides of the account. Wages and salaries paid by government are an expense of government and a receipt of households.

In addition to direct services, government purchases goods and services from business and from abroad. This total is shown as net purchases of goods and services. The meaning of the word "net," as used here, is not the same as in the phrase "net value added," for government is considered a final consumer because it purchases no intermediate product. It is net in the sense that sales to business and foreigners are deducted from government purchases from those sectors to derive the net flow of product.[1]

The final two expenditure items are transfer payments (foreign and domestic) and net interest paid by government. The government makes interest payments on public debt not only to the personal sector, but to other sectors as well; but because it is impossible to segregate government interest payments by the sector that receives them, the Department of Commerce considers that any interest payment outside the government sector will eventually arrive at the personal sector. Thus interest payments to business will increase business profits and will be distributed to the personal sector in the form of dividends. Therefore, the whole net interest figure of $9 billion appears as a receipt of the

[1] These are sales resulting from general government activity. Sales by government business enterprises are included in the business sector. Sales of surplus materials would be an example of general government sales to business.

11. Personal taxes			$ 66	(2.1)
12. Profits tax liability			31	(1.7)
13. Indirect business taxes			62	(1.12)
14. Social security receipts			29	
15.	Business	$14	(1.2)	
16.	Government	2	(3.3)	
17.	Personal	*	(2.4)	
18.	Employees	13	(2.25)	
19. Government receipts			$188	

personal sector. The final item—the balancing item—is the surplus or deficit on current government activity. In 1965 there was a government surplus on a national accounts basis of $3 billion.

The foreign sector   The account for the foreign sector shown in Table 4–4 is identical with that of Table 2–8. As explained there, the account is entirely in net terms; on the left side is recorded the net residual of the flows of currently produced goods and services into and out of the United States. If the net flow is into the United States, it is recorded with a positive sign. The total of $7 billion shown in Table 4–4 means that in

Table 4–4   Foreign transactions account, 1965   (Billions of dollars)

1. Net income payments to the					8. Transfer payments from		
United States			$4		United States government	$3	(3.7)
2.	Wages, salaries	*	(2.13)		9. Net foreign investment	4	(5.4)
3.	Interest	1	(2.23)				
4.	Dividends	1	(2.18)				
5.	Branch profits	2	(5.9)				
6. Net purchases from the							
United States			3				
7. Net export of goods and services			$7		10. Payments to foreigners		$7

* Less than $0.5 billion.

Source: See Table 2–3. The code numbers used in this table refer to entries in Tables 4–2 to 4–5.

1965 the United States earned through the sale of goods and through the receipt of income payments $7 billion more than was spent abroad for imports and the services of foreign factors of production. This deficit on current transactions owed by foreigners to the United States was met by transfer payments from the United States government of $3 billion plus the investment abroad by Americans of $4 billion more than foreigners invested in the United States. Neither of these last two items appears as part of national product, but the transfer payments are part of government expenditures and the net investment of $4 billion represents a use of American saving that will appear in Table 4–5.

The gross saving and investment account   This final account, shown in Table 4–5, does not record the transactions of a separate sector. However, the account is of particular importance. Each of the sector accounts given above includes a balancing item, representing some form of saving, which appears only once in the sector accounts, while every other item appears twice—once as a receipt and once as an expenditure. The saving items appear only once because they represent transactions with capital rather than transactions with current accounts. Thus personal saving does not represent the purchase of a currently produced good or service. It shows that $24 billion of personal receipts were not spent. The purpose of the gross saving and investment account is to draw together all these capital items.

Much will be said in later chapters about the equality of saving and investment. It should be clearly understood that the two sides of Table 4–5 balance because only realized, or actual, saving and investment are recorded. The account must of necessity balance.

Table 4–5   Gross saving and investment account, 1965
(Billions of dollars)

1. Gross private domestic investment			$107	
2. Business purchases on				
capital account	$98	(1.17)		
3. Net change in inventory	9	(1.18)		
4. Net foreign investment			4	(4.9)
			___	
5. Gross investment			$111	

Source: See Table 2–3. The code numbers used in this table refer to entries in Tables 4–1 to 4–4.

The right side of the account lists personal saving, the government surplus or deficit, and gross corporate saving which includes undistributed earnings of domestic corporations, the corporate inventory valuation adjustment, and net foreign branch profits. This last item is included because we are dealing with national accounts and are therefore concerned with the activity of resources owned by Americans, wherever those resources are located. Because the profits of proprietor's activities cannot be separated from proprietor's net income, such undistributed profits (and inventory valuation adjustment) from the operation of unincorporated business enterprises appear as part of personal saving.

It will be noted that the saving-investment account is given in gross terms. As explained in Chapter 3, the Department of Commerce has not been successful in deriving a net investment total because to derive an adequate current price estimate of depreciation has proved impossible. For this reason the depreciation item of $60 billion must be added to the right side to balance the gross business purchases on capital account shown on the left side. The other investment items are net changes in business inventories and net investment by the United States in the rest of the world, i.e., the net increase (or decrease) in claims by the United States against foreigners.

A full understanding of the interrelation between current and capital transactions of the economy is facilitated by an examination of the five accounts given here in conjunction with the gross national product account given in Chapter 2. That account taken by itself leaves out many transactions that do not result from current economic activity. Moreover, the consolidation of the data in one account hides many

6.	Personal saving		$ 24	(2.7)
7.	Gross corporate saving		84	
8.	Undistributed profits	$24 (1.9)		
9.	Branch profits	2 (4.5)		
10.	Inventory valuation adjustment	−2 (1.10)		
11.	Depreciation	60 (1.14)		
12.	Government surplus or deficit (−)		3	(3.9)
13.	Gross saving		$111	

flows between sectors. The sector accounts presented in this chapter supplement the gross national product account by including flows that would otherwise be ignored and by making explicit other transactions that are important in economic analysis.[1]

4–2 A SIMPLIFIED SYSTEM OF ACCOUNTS

The sector accounts presented above are devised to present the maximum amount of statistical information in such a way that they can be used readily for a number of different purposes. For the purposes of this book, further consolidation to reduce the complexity of the accounts will facilitate subsequent analysis.

The basis of this further consolidation divides the economy into the same four sectors, but assumes that all income and product originate in the business sector. Thus the incomes originating in the business and personal sectors shown in Tables 4–2 and 4–3 are now assumed to be purchases of services from the business sector, with the factor payments then being paid by the business sector to persons. In essence, we assume that employees of nonprofit institutions sell their services as part of the business sector, although we retain the previous definitions of net returns. Thus the employee is still not assumed to purchase any intermediate product even though we define him as operating a business. Finally, the business sector is assumed to handle all foreign transactions. Under these assumptions, the consolidated income and product account of the business sector will be the same as the gross national product account shown in Table 1–9.

In the business sector account of Table 4–6 the item "payments to the personal sector" of $488 billion is made up of wages and salaries originating in the personal sector ($18 billion) and the government sector ($66 billion) plus income originating in the business sector ($404 billion). This last item is composed of wages, salaries, and supplements ($293 billion), proprietor's income ($56 billion), rental income of persons ($18 billion), net interest payments ($17 billion domestic, $1 billion foreign), and dividends ($18 billion domestic, $1 billion foreign). Direct taxes are composed of the corporate profits tax liability ($31 billion) plus employer social security payments from the business, government, and personal sectors ($16 billion), all of which are now assumed to be paid by business. Business saving of $24 billion is the

---

[1] Gains resulting from illegal activities and capital gains and losses are excluded from both the gross national product and the sector accounts.

Table 4–6 Business sector and gross national product, 1965 (Billions of dollars)

Payments to personal sector	$488	Consumption expenditures	$431
Direct taxes	47	Government purchases	136
Business saving	24	Net exports	7
National income	559	Gross private domestic	
Indirect business taxes	62	investment	107
Depreciation	60		
Charges against gross national product	$681	Gross national product	$681

Source: See text.

algebraic sum of undistributed corporate profits ($24 billion), corporate inventory valuation adjustment (−$2 billion), and foreign branch profits ($2 billion).

The subtotal of $559 billion shown in Table 4–6 is therefore national income at factor cost—the factor cost of producing the nation's output. The addition of the nonfactor costs, indirect business taxes, and depreciation gives the total charges against gross national product.

The right side of Table 4–6 shows the receipts from the sale of all goods and services in the economy as receipts of the business sector. Sales to consumers of $431 billion is the sum of purchases of consumption goods from the business and foreign sectors and the purchases of direct services by households and institutions ($18 billion). Similarly, government purchases of $136 billion are made up of purchases from the business and foreign sectors ($68 billion) and purchases of direct services ($68 billion). Finally, the net change in inventory ($9 billion) has been added to business purchases on capital account ($98 billion) to derive a gross private domestic total of $107 billion. The net export of goods and services has been left as a separate item.

Table 4–7 presents the summary account for the personal sector. The transactions between this sector and the business sector have already been explained in connection with Table 4–6, but two points

Table 4–7 Personal sector account, 1965 (Billions of dollars)

Payments to business	$431	Receipts from business	$488
Taxes	79	Receipts from government	46
Personal saving	24		
Personal outlays and saving	$534	Personal receipts	$534

Source: See text.

Table 4–8   Government sector account, 1965   (Billions of dollars)

Payments to business		$136	Receipts from persons		$ 79
Transfer payments		49	Receipts from business		109
Domestic	$46		Direct taxes	$47	
Foreign	3		Indirect taxes	62	
Surplus or deficit (—)		3			
Government payments and surplus		$188	Government receipts		$188

Source: See text.

require explanation. First, taxes are shown as $79 billion, although in Table 4–2 they are shown as $66 billion. The $13 billion difference results from transferring employee social security contributions from the receipts side of the personal sector account, where the Department of Commerce places it, to the expense side and including it with personal taxes. Second, intrasectoral interest payments by consumers ($11 billion) shown in Table 4–2 have been dropped from both sides of the summary account. The net result of these two changes is to increase personal receipts (and personal outlays and saving) from $532 billion to $534 billion. On the right side of Table 4–7, the receipts of the personal sector from government are the sum of transfer payments ($37 billion) and net interest, excluding interest paid by consumers ($9 billion). The personal sector shows an excess of receipts over expenditures of $24 billion.

All the items of the government sector account shown in Table 4–8 have already been explained in connection with Tables 4–6 and 4–7.

The foreign sector account of Table 4–9 requires no explanation.

The capital account shown in Table 4–10 is presented in a different form than in Table 4–5. The depreciation item has been separated from business purchases on capital account to show a net investment figure. This is done in spite of the warnings given above about the practical difficulties faced in estimating the current value of depreciation. The concept of net investment is such an important one in subsequent

Table 4–9   Foreign sector account, 1965   (Billions of dollars)

		Transfer payments from United States government	$3
		Net foreign investment	4
Net export of goods and services	$7	Net payments to foreigners	$7

Source: See text.

Table 4–10 Gross saving and investment account, 1965 (Billions of dollars)

Net investment	$ 47	Business saving	$ 24
Depreciation	60	Personal saving	24
Net foreign investment	4	Government surplus	3
		Depreciation	60
Gross investment	$111	Gross saving	$111

Source: See text.

analysis that even though it has no operational equivalent, we shall nevertheless assume that it is equal to gross investment minus depreciation.

4–3 INCOME IDENTITIES

Since each transaction between the sectors of the economy appears twice in the sector accounts, the form of a matrix is a convenient way to present an overall picture of the economy. Table 4–11 presents a matrix based on the accounts shown in Tables 4–6 to 4–10. Although the sector accounts have a total of 30 items, the matrix shows only 18 items. In fact, the matrix would have shown only 16 items if indirect business taxes and depreciation had not been separated out for special purposes. In Table 4–11 each row represents a payment, the left side of a sector account, while each column shows the corresponding receipt entered on the right side of another sector account. For example, consumption expenditure of $431 billion is shown, reading across the table, as an expense of the personal sector and also, reading down the table, as a business receipt.

Some basic income identities can be readily derived from Table 4–11. The following notation is used for ease of presentation:

Gross national product = GNP
Net national product = Y
National income = NI
Disposable income = Y_d
Consumption expenditure = C
Government expenditure = G
Net exports = $X - Z$
Net foreign investment = I_f
Net domestic investment = I_r
Personal receipts = R_p

Transfer payments (domestic) $= T_r$
Transfers to foreigners $= T_f$
Personal saving $= S_p$
Government saving $= S_g$
Business saving $= S_b$
Direct taxes (persons) $= T_p$
Direct taxes (business) $= T_b$
Indirect taxes $= T_i$
Depreciation $= D$

From column 1 of Table 4–11,

$$GNP \equiv C + G + (X - Z) + I_r + D \qquad (4-1)$$
$$681 \equiv 431 + 136 + 7 + 47 + 60$$

Gross national product is the sum of the expenditures by all sectors in the economy. Again, from column 1,

$$Y \equiv GNP - D$$

or

$$Y \equiv C + G + (X - Z) + I_r \qquad (4-2)$$
$$621 \equiv 431 + 136 + 7 + 47$$

The net national product total represents the net additions to the flow of goods and services to individuals, either directly from business (domestic and foreign) or through government, and to the capital stock.

Table 4–11 Income and product flow matrix (Billions of dollars)

	Receipts				
Payments	_Business_	_Persons_	_Govern-ment_	_Net foreign payments_	_Net saving_
Business		488 (R_p)	47 (T_b)		24 (S_b)
Persons	431 (C)		79 (T_p)		24 (S_p)
Government	136 (G)	46 (T_r)		3 (T_f)	3 (S_g)
Net exports	7 (X − Z)				
Net investment	47 (I_r)			4 (I_f)	
Net national product	621 (Y)				
Indirect business taxes			62 (T_i)		
Depreciation	60 (D)				
Total	681 (GNP)	534	188	7	51

Source: See text.

That is, net national product is gross national product less depreciation or, alternatively, the expenditures by the personal and government sectors and the net additions to the capital stock.[1]

From row 1

$$\text{GNP} \equiv R_p + T_b + S_b + T_i + D \tag{4-3}$$

but from column 2 and row 2,

$$R_p + T_r \equiv C + T_p + S_p$$

or

$$R_p \equiv C + T_p + S_p - T_r \tag{4-4}$$

and from column 3 and row 3,

$$T_b + T_p + T_i \equiv G + T_r + T_f + S_g$$

or

$$T_b + T_i \equiv G + T_r + T_f + S_g - T_p \tag{4-5}$$

Substituting (4–4) and (4–5) into (4–3), we have

$$\text{GNP} \equiv C + T_p + S_p - T_r + G + T_r + T_f + S_g - T_p + S_b + D$$

or

$$\text{GNP} \equiv C + S_p + G + T_f + S_g + S_b + D \tag{4-6}$$

Equating (4–1) and (4–6), we have

$$(X - Z) + I_r + D \equiv S_p + S_g + T_f + S_b + D$$

[1] Both the change in inventory and the net exports are given in net terms.

National income	Indirect business taxes	Depreciation	Total
559 (NI)	62 (T_i)	60 (D)	681
			534
			188
			7
			51

Remembering that $(X - Z) - T_f \equiv I_f$, we have

$$I_f + I_r + D \equiv S_p + S_g + S_b + D \qquad (4\text{--}7)$$
$$4 + 47 + 60 \equiv 24 + 3 + 24 + 60$$
$$111 \equiv 111$$

This identity represents both sides of the gross saving and investment account (Table 4–10).

Netting depreciation out of identity (4–7), we have

$$I_f + I_r \equiv S_p + S_g + S_b$$
$$4 + 47 \equiv 24 + 3 + 24$$
$$51 \equiv 51$$

which represents the equality of net saving and net investment.

The identity of saving and investment plays a large part in the subsequent analysis. In the accounts it is clear that saving and investment have been defined as equal. That part of final output not purchased by consumers and government has been called "investment" and must by definition be equal to that amount of receipts not paid out for final goods or services by persons, government, or business.

National income may also be obtained by subtracting indirect taxes from Y.

$$Y - T_i \equiv NI$$
$$621 - 62 \equiv 559$$

National income may also be obtained by adding total personal income payments to direct business taxes and net business savings. Accordingly, from row 1,

$$NI \equiv R_p + T_b + S_b$$
$$559 \equiv 488 + 47 + 24$$

Further, from column 2 and row 2,

$$R_p + T_r \equiv C + T_p + S_p \qquad (4\text{--}8)$$
$$488 + 46 \equiv 431 + 79 + 24$$

The left side of identity (4–8) lists personal income (factor payments plus transfers to persons from government); the right side shows the way persons dispose of their income: consumption expenditures for goods and services, direct taxes, and saving.

If personal taxes are transposed in identity (4–8), the left side becomes personal disposable income, i.e., total income receipts of persons minus their tax payments.

$$R_p + T_r - T_p \equiv C + S_p \equiv Y_d$$
$$488 + 46 - 79 \equiv 431 + 24 \equiv 455$$

Disposable income, as shown by this identity, can be either spent (C) or saved (S_p).

Disposable income can be derived from the net national product total by subtracting from Y that part which does not accrue to persons and adding government transfer payments to persons. Thus

$$Y_d \equiv Y - (T_i + T_p + T_b) + T_r - S_b$$
$$455 \equiv 621 - (62 + 79 + 47) + 46 - 24$$

Finally, let

$$T_i + T_p + T_b - T_r \equiv T$$
$$62 + 79 + 47 - 46 \equiv 142$$

where T is defined as net taxes, so that

$$Y_d \equiv Y - T - S_b$$
$$455 \equiv 621 - 142 - 24$$

Notice, moreover, that the government surplus can be calculated by subtracting government expenditures and transfers to foreigners from net taxes. Thus

$$S_g \equiv T - (G + T_f)$$
$$3 \equiv 142 - (136 + 3)$$

4-4 SUMMARY

In this first part of the book we have presented a fairly detailed picture of the national income and product accounts as developed by the Department of Commerce. At various stages in the discussion we pointed out that in some details the accounts are, for practical reasons, not always consistent. At the same time, there is an underlying rationale to the accounts that overrides the practical difficulties of estimation. The underlying rationale derives from the attempt to measure the annual flows of income and final product in the economy as a basis for evaluating the economy's utilization of its economic resources. In presenting figures, the Department of Commerce tries at the same time to give those that will fit into the body of economic theory from which evaluation and predictions can arise.

As the discussion in Chapter 1 indicated, the annual volume of output is determined by the expenditures for final goods and services, which, in turn, are related in part to the incomes received by the units making expenditure decisions. Therefore, the GNP account is broken down by the Department of Commerce in terms of income receipts by economic units and expenditures by the same units.

In Part 2 we shall examine the factors underlying the expenditure decisions of the economic units and the effects of these decisions upon the volume of final output. From such a study, and with the picture of the economy derived from the national accounts in mind, we shall be in a position to understand what determines the level of national output and to suggest measures that may be employed to affect that level.

PART

TWO

THE LEVEL OF
ECONOMIC ACTIVITY

5

CONSUMPTION, SAVING, AND THE SIMPLE THEORY OF INCOME DETERMINATION

5-1 THE CONSUMPTION FUNCTION

In Chapter 1 we observed that there is a close relationship between aggregate consumption expenditure and the level of disposable income. This relationship leads to one of the central propositions of the theory of income determination: The consumption expenditure of the community is determined principally by the community's level of disposable income. The schedule that relates consumption to disposable income is called the "propensity to consume" or "the consumption function," or sometimes also the schedule of "intended consumption."

A consumption function for a hypothetical economy is shown in Figure 5-1. Disposable income is measured on the horizontal axis. Consumption is measured on the vertical axis. The 45-degree line is a

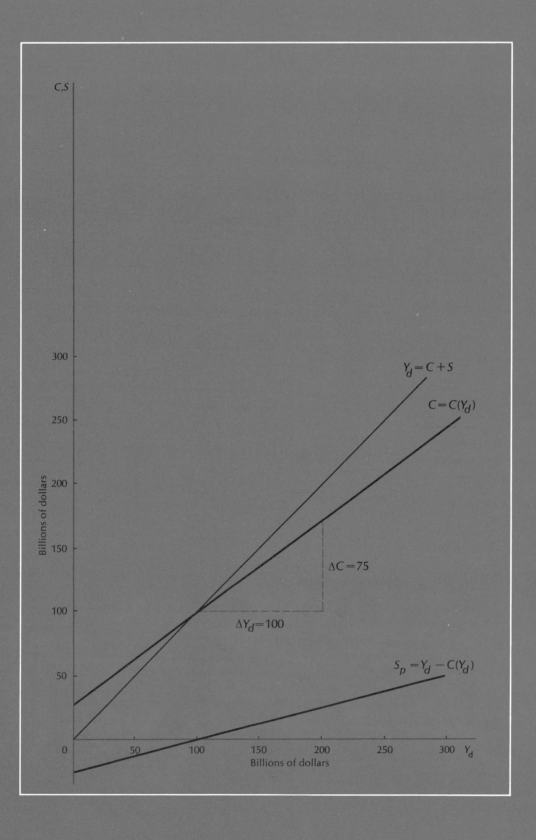

guideline which denotes that any point on the line is equidistant from the two axes. This means that the distance from the origin to some point on the horizontal axis will be the same as the vertical distance from that point on the horizontal axis to the 45-degree line. The level of disposable income can therefore be measured either vertically to the 45-degree line or along the horizontal axis.

The consumption function is drawn as a straight line with a slope of less than one. Although no one would seriously argue that the straight-line assumption is not an oversimplification, it is not enough of a distortion to justify the added complication of introducing a nonlinear schedule. The slope of the consumption function, or "marginal propensity to consume," indicates the percentage of each additional dollar of disposable income that will be consumed. The value of the marginal propensity to consume is less than unity because it is assumed that out of each additional dollar of disposable income received the community will increase its consumption by some percentage of the dollar and save the remainder.

An additional assumption is that there is some level of disposable income ($100 billion in Figure 5–1) at which all disposable income is consumed. Below this disposable income level (often called the "point of zero saving") consumers will make expenditures in excess of their disposable income even though this means dissaving, i.e., dipping into past saving or going into debt.

The marginal propensity to consume is, in the example of Figure 5–1, assumed to be 0.75. The point of zero saving is assumed to occur when disposable income is $100 billion. But as disposable income rises to $200 billion, consumption rises by only 0.75×100, which means that saving must rise by 0.25×100. When disposable income is $200 billion, consumption expenditure must therefore be $175 billion, and saving must be $25 billion. At disposable income levels below $100 billion the community is so poor that it prefers to go into debt rather than spend only its current disposable income on consumption. If it were possible to reduce disposable income to zero dollars, consumption would fall to $25 billion. Personal saving would therefore be −$25 billion.

In addition to the consumption function, Figure 5–1 also includes the schedule of intended personal saving S_p. This schedule is simply the difference between the consumption function and the 45-degree line. The slope of the saving schedule, called the "marginal propensity to save," is always 1 minus the marginal propensity to consume. In the

Figure 5–1   The consumption and saving functions (all values in real terms)

present example, the marginal propensity to consume is 0.75. The marginal propensity to save is therefore 0.25 because any addition to disposable income that is not spent must, by definition, be saved.[1]

5-2 SIMPLE INCOME DETERMINATION

As a means of getting the analysis off the ground in an uncomplicated manner, let us visualize an economy in which there is no government, in which corporations retain no earnings, in which there is no foreign trade, and in which the level of net intended investment is geared to long-term expectations and is therefore independent of the level of current income. Without any government or retained earnings, disposable income and real NNP (Y) are identical. The national income accountant's framework in this economy is

$$Y \equiv C + I_r \tag{5-1}$$

---

[1] Algebraically we may summarize what has been said thus far as follows: The hypothesis that consumption is a function of disposable income can be written

$C = C(Y_d)$

where C stands for aggregate real consumption and Y_d represents aggregate real disposable income. In the event that the consumption function is linear,

$C = C_0 + bY_d$

where b is the marginal propensity to consume and C_0 is the level of consumption at zero disposable income. In the present example $b = 0.75$. Therefore,

$C = C_0 + 0.75Y_d$

From Figure 5-1 it is evident that at an income level of $100 billion savings are zero. Consumption is therefore equal to disposable income at this point. Accordingly,

$100 = C_0 + 0.75 \times 100$

so that

$C_0 = 25$

The equation for the schedule of intended consumption therefore becomes

$C = 25 + 0.75Y_d$

Because personal savings are simply the difference between consumption and disposable income,

$S_p = Y_d - C = Y_d - 25 - 0.75Y_d = -25 + 0.25Y_d$

is the equation for the saving function.

where C is real consumption and I_r is net realized investment. By "realized investment" we mean all net investment regardless of whether it is intentional or unintentional. All income becomes disposable income under present assumptions, so that

$$Y \equiv C + S_p \tag{5-2}$$

Since there are no corporate savings, net private savings S becomes identical with net personal saving S_p. By equating (5-1) with (5-2) and substituting S for S_p, we note that

$$I_r \equiv S \tag{5-3}$$

which becomes the fundamental accounting identity in this simplified economy.

Now suppose that the community's consumption function is that of Figure 5-1 and that producers desire to spend $20 billion on investment goods (net of depreciation) at all levels of income.[1] Under these conditions, what will the equilibrium level of income be?

One way to determine the equilibrium level of income is to add the schedule of intended investment to the consumption schedule and to observe at what points this "aggregate demand" function $C + I$ intersects the 45-degree line.[2] Another way of finding equilibrium is to find the point where the schedule of intended investment cuts the saving schedule. In both cases equilibrium is at $180 billion.

What is the logic behind the equilibrium solution? Suppose that producers believe they will be able to sell $220 billion worth of goods. With production at $220 billion, disposable income will be $220 billion. The consumption function indicates that at an income level of $220 billion, consumers will spend $190 billion on consumption goods and save $30 billion. (Observe the situation at an income of $220 billion in Figure 5-2.) The intended investment schedule shows that businessmen wish to purchase $20 billion worth of investment goods. The total demand for goods and services (aggregate demand) at an income level of $220 billion is therefore $210 billion. But since production is greater than sales by $10 billion, the extra $10 billion worth of goods will be accumulated by businesses in the form of unintended investment in inventories I_u. If businessmen continue to produce $220 billion worth of

---

[1] Note that we now have Y instead of Y_d on the horizontal axis.

[2] Algebraically, if $C = 0.75Y + 25$ and if $I = 20$, then by substituting into $Y = C + I$, we have

$$Y = \frac{25 + 20}{1 - 0.75} = 180$$

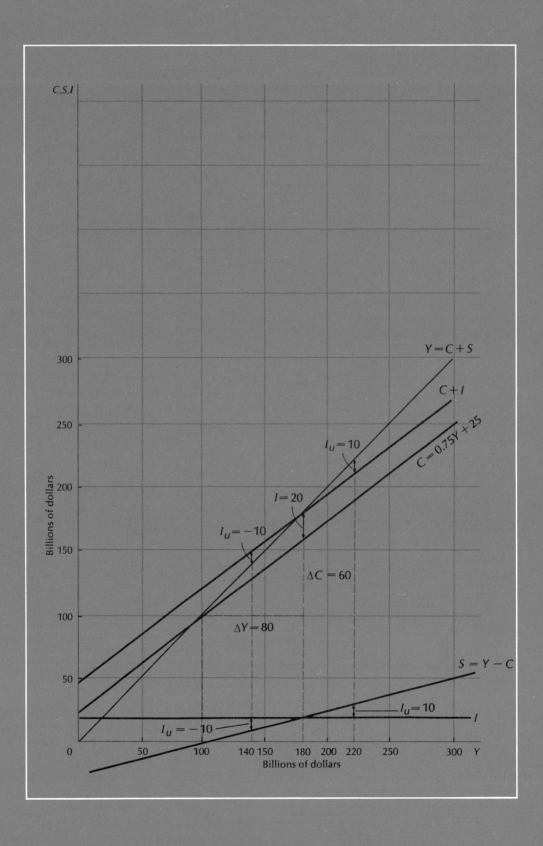

goods, inventories will continue to pile up at the rate of $10 billion per year. There will thus be a tendency for business to cut back production.

At the $220 billion income level the level of saving is $30 billion, intended investment I is $20 billion, and unintended investment I_u is $10 billion. Consequently the national income accountant will note that realized investment (I_r = intended + unintended investment) is exactly equal to the level of realized saving. It must always be true that

$$I + I_u = I_r = S$$

but only in equilibrium will it be true that intended investment equals saving, or

$$I = S$$

because the existence of unintended inventory investment or disinvestment indicates that production and sales are not synchronized.

Again, consider the situation that will arise if businessmen underestimate the demand for goods and services and therefore produce only $140 billion worth of goods while intended investment remains unchanged at $20 billion (see Figure 5–2 again at $Y = 140$). When $Y = 140$, $C = 130$, with the consequence that aggregate demand $C + I$ = 150; thus there will be a $10 billion reduction in inventories not anticipated by businessmen. Since saving is $10 billion and unintended investment is −$10 billion,

$$I + I_u = 10 = S$$

There will now be a tendency for production and income to increase to a level of $180 billion where $C = 160$, $S = 20$, $I = 20$, and $I_u = 0$. The equilibrium level of income, it appears, necessarily requires equality between intended investment and saving.

5–3   THE MULTIPLIER

Suppose that the level of intended investment expenditure is zero. The equilibrium level of income would, in this case, be $100 billion (see Figure 5–2 again). Next pretend that businessmen suddenly decide to spend $20 billion each year on new plants and equipment. The aggregate demand schedule $C + I$ would therefore shift up by $20 billion. Notice, however, that the level of income rises not by $20 billion but

Figure 5–2   Simple income determination
(all values in real terms)

by $80 billion. Observe, finally, that the overall change in income of $80 billion consists of two components—the change in investment expenditure of $20 billion and an additional increase in consumption expenditure of $60 billion. How does this change in consumption of $60 billion come about?

To illustrate this "multiplier" effect let us suppose that changes in expenditure are instantaneously translated into income receipts, but that income recipients do not spend today's income until tomorrow. Suppose next that, instead of a permanent shift in the investment demand schedule, an increase in investment spending of $1 takes place in day 1. This $1 is immediately paid out to the wage earners, stockholders, etc., of the investment goods industry. The marginal propensity to consume b tells us that on day 2, b percent of the additional income earned in day 1 will be spent on consumption goods. Consequently, income originating in consumption goods industries rises by b dollars on day 2, of which b percent, or b^2, is spent in day 3, of which b percent, or b^3, will be spent in day 4, and so on indefinitely. The day-by-day income changes, in excess of the original equilibrium level, resulting from the $1 increase in investment expenditures in day 1 will therefore be

$$1, b, b^2, b^3, \ldots, b^t$$

Since b is a fraction, the differences between the initial equilibrium income level and the actual income level become successively smaller as time passes. Note that as t becomes very large, b^t becomes very small so that income returns to its initial equilibrium.

The time path of income for a value of $b = 0.75$ is traced in Figure 5–3. In day 1 the $1 increase in spending raises the income level by $1 over the initial value of Y_0. In day 2 the amount of $0.75 \times \$1$, or 75 cents, is respent on consumption goods. Income in day 2 is therefore $Y_0 + 75$ cents. In day 3 income will be 0.75×0.75, or $(0.75)^2 \times \$1$, in excess of the initial level, and in day t it will be $(0.75)^{t-1} \times \$1$ in excess of the initial level. As t grows very large, the difference between the initial level and the actual level of income approaches zero.

The case just considered may be visualized most easily by imagining an automobile cruising down a level road at a constant speed of 40 miles per hour with the accelerator held steady exactly halfway from the floor of the car. Imagine that the driver pushes the accelerator to the floor but that he then immediately releases it and holds it steady in its original position. The car will first lurch forward, picking up speed, but

Figure 5–3   The multiplier with a single expenditure (all values in real terms)

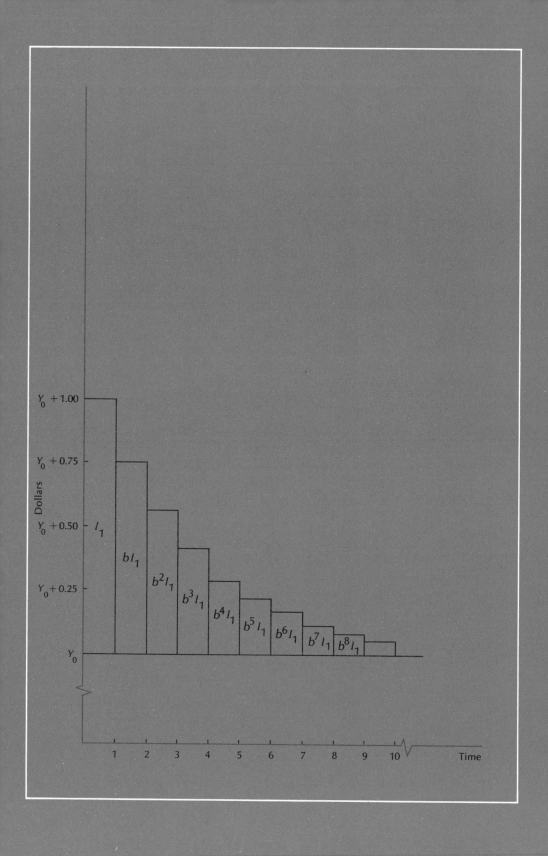

will immediately begin to decelerate and gradually approach its previous 40 mile per hour speed.

What will happen if the driver pushes the accelerator to the floor and keeps it there? The car will pick up speed and continue to accelerate, but at a decreasing rate, until gradually the speed of the car approaches a new constant velocity. This latter case, in which the accelerator is pressed to the floor and held there, is exactly the kind of thing that happens when investment expenditure is increased by some amount and is then maintained at the new higher level permanently. In other words, an upward shift of the investment demand schedule of $1 implies that there will be a $1 increase in investment spending in period 1; another dollar will be spent in period 2, another dollar in period 3, and so on indefinitely.

How will the level of income change over time under this new set of assumptions? In day 1 the investment schedule shifts up so that on this first day the level of income rises by $1. The level of income in day 1 is therefore

$$Y_1 = Y_0 + 1$$

where Y_0 is the initial income level. In day 2 another dollar of investment expenditures is added to the income stream. But in addition to this extra dollar, b percent of the dollar of the investment expenditures of the first day will be spent on consumption. Consequently on day 2 the level of income is

$$Y_2 = Y_0 + 1 + b$$

In day 3, b percent of the income change in day 2 over the initial level, or $b(1 + b) = b + b^2$, will be respent on consumption, in addition to which another dollar of investment expenditure is added to the income stream. Consequently on day 3 the level of income rises to

$$Y_3 = Y_0 + 1 + b + b^2$$

The process repeats itself indefinitely so that in day t

$$Y_t = Y_0 + 1 + b + b^2 + b^3 + \cdots + b^{t-1}$$

which, as can easily be shown,[1] simplifies to

$$Y_t = Y_0 + \frac{1 - b^t}{1 - b}$$

---

[1] Note that

$$Y_t = Y_0 + 1 + b + b^2 + b^3 + \cdots + b^{t-1}$$

As t grows very large, b^t becomes very small so that in the limit the new equilibrium value of income Y_t is

$$Y_t = Y_0 + \frac{1}{1 - b}$$

The change in income $Y_t - Y_0$ due to a $1 per day increase in investment spending therefore is $1/(1 - b)$, which is known as the "multiplier." Remembering that b is the marginal propensity to consume, we can calculate the value of the multiplier by simply measuring the slope of the consumption function. If $b = 0.75$, the multiplier is 4, that is, a $1 increase in investment spending raises the level of income by $4. If $b = 0.50$, the multiplier is 2. If $b = 0$, the multiplier is 1. In this last case, all additional income that results from the increase in investment will be saved, so that there is no respending on consumption, and consequently the level of income rises only by the amount of the increase in investment expenditure.

A diagram similar to Figure 5–4 may help to illustrate the process of adjustment to the new equilibrium level. Assume that $b = 0.50$ and that each day $1 of new investment expenditure materializes. In the first day the level of income rises by $1. In the second day 0.50 of this is respent, in addition to which another dollar of investment expenditure takes place. In the third day 0.50 of the $1.50 is respent on consumption and added to the $1 of investment spending which materialized on day 3. This gives an increase in income, over the initial level, of $1.75. The successive day-to-day increases over the previous day become smaller and smaller and gradually the level of income approaches its new equilibrium level of $Y_0 + 2$.

One of the most useful ways to visualize the multiplier is as follows: We know from our previous discussion that income cannot be in equi-

---

is a geometric series. In order to sum such a series, we need merely multiply each term by b:

$$bY_t = bY_0 + b + b^2 + b^3 + \cdots + b^{t-1} + b^t$$

and observe that when the second series is subtracted from the first series, all but the first two terms from the right-hand side of the first series drop out, while only the first and last terms of the right-hand side of the second series remain, i.e.,

$$Y_t - bY_t = Y_0 - bY_0 + 1 - b^t$$

which simplifies to

$$Y_t = Y_0 + \frac{1 - b^t}{1 - b}$$

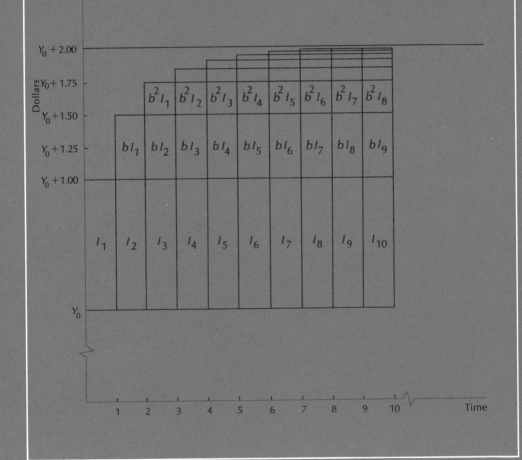

librium unless intended investment and saving are equal. If, therefore, we begin in a position of equilibrium and if intended investment now rises permanently by $1, we know from the equilibrium condition that unless saving also rises by $1, equilibrium will not have been restored. Thus all we need to do is ask: By how much must income rise in order that one more dollar of saving be generated? And this question is identical to asking what the value of the multiplier is. If the marginal propensity to consume is 0.75, the marginal propensity to save is 0.25. This means that each time income rises by $1, saving rises by 25 cents. But since we require saving to rise by $1, and since a $1 rise in income generates only a 25-cent increase in saving, the necessary income increase must be 1/0.25, or $4. Had the marginal propensity to save been 0.5, an additional dollar of income would generate an additional 50-cent saving so that the multiplier would be 1/0.50 = $2. In general, if the marginal propensity to save is $1 - b$, an additional dollar of income creates added saving in an amount $1 - b$ so that a $1 increase in saving would be generated by an income increase of $1/(1 - b)$.

5–4 FACTORS AFFECTING THE LEVEL OF AGGREGATE CONSUMPTION

The proposition that aggregate consumption is a function of the aggregate level of disposable income stems from the revolutionary work of Lord Keynes.[1] Keynes's theory of the consumption function held out the hope that a firm basis for forecasting consumption expenditure had at last been discovered. However, forecasts of post-World War II consumption were quite far off the mark. The forecasts failed because they did not take into account the fact that the consumption behavior of the community depends on many more factors than the current level of disposable income.

It would be impossible to do justice to the entire subject of the consumption function without going far afield. Our purpose in this section is the modest one of bringing to the reader's attention some additional factors that the economist must consider when he attempts to predict

---

[1] J. M. Keynes, *The General Theory of Employment, Interest and Money,* Harcourt, Brace, & World, Inc., New York, 1936.

Figure 5–4   The multiplier with a continuous injection (all values in real terms)

the level of consumption and to suggest the directions which think-ing and research on the subject have taken in recent years.[1]

Some of the variables that may be relevant are ignored in this dis-cussion. It has long been supposed, for example, that an increase in the rate of interest would lead to an increase in saving and therefore to a reduction in consumption. Since this will be treated at some length in Chapter 13, we shall ignore the effects of interest rate changes on con-sumption. Similarly, it has been argued that a fall in the general level of prices will cause the real value of the stocks of currency and govern-ment bonds to rise and that this increase in "wealth" will serve to stimulate consumption. This subject is considered in Chapter 11 and may be passed over here.

It was Keynes's belief that the marginal propensity to consume of low-income groups would be higher than the marginal propensity to consume of high-income groups. This belief suggested that aggregate demand might be raised by a policy of income redistribution. If the marginal propensity to consume of a rich man is 0.60 while the marginal propensity to consume of a poor man is 0.90, a redistribution of income of $1 from the rich to the poor man would raise aggregate consumption by 30 cents. If a redistribution of a given level of disposable income will change the level of consumption, the consumption function for the community as a whole would have to be considered a function of both the level of disposable income and the way in which disposable income is distributed.

In a study of German time-series data, Staehle[2] found that the dis-tribution of income was an important factor in determining aggregate consumption. However, investigations using American "cross-section" data failed to find any significant relationship between income distribu-tion and aggregate consumption.[3] As a result of these studies, many economists no longer feel that an income-leveling policy will signifi-cantly help raise total consumption.

Statistical studies have shown that the shape of the consumption function differs radically, depending upon the type of data used to plot the function. When aggregate consumption expenditures are plotted

---

[1] For a careful and comprehensive survey of the material discussed in this section see R. Ferber, "Research on Household Behavior," *American Economic Review*, 52:19–63, 1962.

[2] H. Staehle, "Short Period Variations in the Distribution of Incomes," *Review of Economic Statistics*, 19:133–143, 1937.

[3] H. Lubell, "Effects of Income Redistribution on Consumers' Expenditures," *American Economic Review*, 37:157–170, 1947. See also J. Marschak's classic paper, "Personal and Collective Budget Functions," *Review of Economic Statistics*, 21:161–170, 1939.

against disposable income for different years, the consumption function appears as a line (C_L in Figure 5–5) emanating from the origin with a slope of approximately 0.9. But when consumption expenditures are plotted for a cross section of family-income groups at one point in time, the shape is more in line with the consumption function plotted in Figure 5–1 and corresponds to the functions C_{S_0}, C_{S_1}, C_{S_2} of Figure 5–5. The poorest families do indeed dissave in the short run, and, as became evident in 1932, the community as a whole may dissave for a time under the pressure of a drastic income shrinkage.

How can these differently shaped consumption schedules be reconciled? One possible approach is to suppose that the observed community consumption level for a period of time is but one point on an existing schedule of intentions and that the short-run schedules drift upward over time. In Figure 5–5 points (C_0,Y_0), (C_1,Y_1), and (C_2,Y_2) are observed points in the years 0, 1, and 2. The schedules C_{S_0}, C_{S_1}, and C_{S_2} are the schedules that reflect the true propensity to consume in years 0, 1, and 2. If a hypothesis can be introduced that explains why the short-run consumption function drifts upward over time, the cross section and time-series observations can be reconciled.

One possible explanation for the secular upward drift of the consumption function is Duesenberry's "relative income" hypothesis.[1] Duesenberry observed that a Negro family with an income of $5,000 saves more than a white family with a comparable level of income. Since the Negro family is likely to reside in a lower rent district than the white family and since a Negro with a $5,000 income is likely to be on a higher point in the distribution of income in his neighborhood, Duesenberry concluded that the difference in consumption behavior could be explained by differences in the level of relative income, i.e., income in relation to what one is accustomed to. These observations then led Duesenberry to formulate the following hypothesis with respect to aggregate consumption behavior. Suppose that in Figure 5–5 the community's level of income is Y_0. A fall in income from Y_0 causes consumers, accustomed to this standard of living, to defend their living standards by maintaining their consumption expenditures. They therefore move backward along the function C_{S_0}, reducing saving drastically while maintaining consumption. Should income rise back toward Y_0, consumption rises by only a little because consumers attempt to recover

[1] J. S. Duesenberry, *Income, Saving, and the Theory of Consumer Behavior*, Harvard University Press, Cambridge, Mass., 1949. F. Modigliani, "Fluctuations in the Savings–Income Ratio: A Problem in Economic Forecasting," in *Studies in Income and Wealth*, Vol. 11, National Bureau of Economic Research, Inc., New York, 1949.

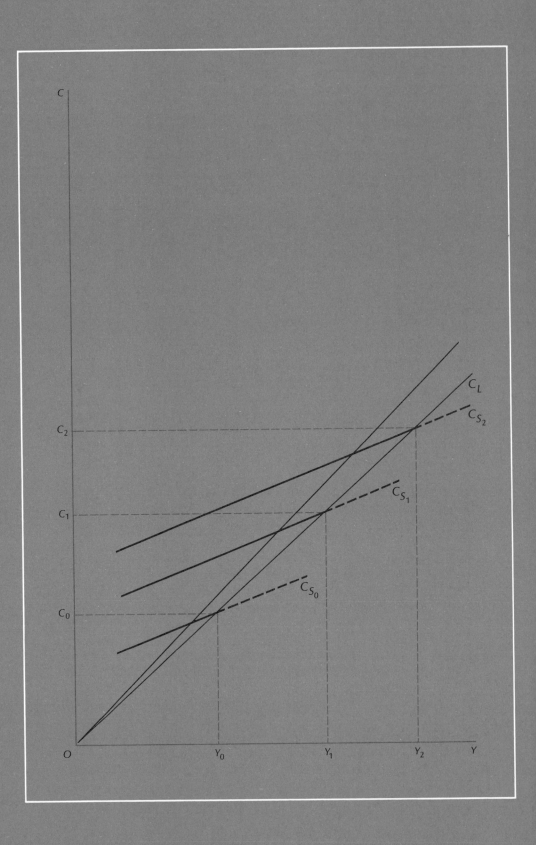

the preceding peak level of saving. This implies that as income rises the community moves upward along the C_{s_0} schedule. But when Y_0 is reached, the previous highest standard of consumption and saving to which the community is accustomed is restored. Further increases in income therefore cause a sharp rise in the marginal propensity to consume. Additions to income are then split so as to maintain a constant consumption-income ratio. When income is above the highest past peak, the community moves along C_L. If income reaches Y_1 but subsequently falls, the community repeats its attempt to preserve its newly acquired higher living standard and moves backward along C_{s_1}.

While Duesenberry's hypothesis explains the secular upward drift of the consumption function, his "relative income" hypothesis is by no means the only explanation. Tobin,[1] for example, showed that the difference in the saving habits between Negroes and whites could be explained by the fact that although a Negro and a white family might have the same current income, the white family is likely to be wealthier and more secure and will therefore tend to save less.

Another factor that helps explain the upward drift of the consumption function is the introduction of new products. New products may so change consumer preferences that consumers are willing to revise their expenditure plans and purchase the new commodity at the expense of saving. A comparison, by one of the authors,[2] of the buyers of television in 1950 with groups of nonbuyers confirmed the suspicion that this particular new product was purchased primarily at the expense of saving rather than at the expense of alternative consumption expenditures.

Dissatisfaction with the hypothesis that consumption is primarily a function of current income arises from a number of additional sources. One difficulty is that if we plot consumption against income over a six-month period, we shall obtain a substantially less steeply sloped consumption function than if we choose one year as our time period. Indeed, the longer the time period we choose, the steeper the observed

[1] J. Tobin, "Relative Income, Absolute Income, and Savings," in *Money, Trade and Economic Growth, Essays in Honor of John H. Williams*, The Macmillan Company, New York, 1951.

[2] T. F. Dernburg, "The Consumption–Income Ratio and Product Innovation," Purdue University, Institute for Quantitative Research in Economics and Management, Institute Paper No. 9, 1960. See also T. F. Dernburg, "Consumer Response to Innovation," in T. F. Dernburg and others, *Studies in Household Economic Behavior*, Yale University Press, New Haven, Conn., 1958.

Figure 5–5 Long-run and short-run consumption functions (all values in real terms)

consumption function becomes. The presumption is that lengthening the period over which the flow of income and consumption are measured tends to eliminate the effects of short-run variations in income and of lags in the adjustment of consumption to changes in income. Mrs. Mack[1] has shown that if we divide families according to income class, the higher-income groups will contain a larger proportion of people whose incomes have recently risen, while the lower-income groups will contain a larger proportion of families whose incomes have recently fallen. Since some of these income changes may be temporary and since it takes time to adjust consumption expenditures even to income changes that are permanent, the measured consumption level of the higher-income groups will be lower than would be true in the long run, while the measured consumption levels of the lower-income groups will be higher than would be true in the long run. Therefore, a cross-section consumption function of consumption plotted against income over some fairly short period of time will tend to make the observed consumption function a good deal flatter than the "true" propensity to consume.

A related finding is the discovery that groups with very variable incomes, such as farm families, seem to have lower marginal propensities to consume than groups with more stable incomes. Similarly, there is a much looser correlation between consumption and income for farm families than for most other groups in the population.

These findings suggest that perhaps consumption ought to be related to some longer-run measure of income or wealth than current income. Indeed, attempts to derive the consumption function from the basic microeconomic theory of consumer utility maximization suggest that the rational consumer will make his current consumption be a function of his "normal" rather than his actual income. Actual income is subject to temporary windfall gains and losses and should therefore be broken down into a "permanent" and a "transitory" component. In principle, consumption should also be broken down in this way, and one should then relate permanent consumption to permanent income.[2]

[1] R. P. Mack, "The Direction of Change in Income and the Consumption Function," *Review of Economics and Statistics*, 30:239–258, 1948.

[2] M. Friedman, *A Theory of the Consumption Function*, National Bureau of Economic Research, Inc., New York, 1955. A similar hypothesis is advanced by F. Modigliani and R. Brumberg, "Utility Analysis and the Consumption Function: An Interpretation of Cross-section Data," in K. K. Kurihara, ed., *Post-Keynesian Economics*, Rutgers University Press, New Brunswick, N.J., 1954. See also R. Brumberg, "An Approximation to the Aggregate Savings Function," *Economic Journal*, 66:66–72, 1956; A. Ando and F. Modigliani, "The 'Life Cycle' Hypothesis of Saving: Aggregate Implications and Tests," *American Economic Review*, 53:55–84, 1963; and M. J. Farrell, "The New Theories of the Consumption Function," *Economic Journal*, 69:678–696, 1959.

It is statistically impossible to isolate permanent from transitory income. However, some idea of a consumer's permanent or normal income can be derived in the following way. Imagine a consumer who contemplates the sale of all his future earnings for a lump-sum payment to be made immediately.[1] Add to this the value of his accumulated wealth, and imagine that the entire sum is then invested at interest. The annual interest earning on this sum is what we should call the consumer's permanent income.

If consumption is a function of permanent income, a rise in actual income would be expected to affect consumption only insofar as the rise in income raises the consumer's permanent income. Since the direct effect of a change in current income on permanent income is very small, one would expect a low marginal propensity to consume since changes in income would be reflected primarily in fluctuations in the level of saving. On the other hand, an increase in income may give rise to the expectation that permanent income will be greater than it was originally thought to be, and if this is the case, the marginal propensity to consume may be quite high. Thus the new theories suggest that because it is difficult to estimate the effect of a change in actual income on permanent income, it will be difficult to predict its effect on consumption. The marginal propensity to consume may therefore be very unstable and unpredictable. In any case the simple rule that a given change in income will always produce a given predictable change in consumption cannot be relied upon.

If it is true that consumers gear their consumption expenditures to their lifetime earning prospects rather than to their current incomes, one ought to be able to find an association between consumption and the age of individuals. Young families, for example, will have a low current income but a high permanent income, and they are therefore likely to consume a larger fraction of their income than older families whose actual incomes may be equal to or below their permanent incomes. These and other presumptions are confirmed by numerous studies. One of the most interesting is the study by Watts.[2] He proposes the hypothesis that current consumption spending is primarily a matter of expected income, where expected income E is, in principle, very similar to permanent income as we previously described it. A high E implies a high level of current consumption, while a low E implies the opposite. Among the factors affecting E, Watts finds age, education,

---

[1] In Chap. 7 we shall learn how to calculate the current value of a stream of future receipts.

[2] H. Watts, "Long-run Income Expectations and Consumer Savings," in T. F. Dernburg and others, *op. cit.*

occupation, race, and location to be significant. Spending units with younger heads who have a college education save the least because their expected income is greatest. Professional and business people have a higher expected income and therefore save a smaller part of their income than unskilled workers. Opportunities for high future income are presumably greater in urban areas, and in areas of high population density there are likely to be stronger imitative effects. Urban households therefore generally save less than rural households with the same income. Spending units close to retirement save more than younger units because their expected income and their current income are tending to equality. However, the age group that is currently putting its children through college saves less than other older age groups.

In order to put together the foundation stones of macroeconomic theory in as simple a manner as possible, we shall return, throughout the next few chapters, to the simple hypothesis that consumption is a function of current disposable income. But it should be borne in mind, as the foregoing discussion has suggested, that the determination of aggregate consumption expenditure is no simple matter.

6

FISCAL POLICY
AND INCOME
DETERMINATION

6–1 GOVERNMENT PURCHASES, TAXES,
AND THE EQUILIBRIUM CONDITION

In this chapter we turn our attention to the effect of government purchases and taxation on the level of income. The assumptions that corporate saving is negligible and that the economy does not engage in foreign trade are retained. Under these conditions real net national product Y is the sum of personal consumption expenditure, net private domestic investment, and government purchases of goods and services, or

$$Y \equiv C + I_r + G$$

The level of income is divided between the government (net taxes) and the household sector (disposable income). Hence

$$Y = Y_d + T \qquad (6-1)$$

and since households are free either to spend or to save their disposable income,

$$Y = C + S + T$$

When government purchases and taxes are introduced, the equilibrium condition is that intended investment plus government purchases must equal saving plus taxes. That this must be true can easily be seen by introducing the notions of an income leakage and an injection. In the simplified model of Chapter 5, where government did not enter the picture, a portion of the current income stream was spent on consumption and therefore reentered the flow of spending. A portion, however, "leaked" into saving. It was noted that if an amount of intended investment just sufficient to balance the saving took place, the level of income would remain unchanged because production and sales plus intended changes in inventories would then be synchronized. But this is the same as saying that investment expenditure is just sufficient to make up for the leakage, due to saving, from the spending stream. If the level of saving is greater than the level of intended investment, more will leak out of the spending stream than is pumped in via intended investment. Taxes, like saving, are income leakages, while government purchases, like intended investment, are injections. If the sum of taxes and saving is greater than the sum of government purchases and intended investment, more will have been produced than sold or intentionally accumulated because insufficient expenditures will have been made to compensate for the leakages.

To summarize: By the definition of the national accounts it must always be true that

$$Y \equiv C + I_r + G$$

and

$$I_r + G \equiv S + T$$

but only in equilibrium is it true that the level of output equals the level of aggregate demand so that

$$Y = C + I + G$$

and that total injections equal total leakages so that

$$I + G = S + T \qquad (6-2)$$

6–2 GAP ANALYSIS AND THE EFFECT OF CHANGES IN THE LEVEL OF GOVERNMENT PURCHASES

Throughout the analysis of this chapter it will be useful to follow the procedure of the previous chapter and to imagine a hypothetical economy in which consumption is a linear function of disposable income and in which the level of investment is independent of the level of income. It should be borne in mind that our assumed numerical values bear no relation whatever to reality and are picked in order to facilitate the exposition and to assist the reader to grasp the fundamentals. Our purpose here is to understand the mechanics of fiscal policy. The practical difficulties of implementation will be considered in Part 4.

Consider the situation depicted in Figure 6–1. The consumption function is linear, and the marginal propensity to consume is assumed to have a value of 2/3. We assume also that the point of zero saving is at an income level of $75 billion. Consequently, the level of consumption associated with $Y = 0$ is $25 billion, and when $Y = 375$, $C = 275$.[1]

The level of intended investment is assumed to be $25 billion at all levels of income. Thus the intersection of the aggregate demand schedule with the 45-degree line is at an income level of $150 billion. Inspection of the diagram also confirms that $150 billion is the income level at which intended investment equals saving.

This situation, which we shall call state I, is the basic starting point against which we intend to compare the effects of various fiscal policies. To summarize the situation we have:

State I

$Y = 150 = Y_d$

$C = 125$

$I = S = 25$

$G = T = 0$

Economists have found the concept of an inflationary or a deflationary gap useful in conducting national income analysis. To illustrate this concept, let us imagine that the full-employment level of income in our present hypothetical economy is $375 billion. The gap is then defined as the difference between the actual level of aggregate demand at the *full-employment level of income* and the amount of aggregate demand that would be needed to attain full employment. If we erect a vertical

---

[1]The equation for the consumption function is

$C = C_0 + bY_d = 25 + 2/3\, Y_d$

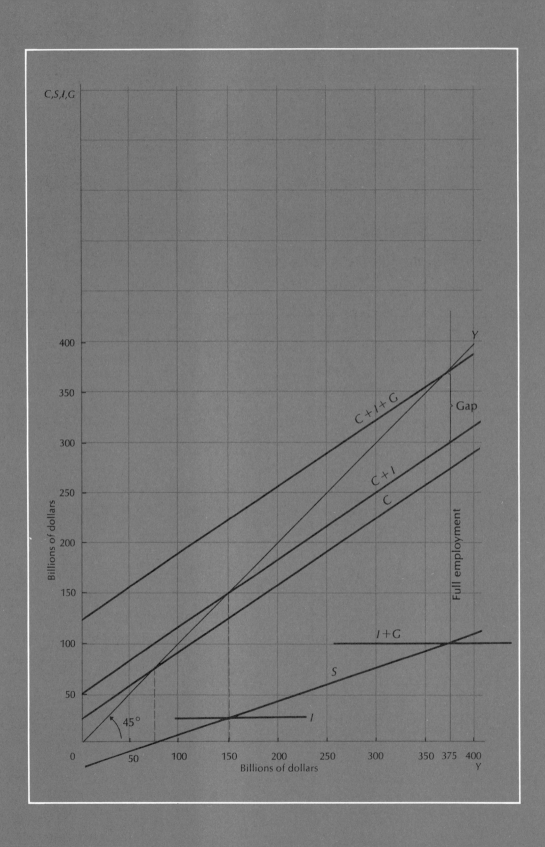

line at the full-employment level of income, we see that full employment would require the aggregate demand schedule to cut the 45-
degree line where it intersects the full-employment vertical line. In
other words, aggregate demand would have to be $375 billion at the
full-employment level of income. In the present example, however, we
see that, at the full-employment level of income, consumption would
be $275 billion and investment would be $25 billion. Consequently,
aggregate demand at full employment would be $300 billion, and there
is a deflationary gap of $75 billion. Had the aggregate demand schedule
cut the vertical line at full employment above the intersection of the
vertical with the 45-degree line, aggregate demand would have been
in excess of what is required for full employment, and we should then
say that an inflationary gap was present. For example if aggregate demand at full employment is $400 billion and the full-employment level
of income is $375 billion, the inflationary gap would be $25 billion.

Knowledge of the magnitude of the gap and the value of the multiplier provides yet another way of locating the equilibrium level of income. Imagine that the economy is at full employment and that a gap
of $75 billion develops because of a downward shift of the investment
function. The level of income would fall by the amount of this decline
in aggregate demand times the multiplier. Because the marginal propensity to consume in this hypothetical economy is 2/3, the multiplier
has a value of 3, and this means that a fall in aggregate demand of $75
billion would cause income to fall by $225 billion to a level of $150
billion. Thus the presence of a deflationary gap of $75 billion implies
that the level of income falls short of the full-employment level by an
amount equal to the magnitude of the gap times the multiplier. We
may therefore state quite generally that the equilibrium level of income
may be calculated by the formula

$$Y = Y^* - \text{gap} \times \text{multiplier} \tag{6–3}$$

where Y^* is the full-employment level of income. Using the numerical
values of our example, we have

$$Y = 375 - (75 \times 3) = 150$$

The magnitude of the deflationary gap is equivalent to the amount
by which aggregate demand must be raised in order to lift income to
the full-employment level. In the present example the deflationary gap

Figure 6–1   The deflationary gap and the effect
of government purchases on the level of
income (all values in real terms)

is $75 billion, and this means that aggregate demand must *shift up* by $75 billion. If such a shift materializes, the level of income would rise by the amount of the increase in aggregate demand times the multiplier. Let the level of aggregate demand be denoted by the symbol D. We can then state a general multiplier formula,

$$\frac{\Delta Y}{\Delta D} = \frac{1}{1-b} \tag{6-4}$$

where ΔY is the change in income and ΔD is the change (vertical shift) in the aggregate demand schedule.

As far as its effect on the level of income is concerned, the source of an increase in aggregate demand is irrelevant. Aggregate demand could rise because consumer tastes change or because consumers have more disposable income as the result of a tax cut. Aggregate demand could rise because of an increase in the desire of business to invest or, finally, because of an increase in government purchases. Regardless of the source, an upward shift in the aggregate demand schedule will raise the equilibrium level of income by the amount of the shift in aggregate demand times the multiplier. In the present example, this would mean that for every $1 billion increase in aggregate demand, the equilibrium level of income would rise by $3 billion.

Suppose now that we return to the situation of state I. The equilibrium level of income is $150 billion, the full-employment level of income is $375 billion, and the economy finds itself suffering from a deflationary gap of $75 billion. Assume next that it is decided to close the gap by raising the level of government purchases by $75 billion.[1] As a consequence, the aggregate demand schedule shifts up by $75 billion, i.e., the $C + I + G$ schedule is now the relevant aggregate demand schedule, and the equilibrium level of income rises by $225 billion to the full-employment level of $375 billion.

The new situation is depicted in Figure 6–1. The aggregate demand schedule, $C + I + G$, cuts the 45-degree line at an income level of $375 billion, and this income level is where total injections $I + G$ now equal $100 billion. Since the level of saving is $100 billion, these injections are balanced by an equal amount of leakages. Call this new situation state II and observe that:

State II

$Y = 375$

---

[1] Here again we should remind ourselves that we are not concerned with the practical difficulties of putting such an enormous increase in G into effect.

$C = 275$

$I = 25$

$G = 75$

$S = 100$

$T = 0$

Therefore,

$I + G = S + T$

$25 + 75 = 100 + 0$

In summary: (1) An increase in the level of aggregate demand will raise the equilibrium level of income by the amount of the increase in aggregate demand times the multiplier regardless of the source of the increase in demand; (2) the deflationary gap is a measure of the deficiency of aggregate demand at full employment; (3) one way to close the gap is to raise the level of government purchases by an amount equal to the size of the gap.

6-3 LUMP-SUM TAXATION AND THE BALANCED BUDGET MULTIPLIER

In this section we shall examine the effect of lump-sum taxation. By a lump-sum (or "head" or "poll") tax we mean that each taxpayer must pay a sum which is independent of the economic circumstances of the payer. In the next section we shall extend the analysis to cover the case of proportional income taxation.

Consider Figure 6–2, where the consumption function of Figure 6–1 is reproduced as the function C_0, and assume that the economy is presently in state II. With government purchases at a level of $75 billion and with no tax collection, there is an annual budgetary deficit of $75 billion. Let us assume that Congress legislates a lump-sum tax, the yield (i.e., the value of collections) of which is $75 billion. The tax reduces disposable income at all income levels by $75 billion. Since the marginal propensity to consume is 2/3, the loss of disposable income causes consumers to reduce consumption spending by $50 billion, that is, $2/3 \times \$75$ billion, and saving by $25 billion. Consequently, the consumption function shifts down by $50 billion at all levels of income.

The new consumption function is the function C_1 in Figure 6–2. The vertical distance between C_1 and C_0 is $50 billion, which in general equals the amount of the change in tax yield multiplied by the marginal

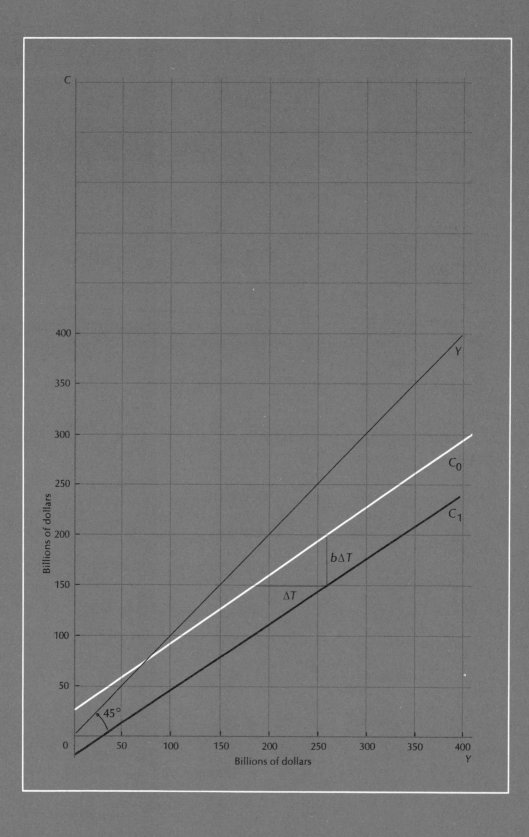

propensity to consume. The horizontal distance between the two functions is equal to the amount of the change in tax yield.[1]

We saw in the last section that an increase in government purchases of $1 would shift the aggregate demand schedule up by $1. We now discover, however, that a similar rule does not apply to taxation. Because a fraction of the increase in tax yield comes out of income that would have been saved anyway, the shift in the consumption function and therefore in the aggregate demand schedule is not equal to 1. It is, rather, equal to the change in tax yield times the marginal propensity to consume.

Since the initial change in aggregate demand due to the increase in taxes is

$$\Delta D = \Delta C = -b \, \Delta T$$

we may substitute this change into Eq. 6–4 and calculate the effect of the change on the equilibrium level of income. This substitution yields

$$\frac{\Delta Y}{\Delta T} = \frac{-b}{1-b} = \frac{-2/3}{1-2/3} = 2$$

and we therefore see that the multiplier with respect to taxation is exactly 1 less than the multiplier with respect to a change in government purchases. Thus for each $1 of increased tax yield, we expect the level of income to decline by $2, and if the total increase in taxes is $75 billion, the equilibrium level of income ought to drop by $150 to a new equilibrium level of $225.

[1] Analytically, consumption is a function of disposable income. Consequently,

$$C = a + bY_d$$

However, disposable income is given by

$$Y_d = Y - T$$

and the consumption function may therefore be written as

$$C = a + b(Y - T)$$

At a given level of income, the change in consumption associated with a change in T is

$$\Delta C = -b\Delta T$$

which, since we have fixed the level of income, represents the magnitude of the vertical shift in the consumption function.

Figure 6–2   Effect of a lump-sum tax on the consumption function (all values in real terms)

Figure 6–3 confirms this result. Let C_0 be the original consumption function, and let $C_0 + I + G$ be the aggregate demand function of state II. Imposition of the tax causes the consumption function to shift down by $50 billion to C_1, and this causes the entire aggregate demand schedule to shift down to where it is represented by $C_1 + I + G$. The downward shift of $50 billion produces a deflationary gap of $50 billion, and given a multiplier with respect to aggregate demand of 3, the level of income ought to drop by $150 billion to a new level of $225 billion. Figure 6–3 does, in fact, show that the new aggregate demand schedule cuts the 45-degree line at an income level of $225 billion. To check whether the result is correct, we calculate the equilibrium magnitudes of our variables in this new situation and note that with $Y = 225$ and $T = 75$, $Y_d = 150$. But with disposable income at $150 billion, consumption is $125 billion, and the level of saving is therefore $25 billion. Thus we see that government purchases of $75 billion plus investment of $25 billion are exactly balanced by $25 billion worth of saving and $75 billion of tax collections.

To summarize this new situation which we describe as state III, we see that:

State III

$Y = 225$

$Y_d = Y - T = 225 - 75 = 150$

$C = 25 + 2/3\, Y_d = 25 + 2/3\, (Y - T) = 25 + 2/3\, (150) = 125$

$S = Y_d - C = 150 - 125 = 25$

$I = 25$

$G = 75$

Therefore,

$I + G = S + T$

$25 + 75 = 25 + 75$

Let us take another look at this result. We have seen that if we begin in state I with the level of income at $150 billion and with government purchases and taxes both at levels of zero, an increase in government purchases balanced by an equal increase in tax collections will not leave the level of income unaffected. The simultaneous effect of

Figure 6–3   The balanced budget multiplier
(all values in real terms)

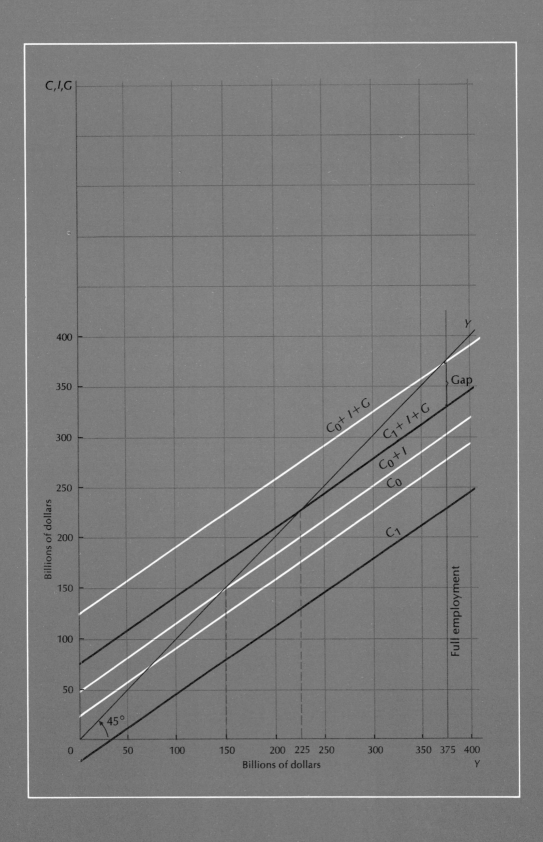

both policies is, in fact, to raise the level of income by exactly the amount of the increase in government purchases and taxes. And it therefore appears that the multiplier for such a simultaneous equal increase in G and T is exactly equal to 1. This result is no accident. It would occur regardless of the value of the marginal propensity to consume. To see why this is the case, note that the multiplier for an increase in government purchases is

$$\frac{\Delta Y}{\Delta G} = \frac{1}{1 - b}$$

while the multiplier for a change in taxes is

$$\frac{\Delta Y}{\Delta T} = \frac{-b}{1 - b}$$

When we add the two together, we have

$$\frac{\Delta Y}{\Delta G} + \frac{\Delta Y}{\Delta T} = \frac{1}{1 - b} - \frac{b}{1 - b} = \frac{1 - b}{1 - b} = 1$$

To make absolutely sure that we understand this result, let us look at it purely from the point of view of the effect of the policies on the deflationary gap. Starting with state I, we have a deflationary gap of $75. When we increase government purchases by $75, we eliminate the gap; however, when we raise taxes by $75 billion, the consumption function and therefore the aggregate demand function shift down by $50 billion. Thus, in combination, the two policies cause the aggregate demand schedule to shift up by $25 billion (compare $C_0 + I$ of state I with $C_1 + I + G$ of state III). Since the net change in aggregate demand is $25 billion, we apply our multiplier formula to this change and see that the net change in income must be $3 \times 25 = 75$.

To see why the result is independent of the value of the marginal propensity to consume, imagine that the marginal propensity to consume has a value of 4/5. The multiplier with respect to aggregate demand would, in this case, have a value of 5. If the level of government purchases rises by $1, the aggregate demand schedule would shift up by $1. If this is balanced by an increase in tax yield of $1, the consumption function would shift down by 80 cents. Consequently, the net change in aggregate demand would be 20 cents, so that when we apply our multiplier of 5 to this change in aggregate demand, we find that income again changes by exactly the amount of the simultaneous increase in G and T.

In summary: The result that we have been discussing is known as the "balanced budget" or "unit" multiplier theorem. It states that equal increases in the level of government purchases and taxes will raise the level of income by exactly the amount of the increase in G and T. It implies that government purchases and equivalent changes in taxes do not exactly offset one another and that therefore it is incorrect to say that government has no effect on the level of income if the budget is balanced. Budgetary balance is not enough; it is important also to consider the level at which the budget is balanced.

6–4   INCOME TAXATION AND AUTOMATIC STABILITY

We propose to consider, in this section, the effect of income taxation. We shall assume that the lump-sum tax is removed and that it is replaced by a proportional 25 percent income tax. Thus the tax function might be written

$$T = tY = 0.25Y$$

where t is the tax rate.

Consider first the effect of the income tax on the consumption function. We saw earlier that a lump-sum tax produces a parallel downward shift of the consumption function. The effect of an income tax, on the other hand, is to rotate the function. The situation is illustrated in Figure 6–4, where C_0 is the original consumption function and C_2 is the consumption function after the imposition of the tax.

The reason for the rotation is not difficult to grasp. The magnitude of the yield from the tax is proportional to the level of income. Consequently, the magnitude of the associated change in disposable income and consumption will also be proportional to the level of income. If the level of income is zero, an income tax will produce no revenue at all, and the level of consumption will be exactly the same as if there had been no tax legislation. However at an income level of $300 billion, the tax yield would be $75 billion, that is, $0.25 \times \$300$. Because disposable income would therefore fall by $75 billion and because the marginal propensity to consume is 2/3, the level of consumption would decline by $50 billion. Thus C_2 lies below C_0 by $50 billion at an income level of $300 billion.

As we have seen, the proportional income tax rotates the consumption function and thereby reduces consumption in direct proportion to the level of income. As in the case of the lump-sum tax, the vertical distance between the consumption functions equals the tax yield times the marginal propensity to consume. As can be seen in Figure 6–4, when the level of income is $300 billion, the level of consumption after the

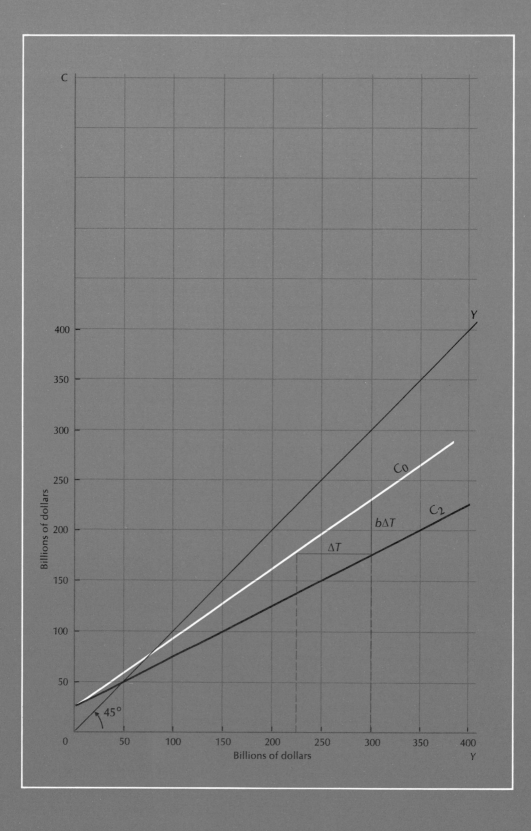

imposition of the tax is $50 billion less than it would have been had the tax not been imposed. The horizontal distance between the two consumption functions measures the tax yield of $75 billion. Thus the intersection of C_0 with the horizontal line that connects the two consumption functions identifies the level of disposable income of $225 billion.

It is important to note that income taxation reduces the slope of the consumption function and therefore lowers the value of the multiplier. The slope of C_0 is the marginal propensity to consume, the value of which we earlier represented by the symbol b and which we have here assumed to equal 2/3. To keep the distinction between the slopes of C_0 and C_2 clear, we shall now call b the *marginal propensity to consume disposable income,* and we shall call the slope of C_2 the *marginal propensity to consume national product.*

To calculate the slope of C_2, we need merely notice that if the level of income (national product) rises by $1, this will raise tax yield by 25 cents. Disposable income therefore rises by 75 cents. Since the marginal propensity to consume disposable income is 2/3, consumption will rise by 50 cents, that is, $2/3 \times 3/4$, and it is therefore evident that a $1 increase in income is now associated with a 50-cent increase in consumption. Thus we see that the marginal propensity to consume national product is 1/2, whereas the marginal propensity to consume disposable income is 2/3. Figure 6–4 shows that the slope of C_2 is, in fact, exactly equal to 1/2.

As a general matter we may say that if the tax rate is t percent, an increase in income of ΔY will raise tax yield by $\Delta T = t\, \Delta Y$, and the change in disposable income will therefore be

$$\Delta Y_d = \Delta Y - \Delta T = (1 - t)\, \Delta Y$$

If the marginal propensity to consume disposable income has a value of b, the change in consumption will be

$$\Delta C = b\, \Delta Y_d = b(1 - t)\, \Delta Y$$

from which it follows that the slope of the consumption function $\Delta C/\Delta Y$ is $b(1 - t)$. Thus the marginal propensity to consume national product is $b(1 - t)$, which in our numerical example is $2/3(1 - 1/4) = 1/2$.

The fact that income taxation causes the marginal propensity to consume national product to decline means that income taxation reduces the value of the multiplier. From the equilibrium condition it follows that if injections increase by some amount, the level of leakages must

Figure 6–4   Effect of proportional income taxation
on the consumption function (all values in real terms)

rise by exactly that same amount if equilibrium is to be restored. Therefore, suppose that government purchases rise by \$1, and consider by
how much income must rise in order to generate an additional \$1 of
saving and taxes. If income rises by \$1, tax yield rises by 25 cents:

$$\Delta T = t \, \Delta Y = 0.25$$

Disposable income rises by 75 cents:

$$\Delta Y_d = (1 - t) \, \Delta Y = 0.75$$

and consumption rises by 50 cents:

$$\Delta C = b \, \Delta Y_d = b(1 - t) \, \Delta Y = 0.50$$

This means that saving rises by 25 cents:

$$\Delta S = \Delta Y_d - \Delta C = (1 - b)(1 - t) \, \Delta Y = 0.25$$

Consequently, an increase in income of \$1 raises taxes by 25 cents and
savings by 25 cents. Total leakages therefore increase by 50 cents:

$$\Delta T + \Delta S = t \, \Delta Y + (1 - b)(1 - t) \, \Delta Y = [1 - b(1 - t)] \, \Delta Y = 0.50$$

and this implies that if total leakages are to rise by \$1, income must rise
by \$2. It follows that our multiplier formula now becomes

$$\frac{\Delta Y}{\Delta G} = \frac{1}{1 - b \, (1 - t)} = \frac{1}{1 - 2/3(1 - 1/4)} = \frac{1}{1/2} = 2$$

The term $b(1 - t)$ is the marginal propensity to consume national
product. The term $1 - b(1 - t)$ measures the fraction of each dollar of
additional national product that leaks into saving and taxes. The multiplier is therefore the reciprocal of the sum of these marginal leakage
propensities.

Let us make sure we understand these results. When taxation is
absent or when taxation is of the lump-sum variety, an increase in government purchases initially raises disposable income by \$1, of which
b percent is then respent on consumption. Summing up the entire
respending chain, we get the multiplier

$$\frac{\Delta Y}{\Delta G} = \frac{1}{1 - b}$$

However, when taxes become a function of income, an increase in government purchases raises the level of disposable income only by $1 - t$
percent of the increase in income because t percent flows right back to
the Treasury in the form of tax collections. Since disposable income rises

by only $1 - t$ percent and since b percent of the change in disposable income is respent on consumption, $b(1 - t)$ percent of the dollar, instead of b percent, will be respent on consumption. Thus the marginal propensity to consume national product is reduced, and the multiplier takes on the lower value, which is given by the formula

$$\frac{\Delta Y}{\Delta G} = \frac{1}{1 - b(1 - t)}$$

This analysis illustrates an important point that is frequently overlooked in discussions of economic policy. An increase in government purchases of X dollars will not necessarily create a budgetary deficit of X dollars because part of the increase in income that results from the increase in government purchases flows right back to the Treasury in the form of taxes. This analysis also suggests that efforts to balance the budget by means of tax rate increases may, to some extent, defeat themselves because the tax rate increases lower the level of disposable income, and tax collections may therefore not increase by as much as anticipated. In our present hypothetical economy, an increase in government purchases of $1 would raise the level of income by $2. Consequently, tax collections would rise by 50 cents, and this means that a $1 increase in government purchases will produce a net addition to the deficit of only 50 cents.

Another important concept illustrated by our present model is the idea of built-in or automatic stability. By reducing the marginal propensity to consume national product, the income tax reduces the value of the multiplier and therefore makes the economy less sensitive to changes in aggregate demand. The stabilizing effects are even more pronounced when tax rates are progressively graduated. This is because as personal incomes rise, taxpayers shift into higher brackets, and a higher proportion of their income is taken away in taxes. Similarly, when personal incomes fall, taxpayers shift into lower brackets. The effect of this is that disposable income and consumption tend to be stabilized even more than they would have been under proportional income taxation.

An automatic stabilizer may be thought of as a mechanism that is built into the economy and that produces an automatic Treasury deficit (and corresponding increase in disposable income) whenever national product falls. The consequence of such automatically induced deficits is that disposable income and consumption are kept from falling by as much as would otherwise be the case. The personal and corporate income taxes are important sources of built-in stability. Also of importance are unemployment compensation programs which bolster the disposable incomes of laid-off workers. Farm price support programs prevent farm prices and incomes from falling during recession. Finally, the social security program helps stabilize disposable income because social security tax collections decline during recessions.

To complete the analysis, let us now consider the effect of the imposition of the 25 percent income tax on the level of income and from there move on to see whether the balanced budget multiplier theorem remains valid under conditions of income taxation. We assume, at the outset, that the economy is in state II. Thus the equilibrium level of income is at the full-employment level of $375 billion, and the aggregate demand function is the function $C_0 + I + G$ of Figure 6–1. This function is redrawn in Figure 6–5 and labeled $C_0 + I + G_0$. At an income level of $375 billion, $C = 275$, $I = 25$, and $G = 75$. In state II there are no taxes. The level of disposable income is therefore $375 billion, the level of saving is $100 billion, and the budgetary deficit is $75 billion.

Given this situation, we now impose the 25 percent income tax. The tax causes the consumption function to rotate downward from C_0 to C_2, and the entire aggregate demand schedule therefore rotates downward and becomes the schedule $C_2 + I + G_0$. At the full-employment level of income of $375 billion, a 25 percent tax implies a tax yield of $93.75 billion and a reduction in disposable income of the same amount. Given a marginal propensity to consume disposable income of 2/3, this means that consumption declines by $62.50 billion. Aggregate demand at the full-employment level of income therefore declines by $62.50 billion, and a deflationary gap in this amount therefore develops.

With a deflationary gap of $62.50 billion and a multiplier with respect to aggregate demand of 2, we expect the level of income to drop by $125 billion, that is, 2 × $62.50, from the full-employment level ($375 billion) of state II. Thus the equilibrium level of income should turn out to be $250 billion, and this is where the new aggregate demand schedule $C_2 + I + G_0$ cuts the 45-degree line.

This new situation is state IV. To check the results, we again inquire whether the equilibrium condition is met and note that,

State IV

$Y = 250$

$I = 25$

$G = 75$

Figure 6–5 The balanced budget multiplier under income taxation (all values in real terms)

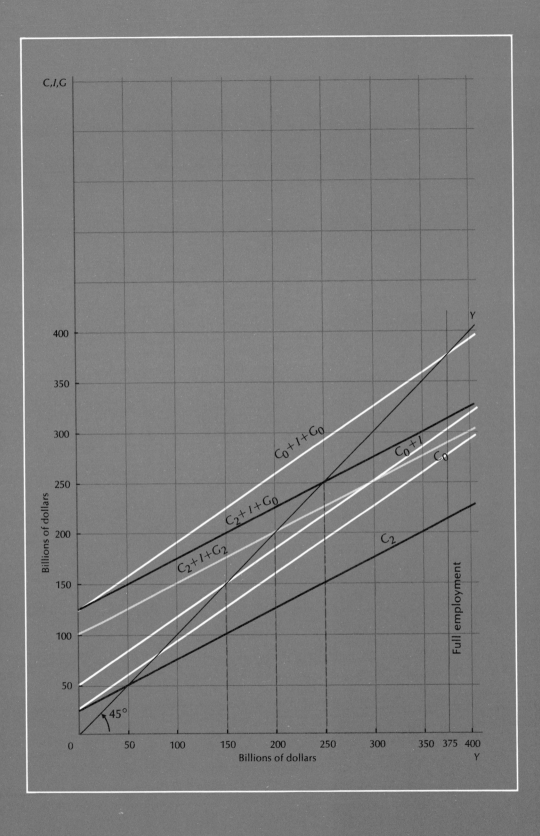

$T = 0.25\ (250) = 62.5$

$Y_d = Y - T = 250 - 62.5 = 187.5$

$C = 25 + 2/3\ Y_d = 150$

$S = Y_d - C = 37.5$

Therefore,

$$S + T = I + G$$

$37.5 + 62.5 = 25 + 75$

and the deficit

$G - T = 75 - 62.5 = 12.5$

To summarize this result: The change in the equilibrium level of income that results from a change in the rate of income taxation can be derived by calculating the magnitude of the deflationary gap the tax creates and by multiplying this gap by the multiplier with respect to changes in aggregate demand that apply *after* the imposition of the tax. In the present example, a 25 percent tax reduces the multiplier to a value of 2. The tax creates a deflationary gap of $62.5 billion. The level of income therefore drops by $125 billion to a level of $250 billion.

State IV finds the economy with a level of government purchases of $75 billion and a tax yield of $62.5 billion. There is therefore a budgetary deficit of $12.5 billion. Imagine as state V that government purchases are adjusted in such a way as to eliminate the deficit.

A reduction in government purchases of $1 lowers income by $2 and therefore induces a fall in tax yield of 50 cents. Consequently, those who believe that the deficit will decline by the full amount of the decline in the value of government purchases will be disappointed. What they will discover is that for each dollar by which G is reduced T will also fall by 50 cents and that the deficit will therefore decline by only 50 cents. From this reasoning, it follows that if the deficit of $12.5 billion is to be eliminated, the level of government purchases will have to be cut by $25 billion, that is, 12.5/0.5.

If G is cut by $25 billion, the level of income will drop by $50 billion to a new level of $200 billion. Figure 6–5 confirms that the new aggregate demand schedule $(C_2 + I + G_2)$ cuts the 45-degree line at an income level of $200. This situation is state V, where we again see that injections equal leakages because

State V

$Y = 200$

$I = 25$

$G = 50$

$T = 0.25\ (200) = 50$

$Y_d = Y - T = 150$

$C = 25 + 2/3\ Y_d = 125$

$S = Y_d - C = 25$

Therefore,

$S + T = I + G$

$25 + 50 = 25 + 50$

and

$T = 50 = G$

Notice now that when we started in state I with $G = T = 0$, the equilibrium level of income was $150 billion. In state V we find the equilibrium level of income to be $200 billion and the levels of G and T to be balanced at values of $50 billion. Observe also that this $50 billion turns out to be the difference between the income levels of states I and V. We conclude from this result that the balanced budget multiplier theorem holds under conditions of income taxation just as it held in the lump-sum tax economy. The proposition may be put as follows: Given any income tax rate, the level of government purchases that balances the budget will result in a new equilibrium income level that will exceed the level that would be attained if $G = T = 0$ by exactly the amount of the balanced budget. Or, to turn the proposition around, if for any level of government purchases one can find a tax rate that balances the budget, the resulting equilibrium level of income will exceed the level at which the economy would be if G and T were both zero by the amount of the level of G and T.[1]

6–5 SUMMARY AND FINAL NOTES

In this chapter we have focused upon the purely mechanical aspects of fiscal policy. We have seen that government purchases have a more high-powered effect on the level of income than an equivalent level of

---

[1] These propositions are proved in the appendix to this chapter. The interested reader should also consult Richard A. Musgrave, *The Theory of Public Finance*, Chap. 18, McGraw-Hill Book Company, 1959; and William A. Salant, "Taxes, Income Determination, and the Balanced Budget Theorem," *Review of Economics and Statistics*, 39:152–61, 1957.

tax yield. This implies that the full impact of fiscal policy on the level of income cannot be measured purely by the size of the budgetary deficit. We saw also that income taxation reduces the size of the multiplier and therefore introduces an automatically stabilizing element.

Although the analysis has emphasized the mechanical aspects of fiscal policy, it nevertheless provides us with some useful and important policy implications. For example, if the economy enters a slump, many minds turn to the thought of a tax cut. But standing in the way of such a cut is the fact that when income drops, tax collections automatically fall. Since many public officials are wedded to the notion that a time of budgetary deficit is a poor time to cut taxes, there is danger that tax cuts will arouse opposition just at the time when they are most needed. During the late 1950s, moreover, the theory was advanced that if Congress were to cut taxes, it would never have the fortitude to raise them again. Finally, the fear is often expressed that a tax cut, after only a mild business downturn, may lead to excessive stimulation of consumption and therefore create inflationary pressures.

The citizen who understands the ABC's of fiscal policy will know that there is considerable danger in these attitudes. If the business slump is allowed to become aggravated, the ultimate tax cut that will be required to bring the economy back to full employment will be much greater than would have been needed had immediate action been taken. Moreover, an additional fall in income, due to the reluctance to cut taxes, may cause a greater budgetary imbalance and even greater reluctance to cut taxes. Finally, the more taxes are cut, the more they have to be raised once full employment is restored.

Political capital can unfortunately be made of our failure to understand the mechanics of fiscal policy. It is common practice for politicians to attract votes during a period of recession by informing the public that the opposition party not only cannot maintain prosperity but also runs a slovenly fiscal system. The logic of the argument is impeccable because a recession is always accompanied by a budgetary deficit. If we would realize that government revenues fall as a recession develops and that a budgetary deficit is therefore practically inevitable, we should soon learn to discount such political skulduggery.

7
THE LEVEL OF INVESTMENT

7–1   INTRODUCTION

Thus far we have examined two of the components of aggregate expenditure—consumption and government purchases. Consumption depends primarily on the level of disposable income, which in turn depends on the level of NNP, on the tax structure, and on the magnitude and nature of the various government transfer payment schemes. About government purchases we have little to say, at the moment, because these must be considered "autonomous"; i.e., they are determined by Congress and are not directly related to the internal structure of the economic system.[1] Investment, like government purchases, has so far been treated as autonomous. In this chapter we abandon the simple notion that the level of investment is fixed.

In deciding how to arrange his portfolio to give him maximum satisfaction, a holder of wealth must remember that different assets yield different returns and have different risks attached to them. He must, for example, decide whether the disutility of the risk of holding an equity as opposed to a bond is balanced by the utility of the higher earnings on the equity. The wealth holder must decide whether, and in what proportion, to hold long-term bonds, short-term bonds, equities, or other types of asset. A businessman must decide whether it is more profitable to use his funds for capital expansion or for the purchase of some existing asset, say an equity in another company. Similarly, he must decide whether the cost of borrowing for purposes of capital expansion is more than compensated for by the expected return on the new investment. The problem of determining the demand for new investment goods may therefore be looked at as a problem in portfolio management, because the decision to invest depends on the profitability of the new investment as opposed to the profitability of holding existing earning assets. If, for example, an investor is able to earn 5 percent on a government bond and can expect to earn only 4 percent on the purchase of a new machine, he will certainly not buy the machine, unless the bond is a far more risky venture than the machine. If, furthermore, the monetary authority would like to see him purchase the machine because that will raise the level of income, it must somehow contrive to change his asset preference in such a way that the machine becomes a more appealing alternative than other earning assets. The first step that needs to be taken if we are to understand this relationship between different types of assets is to inquire into the relationship between the market value of an asset and the rate of return, or yield, of the asset.

7–2 DISCOUNTING AND THE PRESENT VALUE OF AN ASSET

Suppose that the rate of interest is 5 percent. If today an individual lends $100, he will at the end of one year get back the original $100 plus the original sum multiplied by the rate of interest. Arithmetically,

$$100 + 100 \times 0.05 = 100 (1 + 0.05) = \$105$$

---

[1] It is, of course, true that government purchases may be raised in response to a fall in income. But since there is nothing automatic about most such increases, government purchases must be treated as an "autonomous" or "exogenous" variable.

In general, if the interest rate is denoted by i and the sum lent is denoted by P_0, the individual will get back at the end of one year

$$P_1 = P_0(1 + i) \tag{7--1}$$

If he lends the whole sum P_1 for a second year, he will receive

$$P_2 = P_1(1 + i)$$

But since $P_1 = P_0(1 + i)$,

$$P_2 = P_0(1 + i)(1 + i) = P_0(1 + i)^2$$

If he lends P_0 for three years, he will get back

$$P_3 = P_0(1 + i)^3$$

from which we may infer that a sum P_0 lent at interest for t years will pay back at the end of t years[1]

$$P_t = P_0(1 + i)^t \tag{7--2}$$

[1] In Eq. 7–2 it is assumed that interest is compounded once a year. Often, however, interest is compounded semiannually. In the latter case interest for the first six months is figured on P_0. But since only a half year's interest is earned, the effective rate on P_0 is not i but $i/2$. This means that the value of the claim at the end of six months is $P_0(1 + i/2)$, which becomes the principal on which interest for the next six months is figured. At the end of the year

$$P_1 = P_0 \left(1 + \frac{i}{2}\right)\left(1 + \frac{i}{2}\right) = P_0 \left(1 + \frac{i}{2}\right)^2$$

from which we may infer that

$$P_t = P_0 \left(1 + \frac{i}{2}\right)^{2t}$$

If interest is compounded g times a year, we have

$$P_t = P_0 \left(1 + \frac{i}{g}\right)^{gt}$$

For some purposes it is useful to know P_t if compounding takes place instantaneously. Rewrite the last equation as

$$P_t = P_0 \left[\left(1 + \frac{i}{g}\right)^{g/i}\right]^{it}$$

The term $(1 + i/g)^{g/i}$ approachs the number 2.7183 when g grows very large. This number is often referred to as e and forms the base of the natural logarithmic system just as 10 forms the base of the common logarithmic system. Hence we have

$$P_t = P_0 e^{it}$$

Notice that

$$\log_e P_t = \log_e P_0 + it \log_e e$$

But since $\log_e e = 1$, we have the straight-line function,

$$\log_e P_t = \log_e P_0 + it$$

The next step is to turn the original question around and ask: If an individual gets back P_1 dollars in one year, what is today's value of that claim? The answer can be found by solving for P_0 in Eq. (7–1). This yields

$$P_0 = \frac{P_1}{1 + i}$$

which indicates that a claim worth $105 in one year, with the current market rate of interest at 5 percent, has a value today of $100. If the owner tried to sell this future claim for anything more than $100, he would not be able to find a buyer because with an outlay of $100 today the potential buyer can get back $105 in a year and therefore would be foolish to give him more than $100 for this claim. Similarly, the owner would be unwise to sell his future claim for anything less than $100. If he sells the claim for less than $100 and reinvests the proceeds, he would end up with less than $105 at the end of the year, assuming a market rate of 5 percent. The only possible value that the $105 future claim can therefore have is $100. Notice that if the market rate of interest falls to 2 percent, the present value of the claim which pays $105 would increase to $102.94 because this is the amount that would have to be lent at the new rate of interest in order to get back $105 at the end of one year.

A sum P_0 lent today will be worth $P_2 = P_0(1 + i)^2$ at the end of two years. Such a claim could today be sold for P_0. Anyone foolish enough to give more than P_0 for the claim would, at the market rate, have been able to earn more than P_2 in two years with the sum he has paid. On the other hand, if the owner were foolish enough to sell the claim for less than P_0, he could not get back as much as P_2 in two years by lending the amount he sold the claim for. In general, if in t years a claim of P_t is collectible, the present value of that claim is

$$P_0 = \frac{P_t}{(1 + i)^t} \tag{7-3}$$

A claim that is not collectible until far in the future must have very little present value, as compared with the collection sum. Although the Indians who sold Manhattan Island for $24 in wampum in 1624 are now derided for having made a foolish bargain, they could theoretically, by lending the $24 out at interest and waiting 344 years, have earned a sum which might compare favorably with what Manhattan Island could be sold for in 1968.

Consider next the determination of the present value of a bond. Instead of one claim collectible at a certain future date, a bond represents a series of claims collectible at different times in the future. Suppose that each year a coupon can be clipped from the bond and cashed in for a fixed sum R. When there are no more coupons left, the bond reaches maturity and is cashed in for its par value P. Today's value of the bond must be the present value of the sum of all the discounted future returns plus the discounted value of the maturity value. The coupon that is to be clipped in one year and that will have a value of R could be sold today for $R/(1 + i)$; the coupon which is to be clipped two years from now could be sold today for $R/(1 + i)^2$; the last coupon to be clipped could be sold for $R/(1 + i)^n$, where n is the number of years from the present to maturity; and the claim over the maturity value can be sold for $P/(1 + i)^n$. Consequently the present value of the bond is

$$V = \frac{R}{(1 + i)} + \frac{R}{(1 + i)^2} + \cdots + \frac{R}{(1 + i)^n} + \frac{P}{(1 + i)^n}$$

which, by applying the simple technique used to sum a geometric series, reduces to[1]

$$V = \frac{R}{i}\left[1 - \frac{1}{(1 + i)^n}\right] + \frac{P}{(1 + i)^n} \tag{7-4}$$

Notice that when the maturity date is far off in the future (when a bond has no maturity date it is called a "consol"), n becomes very large so that

$$V = \frac{R}{i} \tag{7-5}$$

Equation (7–5) says that if a consol earns $50 each year and if the market rate of interest is 5 percent, the value of the bond must be $1,000. Even if the owner is not familiar with the mathematics of compound interest, he will soon find through painful experience that there can be only one price for the bond. If he tries to sell the bond for more than $1,000, prospective buyers will scoff because they could earn $50 by lending $1,000 on the market; since that is all the bond will yield, it would be quite senseless to pay more than $1,000 for it. If he were foolish enough to accept $900 for the bond, he would discover to his dismay that when he lent the $900 for one year, he would get only $45 in return; if he had kept the bond, he would have received $50 at the end of the year.

---

[1] Note that when the market rate of interest just equals the rate earned on the par value of the bond, $R = iP$ so that

$$V = \frac{iP}{i}\left[1 - \frac{1}{(1 + i)^n}\right] + \frac{P}{(1 + i)^n} = P$$

Equations (7–4) and (7–5) show that there is an inverse relationship between bond prices and interest rates. Suppose that the interest rate falls to 2 percent. The value of the consol that previously sold for $1,000, to yield 5 percent or $50 per year, now increases in value to $2,500. The reason for this is that with an interest rate of 2 percent a potential buyer would have to put up $2,500 to earn $50 per year, whereas at the 5 percent rate he has to put up only $1,000. Again the owner would be foolish to sell the bond for $2,000 because if he lent this sum he would earn only $40 in interest, whereas if he keeps the bond he can earn $50.

The value of a very long-term bond can be approximated by Eq. (7–5). If, on the other hand, the bond is practically ready to be cashed in for its maturity value, n will be very small and when $n = 0$, Eq. (7–4) reduces to

$$V = P$$

This result, of course, is just what we expect. A bond that is on the verge of maturity can hardly have a market value that differs from the par value.

From the foregoing analysis we can infer that the longer the date from present to maturity, the more important the market rate of interest in determining the value of the bond and the less important the par value. Similarly, the closer to maturity, the less important the market rate of interest and the more important the par value.

7–3 THE DECISION TO INVEST

The decision to invest in new machinery or equipment depends on whether the expected rate of return on the machine is greater than the cost of borrowing the necessary funds or, if the funds are already available, the cost of the earnings lost by purchasing the machine rather than by lending out the funds. But what is the expected rate of return on a machine which may not yield any return at all for n years and which yields a return of x dollars in year $n + 1$, a return of y dollars in $n + 2$, a return of z dollars in $n + j$—in short, a return in any given year which may not be the same as the return in any other year? One way of finding out is to ask the question: What rate of interest would make the discounted value of all expected future earnings exactly equal to the cost of the machine? If this rate is r and is the same as the rate at which money can be borrowed, then it is a matter of indifference whether funds are used to purchase a machine or to lend at interest. On the other hand, if $r > i$, the present value of the future earnings of the machine is greater than the present value of a bond (the bond is simply the I.O.U. given in return for the loan of funds), so that it will be more profitable to buy the machine than to lend funds to someone else. Similarly, if $r > i$ and if the prospective purchaser does not have the funds with which to buy the machine, it will pay to borrow in order to purchase the machine.

The rate of return over cost, r, is called the "marginal efficiency of capital." It may be calculated as follows: Let $R_1, R_2, \ldots, R_n$ be the expected earnings of a new capital asset in year $1, 2, \ldots, n$, respectively; let J be the scrap value of the machine at the time of replacement; Q the initial cost of the machine; and r the rate of return over cost. Then

$$Q = \frac{R_1}{(1 + r)} + \frac{R_2}{(1 + r)^2} + \cdots + \frac{R_n}{(1 + r)^n} + \frac{J}{(1 + r)^n}$$

Therefore if Q, J, and the R's are known, r can be calculated.

Consider the simplest case of a machine with an indefinite expected lifetime which yields an identical return R each year. In this case, $Q = R/r$ so that if the machine costs \$1,000 and R is \$100, the expected rate of return over cost of the machine is 10 percent. If the market rate of interest is 5 percent, the \$1,000 would bring a return of \$50 if lent on the market. But if the \$1,000 is invested in the new machine, the annual return is \$100. Consequently, it pays to invest in the machine rather than in the bond. Similarly, if the \$1,000 is not available, it would pay to borrow at 5 percent in order to purchase the machine on which 10 percent can be earned.

It is evident that, given Q and the R's, the number of new machines that will be bought in any period of time will depend on the market rate of interest. It is for this reason that economists frequently write the investment demand function as

$$I = I(i) \tag{7-6}$$

A ranking of prospective investment projects in order of decreasing profitability permits us to define an investment demand schedule of the type presented in Figure 7–1. The rate of interest and the marginal efficiency of capital are measured on the vertical axis, while the level of investment in some arbitrary period of time is measured horizontally. At i_0 the level of investment will be I_0. Additional projects will not be undertaken because the rate of return on those projects is less than the cost of borrowing or the return from lending funds at interest. If the interest rate falls to i_1, it pays to increase the level of investment by $I_1 - I_0$ to I_1 until the return on the marginal project again equals the cost of borrowing.

7-4 FACTORS AFFECTING INVESTMENT SPENDING

There has been a great deal of discussion about the relationship between the rate of interest and the volume of investment spending per unit of time. Traditionally economists have been inclined to the view that investment was highly sensitive to interest rate changes. Skepticism of this view, however, developed during the 1930s. Subsequent statistical investigations, though inconclusive, seem to corroborate the view that the interest rate is an unimportant determinant of the level of investment.[1]

The empirical investigations were conducted by asking businessmen to list the factors that determine their decision to invest. The replies placed very little emphasis upon the cost (the interest rate) of borrowing funds. Such a conclusion, obtained by means of questionnaires, is not very startling. First of all, the supply of funds to an individual firm may be quite interest-inelastic; i.e., the rate of interest may be irrelevant to the firm because it cannot get additional funds at that rate of interest. Second, we do not really expect most firms to regard the cost of borrowing as important since most of their prospective investment projects have expected returns substantially in excess of that cost. In Figure 7-1 if a firm has an investment project that promises to yield a rate of return equivalent to i_0, and if the rate of interest at the time the questionnaire is answered is i_1, the firm will undoubtedly regard the cost of borrowing as a trivial consideration. The rate of interest is important only to the firms with marginal investment projects, namely, those whose yields are in the neighborhood of i_1. The questionnaire approach may, therefore, be misleading. It lumps all firms and all investment projects together when we should be attempting instead to observe the effect of interest rate changes on marginal projects.

It is our belief that the effect of the interest rate on the level of investment will vary with the stage of the business cycle and the rate of technical change. As we shall show in Chapter 12, the interest rate will

[1] J. E. Meade and P. W. S. Andrews, "Summary of Replies to Questions on the Effects of Interest Rates," *Oxford Economic Papers,* 1:14–31, 1938; R. S. Sayers, "Businessmen and the Terms of Borrowing," *Oxford Economic Papers,* 3:23–31, 1940; P. W. S. Andrews, "A Further Inquiry into the Effects of Rates of Interest," *Oxford Economic Papers,* 3:32–73, 1940; J. F. Ebersole, "The Influence of Interest Rates upon Entrepreneurial Decisions in Business: A Case Study," *Harvard Business Review,* 17:35–43, 1938. For a critical survey of these studies, see W. H. White, "Interest Inelasticity of Investment Demand," *American Economic Review,* 46:565–587, 1956.

Figure 7-1 The investment demand function
(all values in real terms)

be irrelevant as an economic calculator during depressions since such periods will be marked by the existence of excess capacity. If we have 100 machines available for use and if the present level of demand is depressed so that we only need 60 machines, a fall in the rate of interest is certainly not going to induce us to invest.

What then determines the position of the investment demand schedule? It is clear that expectations play a large role.[1] A firm with optimistic views of future sales prospects will be more willing to invest than one with pessimistic views of the future. Because past experience is the only basis upon which projections can be made, a firm's expectations about the future course of events will be a function of its past experience. Thus a firm that has recently experienced increases in the demand for its product is likely to be more optimistic about the future than a firm with a stagnant demand. However, even though a firm is optimistic about the expected demand for its product, it may not increase its capital equipment if it has sufficient excess capacity today to handle the expected future demand. Finally, technical progress will affect the current level of investment. A firm's whole view of the future and its ability to compete effectively will be shifted if an invention occurs that renders part of its capital stock obsolete.

All these factors taken together determine the position of the investment demand schedule for a firm. Thus if falling interest rates coincide with a downward shift of the investment demand schedule, the net effect may well be a decrease in the annual volume of investment expenditure. The importance of expectations in investment decisions is a large part of the explanation of the cyclical variations in the volume of investment. Changes in current economic conditions induce cumulative movements in business expectations, causing sharp changes in the aggregate investment demand schedule.

It does not necessarily follow that a firm will borrow even if it has productive outlets for funds (its own or somebody else's) at the going rate of interest. If a firm sells bonds and if the investment for which the funds are used proves unprofitable, the future earnings on the equity issue of the firm are reduced because of the increased obligatory fixed interest payments. This would be a real cost to the firm in the future; although it is in part a function of the cost of borrowing, it is also a function of past financing decisions and therefore is independent of the

---

[1] J. S. Duesenberry, *Business Cycles and Economic Growth,* Chaps. 4 and 5, McGraw-Hill Book Company, New York, 1958; and M. Kalecki, *Theory of Economic Dynamics,* Chaps. 6–10, George Allen & Unwin, Ltd., London, 1954, are useful supplements to the following discussion.

current cost of borrowing. There is, of course, the alternative of increasing the ordinary stock issue. Again, if the proceeds of the new issue are not used so that they increase profits proportionately as much as the increase in share capital, the project is not likely to be attractive to management. Furthermore, there are definite limits to any firm's ability to increase its equity issue. There is finally the alternative that the firm can "plough back" its accumulated reserves. Although this protects the firm from the necessity of going to the market, internally financed investment, if unprofitable, is no more likely to be undertaken than the same investment with borrowed funds.[1] These possible future costs of present borrowing are factors influencing a firm's decision to invest and have little, if anything, to do with the current cost of borrowing. Thus, while the supply of funds for the economy as a whole may be interest-elastic, for any one firm the risks involved when it increases its debt may preclude further investment, even though the investment demand schedule for the firm shifts outward.

Taking these various factors into account, what can be done in the way of formal amendment of Eq. (7–6)? Empirical studies have shown that the level of investment is highly correlated with the level of profits. This may be because profits are only partly paid out in the form of dividends; an increase in profits therefore provides the firm with a larger pool of internal finance. A rise in profits, moreover, indicates improvement in business conditions which calls for expansion of capacity and enhances the state of business "confidence." Because profits and the level of income are highly correlated, economists often rewrite the investment demand equation as

$$I = I(i,Y) \qquad\qquad (7\text{–}7)$$

It is assumed in this formulation that investment is inversely associated with the rate of interest and directly associated with the level of income. If we now redraw Figure 7–1 (see Figure 7–2), we shall have a whole family of investment demand schedules. Each schedule is associated with a particular level of income. At interest rate i_0 the level of investment will be I_0 when the level of income is Y_0. If income rises to Y_1, investment rises to I_1, and when income rises to Y_2, investment rises to I_2.

The hypothesis that investment is a function both of the rate of interest and of the level of income explains the circumstance that invest-

---

[1] See J. R. Meyer and E. Kuh, *The Investment Decision*, Harvard University Press, Cambridge, Mass., 1957, for a comprehensive analysis of the role played by internal sources of funds in the investment decision of firms.

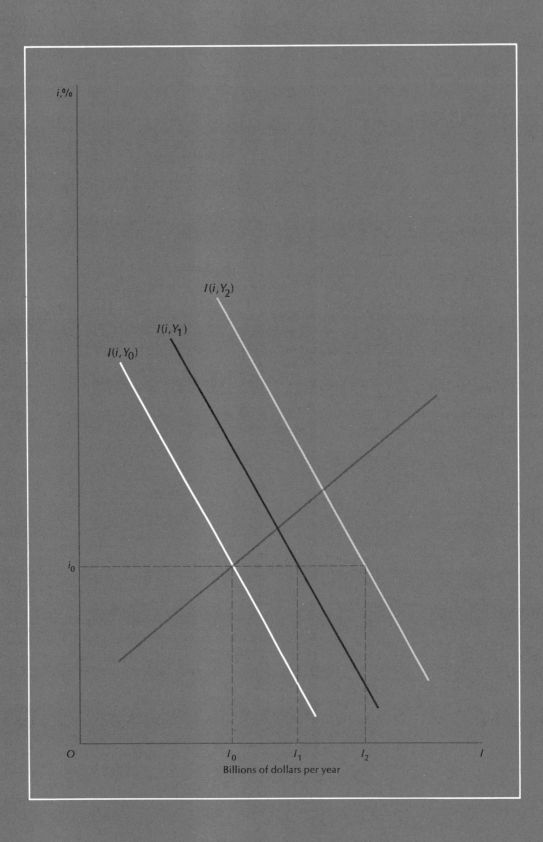

ment and interest rates are positively correlated during the course of a business cycle. If the investment demand schedule were always fixed at $I(i,Y_0)$, investment could not rise without a decline in the rate of interest. However, if a rise in income causes the investment demand schedule to shift to the right, it can easily be seen by drawing a positively sloped line through the investment demand schedules of Figure 7–2 (gray line) that the level of investment and the rate of interest may move in the same direction.

An alternative formulation of the investment demand equation is

$$I = I(i, \Delta Y) \tag{7–8}$$

where the change in income ΔY replaces the level of income. This formulation is based on the notion that business will need to expand its productive capacity only if output *increases,* whereas a constant level of output requires no additional capacity. This hypothesis is called the "acceleration principle." It is often said that in the present case investment is "change-induced," whereas in Eq. (7–7) investment is said to be "level-induced."

Throughout the analysis of Part 2 we shall retain Eq. (7–6) as our investment demand hypothesis. The level- and change-induced hypotheses become relevant and interesting when we take up the dynamic problems of Part 3.

Figure 7–2   Investment as a function of the
interest rate and the level of income
(all values in real terms)

8

INTEREST
AND MONEY

8–1 INTRODUCTION

In the previous chapter we called attention to the fact that there is a definite link between the rate of interest or yield on an asset and the market value of the asset. From this it would appear that the problem of determining the equilibrium rate of interest might be looked on as a matter of determining the supply of and the demand for different types of earning assets. The problem might also be looked at in another way. The supply of and the demand for different types of earning assets will not be in equilibrium unless the supply of and the demand for money (non-interest-bearing assets) are in equilibrium. A wealth holder who has deposits in his bank and cash in his pocket in excess of the amount he wishes to hold for various purposes will try to trade these deposits and cash in return for earning assets. An excess supply of money, other things being equal, implies the presence of excess demand for bonds and other earning assets, and this, in turn, implies that bond prices will be rising and interest rates will be falling. The question of determining equilibrium interest rates may therefore be viewed in terms of the supply of and the demand for bonds, and it may also be viewed as a problem of determining the supply of and the demand for money. The latter approach is the simplest and the one most often followed.

To begin, assume that the financial sector of the economy is competitive and that there is no risk whatsoever attached to the making of loans. We assume, in other words, that a bank takes no risk of default when it makes a loan; a bondholder encounters no risk of capital loss; and the expected future returns on new investment projects are, in fact, certain returns. Under these conditions it must be the case that the bank lending rate i_l, the bond rate i_b, and the rate of return on the least profitable (marginal) investment projects undertaken r must all be equal. If the bond rate is 5 percent, the rate of return on new investment is 7 percent, and banks try to charge 10 percent on their loans, the banks will be unable to find borrowers, while bondholders will attempt to sell their bonds and use the proceeds to make loans for current investment projects; i.e., they will try to trade existing securities for new securities. The effect of these arbitrage operations will be to force bond prices down and bond rates up. Meanwhile the banks, in order not to lose business, would be obliged to lower their loan rate. The bond rate and the loan rate must therefore tend to equality. Alternatively, if the bond rate and loan rate are less than the rate of return on the least profitable investment project, businessmen will be tempted to purchase additional new machines with borrowed funds and to sell their bondholdings in order to buy machines. The effect of this operation will be to lower the rate of return on the marginal investment project, and at the same time raise the bond and bank rates.

In reality there are many different bond rates, none of which is likely to correspond to the bank lending rate or to the rate of return on the marginal investment project. This simply follows from the fact that there are different degrees of risk attached to different types of assets; that imperfect knowledge as to the most profitable opportunity for the investment of funds prevails; and that funds, once committed, may be recovered only on pain of capital loss if more profitable opportunities arise in the future. A bank takes a greater risk when it makes a business loan than it does when it buys a government bond. Similarly, the bank takes a greater risk by buying a long-term bond than a 60-day Treasury bill. If bond prices fall, a holder of a short-term bond need merely hold the bond to its maturity date (say 60 days) in order to collect the face value. However, if he holds a 20-year bond, he may not be so lucky. The price of the bond may not, within the near future, rise to what he paid for it. He may therefore be "pinned in" in the sense that if he wants to recover the par value of the bond, he must hold it for 20 years, meanwhile foregoing the possibility of more profitable ways to use his funds. In order to get bondholders to take the risk of capital loss on a long-term bond when they do not take such a risk with a short-term security, the yield on long-term bonds must be greater than on short-term bonds.[1] Similarly, since the future returns on a new machine can only be guessed at, investment in a new machine involves a considerable risk. Some wealth holders therefore prefer a fairly safe bond on which they earn 3 percent to an equity on which they are likely, but less certain, to earn 6 percent. Similarly, entrepreneurs may be unwilling to risk investment in a new machine unless the expected rate of return over cost is 15 percent, when in fact the cost of borrowing is only 7 percent.

The upshot is that if account is taken of differences in risk and of ignorance and immobility, the rates of return on all types of assets will tend to be equalized at the margin. Under such conditions the structure of interest rates may be thought of as one common rate, and we may suppose that there is no difference between a long-term and a short-term bond and no difference between the I.O.U. which a bank gets in return for the loan of funds and the bond which you or I might get from the United States Treasury or from a corporation in return for the loan of our funds. Since the yield i on this typical I.O.U. is simply the amount required to induce the public and the banks to part with funds—i.e., the cost of borrowing—and since excess supply of money implies excess demand for earning assets, the problem of interest rate determination may provisionally be viewed as a problem of determining the supply of and the demand for money.

Before proceeding to an analysis of the determinants of the demand for and supply of money, we need to be certain that we are agreed on a definition of money. The conventional definition is the following: Money is the sum total of currency and bank deposits, but not saving (time) deposits, held by the nonbank public. This means in effect that money amounts to the stock of non-interest-bearing liquid assets held by the nonbank public.

---

[1] This is not always true. A large increase in the supply of short-term bonds may force the short rate above the long rate. Because of imperfections in the capital market, this relationship between short and long rates may persist for considerable periods of time.

8-2   THE DEMAND FOR MONEY

In his *General Theory of Employment, Interest and Money*,[1] Lord Keynes suggested that the demand for money could be divided into three separate demands or "motives." People hold money, according to Keynes, because they need cash balances to make day-to-day transactions, because it is important to have money balances on hand to meet unforeseen contingencies, and because, for various reasons, they prefer to hold money balances as an asset in preference to, or in combination with, other forms of wealth. Thus the demand for money is a combination of the *transactions*, the *precautionary*, and the *speculative* or *liquidity preference* demands. Although modern monetary theory suggests that these distributions are arbitrary, they are nevertheless useful for the purpose of organizing our discussion.

The transactions demand for money   Individuals and business enterprises maintain certain average levels of cash and deposits because of the need to make day-to-day transactions. If receipts of income and expenditures were always synchronized perfectly with respect to time, there would be no need for such idle balances. Because the typical person is paid once a month or once a week and because he does not make all his disbursements at exactly the time he receives his income, he must maintain some amount of cash for the purpose of meeting his transactions needs.

Consider the hypothetical bank account depicted in Figure 8–1. Time is measured horizontally, and the amount in the bank account at any time is measured vertically. We assume that the individual receives y dollars of income at the beginning of the period (time zero), that he spends the entire amount at a uniform rate throughout the period, and that he ends up with a zero balance at the end of the period (time one). At the beginning of the month he holds y dollars; at the end he holds no money; and since he spends at a uniform rate throughout the period, his average idle balance is $y/2$ dollars. It is this average idle balance that we call his transactions demand for money.

The size of the transactions demand for money obviously depends upon the magnitude of the individual's money income. If his income and his expenditures both rise by Δy dollars, his average idle bank bal-

[1] J. M. Keynes, *The General Theory of Employment, Interest and Money*, Chap. 13, Harcourt, Brace & World, Inc., New York, 1936.

Figure 8–1   Time profile of a hypothetical bank account

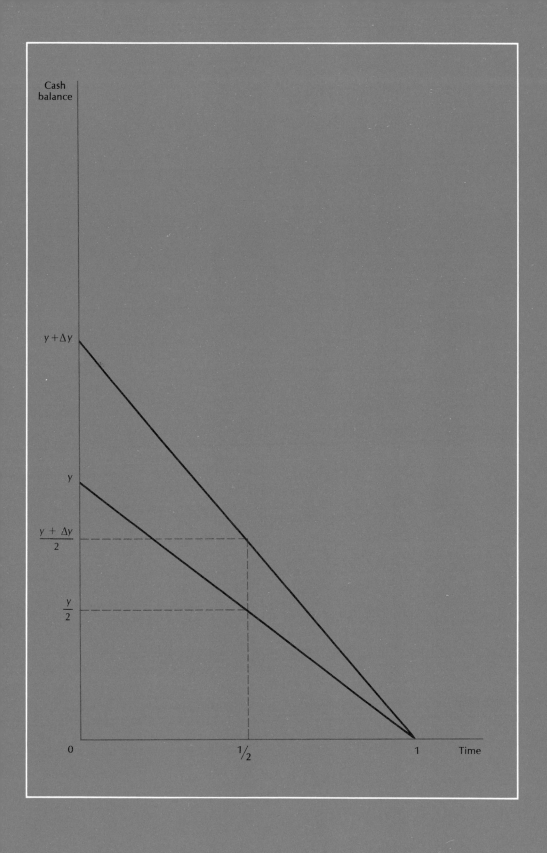

ance will tend to rise by $\Delta y/2$ dollars. Thus, as a first approximation, we may say that the transactions demand for money is a function of the level of money income.

If our concern is with the long run, we have to take changes in institutional payments practices into account. If an individual begins to receive his paycheck each week instead of each month, he would have to maintain approximately one-fourth of the average balance he had previously maintained. Thus, even though his income remains the same, the fact that he is paid more frequently implies that his transactions demand 'for money falls by roughly three-fourths. Similarly, individuals who pay all their bills at the beginning of the month would have very little need for transactions cash, and individuals who pay their taxes as they go need not accumulate cash balances in anticipation of the need to meet a forthcoming tax liability.

Recent developments in monetary theory suggest that the transactions demand for money may be a function not only of the level of income but also of the rate of interest.[1] To see why this might be the case, consider the individual whose bank account is plotted in Figure 8–2. Of the y dollars he receives at the beginning of the period, three-quarters will be idle for one-fourth of the period; one-half of the balance will be idle for half the period; and one-quarter of the balance will be idle for three-fourths of the period. Under these circumstances, it might be profitable for the individual to take some fraction of these idle funds and purchase earning assets which he then sells when he runs out of cash.

It is evident from inspection of Figure 8–2 that if the individual contemplates one bond purchase and one sale during the period, he will maximize his interest earnings if, at the beginning of the period, he puts exactly one-half of his income into bonds which he then sells when he runs out of cash at $t = 1/2$. The shaded rectangle in Figure 8–2 represents the time profile of his bond holdings. The largest such rectangle that can be drawn under the cash balance curve is the one that makes the initial balance equal to $y/2$ and implies sale at $t = 1/2$. Any other date of purchase or sale, and any other value for the bond purchase, would be suboptimal.

---

[1] W. J. Baumol, "The Transactions Demand for Cash: An Inventory Theoretic Approach," *Quarterly Journal of Economics,* 66:545–556, 1952; and J. Tobin, "The Interest Elasticity of the Transactions Demand for Cash," *Review of Economics and Statistics,* 38:241–247, 1956. The present discussion is based on Tobin's analysis.

Figure 8–2 Optimal program for two transactions

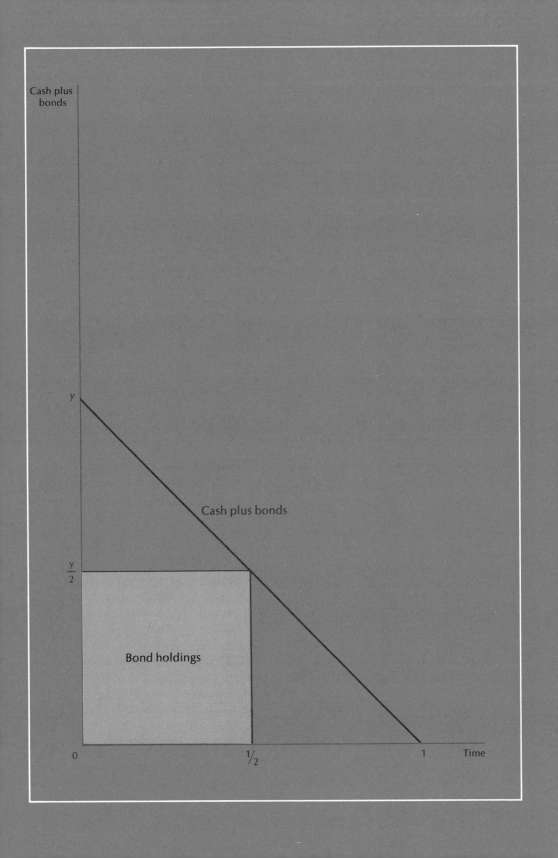

If the individual wishes to make three transactions, the optimal program is to buy bonds at $t = 0$ with two-thirds of his income. He should then sell one-half of his bond holdings when he runs out of cash at $t = 1/3$ and sell the remainder when he again runs out of cash at $t = 2/3$. This program is illustrated in Figure 8–3. In the case of four transactions his initial purchases should equal $3/4y$, which he then sells off in equal amounts of $1/4y$ at times $1/4$, $1/2$, and $3/4$.

The initial bond purchase for two transactions is $1/2y$; for three transactions it is $2/3y$; and for four transactions it is $3/4y$. From this we can readily infer that if the wealth holder makes n transactions, the value of the individual's initial purchase of bonds should be $[(n - 1)/n]y$. Because he begins the period with initial bond holdings of $[(n - 1)/n]y$ and ends the period with zero holdings, the average value of his bond holdings must be

$$\frac{n - 1}{2n}\, y$$

Consequently, if the interest return is i percent per period, his revenue will be

$$R = \frac{n - 1}{2n}\, iy$$

The revenue function is plotted in Figure 8–4. As can be seen there, revenue rises continuously as the number of transactions rises. The rise proceeds at a diminishing rate, however, and revenue therefore approaches a limiting value of $iy/2$. This maximum revenue is obtained if the bondholder puts his entire initial income into bonds and sells these bonds off continuously in infinitely small amounts as he needs cash. In this case his initial purchase of bonds equals y; his average holding is $y/2$; and his revenue therefore is $iy/2$. If the wealth holder were to follow this plan, he would never hold any money balances at all and his transactions demand for money would therefore be zero.

What prevents the wealth holder from making an infinite number of small transactions is the circumstance that there are costs associated with each transaction. Such costs tend to have a variable component that is related to the size of the transaction and a fixed component that is the same for each transaction regardless of its value. It is this fixed cost that makes small transactions unprofitable and that limits the number of bond purchases and sales that wealth holders will make.

Figure 8–3 Optimal program for three transactions

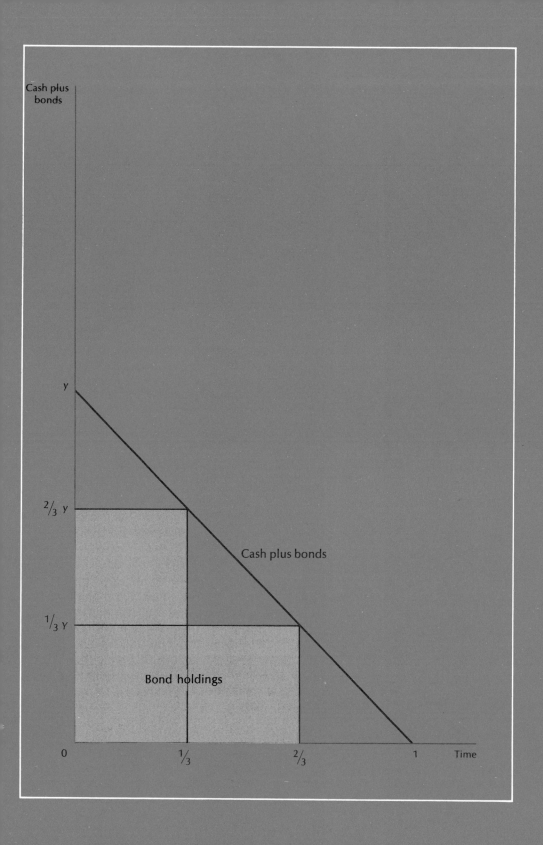

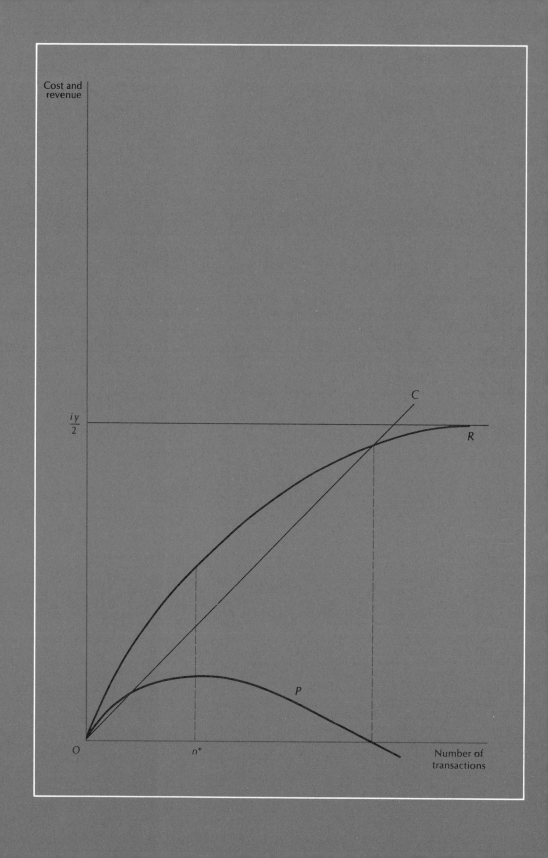

A sophisticated analysis[1] would take into account both the fixed and variable costs. However, for present purposes it is sufficient to assume that transactions costs are exclusively of the fixed variety. Consequently, we assume that for each transaction there is a cost of *a* dollars and that total transactions costs are therefore given by the linear function

$$C = na$$

The profit-maximizing investor will pick the number of transactions that maximizes the difference between cost and revenue. As can be seen in Figure 8–4, the maximum point on the profit function *P*, where $P = R - C$, is at a level of *n** transactions.[2] This is the value of *n* at which the slopes of the *R* and *C* functions are equal. This means that the marginal revenue of the next transaction just equals the marginal cost of making the transaction. Profits are therefore at a maximum.

As the reader can easily verify by inspecting Figure 8–4, the optimum number of transactions will increase if income and the rate of interest rise, and it will decrease if the cost per transaction increases. A rise in *i* or *y* will rotate the revenue curve upwards and to the left, and the maximum profit will therefore be obtained with a higher volume of transactions. On the other hand, a higher *a* will rotate the cost function counterclockwise, and *n** will therefore be reduced.

The fact that the optimum number of transactions is influenced by the income of the individual is explained by the presence of the fixed transactions cost. It probably will not pay a person with an initial balance of $1,000, which he will spend in a month, to use a fraction of

[1] Tobin, *ibid.*, incorporates the effect of both fixed and variable transactions costs into his analysis.

[2] The optimum number of transactions *n** can be calculated by noting that the profit function is

$$P = \frac{n-1}{n} iy - na$$

by differentiating the function with respect to *n*, and by setting the resulting derivative equal to zero. The result is

$$n^* = \sqrt{\frac{iy}{2a}}$$

The optimum number of transactions therefore increases with increases in *i* and *y*, and decreases with increases in transactions costs.

Figure 8–4   Interest revenue and fixed transactions costs as functions of the number of transactions

this balance to purchase bonds because he cannot hold the bonds long enough to earn the interest needed to overcome the fixed transactions cost. On the other hand, a large corporation faced with the need to accumulate sizable cash balances in anticipation of a quarterly income tax payment may very well find that it is profitable to invest these funds temporarily in short-term bonds.

The most important result of this analysis is that the transactions demand for money is a decreasing function of the rate of interest. A rise in the rate of interest increases the number of times during the income-expenditure period that bond holders find it worthwhile to enter the bond market. And this implies that a rise in the rate of interest reduces the wealth holder's average holding of idle cash balances. If he buys bonds in an amount $[(n - 1)/n]y$ at the beginning of the period, he retains y/n dollars of cash. Since he spends all this before replenishing his cash balance, his average holding of money must be $y/2n$ dollars, and this clearly implies that his average cash balance is inversely proportional to n^*.

To summarize: The traditional theory of the transactions demand for money assumes that this demand is proportional to the level of income. However, because a rise in the rate of interest raises the optimum number of times that wealth holders find it profitable to enter the bond market and because this has the effect of reducing their average level of money holding, it follows that the transactions demand for money is a decreasing function of the rate of interest. The higher the rate of interest, the more costly it is to hold money relative to other assets, and a rise in the rate of interest therefore produces an incentive to economize money balances and to substitute earning assets in their place.

The precautionary demand for money   A salesman about to embark on a business trip from Chicago to New Orleans will have to take with him a certain amount of (transactions) cash to pay for travel and living expenses. However, if he is a prudent person, he will probably take along more money than the amount he actually plans to spend on the trip. If, for example, his car breaks down and he is unable to pay for the repairs, he may never get to New Orleans to conduct his business. Because of this failure he may miss out on a promotion or he may even lose his job. Because his reputation will be damaged, he may have difficulty finding a new job. All these misfortunes befall him because he has failed to maintain some precautionary balance of money and has therefore fallen prey to what economists describe as the "linkage of risks."

The precautionary demand for money, like the transactions demand, is probably quite closely related to the level of money income. If the cost of automobile repairs rises or if the number of business trips taken each year increases, the salesman's precautionary requirements will probably rise in proportion. However, as in the case of the transactions demand, the precautionary demand may be responsive to changes in the rate of interest. An increase in interest rates may make the purchase of earning assets so tempting that the salesman may be willing to assume a slightly greater risk in the form of a lower precautionary balance in return for the added interest earnings.

The speculative demand for money To hold money balances for reasons unconnected with transactions and precautionary needs appears irrational because money balances that exceed required transactions and precautionary holdings may be exchanged for earning assets. Nonetheless there are grounds for believing that wealth holders do include money as one of the assets in their portfolios and that there is therefore a speculative or liquidity preference demand for money.

When the rate of interest is very low, security prices are very high. Consequently, a small yield can be earned only at the expense of a relatively large outlay. In such a situation a bond purchase does not look like a very attractive bargain. Moreover, if in the past the rate of interest was high but has since fallen to a lower level below which it is not expected to go, the balance of expectations will be in favor of a future rise in the rate. Anyone owning a bond at a time when the rate rises will suffer a capital loss. Consequently, if there is a general expectation that the rate of interest will rise, there will be a preference for liquidity. Since a capital loss cannot be taken on cash (except through a rise in the price level),[1] a situation may arise in which individuals will prefer to hold onto their cash rather than invest in earning assets. They do this in the expectation that interest rates in the future will be higher than at present and that they will therefore be able to strike a better bargain at a subsequent date.

This argument, first presented by Lord Keynes, has been criticized on the ground that it implies an all-or-none kind of behavior. If the interest earnings of a bond are in excess of the expected capital loss, it will pay to invest all one's funds in bonds. If the expected capital loss is greater than the interest earnings, no bonds will be held. Consequently, the

---

[1] The expectation of a fall in the price level will make money a relatively more attractive way to hold wealth than physical assets. But this is true of any kind of liquid asset whose money value does not vary with the price level. Price expectations help explain relative preferences between physical and liquid assets but do not explain relative preferences among different types of liquid assets.

minute the critical point is reached where the scales tip in favor of bonds, we would expect a mass exodus from cash into bonds. Keynes's explanation for the fact that this mass exodus does not occur was based on the assumption that different people have different expectations with regard to the future. This view, however, is open to the criticism that if the low rate of interest persists long enough, it will begin to be viewed as permanent so that expectations will converge, the fear of capital loss will disappear, and the speculative demand for money will fade out.

The modern theory of liquidity preference[1] has liberated the concept of a speculative or asset demand for money from reliance upon the expectation that interest rates will rise in the future. Even if no future change in asset prices or yields is expected, wealth holders cannot be certain of what the future will bring. The extent of such *uncertainty* varies with the nature of the asset and tends to run in the same direction as the expected yield of the asset. The expected return on an oil well or a uranium mine may be very high; however, the probability that this return will in fact be realized is quite low. The expected return on cash, on the other hand, is zero; and there is no uncertainty about this at all.

Any wealth holder who suffers no disutility from uncertainty would put all his assets into oil wells and uranium mines. Such persons are "plungers." However, most investors are "risk averters" who attempt to arrange their portfolios in such a way as to balance, at the margin, the utility of additional return against the disutility of additional uncertainty. Such wealth holders will diversify their portfolios. They will hold some highly speculative stocks on which the expected return and the degree of uncertainty are high; they will hold some blue-chip stocks and bonds that are characterized by lower, but more certain, returns; and they may also hold some cash. Although the cash earns no interest, it has the valuable property of being the most liquid of all assets. This means that one can always convert cash into other assets, but that one might have to wait or to take a lower price if he attempts to reverse the process. Individuals who have cash on hand are therefore in a better position to take advantage of the unexpected opportunities that may arise.

Now consider the effect that a rise in the general level of yields would have upon the composition of an investor's portfolio. The rise in interest rates causes the potential interest that is foregone by holding

---

[1] This discussion follows the line of J. Tobin, "Liquidity Preference as Behavior towards Risk," *Review of Economic Studies*, 25(2):65–86, 1958. The current view seems to have been quite clearly foreshadowed by J. R. Hicks, "A Suggestion for Simplifying the Theory of Money," *Economica*, New Series, 5:1–19, 1935.

cash to increase, and it therefore becomes more expensive to hold cash. Returns being higher, some of the investor's risk aversion will be overcome, and he will tend to substitute some oil-well stocks for blue chips; some blue chips for long-term bonds; some long-term bonds for Treasury bills; and some Treasury bills for cash. The composition of this portfolio will therefore move in the direction of decreased liquidity. On the other hand, if yields generally fall, the return on oil wells no longer compensates for the risk, while the loss of interest due to the holding of cash and the low-yield assets becomes smaller. The investor will therefore tend to adjust his portfolio in the direction of increased liquidity. The investor's preference for liquidity can therefore be seen to increase with a fall in the rate of interest, and his asset demand for money may also be a decreasing function of the rate of interest.

8–3   ALTERNATIVE THEORIES OF THE DEMAND FOR MONEY

One of the major questions that we shall attempt to answer in this book is why some economists have supreme faith in the ability of the competitive market system to bring the economy out of recession and back to full employment automatically, while other economists are skeptical of the ability of the patient to cure himself and believe that the monetary-fiscal doctors must be called upon. A closely related question is the issue of why some economists would put their faith in the effectiveness of monetary policy, while others regard fiscal policy as the salvation. As we shall see in Chapters 10 and 11, both questions hinge, to a considerable extent, on the nature of the demand for money. It is therefore exceedingly important that we take care to classify the assumptions that different groups of economists make about the demand for money.

One of the most familiar expressions in monetary economics is the "quantity equation"

$$MV = pY$$

The equation is a simple truism which states that the quantity of money M times the velocity of turnover of money in the purchase of newly produced goods and services V must equal the value of money income pY, where p is an index of prices and Y is the level of real income measured in base-period prices.

In some interpretations it is assumed that V is a constant. Velocity may change because institutional payment practices change, because a change in the rate of interest causes a change in the quantity of money demanded for various purposes, or because of many other factors. In any case, the assumption that V is a constant amounts to a clear denial of a possible existence of a speculative demand for money because it implies that the demand for money is independent of the rate of interest. The theory seems to assume that no wealth holder will be irrational enough to hold money balances in excess of transactions and precautionary needs when he could use the balances to purchase earning assets. Under these "classical" assumptions, the quantity equation becomes more than a mere truism and becomes instead the well-known quantity theory, according to which an increase in the money supply must lead either to an increase in real income Y or to an increase in the price level p, or to some combination of the two. An increase in the supply of money, the velocity of turnover being fixed, implies that wealth holders will attempt to rid themselves of the idle balances by purchasing earning assets. This means that the prices of earning assets will be bid up, interest rates will fall, and investment and income will increase. If idle resources are available, Y may rise. If, instead, the economy is already at full employment, competition for the available supply of output will raise prices. Since competition for earning assets will continue until all the excess money balances are absorbed into transactions demands, we may infer that with V fixed, the level of money income will always be proportional to the money supply.

The quantity equation can be written as

$$m = \frac{M}{p} = kY$$

where M/p is the real value of the money supply and k is the reciprocal of V, and therefore represents the fraction of a time period the average dollar is held between transactions. In this form the equation has been called the "Cambridge quantity equation," and k has been denoted as the "Marshallian k ratio."

By introducing the speculative demand for money, Keynes specifically denied the constant velocity assumption. Like his predecessors, however, Keynes believed that the transactions and precautionary demands were dependent on the level of income and not specifically associated with the rate of interest. The Keynesian variant of the demand for money may therefore be written as

$$m = \frac{M}{p} = kY + L(i)$$

where $L(i)$ is the speculative demand for money which varies inversely with the rate of interest and where k must now be interpreted to mean the ratio of transactions money balances to the volume of transactions.[1]

An interesting feature of the Keynesian variant is that once a critically low rate of interest is reached, increases in the supply of money will not achieve any further reduction in the rate of interest. Such a situation may arise from the fact that at very low rates of interest the yield on earning assets is so low and the risk of holding earning assets is so high that, given the liquidity premium of holding money, wealth holders will be willing to substitute money for earning assets in their portfolios without requiring an inducement in the form of higher bond prices.

Alternatively, consider the following situation: Suppose that the Federal Reserve System attempts to increase the money supply by purchasing government bonds from the public. Under normal circumstances such an increase in the demand for bonds would raise bond prices and lower interest rates. However, if interest rates are so low that wealth holders are undecided whether the cost of not investing compensates for the risk of capital loss, they may be willing to sell their bondholdings at existing prices. The fact that the Federal Reserve is supporting the market and may not continue to do so in the future may be taken as a golden opportunity to unload bondholdings. In the type of "liquidity trap" situation here described, the public's supply of bonds is infinitely elastic, which implies that the demand for speculative money balances will also be infinitely elastic with respect to the rate of interest.

Another monetary variant, which for lack of a better name we shall arbitrarily call the "modified Keynesian" variant, would include in the transactions and precautionary demands the assumption that these demands are inversely related to the rate of interest. Therefore, this variant may be written

$$m = L_1(i,Y) + L_2(i)$$

where L_1 refers to the transactions and precautionary demands and L_2 to the speculative demand. Since all the motives for holding money appear to depend on the rate of interest, the modified Keynesian variant im-

---

[1] This way of writing the demand for money assumes that the speculative demand, as well as the transactions and precautionary demands, is, given a constant rate of interest, proportional to the price level. Although Keynes made no such assumption, we shall follow D. Patinkin, "Keynesian Economics and the Quantity Theory," in K. K. Kurihara, ed., *Post-Keynesian Economics,* Rutgers University Press, New Brunswick, N.J., 1954, and assume that an increase in the price level will lead to a proportional increase in the demand for speculative balances.

plies that the distinction between the various motives is somewhat artificial, so that the above expression may just as well be compressed to

$$m = L(i,Y)$$

Recent developments in monetary theory place emphasis on the importance of wealth in determining the demand for money. The theory of portfolio balance suggests that an increase in the quantity of money demanded will occur not only if income rises and/or the rate of interest falls, but also if wealth holders become richer. An increment to wealth, in other words, causes wealth holders to attempt to distribute this increment over additional holdings of not one, but several forms of wealth. For example, Tobin[1] specifies the demand for money as

$$m = L(i,Y,K)$$

where K, the capital stock, represents the earning power, or productive wealth, of society.[2] Let us denote this final form of the demand for money the "modern Keynesian" variant.

The Keynesian variant is diagramed in Figure 8–5. The rate of interest is measured on the vertical axis. The transactions and precautionary demand for money m_1 is assumed to be inelastic with respect to the rate of interest. When the speculative demand for money m_2 is added, the total demand for money $m_1 + m_2$ is obtained. If the supply of money balances is m_s, the demand and supply schedules intersect at interest rate i_0. If the money supply increases to m_s', wealth holders will be induced to hold the added balances only if the interest rate falls to i_1. At i_1 the liquidity trap, where the demand for money is infinitely elastic, is reached. An increase in the supply of money from m_s' to m_s'' yields no fall in the rate of interest.

In closing this section, we want the reader to note very carefully

[1] J. Tobin, "A Dynamic Aggregative Model," *Journal of Political Economy,* 63:103–115, 1955.

[2] Emphasis on wealth as an important determinant of the demand for money is carried farthest by the so-called modern quantity theorists. The modern quantity theorist as exemplified by Milton Friedman differs from the modern Keynesian in that he regards the rate of interest and the level of current income as of only minor importance in determining the demand for money. See Milton Friedman, "The Quantity Theory of Money: A Restatement," *Studies in the Quantity Theory of Money,* Chap. 1, The University of Chicago Press, Chicago, 1956, and "The Demand for Money: Some Theoretical and Empirical Results," *Journal of Political Economy,* 67:327–351, 1958.

Figure 8–5 Demand and supply for money balances (all values in real terms)

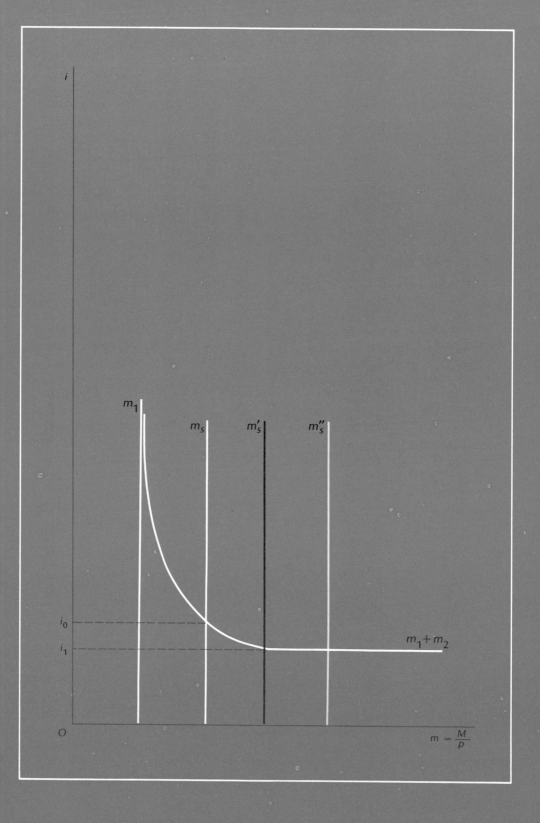

that the demand for money is linked only to current income transactions and not to financial transactions. The reason for this is that the various equations are equilibrium relations that specify the amount of money that wealth holders would hold for various purposes if their portfolios were in balance. General monetary equilibrium is a situation in which all portfolios are balanced and in which there would be no financial transactions at all.

8–4 THE SUPPLY OF MONEY

Recall the definition of money as the sum total of currency and bank deposits, but not savings deposits, held by the nonbank public. In the past there was a direct link between a country's gold stock and its stock, or supply, of money. But with the growth of fractional-reserve-deposit banking, the abandonment of specie as a medium of exchange, and the separation of the currency from specie backing, the connection between the gold stock and the domestic supply of money has become very faint.

While it is not vital for present purposes to ask how the money supply got where it is, it is nevertheless crucial to know how the money supply can be changed. In order to do this, we draw up four balance sheets (Table 8–1) of financial assets and liabilities—a balance sheet for the United States Treasury, a balance sheet for the Federal Reserve System, a consolidated balance sheet for the commercial banking system, and a balance sheet for the general public. The balance sheets are hypothetical statements in which we are going to post only changes in various accounts, since it is only the changes that interest us.

Suppose that a gold miner, by dint of his own hard labor, digs $1,000 worth of gold out of the ground. This $1,000 is an asset to the gold miner which means that the assets of the public increase by $1,000, and so also does the public's net worth. The increase in assets and net worth due to the creation of the new wealth in the form of gold is labeled *a* in the public's balance sheet.

By law, the gold miner must take the gold to the United States Treasury. The Treasury accepts the gold, which becomes an asset in its balance sheet, and in return writes a check to the gold miner. This check will ultimately reduce the Treasury's bank account, which it keeps with the Federal Reserve System. The miner then takes the check and deposits it in his commercial bank. He therefore trades one asset (gold) in favor of another asset (bank deposits). The commercial bank receives the check and credits the gold miner with a deposit. This is entered on the right-hand side of the bank's balance sheet because the deposit is a

Table 8–1

United States Treasury		Federal Reserve banks	
Deposits with Federal Reserve −1,000 b +1,000 c	Gold certificates +1,000 c	Gold certificates +1,000 c	Treasury deposits −1,000 b +1,000 c
Gold +1,000 b			Member bank deposits +1,000 b

Commercial banks		Public	
Loans and securities +800 d +640 f	Deposits +1,000 b + 800 e + 640 g	Deposits +1,000 b + 800 e + 640 g	Net worth +1,000 a
Reserves +1,000 b − 800 d + 800 e − 640 f + 640 g		Securities − 800 d − 640 f	
		Other assets +1,000 a −1,000 b	

debt which the bank must pay the depositor on demand. But while the bank incurs a liability, it also receives a new asset of $1,000 which it deposits in its own bank account (called "reserves") with the Federal Reserve System. The Federal Reserve[1] upon receipt of the check credits the account of the commercial bank and thus increases its deposit liability to the banking system (Member Bank Deposits), but at the same time makes a deduction from the Treasury's account of $1,000. All these transactions, starting with the receipt of the gold by the Treasury, are labeled b in the various balance sheets.

Notice that the Treasury has traded a portion of its bank account in return for the gold, while the gold miner has done the opposite. The net effect therefore is to increase the money supply (measured by the demand deposits and currency held by the public) by $1,000.

How can the Treasury replenish its account? The usual procedure is for the Treasury to print gold certificates which it sells to the Federal

---

[1] The easiest way to think of the Federal Reserve System is as a bank for bankers and for the United States Treasury.

Reserve System for deposit credit. When this operation (labeled c) has been accomplished, the Treasury's account is back where it was previously. The net effect, so far as the Treasury is concerned, is an increase in its assets (gold) and an increase in liabilities (gold certificates) of $1,000. The net effect as far as the Federal Reserve is concerned is a $1,000 increase in its deposit liabilities, in return for which it has gained an asset in the form of a gold certificate. The commercial banks have an increase in deposit liabilities, in return for which they have an added deposit of $1,000 with the Federal Reserve System. The public, finally, has traded $1,000 of gold in return for a bank deposit.

Is the $1,000 change in deposits the net effect on the money supply? Not necessarily: Suppose that the legal minimum reserve requirement is 20 percent. This means that the commercial banks must hold 20 percent of demand deposits (0.20 × $1,000) idle in their Federal Reserve accounts but that the remaining $800, known as "excess reserves," may be used to purchase earning assets. Suppose the bank receiving the $1,000 purchases an $800 bond from a member of the public. The bank writes a check which is received in payment for the bond (d), but the check is redeposited somewhere in the commercial banking system (e). This means that the added reserves due to the Treasury gold sale are still $1,000. But with deposits of $1,800 there are now excess reserves of $640, that is $1,000 − 0.20 × $1,800, which may be used to purchase additional securities (f). But since the proceeds will be redeposited (g), deposits rise to $2,440 or $1,000 + $800 + $640.

Notice that each time excess reserves are used to buy earning assets, the proceeds are redeposited somewhere in the commercial banking system. This means that, after the original $1,000 increase in reserves, which came from outside the commercial banking system, the purchase of earning assets does not change total reserves. But the purchase of earning assets does change required reserves because these purchases cause deposits to increase. Thus we may infer, from the fact that the net change in reserves is $1,000 and from the fact that required reserves are 20 percent of demand deposits, that excess reserves will be exhausted when deposits have risen by $5,000. A 5:1 expansion of deposits will therefore be possible on the basis of the original increase in reserves of $1,000. The final situation is shown in Table 8–2, where it can be seen that after the initial $1,000 increase in deposits and net worth due to the gold production and sale (a) the public has traded the banking system $4,000 worth of earning assets in return for $4,000 of deposits (b). The net effect of the gold purchase on the supply of money is therefore $5,000.

It is not necessary for gold to be discovered in order for the money supply to be increased. Whenever additional reserves are placed in the

Table 8–2

Commercial Banks				Public			
Securities		Deposits		Deposits		Net worth	
	+4,000 b		+1,000 a		+1,000 a		+1,000 a
			+4,000 b		+4,000 b		
Reserves				Securities			
	+1,000 a				−4,000 b		

commercial banking system, deposit expansion may proceed. The identical result could, for example, be achieved by a Federal Reserve open market purchase of government bonds. In this case, the Federal Reserve trades the public a deposit of $1,000 in return for the bond. This, in turn, creates added reserves of $1,000 (see Table 8–1) and leaves the way open for the same kind of multiple expansion as before. The Federal Reserve could also neutralize the monetary effect of the Treasury gold purchase. If the Federal Reserve had sold a government bond of $1,000, this would have reduced deposits and reserves by $1,000 and therefore would have canceled the effect of the gold purchase.

An expansion of the money supply could also result from a net export of goods and services from the economy. The monetary effects of the gold flows received in return are identical to those that result when the gold is dug out of the ground. The expansion could also result from commercial-bank borrowing from the Federal Reserve. In this event, the commercial bank incurs a liability with the Federal Reserve in return for additional reserves. It is important to note that in all cases monetary expansion can take place only if some additional reserves appear from outside the commercial banking system, for if an individual bank wishes to replenish its reserves by selling a security to a member of the public, it does so at the expense of the deposits and reserves of some other commercial bank.

We noted above that with a legal minimum reserve requirement of 20 percent, a $1,000 increase in reserves could lead to a $5,000 expansion of the money supply. The $5,000 is a theoretical maximum that will be realized only as long as there is no hoarding either by the banks or by the public. If, for example, the banks simply hold the added reserves instead of converting them into earning assets, the money supply increases by only $1,000. Similarly, if one of the sellers of the bonds purchased by the banks converts his additional deposits into cash which he hides in a cookie jar, the process of expansion will be arrested at that point.

The foregoing possibilities suggest that although the monetary authority (Federal Reserve) can make the level of member bank reserves whatever it wants, it cannot always be sure that the money supply will rise in a constant proportion to a rise in reserves. Indeed, the ratio of deposits to reserves can be expected to fluctuate considerably. Banks are not likely to utilize all their excess reserves to purchase earning assets. The typical bank operates under conditions of uncertainty. Whether new deposits in any period will exceed withdrawals is never known for certain. Even if the bank regards the chances that deposits will match withdrawals as even, the penalty attached to being caught short is enough to make it hold excess reserves.[1] There is little reason to suppose, moreover, that banks differ fundamentally from other wealth holders. Assuming that their portfolio balance behavior is similar to that of individuals, banks will be likely to hold larger quantities of excess reserves during periods of low interest rates. A rise in bond yields and loan rates will make banks less reluctant to lend and will therefore increase the ratio of earning assets to reserves and also the supply of money. Thus the supply of money, as well as the demand for money, appears to be partially determined by the rate of interest.

In summary, the potential size of the money supply depends in the final analysis on the volume of bank reserves. Since the volume of these reserves is almost entirely dependent on Federal Reserve–Treasury action, the money supply is often treated as a "policy variable," i.e., fixed unless changed by central direction. As we have seen, the ratio between the actual and the potential money supply may fluctuate under the impact of changing interest rates and varying degrees of uncertainty. Consequently, to treat the supply of money as a policy variable is not entirely satisfactory. The main purpose of the following chapter, however, can very well be achieved by assuming that the supply of money is fixed unless changed by central direction. But in Chapter 10 we shall try to become a bit more sophisticated and shall, therefore, drop this simplifying assumption.

8–5 MONETARY EFFECTS OF A FISCAL OPERATION

If we are to gain an understanding of the workings and the effectiveness of monetary and fiscal policies, it is extremely important that we understand the monetary effects of a fiscal operation. A "pure" fiscal policy

[1] For an analysis of the effect of uncertainty on credit expansion see D. Orr and W. J. Mellon, "Stochastic Reserve Losses and Expansion of Bank Credit," *American Economic Review*, 51:614–23, 1961.

can be defined as a Treasury operation that changes the size of the current income stream while leaving the money supply unaffected. A "pure" monetary policy is defined as an operation that affects the money supply without directly altering the current income stream. A Federal Reserve purchase of government bonds from a member of the public alters the money supply but has no direct effect on the level of current income.[1] On the other hand, an increase in government spending directly increases income, while an increase in taxes has the opposite effect.

Insofar as the payment of taxes to the Treasury reduces demand deposits, the fiscal operation will not be "pure" in the sense that there is no effect on the money supply. If we are able to talk about "pure" fiscal policy, we must assume that the tax revenues are utilized to retire debt held by the public, or that government expenditures in an equal amount are made at the same time. In both cases, the monetary effects of the fiscal operation(s) just cancel. Although it may be difficult at the moment to grasp the purpose of these subtleties, it will subsequently become apparent why the distinction must be held firmly in mind.

Consider the monetary effects of an increase in government purchases. Suppose that the Treasury makes a payment of $100 to a mail carrier. The $100 is an income payment and therefore constitutes a fiscal operation. But the $100 payment is also an addition to the money supply; if it is not offset by a corresponding reduction, it must be considered a combined monetary-fiscal change. Whether or not such an offset occurs depends on the method of financing the $100 expenditure.

1. If the Treasury increases tax collections by $100, there will be a reduction in demand deposits of $100. The monetary effects of the expenditure and the tax cancel each other. A tax-financed expenditure can therefore be regarded as a pure fiscal policy.

2. If the Treasury replenishes its account by selling bonds to the public, the public will make payment from its deposits in return for bonds. Again, the monetary effects of the fiscal operation cancel out. A deficit financed by a sale of bonds to the public may therefore be considered a pure fiscal policy. When reference is made to fiscal policy, it should always be assumed that deficits are financed by borrowing from the public and that surpluses are used to retire debt held by the public.

3. It is possible for the Treasury to replenish its account by selling bonds to the Federal Reserve System. In this case, the $100 payment to

[1] The Federal Reserve purchase may, through its effect on interest rates, raise the level of investment and income. We regard such an effect as indirect.

the mail carrier remains as a net increase in the reserves of the banking system. The government expenditure in this case is a combined monetary-fiscal operation since it both increases income and changes the money supply.

8–6 THE PROGRAM

In the next chapter the building blocks of Chapters 5 through 8 are put together into a general equilibrium model of the economic system. The necessity for this stems from the following consideration: Referring again to Figure 8–5, if the rate of interest is i_0, a certain level of investment is thereby implied. This level of investment in turn implies a certain equilibrium level of income. Suppose, however, that the supply of money is increased to m_s'. This increase in the money supply lowers the rate of interest and stimulates the level of investment. But this means that income will rise; if income rises, the transactions demand for money rises, and this in turn will affect the rate of interest. An endless chain of action and reaction can therefore be set off—a chain that cannot be properly analyzed with our existing apparatus. The purpose of the next chapter is to develop a more effective model that will (1) help avoid the pitfalls of partial equilibrium analysis and (2) provide a framework within which to consider the effectiveness of alternative stabilization policies.

9

GENERAL EQUILIBRIUM OF THE PRODUCT AND MONEY MARKETS

9–1 INTRODUCTION

In the last chapter it was suggested that a change in the money supply would affect the rate of interest both directly through the initial change and indirectly through changes induced by the effect of interest rate changes on the level of investment and the level of income. The same kind of reaction can be set off in the market for final goods. An innovation, for example, will shift the investment demand schedule to the right and bring about a change in the level of income. But an increase in investment, by increasing the level of income, leads to an increase in the transactions and precautionary demands for money balances. If wealth holders (including banks) are to be induced to release the necessary balances from speculative hoards, interest rates must rise. But this in turn means that investment will fall, income will fall, and the process will go through another round of action and reaction. Evidently it will help to introduce a model that will give the final equilibrium solution even if it does not trace the process whereby equilibrium is reached.[1]

To simplify matters at the outset, let us again pretend that the government does not exist and that foreign trade does not take place. Under these conditions equilibrium of the market for final goods (product market) requires equality between intended saving and investment. The general form of the saving function can be written

$$S = Y - C(Y) \tag{9-1}$$

which, together with the investment demand schedule

$$I = I(i) \tag{9-2}$$

gives the product market equilibrium condition

$$I(i) = Y - C(Y) \tag{9-3}$$

The condition states that for any arbitrary rate of interest there is some level (or levels) of income that will make intended investment and saving equal. This relationship between the rate of interest and the level of income is referred to as the "*IS* function."

Assuming a Keynesian-type demand for money function (i.e., the real speculative demand for money is a function of the rate of interest, and the real transactions and precautionary demands[2] are proportional to the level of real income), monetary equilibrium will be given by

$$m_s = kY + L(i) \tag{9-4}$$

where m_s, the supply of real money balances, is assumed to be constant. Given the supply of real money balances, there will be some level (or levels) of real income that is (are) associated with a particular rate of interest. This relationship is called the "*LM* function."

Notice that the equilibrium condition in the two markets is a function of two variables—the rate of interest and the level of income. It would therefore be possible to solve the two equations and obtain the final equilibrium solution for the rate of interest and the level of income. Our understanding will be facilitated, however, if we trace the process of solution in a set of simple diagrams.

---

[1] The model used here was first presented by J. R. Hicks, "Mr. Keynes and the 'Classics': A Suggested Interpretation," *Econometrica*, New Series, 5:147–159, 1937.

[2] From now on the combined transactions and precautionary demands will be referred to simply as the "transactions demand."

9–2 GRAPHIC DERIVATION OF THE *IS* AND *LM* FUNCTIONS

The investment demand schedule $I = I(i)$ is plotted as a straight line in the first quadrant of Figure 9–1. The rate of interest is posted on the vertical axis, and the level of investment on the horizontal axis.[1] In quadrant 2 the intended investment-saving equilibrium condition is posted. This curve must be a straight line rising from the origin at a 45-degree angle because intended investment must equal saving at equilibrium. The familiar saving schedule is plotted in quadrant 3. We assume in this case that the level of saving is zero at an income level of $100 billion and that the marginal propensity to save is 0.5.[2]

Starting with an interest rate of 3 percent, we note in quadrant 1 that investment of $50 billion will be undertaken. Moving to quadrant 2, we observe that saving must also be $50 billion. In quadrant 3 the saving function indicates that $50 billion will be saved at an income level of $200 billion. Finally, in quadrant 4 we obtain one point of product market equilibrium; i.e., when the rate of interest is 3 percent, the level of income that will just make intended investment equal saving is $200 billion.

If the rate of interest is raised to 4 percent, the level of investment drops to $25 billion. This means that saving must be $25 billion and therefore that the level of income must be $150 billion. If the rate of interest falls to 2 percent, investment rises to $75 billion, so that the equilibrium level of income must be $250 billion.

If this procedure of selecting arbitrary rates of interest and finding the level of income that is consistent with each rate of interest is continued, a curve known as the "*IS* curve" will be traced out in quadrant 4. This curve is a simple graphic representation of the product market equilibrium condition of Eq. (9–3) and shows the level of income that will yield equality of intended investment and saving at different possible interest rates.[3] Evidently we may also interpret the *IS* schedule as the schedule of aggregate demand for goods and services with respect to the rate of interest.

The identical procedure used above may now be applied to the problem of finding monetary equilibrium. In quadrant 1 of Figure 9–2 the real speculative demand for money, $m_2 = L(i)$, is plotted against the rate

---

[1] The equation for the investment demand schedule is assumed to be $i = 0.05 - 0.0004I$ or, rearranging terms to make I the dependent variable, $I = (i - 0.05)/ -0.0004$.

[2] The equation for the saving function is $S = -50 + 0.5Y$.

[3] The equation for intended investment is $i = 0.05 - 0.0004I$, which may be rewritten $I = (i - 0.05)/ -0.0004$. The saving function is $S = -50 + 0.5Y$; if intended investment is equated with saving, we have $(i - 0.05)/ -0.0004 = -50 + 0.5Y$, which simplifies to $i = 0.07 - 0.0002Y$; this is the equation for the *IS* function and should correspond with the points plotted in Fig. 9–1.

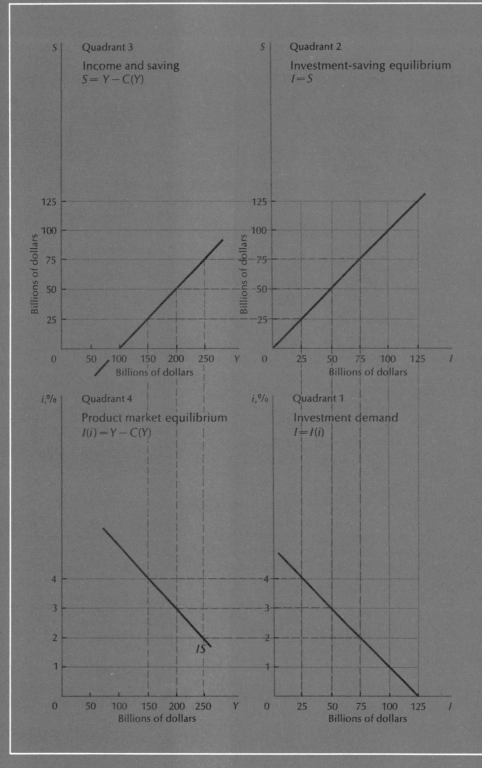

of interest. It is assumed that the inhabitants of the economy balance their portfolios in such a way that when the rate of interest is 3 percent, the speculative demand is $25 billion. At 2 percent it is $50 billion, at 1 percent it is $75 billion, and at 0 percent it is $100 billion or more.

Quadrant 2 shows how the given money supply of $125 billion can be split between transactions and speculative balances. If the transactions demand is $100 billion, then $25 billion will be left over for speculative purposes. If the transactions demand is $75 billion, $50 billion will be left over for speculative balances. In quadrant 3 the transactions demand, assumed to be proportional to the level of income in a 1:2 ratio, is posted. Finally, in quadrant 4 the rate of interest that is consistent with monetary equilibrium is posted against the level of income.

Beginning with an interest rate of 3 percent, we note in quadrant 1 that wealth holders desire to hold $25 billion of idle cash and deposits for speculative purposes. In quadrant 2 we observe that $100 billion will be released for transactions purposes. But quadrant 3 indicates that $100 billion of transactions money is consistent with a level of income of $200 billion. Moving to quadrant 4, we observe that the level of income that yields monetary equilibrium with a money supply of $125 billion and an interest rate of 3 percent is $200 billion.

Now start with an interest rate of 2 percent. At this rate of interest wealth holders will wish to hold idle speculative balances of $50 billion. This means that the amount released for transactions purposes will be $75 billion, which is consistent with a level of income of $150 billion (quadrant 3). Accordingly, we note in quadrant 4 that the level of income that will yield monetary equilibrium at a 2 percent rate of interest is $150 billion.

If this process of selecting arbitrary rates of interest and finding the level of income that is consistent with monetary equilibrium at each rate of interest is continued, a curve known as the "LM curve" will be traced out in quadrant 4.[1] This curve is a simple diagrammatic representation of the monetary equilibrium condition of Eq. (9–4).

---

[1] Inspection of quadrant 1 of Fig. 9–2 indicates that the speculative demand is a straight line with the equation $i = 0.04 - 0.0004m_2$, which may be rewritten as

$m_2 = (i - 0.04)/ -0.0004$

The transactions demand m_1 is $m_1 = 0.5Y$, and since the money supply is $125 billion,

$$m_1 + m_2 = 125 = 0.5Y + \frac{i - 0.04}{-0.0004}$$

from which it follows that the equation for the LM function is $i = -0.01 + 0.0002Y$.

Figure 9–1 Product market equilibrium
(all values in real terms)

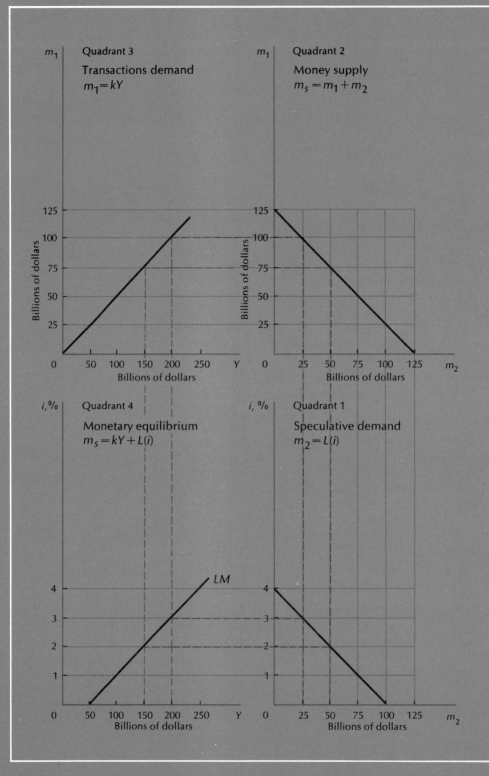

Although the *LM* schedule suggests that several rates of interest are consistent with monetary equilibrium and the *IS* curve suggests that several rates are consistent with product market equilibrium, there is only one rate of interest and one level of income that is consistent with both. In Figure 9–3 the *IS* and *LM* functions of Figures 9–1 and 9–2 are superimposed. The intersection of the two curves is at an income level of $200 billion with an interest rate of 3 percent.[1] Once these equilibrium values have been found, it is easy enough to trace back once again through the product market diagrams and verify that the level of investment is $50 billion and the level of savings is $50 billion. Similarly, if we retrace our steps through the money market, we find that at equilibrium the speculative demand is $25 billion and the transactions demand is $100 billion. General equilibrium prevails: There is no tendency for any magnitude to change.

9–3 GOVERNMENT AND GENERAL EQUILIBRIUM

As was noted previously, the condition that must hold at the equilibrium level of income is that total income leakages must equal total injections.

---

[1] It should be possible to find the equilibrium values by solving the *IS* and *LM* equations simultaneously. The *IS* function is $i = 0.07 - 0.0002Y$, and the *LM* function is $i = -0.01 + 0.0002Y$. When we equate these two functions, we find that $i = 0.03$ and $Y = 200$. Given the solution for the level of income, we can then go to the saving function and note that

$$S = -50 + 0.5Y = -50 + 0.5 \times 200 = 50$$

The equilibrium rate of interest can be substituted into the investment demand function which implies

$$I = \frac{i - 0.05}{-0.0004} = \frac{0.03 - 0.05}{-0.0004} = 50$$

and we therefore see that intended investment equals saving.

Similarly, the level of income of 200 requires transactions balances of

$$m_1 = 0.5Y = 0.5 \times 200 = 100$$

Because the money supply is 125, this releases 25 for speculative purposes. This result is consistent with a 3 percent interest rate because from the speculative demand equation we have

$$m_2 = \frac{i - 0.04}{-0.0004} = \frac{0.03 - 0.04}{-0.0004} = 25$$

**Figure 9–2 Monetary equilibrium
(all values in real terms)**

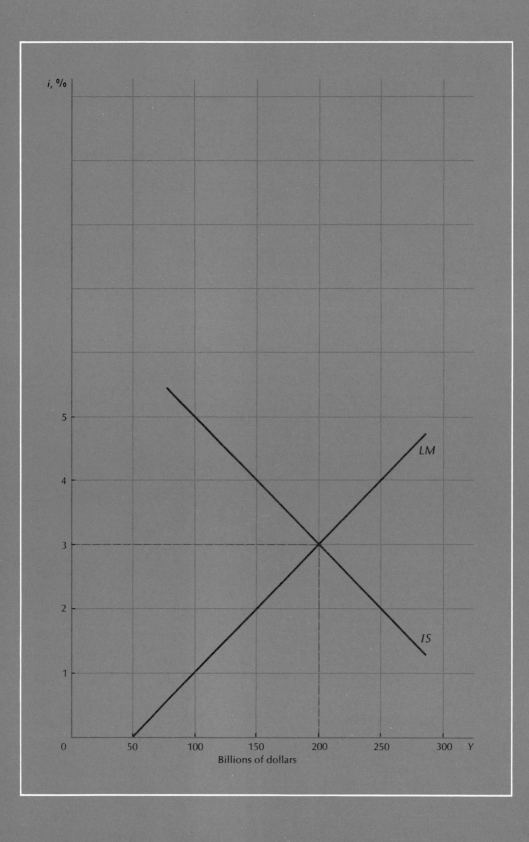

Thus intended investment plus government purchases must equal saving plus taxes. This means that the IS schedule, which represents product market equilibrium, becomes[1]

$$I(i) + G = Y - C(Y - T)$$

In order to observe the effect of fiscal policy, we now take the assumed economy of Section 9–2 and first add $25 billion of government purchases and then $25 billion in the form of lump-sum taxes. In Figure 9–4 the IS schedule prior to the imposition of government purchases and taxes is IS_0.

Government purchases have the same effect on the level of income as investment expenditures. We may therefore add the $25 billion government purchases to the investment demand schedule in quadrant 1. The combined investment demand schedule and government purchases schedule (what we have been calling injections) is now denoted as $I(i) + G$. Note that if G is added to the investment demand schedule, the horizontal axis of both quadrants 1 and 2 must be changed to $I + G$. The new equilibrium condition is that the injections $I + G$ must be balanced by an equal amount of leakages $S + T$ so that $S + T$ becomes the vertical axis in quadrants 2 and 3.

At a 3 percent rate of interest, an investment expenditure of $50 billion will be undertaken, to which must be added the $25 billion government purchases. This means (quadrant 2) that $75 billion of leakages are now required to match the injections. Observe in quadrant 3 that these leakages are generated at an income level of $250 billion. Dropping a per-

---

[1] Since we are ignoring all but personal saving, we may write

$$S = Y_d - C$$

Disposable income is defined as

$$Y_d = Y - T$$

and since consumption is a function of disposable income we have

$$C = C(Y - T)$$

Combining these expressions gives us the savings schedule

$$S = Y - T - C(Y - T)$$

so that upon adding T to both sides of the equation, we obtain the total leakages schedule

$$S + T = Y - C(Y - T)$$

Figure 9–3   General equilibrium (all values in real terms)

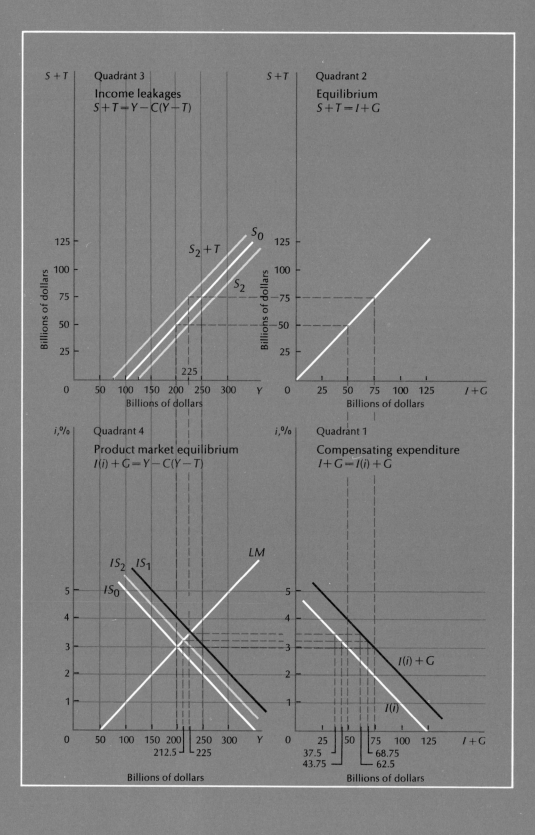

pendicular into quadrant 4, we note that product market equilibrium at a 3 percent rate of interest, instead of being at an income level of $200 billion, is now at $250 billion. If product market equilibrium is found for a number of other interest rates, it will always be the case that for any rate of interest, product market equilibrium is at an income level $50 billion higher than before the addition of the $25 billion of government purchases. Apparently the IS schedule shifts to the right by $50 billion at all rates of interest. This new schedule is denoted as IS_1 in Figure 9–4.

If the $I(i) + G$ schedule of quadrant 1 shifts by $1, the IS schedule of quadrant 4 will shift horizontally by $1 times the multiplier, which in this example is 2. This is so because the increase in investment or government purchases will require an additional dollar of saving to offset it. Income must therefore rise by enough to generate an additional dollar of leakages. Consequently the shift in the IS schedule will always equal the shift in the $I(i) + G$ schedule times the multiplier—a result that would be expected from the analysis of Chapter 6.

Although the IS schedule will shift by the change in investment or government purchases times the multiplier, is it also true that the change in income will be of this magnitude? In Figure 9–4 the IS_1 schedule cuts the LM schedule at an income level of $225 billion. Although the multiplier is 2, the level of income rises by only $25 billion. What accounts for this?

Observe first of all that the rate of interest in the new equilibrium position is 3.5 percent. The increase of 0.5 percent over the original level has been caused by the fact that the government cannot borrow $25 billion from the public without a higher yield inducement. Given the assumption that the money supply is fixed, the funds borrowed by the government must come from a reduction in speculative balances and/or from a reduction in transactions balances. In any event, if wealth holders are to be persuaded that government securities are more attractive than the other forms in which they have been holding wealth, interest rates must rise. But this in turn implies that the level of investment will fall, and this means that the level of income will fall. The stimulus provided by the fiscal policy is therefore partially offset by a decline in investment spending.

At the new equilibrium rate of interest of 3.5 percent, investment expenditures are only $37.5 billion. Add to this the government purchases of $25 billion and note that compensating expenditures in the

Figure 9–4 Government purchases and taxation (all values in real terms)

new equilibrium position are, not $75 billion as originally expected, but only $62.5 billion. Thus the net change in injections is only $12.5 billion (62.5 − 50.0), which means that the change in income will be 2 (the multiplier) times $12.5 billion, or $25 billion.

We can now see that one of the virtues of the *IS-LM* model is that it shows that the crude multipliers of past chapters implicitly assume monetary neutrality, i.e., that any change in government purchases, taxes, or investment would not affect the rate of interest and therefore the level of investment. We now observe, however, that it is conceivable for an increase in government purchases not to affect the level of income at all. If, through monetary repercussions, an increase in government purchases of $1 leads to a fall in investment expenditure of exactly $1, there will be no change in income. If, on the other hand, the deficit spending can be financed with no change in interest rates, a full multiplier effect on the level of income will materialize. It is evident, then, that the simple multipliers of Chapters 5 and 6 will hold only if the added transactions resulting from an increase in expenditure can be financed without changes in interest rates. Observe that if the *LM* function is a horizontal line, changes in income will equal the shifts in the *IS* schedule.

Next let us impose a tax of $25 billion to match the government purchases and assume, as in the simplest fiscal policy model of Chapter 6, that the tax is independent of the level of income. Previous considerations lead us to suppose that $25 billion of taxes will lower the level of income by $25 billion because, the marginal propensity to save being 0.5, $12.5 billion of the tax will be drawn from savings. Leakages therefore rise by a total of only $12.5 billion so that, given a marginal propensity to save of 0.5, the level of income will have to fall by $25 billion in order to eliminate the leakages in excess of injections. We should therefore expect the *IS* schedule to shift to the left by $25 billion.

In Figure 9–4 we observe that the $25 billion tax shifts the saving schedule down by $12.5 billion from S_0 to S_2. If we add the tax function to the saving schedule, we obtain the total leakages schedule $S_2 + T$, which is $12.5 billion greater at all levels of income than the S_0 schedule. The combined investment and government purchases of $75 billion, which are generated at a 3 percent rate of interest, will now be offset by $75 billion of leakages at an income level of $225 billion instead of an income level of $250 billion, as in the previous example. At all other interest rates the same thing will happen: The level of income that yields product market equilibrium at different rates of interest is always $25 billion less than the level prior to the imposition of the tax. The *IS* schedule therefore shifts to the left by the amount of the change in leakages, $b \, \Delta T$, times the multiplier, or by $b \, \Delta T/(1 - b)$. After the imposition of the tax, the *IS* schedule is IS_2 of Figure 9–4.

Although the equilibrium level of income prior to the imposition of the tax was $225 billion and the tax causes a leftward shift in the *IS* schedule of $25 billion, the equilibrium level of income falls to only $212.5 billion. Again, monetary effects have kept the full multiplier from working its way out. If the tax proceeds are used to retire the bonds that were issued to borrow the $25 billion previously spent by the government, there will be no net shrinkage in the money supply, although the reduction in consumption caused by the tax will release some money balances from transactions. If monetary equilibrium is to be established, interest rates must fall, investment will be stimulated, and the level of income will rise. The depressing effect of the tax is therefore partly offset by an increase in investment.

Notice that in the final equilibrium situation, the rate of interest is 3.25 percent. At this rate of interest the level of investment is $43.75 billion, whereas at the previous equilibrium rate of 3.5 percent the level of investment was $37.5 billion. Although the tax would tend to lower the equilibrium level of income by $25 billion, the monetary effects of the tax are such as to raise the level of investment by $6.25 billion (from $37.5 billion to $43.75 billion) and the level of income by $12.5 billion. The net effect, as shown in Figure 9–4, is to lower the equilibrium level of income by $12.5 billion.

9–4   SHIFTS IN THE *IS* AND *LM* FUNCTIONS

In the last section it was seen that the addition of $25 billion of government purchases shifted the *IS* schedule to the right by $50 billion because, the marginal propensity to save being 0.5, income would have to rise by $50 billion to generate the additional leakages needed to offset the added $25 billion of government purchases. Similarly, the addition of a $25 billion tax shifted the *IS* schedule to the left by $25 billion because the level of income would have to fall by $25 billion to offset the additional leakages of $12.5 billion caused by the imposition of the tax. These are but two of the ways in which the *IS* schedule may shift. Some other factors that may cause such a shift in the *IS* schedule, as well as some changes that will shift the *LM* schedule, are considered briefly in this section.

A reduction in intended saving (increase in intended consumption) will shift the saving schedule of quadrant 3 down and thereby reduce the leakages generated at all income levels. This means that the IS schedule will shift to the right. Such a change in the saving schedule may result from the introduction of a new product which consumers feel they must have even if it is at the expense of saving. The downward shift in the saving schedule may also result from an increase in the community's wealth. A persistent governmental deficit, for example, may result in the accumulation of such a large stock of liquid assets in the hands of the public that wealth holders no longer feel the necessity of saving at their previous rate. Similarly, the expectation of price increases and shortages of consumer goods may bring about a fall in the saving schedule and lead to a burst of consumer buying of the kind that occurred at the start of the Korean War.

The IS schedule will shift to the right if the investment demand schedule shifts to the right. Such a shift may occur as a result of an innovation, as the result of additional housing requirements brought about by population increases, and as the result of better profit expectations in the future. In all these cases, the IS schedule will exhibit a horizontal shift equal to the amount of the shift in the investment demand schedule times the multiplier, or, what amounts to the same thing, the reciprocal of the marginal propensity to save.

Shifts in the LM schedule may result from monetary policy, from changes in expectations, and from changes in payments practices. If the Federal Reserve Open Market Committee decides to pursue an expansionary monetary policy, it will purchase government bonds on the open market. Wealth holders trade part of their stock of government bonds to the Federal Reserve System in return for bank deposits. This means that the money supply schedule of quadrant 2 of Figure 9–2 shifts to the right, a greater volume of money is available for both transactions and speculative purposes at all rates of interest, and the LM curve of quadrant 4 shifts to the right.

Changes in expectations are likely to make their presence felt in the money market by shifts in the speculative demand for money. If, for example, investors become accustomed to a low rate of interest, the fear of capital loss that usually accompanies a low rate may gradually become less powerful. Thus the m_2 schedule will shift to the left, and a greater volume of transactions, and therefore income, can be supported at all rates of interest. This means that the LM schedule shifts to the right.

Changes in payments practices will change the volume of transactions that a given money supply will support. If individuals are paid twice as often as before, the average idle deposits that must be held for transactions purposes will decline by one-half. This means that the m_1 schedule of quadrant 3 of Figure 9–2 will rotate in a clockwise fashion, and so also will the LM schedule. In the United States there has been a steady advance in the rapidity with which checks are cleared and in the rapidity with which payments and collections are made. All such changes tend to reduce average transactions balances relative to the volume of transactions. In addition, we may well imagine the size of the reduction in the "k ratio" that has resulted from the increasing use of the pay-as-you-go tax as opposed to the once-a-year payment. Imagine the increase in transactions balances that would be required if, instead of paying taxes each week or each month, we were once again to go back to the system of paying all our income taxes once a year.

9–5 "REAL" VERSUS "MONETARY" SOURCES OF INCOME CHANGE

The present model of income and interest rate determination is a useful tool for the analysis of many macroeconomic problems. One very interesting application, which we present here in order to increase the reader's familiarity with the model, is to the problem of identifying the sources of the disturbances that cause the level of income to change.[1]

Changes in income that occur as the result of shifts in the consumption or investment functions or in government tax and expenditure policies may be denoted as "real" disturbances. Changes in income that stem from changes in the money supply or from changes in liquidity preference may be denoted "monetary" disturbances. In Figure 9–5(a) we assume that the IS schedule shifts from IS_0 to IS_1. This real disturbance causes the level of income to rise from Y_0 to Y_1 and the rate of interest to rise from i_0 to i_1. In Figure 9–5(b) income increases from Y_0 to Y_1 because of a shift in the LM curve caused by, for example, an increase in the money supply. In this case, however, the rate of interest declines. Consequently, it is apparent that a real disturbance may be distinguished from a monetary disturbance by observing that in the case of the former income and the interest rate move in the same direction whereas in the case of the latter they move in opposite directions.

[1] The discussion is adapted from J. L. Stein, "A Method of Identifying Disturbances Which Produce Changes in Money National Income," *Journal of Political Economy,* 68:1–16, 1960.

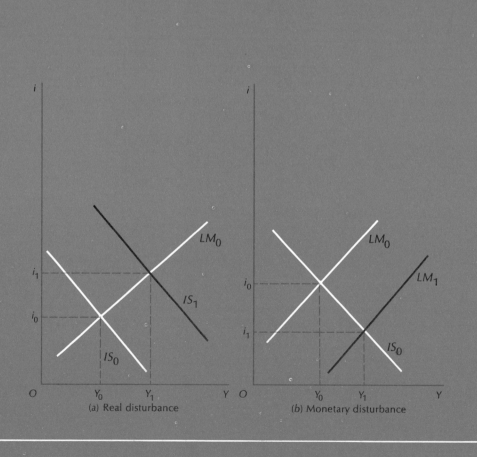

(a) Real disturbance   (b) Monetary disturbance

In general, a shift to the right of the *IS* schedule will tend to raise the level of income and the rate of interest. A shift to the right of the *LM* function, on the other hand, will raise the level of income and lower the rate of interest. There are, however, some extreme cases for which these rules do not hold. Strangely enough, it is these extreme cases that have caused much of the controversy among economists. In the next chapter we shall examine these extremes and their implications for policy.

Figure 9–5   Identifying real and monetary
disturbances (all values in real terms)

10

THE DEMAND FOR
MONEY AND
STABILIZATION POLICY

10–1   INTRODUCTION

Under what conditions is monetary policy effective in changing the level of real income? Under what conditions is it ineffective? Under what conditions is fiscal policy effective? Under what conditions is it ineffective? When should an "integrated" monetary-fiscal policy be used? Do alternative assumptions about the demand for money and the shape of the investment demand schedule make any difference?

10–2   A KEYNESIAN-CLASSICAL-INTERMEDIATE MODEL

Consider the hypothetical speculative demand function of Figure 10–1. It is assumed that between interest rates of 2 and 6 percent the specula-

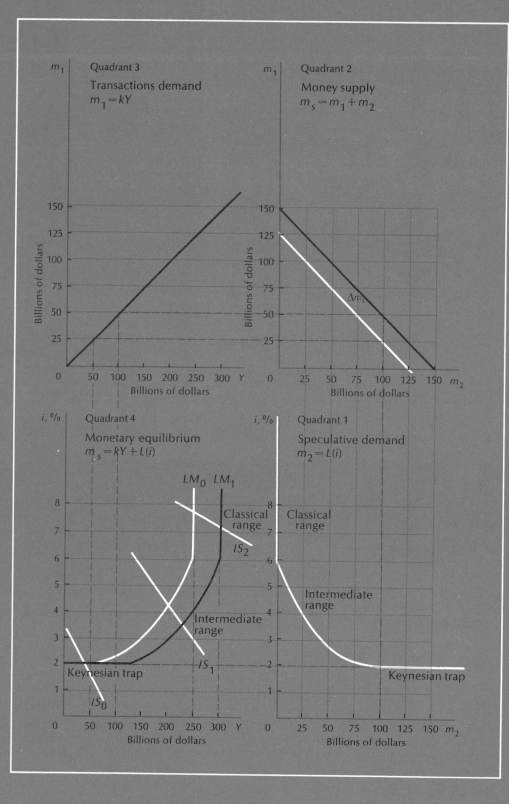

tive demand for money is inversely related to the rate of interest. However, when the rate of interest rises to 6 percent the interest loss from holding idle balances becomes so great and the expected risk of capital loss resulting from a further rise in interest rates becomes so small that the speculative demand disappears. On the other hand, once the rate of interest falls to 2 percent, the interest loss is so low and the risk of capital loss so great that investors would just as soon hold idle money balances as earning assets. When increases in the money supply reduce the interest rate to 2 percent, further increases will not affect the rate of interest. The region above 6 percent will be recognized as the region within which the classical assumption (Chapter 8) of no speculative demand holds, while the region of speculative demands of $100 billion or more will be recognized as the Keynesian liquidity trap region.

Given this speculative demand function, let us trace out the *LM* curve on the assumption that the money supply is $125 billion and the ratio of transactions balances to the level of income is 0.5. For interest rates between 2 and 6 percent the derivation is straightforward, following the lines of the last chapter. But what about the classical range? For an interest rate of 7 or 8 percent the same transactions balances are released as for a 6 percent rate. The same level of income is therefore associated with any rate of interest of 6 percent or more. This means that for all interest rates of 6 percent and above the *LM* curve becomes a vertical line.

Next consider a speculative demand of $125 billion. Evidently this is just as consistent with a 2 percent rate of interest as a speculative demand of $100 billion. But since the available transactions balances would be reduced to zero, the level of income that can be supported would be zero, and thus we observe that monetary equilibrium is consistent with all levels of income between zero and $50 billion at an interest rate of 2 percent. For levels of income below $50 billion the *LM* function must be a horizontal line.

Next consider an increase in the money supply of $25 billion resulting from a Federal Reserve purchase of government bonds on the open market. This purchase produces a shift to the right of $50 billion in the *LM* function because each dollar added to the money supply will support $2 of added transactions. How will this monetary policy affect the level of income?

1. If the *IS* schedule (*IS₀*) cuts the *LM* schedules in the Keynesian

Figure 10–1   **Monetary policy**
(all values in real terms)

liquidity trap region, the increase in the money supply does not affect the level of income at all. In this case wealth holders are quite willing to trade their bonds to the Federal Reserve in return for money without the premium of a higher bond price. The rate of interest therefore remains the same, investment is not stimulated, and the level of income remains unchanged. If the liquidity trap prevails, monetary policy is totally ineffective in changing the level of income.

2. If the IS schedule (IS_2) cuts the LM schedules in the classical range, quite the opposite picture emerges. If sellers are to be found for the bonds that the Federal Reserve wishes to buy, the prices of government bonds must be bid up by enough to persuade wealth holders that other assets are now relatively more attractive than government bonds. Only under these conditions will they accept money balances in exchange for the government bonds. There being no speculative demand for money to hold, wealth holders will take these new money balances and use them to purchase other earning assets. These other assets may take the form of new capital investment (new securities) or of purchase of existing securities. New capital investment will raise the level of income and therefore the transactions demand for money. However, as long as some idle money balances in excess of those required for transactions remain, wealth holders will continue to compete with each other for earning assets. Hence bond prices continue to rise and interest rates continue to fall until the point is reached where new investment raises the level of income by exactly enough to absorb the added money balances into transactions. To repeat, as long as there are some money balances in excess of those needed for transactions, there will be competition for earning assets. This means that interest rates will continue to fall and that investment will continue to rise until the idle balances are absorbed. The level of income must therefore rise by $\Delta m_s/k$, where Δm_s is the change in the money supply measured in real terms.

3. If the IS schedule (IS_1) cuts the LM functions in the intermediate range, the increase in the money supply succeeds in increasing the level of income, but not by as much as in the classical case. In the classical case the rate of interest falls by enough to absorb the whole addition to the supply of money into transactions demands. In the present case, however, part of the increase will be absorbed into speculative holdings because the decline in the rate of interest raises the desire of wealth holders to hold speculative balances. Thus investment will not increase by as much as in the classical case, and the level of income will rise by only a fraction of $\Delta m_s/k$.

The next step is to consider the effectiveness of fiscal policy under our three alternative assumptions about the demand for money. Consider Figure 10–2 in which the three-range *LM* function is reproduced together with six *IS* schedules. IS_0, IS_1, and IS_2 are the same schedules as in Figure 10–1. $IS_{(0+g)}$, $IS_{(1+g)}$, and $IS_{(2+g)}$ are the schedules that emerge after an increase in the level of government purchases of goods and services.

1. In the Keynesian region the increase in government purchases causes the level of income to rise by $Y_0' - Y_0$. This amount is equal to the full multiplier times the increase in G.[1] Since we have assumed that the increase in G is not tax-financed and since we assume a fixed money supply, the funds are obtained by borrowing from the public. The fiscal policy is therefore a "pure" fiscal policy as described in Chapter 8. As long as the liquidity trap prevails, the funds can be borrowed from speculative balances without causing the rate of interest to rise. Consequently, the level of investment will not be affected by government borrowing, and the level of income will therefore rise by the full multiplied amount of the increase in G.

2. In the intermediate range, the increase in G succeeds in increasing the level of income from Y_1 to Y_1'. This increase is not, however, as great as the increase in the Keynesian region. In this intermediate range governmental borrowing will cause the rate of interest to rise since wealth holders would not release the funds at the original rate of interest. But when the rate of interest rises, the level of investment falls, with the consequence that the expansionary effect of fiscal policy is somewhat dampened by an offsetting fall in investment.

3. In the classical range, the increase in the level of government purchases has no effect on the level of income whatsoever. Because there are no idle money balances available in the private sector of the economy, government can borrow funds from the private sector only by making it worthwhile for the sector to reduce investment spending in direct proportion to the amount borrowed by the government. This means that interest rates must rise by enough to make the return on government bonds greater than the prospective yield on private investment. Any increase in G will therefore be matched by an equal reduction in private investment. It is evident therefore that in the classical case fiscal policy is of no use whatsoever. Changes in the levels of government purchases and taxes can change the allocation of resources as

[1] Remember from the discussion of the last chapter that the horizontal shift in the *IS* schedule will equal the multiplier times the horizontal shift in the $I + G$ schedule.

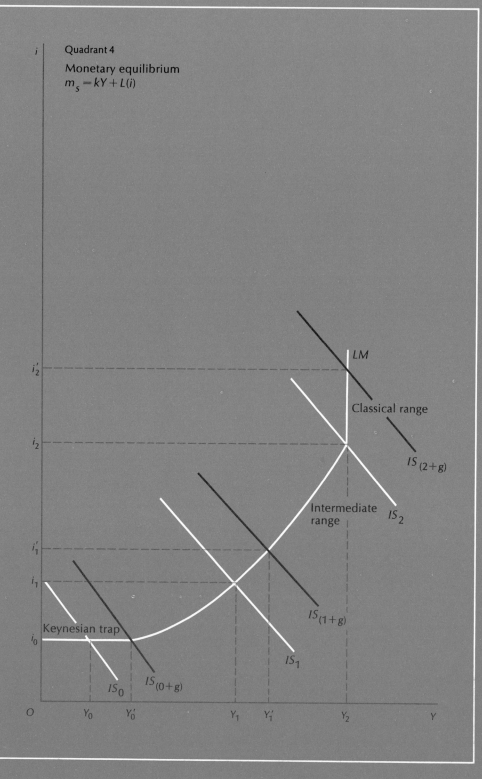

Quadrant 4

Monetary equilibrium

$m_s = kY + L(i)$

between consumption, investment, and government, but they cannot change the level of income.

10–3 FACTORS INFLUENCING THE EFFECTIVENESS OF MONETARY POLICY

Having considered the Keynesian and classical extremes in some detail, let us now consider the implications of some of the alternative assumptions about the demand for and the supply of money that were discussed in Chapter 8. Let us define as our measure of the "effectiveness" of monetary policy the change in income that accompanies a change in the money supply of $1. As we have seen, the range of effectiveness can vary between an extreme Keynesian value of zero and a classical maximum value of $1/k$.

Looking again at Figure 10–1, it is clear that the effectiveness of monetary policy, assuming a given negatively sloped IS curve, depends upon the slope of the LM curve. Although the LM curve always shifted by $\Delta m_s/k$, we found monetary policy to be completely ineffective when the slope of LM was zero; partially effective when it was positive; and completely effective when it was infinite.

The different values of the slope of the LM schedule in the different ranges were the consequence of the speculative demand for money. In the absence of a speculative demand, LM had an infinite slope; with speculative demand inversely related to the rate of interest, LM had a positive slope; and with infinitely elastic speculative demand, LM had a zero slope. Let us now see what happens to the slope of the LM curve when we assume, first, that the transactions demand for money and, second, that the supply of money are both sensitive to interest rate changes.

Considering first the transactions demand, we found in Chapter 8 that it would pay wealth holders to enter the bond market more and more frequently during an income-expenditure period as interest rates rise. This means that as interest rates rise, average transactions balances fall so that the transactions demand for money is inversely related to the rate of interest.

In Figure 10–3, LM_0 is drawn on the assumption that the transactions demand for money is not affected by the rate of interest and that the relevant transactions demand curve in quadrant 3 is m_{t_4}. LM_1, on the

Figure 10–2 Fiscal policy
(all values in real terms)

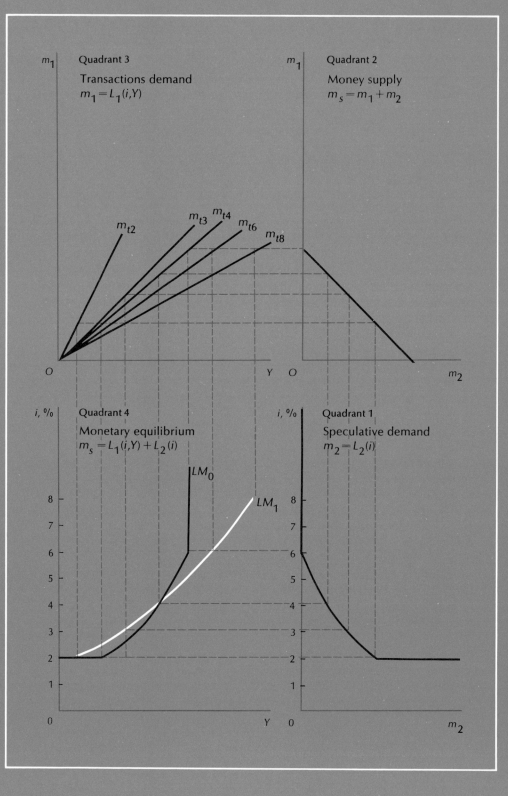

other hand, is drawn on the assumption that at an interest rate of 6 percent m_{t_6} relates the transactions demand to the level of income; m_{t_4} relates the transactions demand to the level of income when the rate of interest is 4 percent; m_{t_2} is appropriate for a 2 percent rate; and m_{t_8} represents an 8 percent rate. Since we now have a whole family of transactions demand schedules, each one appropriate to a particular rate of interest, we must, in deriving the *LM* schedule, trace through the quadrants by starting with different interest rates in quadrant 1 and pick the transactions demand curve in quadrant 3 that is appropriate to the particular interest rate with which we began in quadrant 1.

LM_1 is less steeply sloped than LM_0. There is now no pure classical range because there is no longer a fixed relationship between money balances and the volume of transactions despite the fact that there is no speculative demand. This flattening out of the *LM* schedule implies that the more interest-elastic transactions and precautionary demands become, the less (more) effective does monetary (fiscal) policy become.

Let us consider next the possibility that rising interest rates cause banks to activate excess reserves and thereby increase the money supply. A useful way to approach this problem is to assume that there is no speculative demand for money and that the transactions demand is insensitive to interest rate changes. In this way the effect of interest elasticity of the money supply can be compared with the classical *LM* function.

In Figure 10–4 quadrant 1 is left blank to denote the absence of speculative demand, and the absence of interest sensitivity of transactions demand means that there is only one transactions demand function in quadrant 3. Beginning with interest rate i_0, we assume that the money supply is m_{i_0}. Since there is no speculative demand for money, all balances are available for transactions. Consequently, the level of income that can be supported is Y_0. If the interest rate rises to i_1, banks activate excess reserves so that the money supply now becomes m_{i_1}, and the income level that can be supported becomes Y_1. Similarly, a rise in the interest rate to i_2 causes a further increase in the money supply so that income level Y_2 yields monetary equilibrium. Without any increase in reserves a time must come when interest rate increases induce no further increases in the supply of money. Consequently, the slope of the *LM* curve becomes steeper as the interest rate rises and eventually becomes vertical as in the classical case.

Notice that our present assumption produces an *LM* curve that takes

Figure 10–3   Interest-elastic transactions demand (all values in real terms)

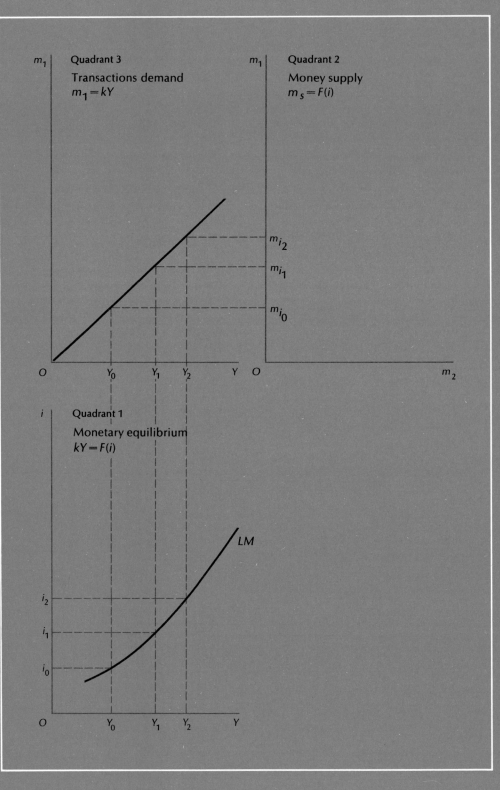

on a shape similar to that attained when we assumed the existence of a speculative demand on the part of the public. Indeed, it may very well have been the case that during the great depression of the 1930s, what appeared to have been a liquidity trap caused by a highly elastic demand for money may have been partially caused by a highly interest-elastic supply of money resulting from bank behavior. Certainly banks held large quantities of excess reserves and appeared to make little effort to convert these reserves into earning assets.

But what does this kind of situation imply about the effectiveness of monetary policy? The money supply function implied by our present discussion might be written

$$m_s = F(i,R)$$

where R is the volume of bank reserves measured in real terms. An increase in bank reserves brought about by Federal Reserve purchase of bonds automatically increases the money supply by an equivalent amount (refer to the discussion of money supply in Chapter 8 if the reasons for this are not clear), and will tend to produce a further increase in the money supply as banks use their excess reserves to purchase earning assets. But the consequence of this is that interest rates fall, producing reluctance to engage in further expansion. During a deep depression interest rates may already be so low that Federal Reserve purchases may not induce banks to use their excess reserves to expand their holdings of earning assets. As a consequence, the ratio of a change in the money supply to a change in reserves will be only 1:1, whereas the potential ratio may be as high as 5:1. Thus the Federal Reserve's leverage effect on the money supply may, during such periods, be severely reduced. What this suggests is that at low interest rates it may take a far more sizable Federal Reserve purchase to shift the LM function to the right by some amount than it would take during periods of higher interest rates.

10–4 MONETARY POLICY AND INTEREST-INELASTIC INVESTMENT DEMAND

Another reason why monetary policy may fail to be effective stems from the circumstance that investment may be insensitive to changes in the interest rate. As we saw in Chapter 7, there is reason to doubt whether

Figure 10–4 Interest-elastic money supply
(all values in real terms)

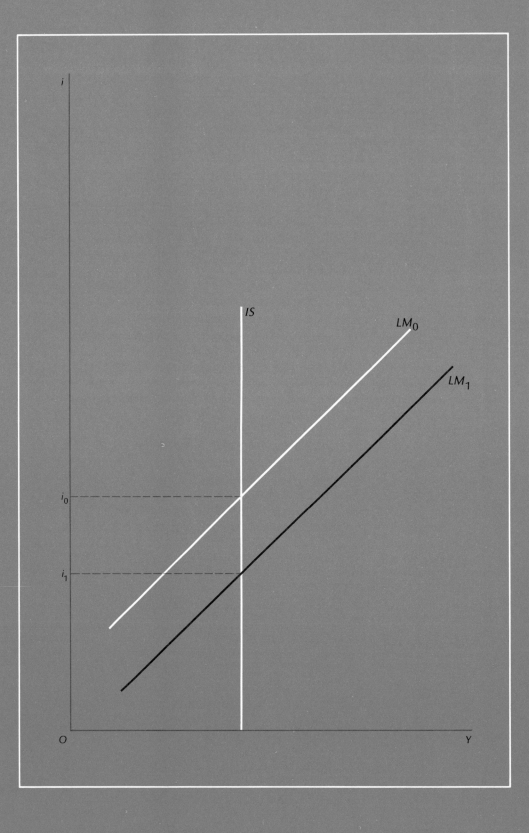

interest rate changes, even if they could be brought about, could make a significant contribution toward raising the level of investment during periods of slack demand. In the extreme case of a vertical investment demand schedule, the *IS* schedule will also be vertical (see Figure 10–5), so that monetary policy, even though interest rates can be made to change, will not affect the level of income.

In classical monetary assumptions it is implicit that the investment demand schedule is interest-elastic.[1] If the ratio of real cash balances to the level of real income is fixed, an increase in the money supply must find its way into new transactions in the form of either consumption or investment expenditures. If consumption expenditures are insensitive to changes in the interest rate, which nearly everyone assumes to be the case, investment must be interest-elastic; if it is not, existing security prices will be bid up to a value of infinity, and interest rates will fall to zero. If this possibility is ruled out, it must follow that either the investment demand schedule or the demand for money is elastic with respect to the rate of interest.

In conclusion, it appears to be the elasticity of demand for money that is crucial from the policy point of view. If the rate of interest cannot be made to fall as a result of Federal Reserve action to increase the supply of money, the shape of the investment demand schedule is irrelevant. If, on the other hand, an increase in the money supply succeeds in reducing the rate of interest, the level of investment must necessarily rise. If it does not, the increase in the supply of money will cause interest rates to continue falling until the liquidity trap is reached.

[1] J. Tobin, "Liquidity Preference and Monetary Policy," *Review of Economics and Statistics,* 29:124–131, 1947.

Figure 10–5 Interest-inelastic investment demand (all values in real terms)

11

THE LEVEL OF EMPLOYMENT (1)

11–1 INTRODUCTION

The discussion thus far has been based on the notion that the economy can be divided into two markets—a market for final goods and services and a market for money. But this is not sufficient. We must add a third—the market for factors of production—in order to determine the level of employment. On the surface the task does not look difficult. Each firm in the economy will have a production function, i.e., a relationship between the level of output and various combinations of factor inputs; and thus we may visualize an aggregative production function for the economy as a whole. Such a function may be written

$$Y = X(N, K^*)$$

where N is the level of employment and K is the size of the capital stock of the economy. In a short-run analysis of the kind we have been performing in this part of the book, it is assumed that K is fixed (this is denoted by the asterisk) so that with a given level of output (or real income) the level of employment will be determined.

However, the matter is not as simple as it appears. The *IS-LM* intersection is a position at which the market for goods and services and the money market are simultaneously cleared. But the level of production that is implied by this intersection may require the use of less labor than is willing to work at the existing rate of remuneration. In other words, equilibrium in the product and money markets may be accompanied by disequilibrium—specifically, excess supply—in the market for labor services. In Figure 11–1 the vertical line labeled Y^* denotes the level of real income that would be produced if all the resources of the economy were fully employed.[1] Since the *IS-LM* intersection is to the left of Y^*, the present situation implies the existence of labor market disequilibrium. In this chapter our problem is to find out whether a situation of the kind depicted in Figure 11–1 can be sustained. Will not excess supply in any market cause prices to fall, and will this not, in turn, set off forces that disrupt the *IS-LM* equilibrium? Finally, will these price adjustments continue until all markets are cleared?

11–2 THE FACTOR MARKET AND THE INTEREST-INVESTMENT MECHANISM

To make headway with our present problem, we need to consider a few elements of the theory of the business firm. The theory teaches that a firm in a competitive industry will hire workers up to the point where the value of the marginal product (marginal product multiplied by the price of output) just equals the cost of the factor. Assuming that pure competition prevails, this profit maximization condition, for the economy as a whole, may be written

---

[1] For simplicity, we are assuming here that there is only one full-employment level of output. Actually, it would be more sensible to speak of a full-employment zone. Output can be expanded by inducing labor to work overtime and by luring additional people into the labor force.

Figure 11–1   An excess supply of labor
(all values in real terms)

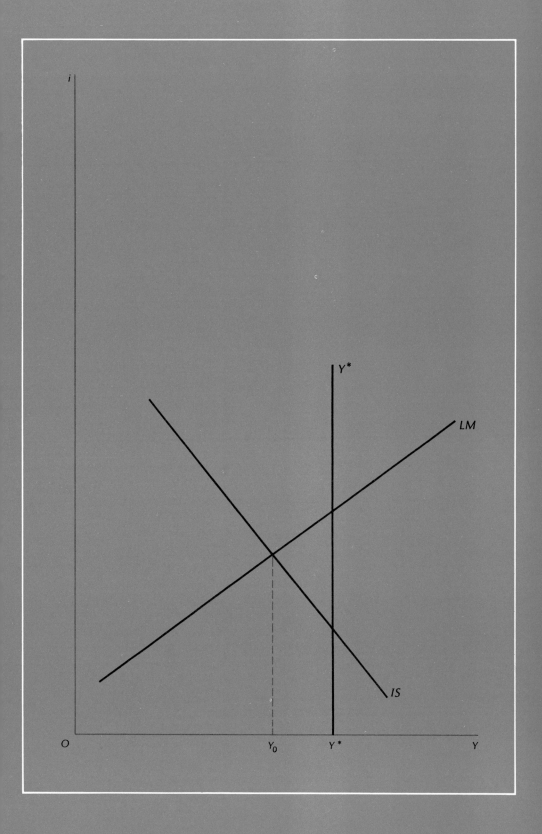

$$w = pX_n$$

or

$$\frac{w}{p} = X_n$$

where w is the money wage rate, p is the level of prices, w/p is the "real" wage rate, and X_n is the marginal physical product of labor. The demand for labor may therefore be written as

$$N_d = D\left(\frac{w}{p}\right)$$

which states that the demand for labor is a function of the real wage rate. According to the law of diminishing returns, the marginal product of labor declines as more workers are hired. It follows that if the level of employment is to be increased, the real wage must fall. The demand for labor is therefore a decreasing function of the real wage rate.

On the supply side the matter is more complicated. For the moment we shall adopt the classical assumption that the supply of labor, as well as the demand, depends upon the real wage. It is argued that in a world of rational human beings no one will be so foolish as to imagine that he will be better off if both wages and prices double. If an individual does feel better off under these conditions, he is said to be subject to "money illusion." In the absence of money illusion a change in the quantity of labor supplied will take place only if the real wage changes. Consequently, the classical labor supply function may be written as

$$N_s = S\left(\frac{w}{p}\right)$$

The labor demand and supply functions are shown in Figure 11–2. The real wage rate is measured on the vertical axis, and the quantity of labor is measured on the horizontal axis. The demand curve for labor is negatively sloped in line with the assumption of diminishing returns. The supply curve is positively sloped on the assumption that higher real wage rates will be needed to induce additional workers to become employed. At real wage rate $(w/p)_0$ the quantity of labor demanded by business is N_0. Workers, however, are willing to offer N_1 units of labor, which means that there is an excess supply of labor. When more workers are willing to work at the going real wage rate than business is willing to hire, we have "involuntary unemployment." Should the real

Figure 11–2   The labor market: classical case

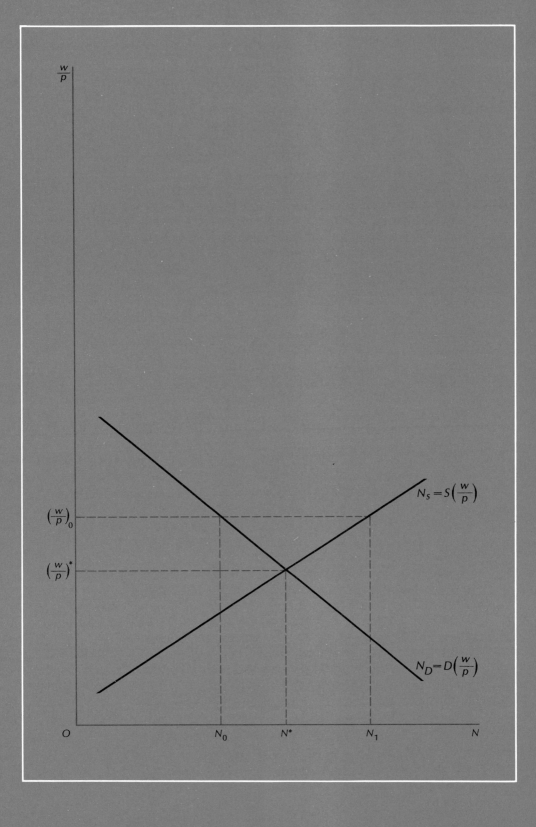

wage fall to $(w/p)*$, involuntary unemployment would be eliminated, and the economy could then be said to be operating at full employment.

From Figure 11–2, it appears that all that is needed to restore full employment is a fall in real wages. Is there a mechanism via which this may happen? If the labor market is competitive, an excess supply of labor would cause workers to compete with each other for the available jobs by offering to work for lower money wage rates. If the level of prices remains constant, the fall in money wages means that real wages will fall and the level of employment will increase. However, if the wage fall should be accompanied by a corresponding fall in the level of prices, real wages will remain the same and employment will not increase. The classical economists believe that real wages could be reduced by a fall in money wage rates, while Keynesians believe that this is not necessarily the case. Let us see where they differ.

A fall in money wages will lower marginal production costs and, as suggested by the theory of the firm, will lead to an increase in output and employment. But will the increase in output be bought? Because the marginal propensity to consume is less than unity, only a fraction of the added output will be taken off the market by consumers, so that the remainder must be in the form of intended investment if the increased level of output and employment is to be sustained.

If intended investment fails to increase, however, unintended inventory accumulation takes place, prices fall, and output and employment fall back to their original levels. In the absence of an increase in intended investment, the level of output at which intended investment and saving are again equal must be the original level of output; since this is associated with a particular real wage, we may infer that prices will fall in proportion to the wage cut.

The present argument can best be illustrated by a diagram similar to those introduced in Chapter 5. In Figure 11–3 the aggregate demand schedule $C + I$ cuts the 45-degree line at income Y_0. The full-employment level of income is at $Y*$. Since the level of income is less than the full-employment level, there must be an excess supply of labor. As a consequence, money wages will be falling. Suppose that the fall in money wages causes business firms to produce $\Delta Y = Y* - Y_0$ additional units of output. If there are no taxes, the increased output creates additional disposable income in the same amount. But since the marginal propensity to consume is less than unity, the increase in consumption

Figure 11–3   Effect of a fall in wages and prices (all values in real terms)

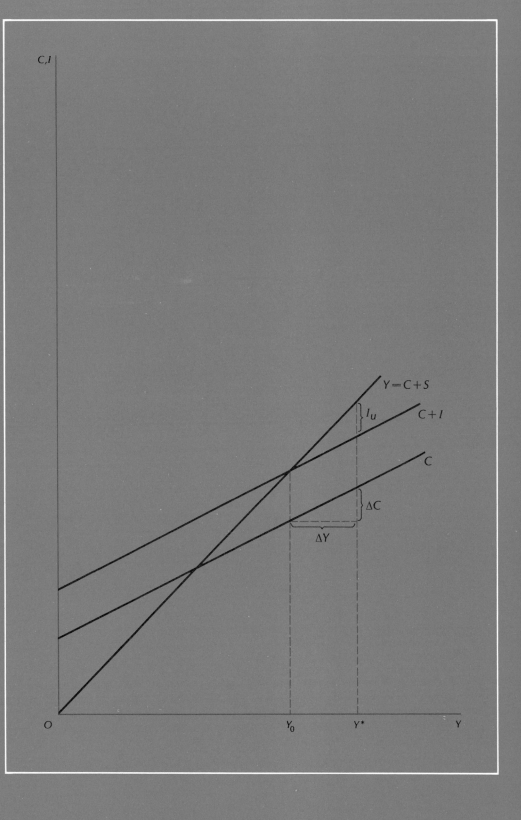

ΔC is less than ΔY and the difference represents unintended accumulation of inventories I_u. As we saw in Chapter 5, equilibrium will not be restored until unintended investment is eliminated, and this means that prices will fall and output will return to the original level Y_0. Because the absence of unintended investment implies that firms are operating at their profit-maximizing output levels, and because the same level of output implies that the same amount of labor will be hired as before the fall in wages, the fall in prices must have been in exact proportion to the fall in money wages. Real wages remain the same; the labor market clearing mechanism fails to operate.[1]

To a classical economist such a result is inconceivable. He would argue that as long as there is an uncleared market, in this case the labor market, and as long as competition puts pressure on wages and prices, the real value of the money supply will increase, and this will force down interest rates, raise the level of investment, and increase the level of income and employment.[2] Since prices and wages must continue to fall as long as there is some involuntary unemployment, investment and income must continue to rise until unemployment is eliminated. In Figure 11–4 the original intersection of IS with LM_0 is at income level Y_0 and interest rate i_0. As wages and prices fall, the real value of the money supply increases, and this means that the LM curve shifts to the right.

[1] J. M. Keynes, *The General Theory of Employment, Interest and Money,* Chap. 19, Harcourt, Brace & World, Inc., New York, 1936; papers by A. P. Lerner and J. Tobin, in S. E. Harris, ed., *The New Economics,* Chaps. 10 and 40, Alfred A. Knopf, Inc., New York, 1950; W. J. Fellner, *Competition Among the Few,* Alfred A. Knopf, Inc., New York, 1949, pp. 266–272; F. Modigliani, "Liquidity Preference and the Theory of Interest and Money," *Econometrica,* 12:45–88, 1944; T. Wilson, *Fluctuations in Income and Employment,* Chap. 10, Sir Isaac Pitman & Sons, Ltd., London, 1942.

[2] Recall from Chap. 8 that the real value of the money supply is given by the ratio of the actual, measurable, or nominal, supply of money M to the price level p. Thus, since

$$m = \frac{M}{p}$$

a fall in the price level would have the same effect on the real value of the money supply as would an increase in nominal money balances due, for example, to a Federal Reserve purchase of securities on the open market. In terms of the four-quadrant money market diagram, the fall in the price level would be represented by an outward shift of the money supply curve in quadrant 2. This would mean that at any arbitrary rate of interest additional money balances would be available for transactions purposes so that a higher level of income would be associated with monetary equilibrium; i.e., the LM curve would shift to the right.

Figure 11–4   Effect of a fall in the price level:
classical case (all values in real terms)

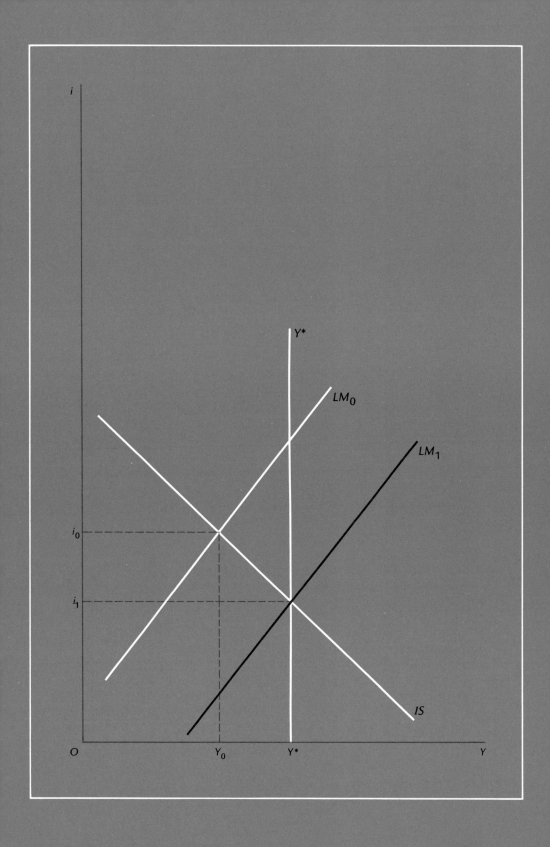

The rate of interest therefore falls, and intended investment and income rise. Since wages and prices continue to fall as long as income is less than Y^*, the LM curve will continue to shift to the right until unemployment is eliminated. Consequently, the final equilibrium position is where LM_1 cuts IS at Y^* and interest rate i_1. In terms of Figure 11–3, wage-price declines will raise the investment schedule to the point where the aggregate demand schedule cuts the 45-degree line at Y^*. Unemployment, apparently, tends to eliminate itself automatically.

The Keynesian would rebut this argument with the theory of liquidity preference. The fall in prices caused by the wage cut will, to be sure, increase the real value of the money supply. But this will not affect the rate of interest or the level of intended investment because in the liquidity trap the demand for money is infinitely elastic at the existing rate of interest. In Figure 11–5 the IS-LM intersection at income Y_0 is in the liquidity trap range. The rise in the real value of the money supply acts to shift the LM curve from LM_0 to LM_1, but this obviously has no effect on the interest rate. The money balances that are released from transactions demands by the fall in the price level are hoarded by wealth holders, who make no attempt to convert them into earning assets. The rate of interest remains the same, and the level of investment and income remains constant at Y_0. The Keynesian therefore believes that an "underemployment equilibrium" level of income, such as Y_0, may persist and that there is no automatic tendency for the economy to return to full employment.

There is a problem in the Keynesian solution. If a fall in wages and prices fails to reduce the level of unemployment, why will wages and prices not continue to fall indefinitely? This apparently does not happen; money wages tend to be sticky in the downward direction. In an environment characterized by widespread unionism workers can defend themselves against wage cuts. A previously hard-won money wage increase, moreover, tends to be maintained despite shrinking employment.

In recognizing these institutional facts of life, Keynes broke away from the classical theory of labor supply. Instead of assuming that the supply of labor depends on the real wage, he assumed that labor is subject to money illusion and that the supply of labor is a function of the money wage rate. In Figure 11–6, w_0 is the historically given money wage rate and p_0 is the ruling price level. At money wage w_0 workers will offer anywhere between zero and N^* units of labor. Thus the labor supply curve is a horizontal line at w_0/p_0. Although the money wage rate

Figure 11–5   Effect of a fall in the price level: Keynesian case (all values in real terms)

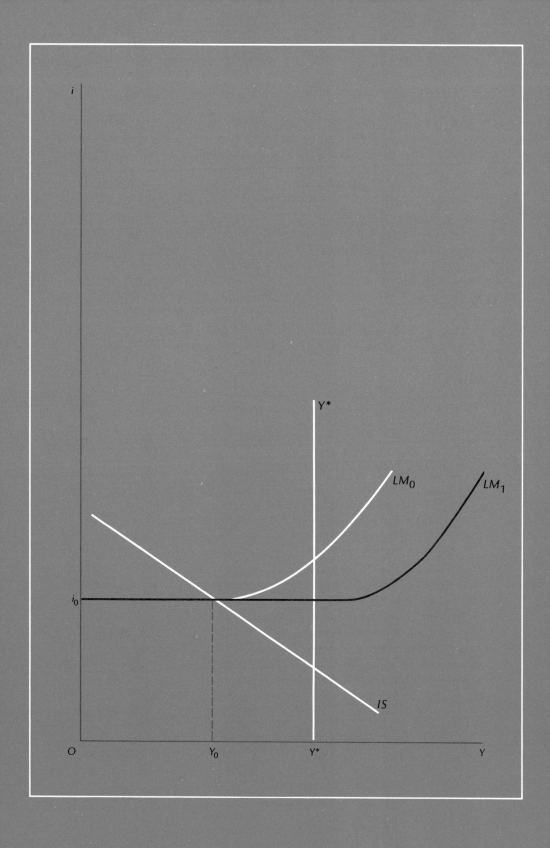

cannot be made to fall, it will rise when all those who are willing to work at w_0 are employed and additional workers are desired. Consequently, the labor supply curve bends up sharply once N^* has been reached. In Figure 11–6 the labor demand schedule cuts the supply schedule at N_0. Consequently, the distance $N^* - N_0$ measures involuntary unemployment—the number of workers willing to work at the existing level of real wages but who do not find employment.

Since the money wage rate is assumed to be downwardly rigid (and since a fall in wages, even if it could be brought about, would produce a proportional drop in the price level), the restoration of full employment can come about only through a real wage fall resulting from an increase in aggregate demand and the price level. If such a rise in the price level materializes, the entire labor supply schedule shifts down, and involuntary unemployment is eliminated. Thus at real wage w_0/p_1 the labor demand schedule cuts the supply schedule at N^*, where all who are willing to work at the new real wage are employed. Notice that even though the real wage has fallen, the number of workers willing to work at the new real wage is the same as at the old real wage, a result that follows from the assumption of money illusion.

In summary, money wage cuts resulting from competition in the labor market leave the level of employment and the real wage unchanged in the Keynesian system. Consequently, we may call the level of employment N_0 in Figure 11–6 an underemployment equilibrium. In the classical analysis, on the other hand, competition on the labor market will continue until the fall in money wages brings about the fall in real wages needed to restore full employment.

We have seen that the issue of whether there is a unique equilibrium level of income and employment or whether there are several possible equilibrium levels seems to hinge primarily on the nature of the demand for money. If the demand for money is infinitely elastic with respect to the rate of interest, there will be no labor market clearing mechanism regardless of the nature of the labor supply function. But the labor supply function is important in another respect: If the demand for money is elastic, if at the same time competition on the labor market leads to money wage reductions, and if no change in the level of employment takes place, the end result would be that money wages and prices would fall indefinitely. It is clear, however, that in our existing institutional framework wages and prices are extremely sticky in the downward direction.

Figure 11–6   The labor market: Keynesian case

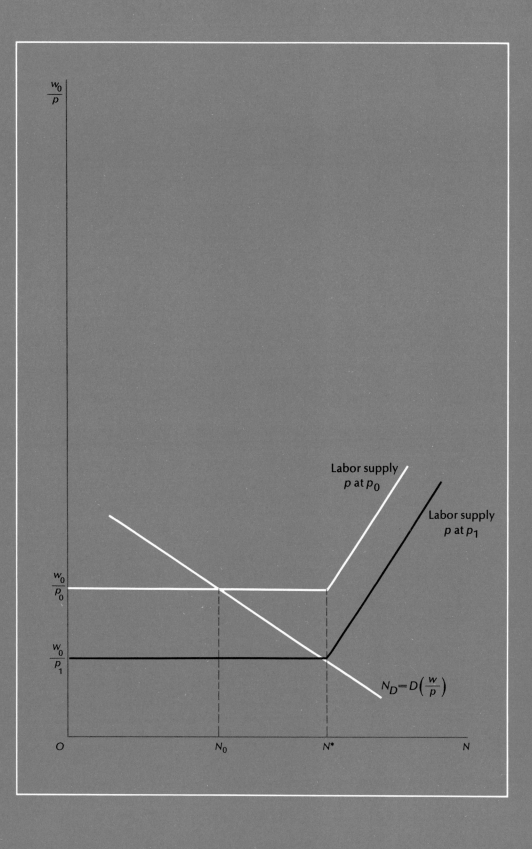

11–3   FORMAL MODELS OF INCOME
AND EMPLOYMENT DETERMINATION

Given a constant capital stock, the production function of the economy

$$Y = X(N,K^*)$$

indicates that once the level of income is known, the level of employment will automatically be determined. Similarly, if the level of employment has been determined, the level of income must be known. Although the Keynesian and classical models are general equilibrium systems in which the equilibrium values of the variables are simultaneously determined, it is nevertheless useful to think of the determination of the equilibrium values in terms of a definite sequence. In the classical model the sequence runs from the level of employment to the level of income, consumption, and investment; then to the rate of interest; and finally to the price level. In the Keynesian system it is helpful to think of the sequence as running in the other direction. The consumption and investment functions, together with the monetary equilibrium relation, determine the rate of interest and the level of income, which, in turn, determine the level of employment.

The Keynesian underemployment system can be formalized as follows: If the price level is initially held constant and the nominal money supply is given, product market equilibrium

$$I(i) = Y - C(Y)$$

together with monetary equilibrium

$$\frac{M}{p} = kY + L(i)$$

serve to determine the level of income, consumption, investment, savings, the rate of interest, and the way money balances are split between transactions and speculative purposes. The level of income being known and the capital stock being fixed, the production function

$$Y = X(N,K^*)$$

determines the level of employment. Consequently, the demand for labor together with the downwardly rigid money wage

$$N = N_d = D\left(\frac{w_0}{p}\right)$$

adds the equation needed to determine the price level.

Next let us formalize the classical system. The real wage and the level of employment are determined by labor market equilibrium

$$D\left(\frac{w}{p}\right) = S\left(\frac{w}{p}\right)$$

Since the level of employment is now known, the level of income is determined by the production function

$$Y = X(N,K^*)$$

Since we know the level of income, the product market equilibrium equation

$$I(i) = Y - C(Y)$$

determines the rate of interest and the way in which aggregate expenditures are divided between consumption and investment. Finally, since both the level of income and the rate of interest are known, the monetary equilibrium equation

$$m_s = \frac{M}{p} = kY$$

serves only to determine the level of prices.

Observe that in the classical model the rate of interest is independent of the size of the money supply and that the sole function of the money supply is to determine the level of prices. The reasons for this, though highly interesting and important, are not pertinent to our immediate line of inquiry, and further discussion of the classical model may profitably be postponed until Chapter 13, where the model will be explored in detail.

11–4 ADDITIONAL NOTES ON MONEY WAGE RATES, MONEY ILLUSION, AND EMPLOYMENT

The Keynesian argument that the liquidity trap would prevent wage-price flexibility from restoring full employment has not gone unchallenged. The distinguished economist A. C. Pigou argued that even though the liquidity trap might bar the way to an increase in employment via the path of changes in interest rates and investment, falls in wages and prices would sooner or later restore full employment because a decline in the price level would cause the consumption function to shift up.[1] The mechanism by which the consumption function shifts up, commonly known as the "Pigou effect," has the following rationale: If consumption is an increasing function of the level of wealth, as well as of the level of income, we can presume that if falling wages and prices cause wealth holders to feel wealthier, they will increase their consumption outlays at all levels of income. Why, however, should a fall in the price level cause wealth holders to feel wealthier?

As the level of prices falls, the real value of the assets whose prices are fixed in nominal terms rises. A fall in the price level makes debtors poorer and creditors richer. Because each $1 of debt is matched by $1 of credit, the presence of a Pigou effect would have to depend upon the presence of a difference between the spending behavior of debtors and creditors in response to a change in the price level. The reason for supposing that there is such a difference in the consumption responses to wealth changes is that the government is a large net debtor while the private sector, which holds a net balance of government obligations, is a net creditor. If, then, it is assumed that the marginal propensity of the government to spend wealth is zero, while the marginal propensity to consume wealth is positive for the private sector, a transfer of wealth from one sector to the other due to a change in the price level will cause the level of total spending to change.

Money wage cuts may have some additional effects on the level of employment. Some of the possibilities follow:

1. A fall in wages and prices will induce foreigners to buy more from us and at the same time will make it easier for domestic producers to sell abroad. This means that the net export of goods and services, and therefore aggregate domestic expenditures, will rise and that the level of employment will increase.

It should be kept in mind, however, that recessions tend to coincide internationally. Improvements in domestic income and employment arising from an increase in net exports generally come from the exportation of domestic unemployment to foreign countries rather than from any overall expansion in the level of total world employment. This subject is discussed in more detail in Chapter 14.

2. A money wage cut represents a redistribution of income from workers to dividend earners. If, as is likely, high-income groups have a lower marginal propensity to consume than low-income groups, each dollar taken from a wage earner and given to a dividend earner will

---

[1] A. C. Pigou, "The Classical Stationary State," *Economic Journal,* 53:343–351, 1943, and "Economic Progress in a Stable Environment," *Economica,* New Series, 14:180–188, 1947.

produce a net decline in aggregate consumption expenditure. A money wage cut may therefore cause aggregate consumption to decline, and if this redistributive effect is dominant, a cut in money wages will reduce, rather than raise, the levels of income and employment.

3. It is difficult to believe that money wage reductions could occur in an instantaneous, across-the-board manner. The piecemeal wage reductions that are more likely to be experienced would foster the expectation that further cuts are in the offing. Acting on this expectation, entrepreneurs will cut back production, make sales out of inventory, and postpone new plant and equipment expenditures. Similarly, consumers might well expect the trend of prices to continue downward and therefore postpone consumption expenditures. The adverse expectations induced by the wage cut may therefore defeat its intended effect.

4. As we have seen, Keynes believed labor to be subject to money illusion. He believed, in other words, that workers were far more conscious of changes in money wage rates than of changes in the price level and that they would therefore be likely to regard an increase in money wages as an increase in real wages even if prices rose in proportion to the wage increase. This implies that if money wages remained unchanged, an increase in the price level would not be noticed by workers, who therefore would offer the same supply of labor even though real wages had fallen.

There is no reason to suppose that money illusion is confined to labor supply. Imagine, for example, the effect of its presence on consumption spending. If money wages and prices fall and consumers notice the fall in money income but not the fall in prices, they will be under the illusion that real income has fallen. However, when real income falls, the percentage of income consumed rises (provided that the consumption function has a positive intercept). Thus if consumers think their real income has fallen, they will spend a greater percentage of their money income than previously. This means that the consumption function in terms of real disposable income will shift up as a result of the wage cut and that the level of income will rise.

The Federal income tax structure is probably the greatest single source of money illusion in the United States economy. Tax rates and brackets are based on money rather than real income. If money income and prices both fall, leaving real income unchanged, taxpayers nevertheless shift into lower brackets and the real value of their tax burden declines. Consequently, a proportional fall in wages and prices will raise real disposable income and the level of consumption spending.

As long as we are on the subject of money illusion, we should point out that the existence of money illusion does not necessarily imply irrational behavior on the part of those whose economic behavior is not in strict conformity with the classical "homogeneity postulate."[1] The primary reason for this is that workers, consumers, and businessmen all make long-term contracts that are fixed, not in real, but in money terms. A wage earner, for example, may still have many years of payments to make on the mortgage on his home. If wages and prices decline in the same proportion, his real wage will be the same. But the real value of his debt burden will increase, and he may therefore be obliged to reduce his current consumption expenditure. Although the worker appears to be subject to money illusion, his decision to consume less may be based on a perfectly rational calculation. Since workers tend, in general, to be debtors, a fall in money wages, even though real wages remain the same, will be regarded as a serious real loss.

[1] A fancy way of saying that the supply of labor is a function of the real wage is to say that the function is homogeneous of degree zero. In general we may write

$$N_s = S(w,p)$$

as the labor supply function. In the absence of money illusion a proportional increase in w and p will not affect the amount of labor supplied. To a mathematician this means that the labor supply function has the property of zero degree homogeneity. In general, an nth order homogeneous function has the property that if all the independent variables are multiplied by a constant, the dependent variable will be multiplied by that same constant raised to the power n.

Mathematically, if

$$y = f(x,z)$$

then

$$yu^n = f(xu,zu)$$

and if $n = 0$, $u^n = 1$, so that

$$y = f(x,z) = f(xu,zu)$$

which means that multiplication of the two independent variables by a constant does not change the value of the dependent variable.

Therefore, in the case of the labor supply function,

$$N_s = S(w,p) = S(uw,up)$$

and since u is an arbitrary constant, we can let $u = 1/p$ so that

$$N_s = S\left(\frac{w}{p},1\right)$$

which is to say that the supply of labor depends only on the ratio of w to p, the real wage rate.

If workers are subject to money illusion, the labor supply function will not be homogeneous, and hence it is said that the homogeneity postulate is denied. In this connection see W. W. Leontieff, "Postulates: Keynes' General Theory and the Classicists," in Harris, ed., *op. cit.*, Chap. 10.

Whether money illusion is rational or not, it is important to emphasize that from the point of view of the economy as a whole, money illusions are in general stabilizing. The Federal income tax structure, for example, causes tax collections to fall by a greater proportion than wage decreases even though prices may fall in the same proportion. Since this raises real disposable income, the effect is stabilizing. Similarly, during inflationary periods tax collections increase in greater proportion than increases in money income even though prices may have risen in proportion. The effect is to reduce real disposable income and real consumption expenditures and is therefore again stabilizing.

11–5   SUMMARY AND CONCLUSIONS

This chapter may be summarized as follows:

1. In the classical view there is only one equilibrium level of employment, which is determined by labor market competition. Since there is only one equilibrium level of employment, there is only one equilibrium level of income, which must necessarily be the full-employment level. In the absence of wage-price rigidities, there will be an automatic tendency for all markets to be cleared and for full employment to be restored.

2. In the Keynesian view the level of employment is determined by the level of income, which in turn depends upon aggregate demand. Since there is no presumption that competition on the labor market exists, or that if it did exist, real wages would fall, "underemployment equilibrium" is a possibility.

3. The question of whether money wage cuts will raise the level of employment depends primarily on the nature of the demand for money. In the absence of other effects, a money wage cut will leave the level of employment unaffected in the liquidity trap extreme, while in the classical extreme of a fixed ratio of money balances to the volume of transactions, money wage cuts will restore full employment.

4. The effect of money wage cuts on the level of employment will depend to some extent on the importance of the Pigou effect, on the significance of foreign trade, on the effect of money illusion on consumption, on money illusion in the tax structure, on the effect of a redistribution of income on consumption, and finally on the nature of the expectations induced by the wage cut.

Although our discussion of the level of employment is not yet finished, it is useful at this juncture to take stock. To suppose that a money wage cut, as a practical policy device, is feasible in our present-day institutional environment would be to lose touch with reality. Apart from other considerations, the fall in real wages needed to restore full employment could always be achieved by monetary and fiscal, as opposed to wage-price, policy. Since these tools are feasible, while money wage cuts are not, they are the ones that will be employed.

But it would be foolish to infer from this that it is pointless to consider the effectiveness of wage cuts on the level of employment. In the first place, the typical classical economist believes that money wage cuts can restore full employment; if that is so and if he is opposed to remedies that restore full employment by raising the price level, he is apt to promote policies designed to restore wage-price flexibility. While centrally enforced wage cuts are unrealistic, a strong antitrust policy, designed to destroy the monopoly power of unions and enterprises, is not beyond the realm of possibility. Because price flexibility is a necessary feature of an automatically regulating economic system, monopoly, apart from other reasons, is anathema to the traditional economist.[1] The Keynesian, less convinced of the importance of wage-price flexibility, is apt to be a less enthusiastic trust buster than his classical counterpart.

Second, the question of whether money wage cuts will be effective in restoring full employment is really the same as the question of whether or not the economy has an automatic steering wheel. An economist who believes that full employment at stable prices is the norm to which the economy will return after a disturbance from equilibrium will prescribe radically different policies than the economist who believes that full employment is an accidental state that cannot be maintained, or even achieved, without considerable assistance from governmental policy.

Third, the discussion of money wage cuts has focused attention on the most vital of the differences between Keynes and traditional economists, namely, the theory of liquidity preference, which, as we saw in Chapter 10, was the vital part of the issue between monetary and fiscal policy. We now see that this is the vital difference between an automatically adjusting economy and one in which several equilibrium levels of employment are possible.

---

[1] The view that stabilization policy of any description is doomed without vigorous action to restore competition is expressed most lucidly by Henry Simons, *Economic Policy for a Free Society*, Chap. 5, The University of Chicago Press, Chicago, 1948.

12

THE LEVEL OF EMPLOYMENT (2)

12–1 INTRODUCTION

The discussion of employment theory between the Keynesians and their critics left a number of loose ends which we shall attempt in this chapter to tie together. By removing the assumption that pure competition prevails in product markets and by adding a few added assumptions, all of which seem to conform to the realities of the world, we can show that:

1. Under depression conditions the level of employment can be changed without changes in real wages.

2. The classical assumption of a labor supply dependent on the real wage does not, contrary to accepted doctrine, determine a unique level of employment, output, and real wage even though a labor market clearing mechanism exists.

3. Money wage cuts and increases in the supply of money through monetary policy will not increase the level of investment even though interest rates can be made to fall. Indeed, the interest rate as an economic calculator is largely irrelevant during depression.

12-2 THE MOVEMENT OF REAL AND MONEY WAGES

It follows directly from the labor demand function

$$N_d = D\left(\frac{w}{p}\right)$$

and the law of diminishing returns that in the short run an increase in the level of employment cannot be brought about without a fall in the real wage. Most economists, accepting the labor demand function as written above, assume that a fall in real wages is a natural by-product of emergence from depression. Noting that money wages rise as output rises, Keynes expressed the opinion that "the change in real wages associated with a change in money wages, so far from being usually in the same direction, is almost always in the opposite direction."[1] In other words, Keynes and most economists believed that even though money wages rise during recovery, prices rise even faster so that real wages fall. But when the issue was subjected to statistical analysis,[2] it was found that real wages actually increase as output and employment increase. Apparently there is something wrong with the notion that the demand for labor is a decreasing function of the real wage.

In a later article[3] Keynes acknowledged the fact that real wages seem to increase as output increases, although he refused to abandon the assumption of diminishing returns in the short run. He suggested instead that real wage increases would be compatible with employment increases if the assumption of pure competition were abandoned. Whereas a pure competitor will hire workers up to the point where the wage equals the value of the marginal product (marginal product multiplied

[1] J. M. Keynes, *The General Theory of Employment, Interest and Money,* Harcourt, Brace & World, Inc., New York, 1936, p. 10.

[2] L. Tarshis, "Changes in Real and Money Wages," *Economic Journal,* 49:150–154, 1939; and J. T. Dunlop, "The Movement of Real and Money Wage Rates," *Economic Journal,* 48:413–434, 1938.

[3] J. M. Keynes, "Relative Movements of Real Wages and Output," *Economic Journal,* 49:34–51, 1939.

by price), a monopolist will hire workers up to the point where the wage equals the marginal revenue product (marginal product multiplied by marginal revenue). Since marginal revenue mr can be written

$$mr = p\left(1 - \frac{1}{e}\right)$$

where p is the price of output and e is the price elasticity of demand, we may write

$$w = p\left(1 - \frac{1}{e}\right)X_n$$

or

$$\frac{w}{p} = \left(1 - \frac{1}{e}\right)X_n$$

as the condition for maximum profit. This implies that the demand for labor can now be written

$$N_d = D\left(\frac{w}{p}, e\right)$$

Under these conditions output increases are compatible with real wage increases as long as demand elasticities increase with increases in aggregate demand.

In the following sections the assumptions of imperfect competition will be retained. It will, however, be shown that even though demand elasticities remain unchanged, employment increases are not incompatible with real wage increases. It will, in fact, be assumed that demand elasticities remain unchanged since this will help to avoid repetition and to simplify the exposition.

12–3 A MODEL OF A DEPRESSION ECONOMY

It should be recognized that although a certain stock of capital goods K^* exists, this does not, unless the stock of capital goods is indivisible, necessarily mean that K^* will be employed in the sense that it is utilized in the production process. A cigarette factory with 100 machines will, in times of slack demand, use somewhat less than 100 machines because substitution between labor and machines is not perfect. The firm may therefore utilize 60 machines together with some labor even though labor costs are variable, whereas machine costs are fixed in the short run.

If the period of slack demand persists, the idle equipment may gradually be reduced. But since this can normally take place only by a slow process of depreciation and obsolescence, the typical depression can be expected to be characterized by widespread excess capacity, which, if equipment is divisible and the production function is characterized by ranges of zero returns, may for purposes of analysis be considered unemployed.

If the present view of the matter is acceptable, the marginal productivity of labor (labor demand) schedule of Figure 11–2 merely becomes one of many possible labor demand schedules. In that figure, if the real wage is $(w/p)_0$, the optimum factor mix may warrant the level of employment N_0. The labor demand schedule shows the increments to output that can be obtained by adding successive units of labor to the given initial factor mix. If, however, it is decided that the additional output can be produced more profitably by bringing another existing machine into operation, the labor demand schedule shifts to the right. Under these assumptions, an increase in aggregate demand can restore full employment by a shift in the demand curve for labor and/or by a fall in the real wage. As long as the stock of capital goods is divisible, as long as excess equipment is available, and as long as zero marginal returns to capital are possible, increases in employment may be achieved without real wage adjustments.

A formal model similar to the models of the previous chapter can be constructed quite simply. Write the production function as

$$Y = X(N,K) \qquad K \leqq K^*$$

where K is to be interpreted as capacity in use, which in the short run may vary between zero and K^*, where K^* is capacity in existence at the beginning of the production period. To find the factor mix, consider the following analogies from the theory of the individual firm. Assume that labor and machinery are the only factors of production used by the firm, that equipment is divisible, that factors are of homogeneous efficiency, and that the firm's production possibilities for the output levels y^*, y_1, and y_0 are as represented by the isoproduct curves of Figure 12–1, in which the quantity of machinery is measured on the vertical axis and the quantity of labor is measured on the horizontal axis.

Suppose that full employment for this firm justifies a level of output y^* and that the tangency of the factor price line is at (k^*, n^*). Now suppose that the desired level of output drops to y_0. Since the firm has available k^* units of capital which can be reduced only by gradual depreciation and obsolescence (which we ignore for the sake of sim-

Figure 12–1 Determination of the factor mix for an individual firm at output levels Y_0, Y_1, and Y^*

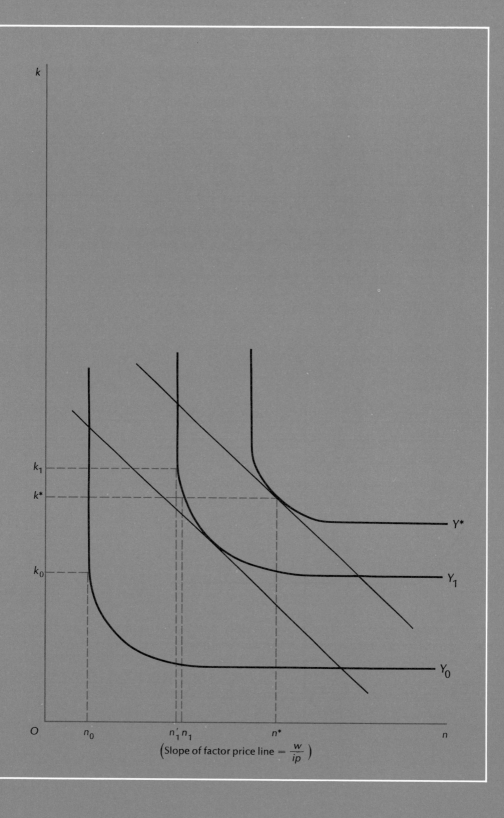

$\left(\text{Slope of factor price line} = \dfrac{w}{ip}\right)$

plicity), output of y_0 will be produced with k_0 units of machinery and n_0 units of labor. Since capital costs are sunk costs and not variable in the short run, the factor price line at less than $k*$ is, in effect vertical; i.e., the variable cost of utilizing another machine is zero. It therefore pays the firm to adjust to a decline in output by laying off workers up to the point where the marginal product of capital is zero. If the level of output in this situation is still greater than the desired amount, it will pay to begin shutting down machinery and laying off workers simultaneously. The process continues until the desired level of output y_0 is achieved, at which point the optimum factor mix warrants the use of k_0 machines and the hiring of n_0 workers.

Let us call this case A and incorporate it into an aggregative model. Assume that a rigid money wage w_0 prevails and that $K < K*$. Under these conditions

$$I(i) = Y - C(Y) \tag{12-1}$$

defines product market equilibrium. Monetary equilibrium is expressed by

$$m = \frac{M}{p} = kY + L(i) \tag{12-2}$$

The production function

$$Y = X(N,K) \qquad K \leqq K* \tag{12-3}$$

gives the relationship between factor inputs and output. To these equations we must add the profit-maximizing relations,

$$\frac{w}{p} = \left(1 - \frac{1}{e}\right) X_n \tag{12-4}$$

and

$$0 = \left(1 - \frac{1}{e}\right) X_k \tag{12-5}$$

Assuming a given real money supply, Eqs. (12–1) and (12–2) give product and monetary equilibrium and therefore determine i, Y, C, S, and I. Y having been determined, the factor mix is given by the production function in Eq. (12–3) and by the condition in Eq. (12–5) that the marginal product of capital equals zero. Finally the addition of Eq. (12–4) gives the price level.

As a consequence of a mild slump the desired level of output may fall only from $y*$ to y_1. In this case—call it case B—the marginal product of capital cannot be made equal to zero by worker layoffs. Since in the short run new equipment cannot be obtained, output of y_1 will be produced with k^* units of capital together with n_1 units of labor. In the aggregate this implies that Eq. (12–3) becomes

$$Y = X(N,K^*) \tag{12–6}$$

which further implies that Eq. (12–5) can be eliminated because the level of employment is now determined by the production function, since Y is known.

Note that case B corresponds to the usual formulation of the Keynesian system because all existing capital equipment is in use while only the intensity of utilization is subject to change. In a modern industrial economy in which factors of production are highly specialized and imperfect competition keeps product prices from being bid down so that excess capacity is absorbed, it is doubtful whether case B has very much relevance unless the fall in demand is slight. It is practically inconceivable that the output adjustment that results from a fall in demand will ever be achieved entirely by a fall in employment. Certainly in a deep depression it is reasonable to suppose that both men and machines will be idle.

12–4   THE IMPLICATIONS

When demand falls from the full-employment level, the existence of divisible capital equipment implies that a portion of the capital stock will be unemployed. From this it follows that output can be expanded by hiring more labor, by bringing additional existing machines into use, or by both. In essence this means that there is more than one attainable marginal productivity of labor schedule and that employment can be increased both by a shift in the schedule and by a movement along it. It follows that there may be many possible real wage rates that are compatible with labor market equilibrium.

The fact that the demand for labor depends not only on the real wage but also on the level of aggregate demand means that regardless of the labor supply schedule, there is no unique equilibrium level of employment. Writing the classical labor supply function as

$$N_s = S\left(\frac{w}{p}\right)$$

and the demand for labor implied by case A as

$$N_d = D\left(\frac{w}{p}, Y\right)$$

a market clearing mechanism such that $N_d = N_s$ will yield some equilibrium level of employment. There is, however, nothing unique about this level of employment since it also depends upon the particular level of aggregate demand that prevails.

The analysis adds weight to Keynes's belief that interest rate changes will not stimulate the level of investment. As long as there is excess capacity, there is no reason why investment should take place because the effective return on new investment, unless in types of equipment not currently in existence, is zero. Additions to the money supply via money wage cuts or monetary policy will therefore succeed only in reducing interest rates to the point where all the added balances are absorbed into speculative holdings.

Monetary policy, even if the conditions of case B prevail, is likely to encounter frustration. Refer once again to Figure 12–1. Assume that the desired level of output is y_1; then consider the point (k^*, n_1'), where k^* is capacity in existence and n_1' is the level of employment that would exist if k could be increased to k_1. In the long run y_1 can be produced (1) by obtaining an additional $k_1 - k^*$ units of capital, i.e., by investing; (2) by hiring an additional $n_1 - n_1'$ units of labor; or (3) by some intermediate combination of investment and additional labor. If relative factor prices do not change as a result of the fall in demand from y^* to y_1, it is clear that y_1 will be produced by adding more labor rather than by investing, for at the point (k^*, n_1)

$$\left| \frac{x_n}{w} \right| > \left| \frac{x_k}{ip} \right|$$

where x_n and x_k are the firm's marginal products of labor and capital, respectively. For investment to be stimulated, the interest rate would have to fall by an amount sufficient to rotate the factor-price line clockwise beyond k^*. As capitalism advances toward heavier industry—which means more specialized factors of production—the necessary change in interest rates becomes greater.

Finally, observe that case A may, after a period of decumulation or as a result of recovery from a slump, merge into case B. This suggests that our model has certain implications for the supply of output with respect to the price level. Where it is possible to increase output by shifting the labor demand schedule, the supply of output will be elastic with respect to the price level. When it is no longer possible to shift the labor demand curve without further capital accumulation, additional increases in output can be realized only by a movement along the labor demand schedule. But since this is possible only if real wages fall and since existing institutional arrangements all but preclude money wage cuts, the point at which case A merges into case B is the point where the supply of output with respect to the price level becomes less elastic.

13

FULL EMPLOYMENT, THE PRICE LEVEL, AND THE THEORY OF INTEREST

13-1   INTRODUCTION

Part 2 has dealt with an environment in which the productive resources of the economy are nearly always assumed to be partly unemployed. It is now time to round out the discussion by supposing that factor markets are cleared so that the supply of output, call it Y^*, is fixed. Given this assumption, let us observe the effects on our aggregative variables of changes such as an increase in the money supply or an increase in investment demand. This procedure will help prepare the ground for subsequent consideration of inflation; and it will help put the real versus monetary interest theory controversy into its proper perspective.

13–2   THE PRICE LEVEL AND THE RATE OF INTEREST AT FULL EMPLOYMENT

Consider the familiar *IS-LM* diagram in Figure 13–1. The diagram is identical with previous figures with the exception that a vertical line is drawn at Y^* to denote the fact that once Y^* is reached, the supply of output is fixed and cannot, as has been assumed thus far, adjust automatically to aggregate demand. At the point where the *IS* curve cuts Y^*, the interest rate i_0 equates the demand for goods and services with the full-employment supply. This interest rate we shall call the "natural" rate. Abstracting from the effects of government revenue and expenditure policies, the natural rate of interest equates the demand for investment funds with the supply of saving at full employment.

If the *LM* curve also happens to cut Y^* at i_0, the *market* rate of interest will equal the *natural* rate. General equilibrium of factor, product, and money markets is established since at that rate the demand for goods and services equals the full-employment supply, and just the right amount of money balances is made available for a Y^* volume of transactions.

Starting with the equilibrium situation specified above, what is the effect of an increase in the money supply? Assume that the nominal money supply is increased by ΔM dollars. The effect of this increase in the money supply is to shift the *LM* curve to LM_1 and to lower the market rate of interest to i_1. But at i_1 the supply and demand for goods and services are no longer in equilibrium because, investment having been stimulated by the fall of the market rate of interest, the total demand for goods and services is $Y_1 - Y^*$ in excess of what can be supplied. Prices are therefore bid up so that the real value of the money supply, $m_s = M/p$, begins to fall. This means that a particular value of nominal money balances is no longer adequate to make the real transactions previously made. Wealth holders are therefore induced to sell earning assets to supplement their transactions balances; interest rates rise; and excess demand is gradually eliminated as the increase in the interest rate causes investment to decline.

What will be the final solution? As long as the *LM* schedule is to the right of the original schedule, LM_0, there will be excess demand for goods and a continuation of price increases. Evidently, then, equilibrium will not be restored until price increases have brought the real value of the money supply back to its original level. In other words, the *LM* curve will shift back to LM_0, where the market rate of interest

Figure 13–1   Full-employment general equilibrium (all values in real terms)

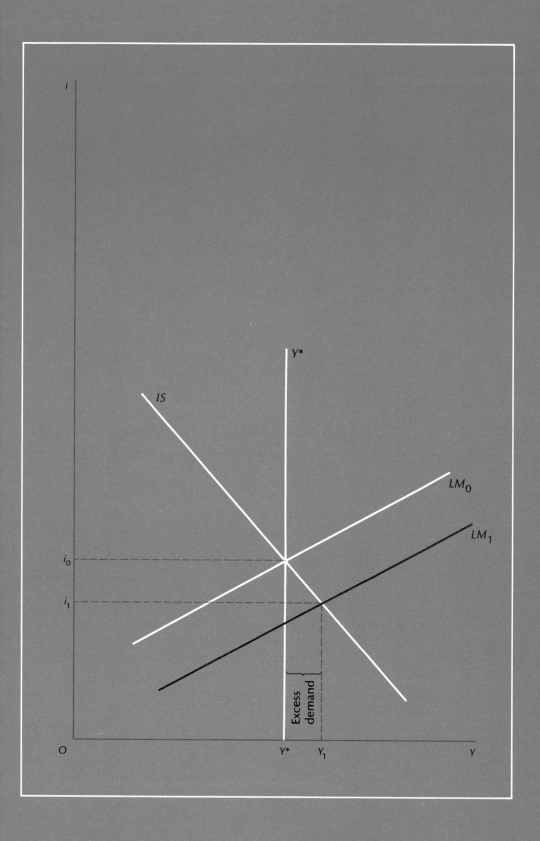

once again coincides with the natural rate. We may therefore conclude that:

1. The increase in the nominal supply of money produces a proportional change in the price level.

2. The natural rate of interest i_0 is reestablished as the equilibrium market rate of interest. Under full-employment conditions the equilibrium rate of interest is independent of monetary factors.[1]

Both conclusions are in direct conformity with the classical view of interest and the price level. Observe, moreover, that these results have been obtained without abandoning Keynes's assumption of a speculative demand for money.

Do these classical results always hold true at full employment? What, for example, would happen in the unlikely event that the assumption of full employment was combined with the liquidity trap hypothesis? In Figure 13–2 the establishment of the liquidity trap at market rate i_1 creates a situation in which excess demand of $Y_1 - Y^*$ prevails. Thus again the price level rises, and the LM schedule shifts to the left. As long as the market rate is below the natural rate, prices will continue to rise, so that ultimately there is no alternative but to suppose that the LM schedule must shift until the trap is escaped. Since final equilibrium is not established until the LM curve shifts to LM_1, we may infer that the liquidity trap is purely a depression phenomenon. At full employment the demand for money cannot possibly be infinitely elastic with respect to the rate of interest except in the practically inconceivable case in which the natural rate of interest happens to be the same as the liquidity trap rate.

Next let us turn to the effect of changes in the demand for goods and services as the result of a decreased desire to save, an increase in investment demand, or an increase in government purchases. If an increase in government purchases causes the IS schedule of Figure 13–3 to shift from IS_0 to IS_1, the natural rate of interest rises to i_1. Thus, if the market rate is at i_0, there must be excess demand for output of $Y_1 - Y^*$ so that competition for the available supply causes prices to rise and the

[1] These results are spelled out by D. Patinkin, "Keynesian Economics and the Quantity Theory," in K. K. Kurihara, ed., *Post-Keynesian Economics*, Rutgers University Press, New Brunswick, N.J., 1954.

Figure 13–2 The liquidity trap and full employment (all values in real terms)

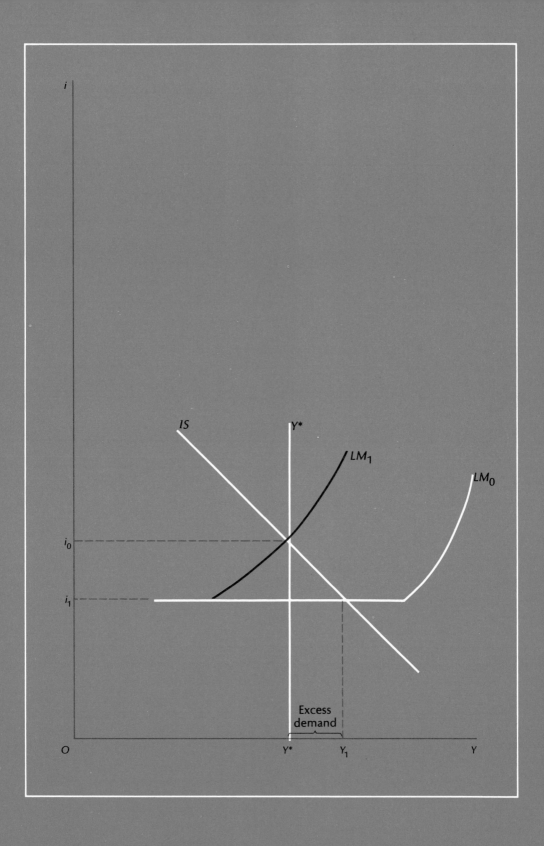

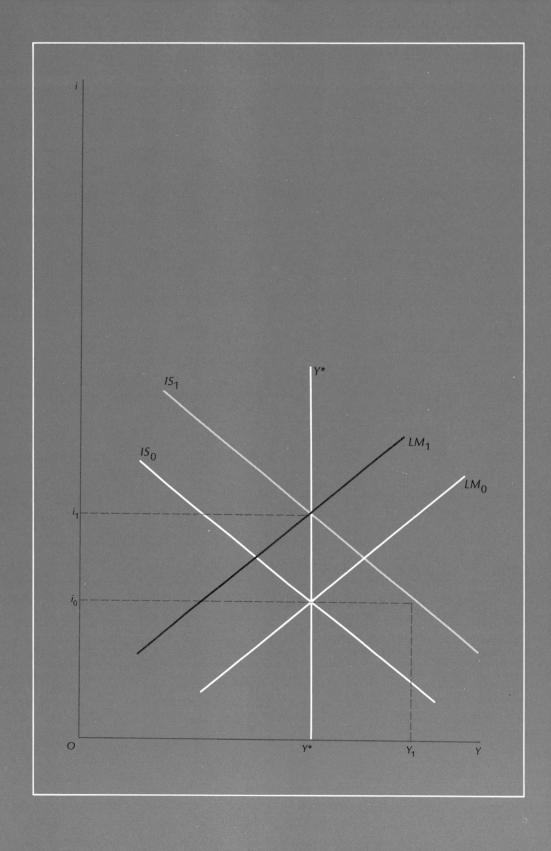

LM curve to shift upward until, at *LM*₁, the market rate of interest coincides with the new natural rate.

In the new equilibrium the same level of real income prevails as before the change except that it is now higher priced. The rise in the interest rate causes money balances to be released from speculative holdings and makes it possible to finance the same volume of real transactions with the same nominal supply of money at a higher level of prices. The existence of the speculative demand for money therefore leaves open the possibility that an increase in investment demand can lead to a rise in the price level—a possibility that could not materialize in the non-speculative demand world of the classical model.[1]

In the full-employment world where the level of output is fixed, we can make the following provisional conclusions:

1. An increase in the money supply will bring about a proportional change in the price level as long as the natural rate of interest is in excess of the rate of interest at which the demand for money is infinitely elastic.

2. The natural rate of interest cannot be altered by monetary changes. The rate depends, rather, on the position of the *IS* schedule in relation to the full-employment supply of output.

3. The price level is uniquely determined by the nominal money supply only in the absence of a speculative demand for money. A shift in investment demand or in the saving function or in government purchases or taxation, by affecting the interest rate, either releases or creates a shortage of speculative balances, thereby affecting transactions balances and the price level.

13–3   REAL AND MONETARY THEORIES OF INTEREST

It seems appropriate to explore further the question of why the assumption of full employment produces such a radical difference in the determination of the rate of interest. The question, moreover, is at the heart of a controversy that has caused much heated debate, namely: Is the

[1] See the appendix to this chapter at the end of the book for proof of these results and derivation of the magnitudes of the changes in the interest rate and the price level.

Figure 13–3   Changes in the natural rate of
interest (all values in real terms)

equilibrium rate of interest determined by real factors such as the productivity of investment and the saving habits of the community, or is interest a purely monetary phenomenon?[1]

Traditionally, it has more or less been taken for granted that the interest rate is determined by real factors and that influences from the monetary sphere were in the nature of short-run disturbances that could not change the natural, and therefore the equilibrium, rate of interest. The natural rate, it will be remembered, is the rate which equates the demand for goods and services with the full-employment supply. Since it is established where the *IS* schedule cuts Y^*, the natural rate must depend on the shape of the investment demand schedule and on the full-employment level of saving. Since the natural rate, in classical theory, is the only possible market *equilibrium* rate of interest and since it depends on the investment demand schedule and the volume of full-employment saving, it is regarded as a "real" phenomenon dependent on the "productivity" of investment (reflected in the shape of the investment demand schedule) and the "thriftiness" or saving habits of the community.

In contrast to this view Keynes argued that since full employment is but one possible equilibrium level of employment, there is nothing natural about the natural rate and that the rate of interest is a monetary phenomenon determined by the intersection of the demand for and the supply of money. This rate, moreover, is an equilibrium rate; if there is no reason why the economic system should automatically adjust to full employment, there is, by the same token, no reason why the market rate should approach the natural rate.

The extremes have been tempered by those writers who regard interest determination as a general equilibrium matter and who therefore

---

[1] The most complete exposition of "real" interest theory is Irving Fisher, *The Theory of Interest,* Kelley and Millman, Inc., New York, 1954. While Fisher thought that both the "impatience to spend income," which necessitates an interest premium if present consumption is to be foregone, and "opportunity to invest it" were the relevant factors, the so-called Austrian school as represented, for example, in F. A. von Hayek, "The Mythology of Capital," *Quarterly Journal of Economics,* 50:199–228, 1936, emphasized the importance of savings, while F. H. Knight, "Capital and Interest," *Encyclopaedia Britannica,* Vol. 4, pp. 779–801, 1946, emphasizes the investment side. The general equilibrium approach is implicit in the famous paper by J. R. Hicks, "Mr. Keynes and the Classics: A Suggested Interpretation," *Econometrica,* 5:147–159, 1937, and is expounded in an interesting fashion by H. M. Somers in "Monetary Policy and the Theory of Interest," *Quarterly Journal of Economics,* 55:488–507, 1941. The papers by F. A. von Hayek, F. H. Knight, J. R. Hicks, and H. M. Somers, as well as an exposition by J. M. Keynes of his own purely monetary theory, may be found in Fellner and Haley, eds. for American Economic Association, *Readings in the Theory of Income Distribution,* McGraw-Hill Book Company, New York, 1946.

hold that the equilibrium rate of interest depends on both real and monetary factors.

Let us first consider the classical real interest theory. To make it more general than we have thus far made it, we should first introduce the possibility that saving may be a function of the rate of interest as well as of the level of income. The average person presumably has a strong preference for present consumption over future consumption. In other words, if he has the choice of receiving a dollar now or a dollar a year from now, he will, barring distortions introduced by taxation, most certainly take the dollar now. If, therefore, he is to be persuaded to forego the dollar now, he must be paid a premium equal to or greater than his marginal rate of time preference, i.e., an amount that will make the utility of the dollar received today equal to or smaller than the utility of the sum he will collect in a year if he lends the dollar. Presumably a higher rate of interest will induce an individual to forego some present consumption in favor of future consumption.

On this basis we may draw the saving schedule $S(i)_0$ plotted against the rate of interest in Figure 13–4, and we may suppose that as the rate of interest rises, the community will be persuaded to increase its level of saving.[1] Superimposed on this saving schedule is plotted the familiar negatively sloped investment demand schedule $I(i)_0$, which defines the expected future rates of return on new investment.

Given the investment demand schedule and the saving schedule, it can easily be seen that the equilibrium rate of interest must be the rate i_0 at which the two schedules cross. If the current market rate of interest happens to be i_1, savers are willing to withhold an amount S_1 from current consumption. But since the demand for investment funds is only I_1, there will be an excess supply of saving, and the interest rate falls. As this happens, the amount of saving offered declines, and what were

---

[1] The whole issue of the effect of interest changes on the volume of saving is rather cloudy. There is no evidence that saving is significantly affected by reasonable changes in interest rates, although large changes could, on a priori grounds, surely be expected to affect saving. A complication arises from the possibility that for some individuals, and for the community as a whole if we assume a high enough interest rate, the saving schedule may assume a negative slope. To some extent this may be due to the fact that some individuals save toward a lump sum of wealth in the future. If an individual's goal is to have available a pool of funds totaling $20,000 when he retires at the age of sixty-five, an increase in the rate of interest will enable him to put aside a smaller sum each year and still reach the desired goal. Similarly, while an increase in the rate of interest will induce him to substitute future consumption in place of current consumption, the high rate so improves his future income prospects that he may tend to save less today. There is thus the possibility that at high enough interest rates the *income* effect may overcome the *substitution* effect and thus produce a backward bend (negative slope) in the saving schedule.

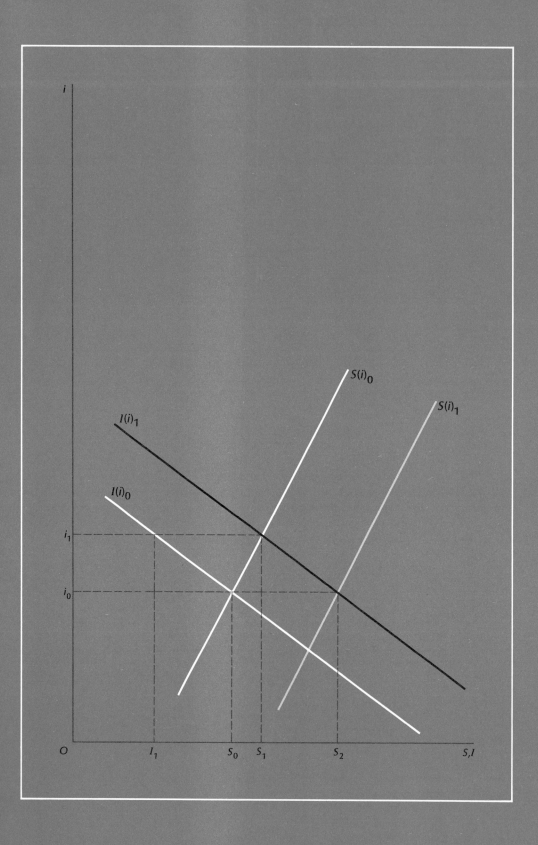

marginal investment projects at i_1 now become profitable. Ultimately the market is cleared at i_0, where evidently the equilibrium rate of interest is that rate that just makes the marginal rate of time preference equal to the return on the last dollar of investment. Notice that the rate i_0 is the natural rate referred to previously; to say that investment equals full-employment saving is the same as to say that aggregate demand equals the full-employment supply of output.

If an innovation shifts the investment demand schedule to $I(i)_1$, the resources required to exploit the innovation must, given the assumption of full employment, come from the willingness of savers to reduce current consumption and increase saving. The inducement to do this is the higher rate of interest that results from the bidding by investors for the available supply of saving. In Figure 13–4 the increase in the interest rate to i_1 induces savers to increase saving by $S_1 - S_0$ (and therefore reduce consumption by an equivalent amount) so that investment may increase by that same amount.

But what would happen if the shift in the investment demand schedule occurred when there were unemployed resources available? In this case the shift in the investment demand schedule need not cause the interest rate to rise at all. The existence of unemployed resources implies that there is no need to induce the public to release resources from consumption. Idle resources may simply be activated by the use of idle money balances held by individuals or by the banking system. When this happens, the level of income rises; and since saving also depends on the level of income, the saving schedule, plotted with respect to the rate of interest, shifts to the right. In Figure 13–4, if the saving schedule shifts to $S(i)_1$ as a result of the increase in income brought about by the increase in investment, the equilibrium rate of interest will not rise at all.

It may clarify matters if we realize, following Horwich,[1] that the investment demand schedule is nothing more than the supply of new securities, while the saving schedule is simply the demand for new securities. Prior to the innovation, the demand and supply for new securities are exactly balanced at i_0. The innovation, by shifting the investment demand schedule to $I(i)_1$, increases the supply of new securities. If the economy is at full employment, the saving schedule (de-

[1] G. Horwich, "Money, Prices, and the Theory of Interest Determination," *Economic Journal*, 67:625–643, 1957.

Figure 13–4   Saving, investment, and the natural rate of interest (all values in real terms)

mand for new securities) cannot shift, so the increased supply of new securities lowers security prices and raises the rate of interest. On the other hand, if unemployed resources exist, it is possible for the investment and saving schedules to shift by equal amounts, which means that the supply of and demand for new securities shift by equal amounts so that the rate of interest will not change. If, in this situation, the interest rate does change, the change must be due to the fact that the higher level of income causes wealth holders to sell some securities in order to supplement their transactions balances. Notice, however, that this will affect the rate of interest only if the demand for money is not perfectly elastic.

What general conclusions can be drawn? In Figure 13–5 the intersection of IS_0 with LM_0 is to the left of Y^* at i_0 and Y_0. Since this is a point of less than full employment, the supply of output is able to adjust to the demand, so that the intersection is a point of general equilibrium. If the IS schedule shifts to IS_1, the level of income rises to Y_1 while the interest rate remains unchanged. This is the case of the liquidity trap in which the equilibrium rate of interest is the rate at which the demand for money becomes infinitely elastic. If the IS schedule shifts further to the right to IS_2, the level of income again rises, but this time the rise is accompanied by an increase in the rate of interest to i_2. Here the liquidity trap is escaped and the equilibrium rate of interest is established at the point of intersection of the IS and LM curves. In this range of the LM function, where the demand for money is neither zero nor infinitely elastic with respect to the rate of interest, the interest rate is determined by the combined equilibria of the product and money markets and can be changed either by monetary factors (a shift in the LM schedule) or by real factors (a shift in the IS schedule).

Finally, suppose that the IS schedule shifts to IS_3 so that the intersection of IS_3 with LM_0 is to the right of the full-employment level of income at interest rate i_3'. Since it is now impossible for the supply of output to adjust to the demand, the price level must rise and the LM curve must shift to the left. In the final equilibrium the LM schedule will have shifted to the point where monetary equilibrium is exactly consistent with equilibrium between the demand for and the supply of goods. This must be the rate i_3 that just balances full-employment saving with investment.

It may reasonably be argued that the Keynesian solution (i_0) and the "general equilibrium" solution (i_2 at Y_2) are not true equilibrium solu-

Figure 13–5   Determination of the equilibrium rate of
interest (all values in real terms)

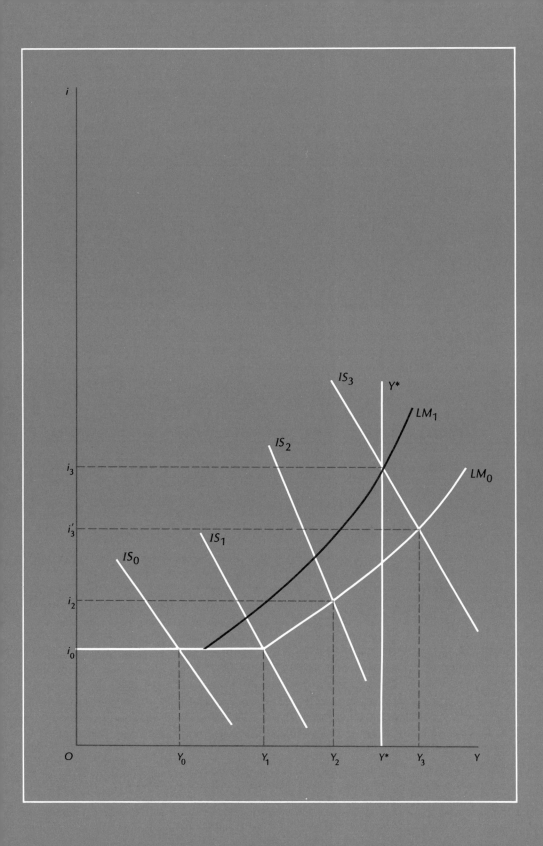

tions because they depend on rigidities in the wage-price structure. In the absence of such rigidities, the existence of uncleared markets would cause prices and wages to fall and would therefore increase the real value of the money supply. In the Keynesian case this would have no effect on the rate of interest and therefore on the level of investment and income. But this would keep markets from becoming cleared, and pressure on wages and prices would continue so that ultimately they would all approach zero. As was seen earlier, compatibility of the liquidity trap with the existence of positive levels of wages and prices necessarily assumes the existence of downward wage-price rigidities.

The case in which the equilibrium rate of interest is determined by both real and monetary factors also depends on the assumption of wage-price rigidities in the downward direction. Since Y_2 is at less than full employment, there are uncleared markets; so that if wages and prices fall, the real value of the money supply will increase. Since the (Y_2, i_2) solution is in a range where the LM curve has a positive slope, the increase in the real value of the money supply will cause the rate of interest to fall either to the point where investment increases by enough to restore full employment or to the point where the demand for money becomes totally elastic (the LM curve becomes horizontal). In the first case the final equilibrium will be the classical natural rate at full employment, and in the latter case it will be the Keynesian liquidity trap rate. The rate i_2 can therefore be permanently maintained only if costs and prices are *absolutely* rigid in the downward direction.

13–4 ASSETS AND THE RATE OF INTEREST

In an economy that suffers from unemployment, additional saving is a bane that reduces aggregate demand and increases unemployment. In a fully employed economy, however, it is the willingness to save that permits resources to be released from current consumption and allows them to flow into capacity-expanding investment. Going back to Figure 13–4, we assume that the natural rate of interest is i_1 and that the level of saving and investment is S_1. A change in saving habits that would shift the saving schedule to $S(i)_1$ would reduce the natural rate of interest to i_0. This would make additional investment profitable and would raise the rate of growth of income.[1] Apparently, then, the rate of growth of income can be accelerated if, with a given investment demand schedule, savers can be induced to be thriftier because this will lower the natural rate of interest.

---

[1] What we are reporting here is a very traditional theory of income growth. As we shall see in Chap. 16, a considerable body of modern theory denies that the rate of income growth can be permanently affected by changes in the level of saving.

The full-employment model we have been studying in this chapter suggests that monetary policy cannot affect the natural rate of interest. A one-time increase in the money supply will temporarily lower the market rate of interest. However, this will be offset by a rise in the price level, and the market rate of interest will return to the original natural rate. It follows that the monetary authority cannot keep the market rate of interest permanently below the natural rate of interest unless it is willing to accept continuous inflation. It follows further that the monetary authority cannot raise the level of investment and income growth without at the same time causing the price level to rise.

This conclusion has been attacked by L. A. Metzler,[1] who invokes the Pigou effect to show that because monetary policy can affect the level of wealth held by the private sector, it can affect the level of saving. If it can affect the level of saving, it can affect the natural rate of interest. And if this is the case, a one-shot monetary policy can permanently affect the level of investment and the rate of income growth. Let us consider Metzler's argument in some detail.

The real wealth of the private sector may be defined as the sum of the net government obligations held by the sector plus the capitalized value of the earnings that result from the ownership of capital. If the full-employment level of income is Y^* and if a proportion α of this income consists of corporate profits and if all profits are paid out as dividends, the real value of common stock will be[2]

$$K' = \frac{\alpha Y^*}{i}$$

If all common stock is in the hands of the private sector, if there is no government debt of the interest-bearing variety, and if all money is in the form of currency, the real value of private wealth W may be written

$$W = \frac{\alpha Y^*}{i} + \frac{M}{p}$$

Now suppose that consumption is an increasing function of the level of wealth as well as of the level of income. This would imply that

$$C = C(Y,W)$$

---

[1] L. A. Metzler, "Wealth, Savings, and the Rate of Interest," *Journal of Political Economy*, 59:93–116, 1951.

[2] The prime is added to distinguish K in the sense of the value of capital ownership from K in the production function sense of units of productive power. In a long-run equilibrium sense the two quantities would be equal. In the short run a fall in the rate of interest raises the real value of K'. But this does not mean that the economy is capable of increasing the level of production.

In combination with the investment demand schedule, this consumption function implies the *IS* curve

$$I(i) = Y - C(Y,W)$$

Since we are assuming full employment (fixing Y at Y^*), the new *IS* schedule implies that the rate of interest is a function of the level of wealth. If wealth increases, consumers will want to spend more for consumption. But if the economy is at full employment, a rise in consumption cannot take place unless investment declines, and this means that the rate of interest must rise. Thus we see that the rate of interest is an increasing function of the level of wealth.

We are now ready to inquire into the effect of an increase in the money supply brought about by Federal Reserve purchases of privately held common stock. In Figure 13–6 we assume that the economy is in equilibrium at full employment with interest rate i_0 and income level Y^*. Now suppose that the Federal Reserve increases the money supply by purchasing securities. The *LM* schedule shifts to the right, and the market rate of interest drops to i_1. Here, however, there is excess demand of $Y_1 - Y^*$ so that the price level begins to rise, as does the rate of interest. The *LM* schedule begins to shift back toward LM_0.

In the analysis of Section 13–2 the *LM* curve would have had to shift all the way back to LM_0 before equilibrium was again restored. But now that consumption depends on wealth, this will not happen. To see why this is so, let us in fact suppose that it does happen. If *LM* shifts back to LM_0, the rate of interest will be back at its original level, which means that each unit of common stock held by the private sector will have the same value as it did before the open market operation. Moreover, the shift back to LM_0 implies that the price level has risen in exact proportion to the increase in the money supply. Consequently, the real value of the money supply is the same as it was before the open market operation. But this must mean that the private sector is poorer. The real value of its stock of money is the same, as is the real value of *each unit* of common stock; but the *number* of units of common stock the private sector now owns is less than before.

These considerations imply that the *IS* curve must shift because the reduction in the level of wealth causes consumption to fall. If full employment is to be sustained, investment must rise to compensate for the fall in consumption, and this means that the rate of interest at which *IS* cuts the Y^* vertical line must fall. In Figure 13–6 the final

Figure 13–6   Wealth and the natural rate of interest (all values in real terms)

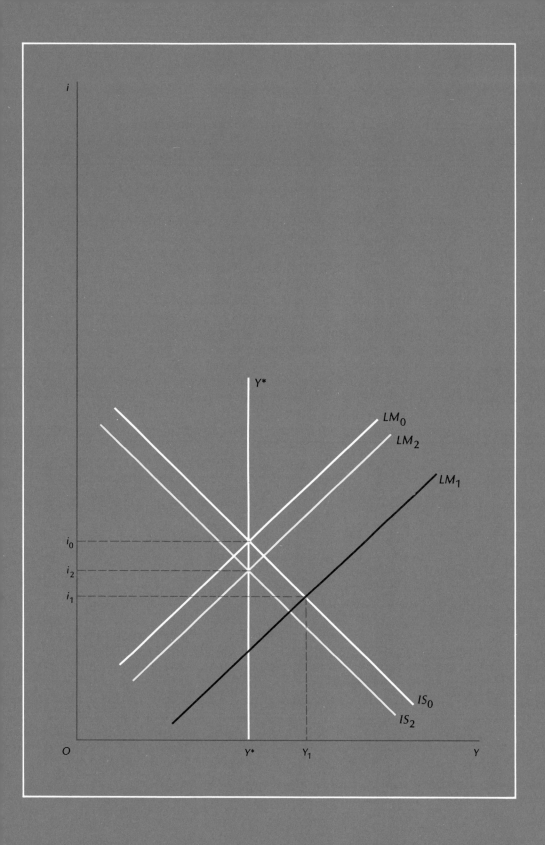

equilibrium might be somewhere in the neighborhood of i_2. The LM curve shifts back, not to LM_0, but to LM_2; and the IS curve shifts to IS_2 as a result of the change in the level of wealth. The monetary authority can, apparently, change the natural rate of interest. And it therefore appears that monetary policy can raise the rate of growth without thereby creating inflation.

Metzler's argument is probably erroneous; at the very least it is incomplete. Let us suppose that the money supply had been increased by dropping newly printed dollar bills out of airplanes. If we ignore the fact that this would involve a temporary increase in disposable income, the increase in the money supply would not be accompanied by a transfer of earning assets. Consequently, a rise in the price level in proportion to the increase in the money supply would leave the real value of private wealth the same as before, and there would, therefore, be no change in the natural rate of interest.

The foregoing argument suggests that it is not the increase in the money supply that is important in determining what happens to the natural rate of interest, but whether or not real wealth has been transferred permanently from the private to the public sector. To complete the analysis, we must consider the alternative uses to which the government puts its newly found wealth.

The private sector is poorer than before because the government now collects dividends that were formerly received by the private sector. The true nature of the policy therefore is that a proportional profit tax has, in effect, been imposed. If the government spends the proceeds, the IS curve shifts up and the natural rate of interest again rises. Or, if the government gives the dividends back to the private sector in the form of a tax reduction, the sector's income and wealth are restored to their former levels and the previous natural rate of interest will therefore be restored. Thus, the traditional view that monetary policy cannot affect the natural rate of interest still appears to be correct.

The reader may feel disappointed that a whole section seems to have been wasted in putting forth a proposition only to have it refuted. The purpose of the exercise, however, is to show that it is extremely important to understand whether a particular policy is a monetary policy, a fiscal policy, or both. In the present case, Metzler's result is comparable (be sure to bear in mind that we are concerned only with a full-employment situation) to increasing the quantity of money and raising taxes simultaneously. The fall in the natural rate of interest that resulted was the consequence of the fiscal, not the monetary, effect of the operation.

14

INTERNATIONAL ASPECTS OF MACROECONOMIC THEORY

14–1 INTRODUCTION

To obtain a well-balanced view of the fundamentals of macroeconomic theory and policy, we must study the effects of income changes abroad upon the level of income of the domestic economy and vice versa. It is the purpose of this chapter to provide a brief survey of some of the more important international aspects of macroeconomic analysis and to consider their implications for domestic stabilization policy.[1]

[1] Among the many excellent general discussions of this topic are L. A. Metzler, "The Theory of International Trade," in H. S. Ellis, ed. for American Economic Association, *A Survey of Contemporary Economics*, Vol. 1, Chap. 6, Richard D. Irwin, Inc., Homewood, Ill., 1949; T. C. Schelling, *International Economics*, Parts III and IV, Allyn and Bacon, Inc., Boston, 1958; and C. P. Kindleberger, *International Economics*, Chap. 4 and Part IV, Richard D. Irwin, Inc., Homewood, Ill., 1953.

It is fair to say that until quite recently American economists have thought of the United States economy as "closed." Because the fraction of our national economic activity which involves the exchange of goods and services with other nations is so small relative to total GNP, it has seemed reasonable enough to ignore foreign influences and, for practical purposes, to think of the economy as functioning in isolation. The course of events since the early and mid-1950s has forced us to revise these attitudes. It has now come to be accepted as commonplace that one of the reasons for the reluctance of the United States government to embark on a full-scale program to eliminate unemployment during the early 1960s was that any action designed to achieve this end would have caused our "balance of payments" problem to be accentuated. It has become painfully evident that international economic developments have a profound effect upon the domestic economy even though the importance of foreign trade to the United States is small relative to its importance for other countries. It is clear, moreover, that international economic developments impose severe restrictions upon the types of national economic policies that can be pursued. Unfortunately, the need to balance our international accounts often stands in the way of the pursuit of exactly those policies that are most badly needed from the point of view of the domestic economy.

Since the early 1950s the United States has suffered from what is variously known as a "balance of payments deficit," a "gold drain," or a "dollar problem." What all these phrases imply is that we have been unable to earn, in return for our sales abroad and from investments by foreigners in the United States, a quantity of foreign money sufficient to balance the quantity of dollars that we have spent abroad for imports, foreign investments, economic aid, and military assistance. The net effect of such a situation is that more dollars have steadily flowed out of the United States than foreign moneys have flowed in. If we imagine trying to balance the books at the end of some accounting period, we should find that once dollars are sent home in exchange for pounds, D. marks, and so forth, foreign countries will be left with a net supply of dollars over and above what they held at the beginning of the accounting period.

If a German exporter earns dollars, he can convert these dollars into D. marks at his bank. The bank, its supply of domestic money having been depleted, may go to the central bank and convert whatever excess amount of dollars it has into domestic money. Because dollars are an acceptable means of paying bills with third countries, the central bank may decide to hold the dollars as "international reserves." On the other hand, if the central bank decides that its dollars holdings are excessive, it can call upon the United States Treasury to buy back the dollars in exchange for D. marks. Finally, if the Treasury is short of D. marks, of foreign exchange, as holdings of foreign money are called, the Treasury will have to buy the dollars back in exchange for gold. When this happens as a steady process, we say that we are suffering from a "gold drain."

Before we get into the complexities of international monetary economics, we need to perform the preliminary chore of integrating international trade into the national accounting framework and of extending our national income equilibrium condition. Real net national product including foreign trade may be defined as

$$Y = C + I_r + G + (X - Z)$$

where $X - Z$ represents the difference between merchandise exports X and merchandise imports Z. A positive net export balance is an addition to income in the same way that a positive level of investment is an addition to income. As before, income receipts are divided into

$$Y = C + S + T$$

When we replace realized investment I_r by intended investment I and equate the two foregoing expressions, we obtain the equilibrium condition

$$I + G + X = S + T + Z$$

which, as always, implies that income leakages must equal injections. Exports, like investment and government purchases, represent injections into the domestic income stream, while imports, like saving and taxes, represent leakages.

14–2 THE DEMAND AND SUPPLY FOR FOREIGN EXCHANGE

The complexities of international monetary economics are such that it is useful to organize the problem in a formal manner. Imagine a world of two countries A and B, where A may be thought of as the "home" country and B as the "rest of the world," and suppose that their respective national currencies are known as alphas and betas. Country A will earn a certain amount of betas from its sales of goods and services to B, from investments by residents of B in A, and from the repatriation of the earnings of investments in B by residents of A. We can call the sum of such earnings the "supply of betas," or, as it is commonly called, the "supply of foreign exchange." Similarly, since A wishes to make purchases and investments in B and since residents of B wish to return profits earned from investments in A, there will be a demand for B's money. Now consider Figure 14–1, where the demand and supply schedules for betas are illustrated. The quantity of betas is measured on the horizontal axis while the price of betas in terms of alphas—the exchange rate as this ratio is known—is measured vertically, and the exchange rate is denoted by the symbol π.

When the price of alphas drops relative to the price of betas, π increases and we say that B's currency has appreciated while A's currency has been "depreciated" or "devalued." If such a change takes place, citizens of A will have to give up a larger number of alphas in order to acquire a given quantity of betas, and the effect of this will be to make B's goods more expensive to the citizens of A even though there may have been no change in the domestic prices of B's goods. As a consequence, we expect the rise in the price of betas to reduce the quantity of betas demanded, and we therefore expect A's demand curve for foreign exchange to be negatively sloped.

On the other side of the market a rise in the price of betas relative to alphas means that citizens of B will have to give up fewer betas to obtain a given quantity of alphas, and this has the effect of making A's goods cheaper in terms of betas (even if there is no change in their domestic alpha prices). Consequently, we expect the demand for imports by B to increase, and this is equivalent to saying that the supply of betas to A increases as the price of betas increases. The supply curve of foreign exchange to A is therefore expected to be positively sloped.[1]

Now imagine that the foreign exchange market is not subject to any governmental interference in either country. Under this assumption the exchange rate would be "flexible" or "free floating," and the market would tend to equilibrate at $\bar{\pi}$ and $\bar{\beta}$, where the bars indicate equilibrium values. Consequently, the demand for and supply of betas would be equated, and there could, in such a situation, be no such thing as a deficit or a surplus in the balance of payments since fluctuations in the exchange rate would wipe out such deficits or surpluses. Finally, note that because the demand for betas is the mirror image of

---

[1] The fact that the supply curve may not actually be positively sloped and the potential consequences of this circumstance are matters for subsequent consideration.

Figure 14–1   The demand and supply for foreign exchange

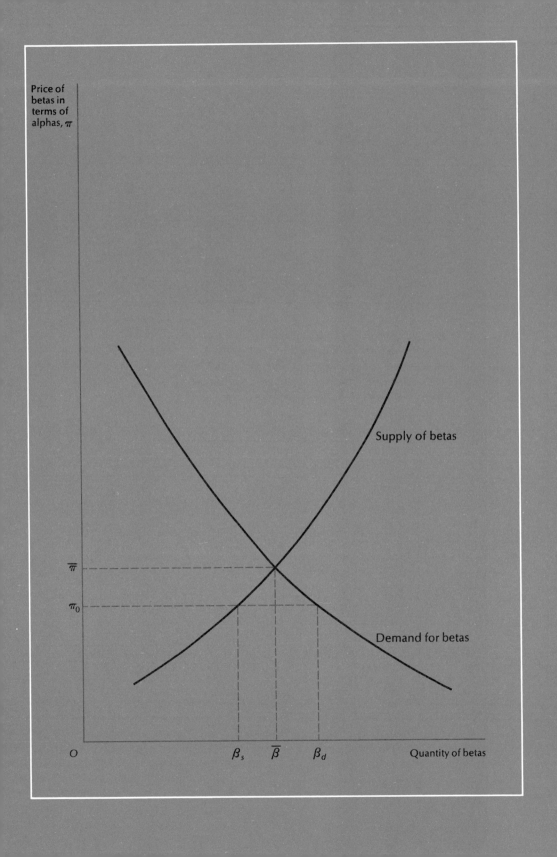

the supply of alphas, the presence of equilibrium in the market for betas must also mean that the market for alphas is in equilibrium.

In practice, the foreign exchange markets are not permitted to operate in such a way as to allow exchange rates to reach their free market values at all times. What happens instead is that countries A and B define the value of their currencies as fixed in terms of a certain weight of gold. In so doing, the countries automatically fix the values of their currencies in terms of each other. The resulting "official" exchange rates may or may not coincide with the rates that would have been established under free market conditions. The chances are, of course, that the official rate will differ from the free market rate. When this happens, balance of payments deficits and surpluses arise, and when one currency is persistently overvalued or undervalued vis-à-vis another currency, difficulties of major proportions are likely to ensue.

Referring again to Figure 14–1, suppose that the official exchange rate has been fixed at π_0. At this rate betas are undervalued in terms of alphas with the result that there is a persistent excess demand for betas together with its mirror image, an excess supply of alphas. Normal market forces would force up the price of betas relative to the price of alphas. Consequently, if the official rate is to be maintained, it will be necessary for governments to intervene. If the excess demand for betas $(\beta_d - \beta_s)$ is to be kept from raising the price of betas, some agency must be willing to fill the gap by supplying the necessary quantity of betas to the market.

Filling these excess demand and supply gaps is exactly what central banks, under the existing international monetary system, attempt to do. If the central bank of country A is willing, and able, to sell betas at a fixed price in exchange for alphas, any tendency for the price of betas to rise would be eliminated because holders of alphas can always buy betas at B's central bank at the official rate.

Although A's central bank may be willing to sell betas at the official rate, it may not always be able to do so. It could certainly not do so if official policy permanently undervalued betas, since the need permanently to accommodate the excess demand for betas would eventually exhaust A's accumulated supply of gold and foreign exchange. What then can country A do to combat the outflow?

If A takes no action before reserves become seriously depleted, speculators are likely to reason that a change in the official price is inevitable. Anticipating the devaluation of alphas, the holders of alphas will attempt to convert their holdings into holdings of betas prior to the anticipated devaluation. Since this increases the excess demand for betas, the effect is to accelerate the rate at which A's foreign exchange reserves are depleted. The system of fixed exchange rates therefore appears to be dangerously unstable.

In order to avert a "run on the pound," or on the dollar, or on alphas, the affected government will usually attempt to seek ways of reducing the drain of gold and foreign exchange well before the situation becomes critical. Let us consider now the kinds of policies that might be pursued. Figure 14–2 is a replica of Figure 14–1 with a few additions. If country A insists on maintaining the official exchange rate, it will either have to deplete its reserves or it will somehow have to contrive a means of shifting the demand curve for betas to the left (for example, from D_0 to D_1) and/or find a means of shifting the supply curve to the right. There are several ways in which this could be accomplished. First, country A might pursue a deflationary fiscal policy. For example, if taxes are raised, the level of consumption in A will decline. Because some of the consumer goods will be imported goods and because some domestically produced goods contain imported materials, the demand for imports will drop and the demand curve for foreign exchange will shift to the left. One way to attack a balance of payments problem therefore appears to be through a reduction in domestic spending via fiscal policy.

A by-product of the deflationary fiscal policy is that prices in country A will decline, or if there is a general worldwide upward trend of prices, prices in A are likely to rise less rapidly than prices in B. The effect of this will be to make A's goods relatively more attractive to A's citizens than imports and to reduce the demand for foreign exchange. Similarly, A's goods become relatively more attractive to citizens of B, thus tending to increase the supply of foreign exchange. Further, if the effect of the policy is to reduce costs in A relative to costs in B, business firms in A may decide that it is more profitable to produce goods for export at home than to establish an overseas subsidiary in B, and the level of investment in B by A's residents therefore declines, while the reverse may happen in the case of firms in country B.

Second, country A might pursue a restrictive monetary policy as a way of shifting the demand and supply curves of foreign exchange. The effect of such a policy would be to raise interest rates in A, making it more attractive for citizens of both countries to invest their funds in the financial markets of country A. Thus we should expect an interest rate differential to produce a capital flow into A that would relieve the pressure on A's foreign exchange reserves.

The reader will undoubtedly have said to himself that neither of the

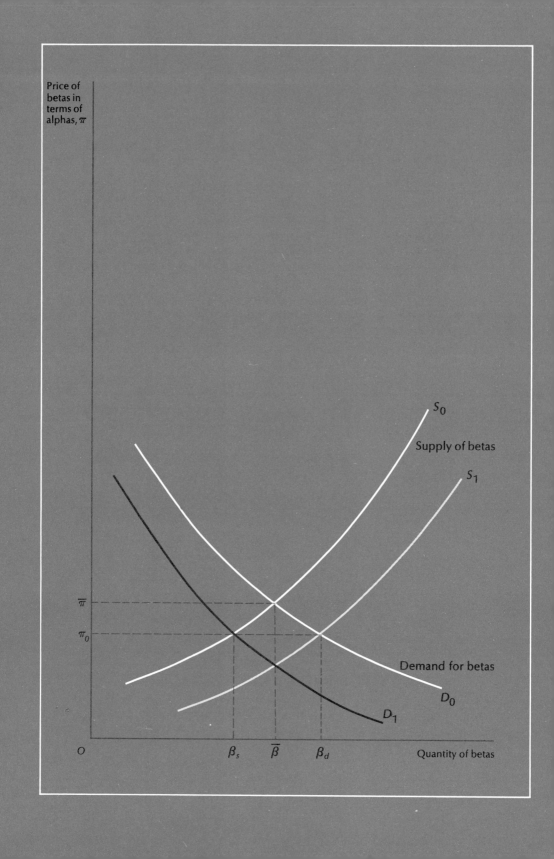

foregoing policies is very attractive. Deflationary fiscal policies lower the level of income and employment in A and are therefore clearly undesirable. Restrictive monetary policy will tend to have the same effects, and because such a policy will work primarily through reducing investment, it may lower the rate of capital accumulation and growth. And if this reduces the rate at which productivity advances, the long-range effects of the policy may be to put A into a progressively less favorable competitive position and ultimately to aggravate the balance of payments problem.

A further unfortunate aspect of the international monetary system as it has evolved since World War II is that a balance of payments problem is nearly always viewed as a problem to be dealt with exclusively by the deficit country which is usually told to "clean its house." Balance of payments disequilibrium, however, is a problem for all countries. In a rational world country B would not continue to tolerate an indefinite surplus for the simple reason that to do so would mean that it was perpetually giving away more goods and services to A than it received. It ought therefore to be in the interests of both countries to seek an end to imbalance. In practice, however, B will rarely assist A in dealing with the problem since to do so would involve permitting a certain amount of domestic inflation and thereby deliberately placing its own exporters at a competitive disadvantage. The citizens of B would be better off if A were not being perennially subsidized; however, the business firms in B would be less profitable, and it is the latter consideration that generally influences the direction of policy.

The effect of placing the adjustment burden entirely on the shoulders of A is to inflict a larger degree of unemployment and deflation on A than would otherwise be necessary; because of this asymmetrical, or one-sided, aspect of the present system, many economists regard it as a system that imposes a deflationary bias upon the world economy.

Third, in order to avert deflation, country A might attempt to close the gap between the demand for and the supply of foreign exchange by pursuing restrictive trade policies. Country A may impose a tariff on B's goods; it may set import quotas; it may subsidize exports; it may impose discriminatory taxes on the overseas earnings of her residents; it may impose restrictions on the uses to which certain alpha holdings may be put; and it may allow the deficit to affect its foreign policy by causing it to reduce or discontinue foreign aid and to restrict

Figure 14–2   Eliminating excess demand
for foreign exchange

its military commitments. Most economists oppose the resort to restrictive policies because such policies inhibit the free flow of resources, of goods and services, and of capital, and they therefore produce inefficient resource allocation and reduce real income throughout the world. These policies, moreover, are really hidden forms of selective devaluation, and since they are selective and discriminatory, they distort the allocation of resources and impair economic efficiency. Domestic producers are sheltered from foreign competition, capital fails to flow into areas of maximum productive use, and consumers are denied access to better and cheaper foreign goods.

To summarize: We have seen so far that a system of fixed exchange rates tends to be unstable because it encourages speculative activity that worsens balance of payments disequilibrium. Second, the system may force countries to pursue monetary-fiscal policies that are undesirable from the point of view of domestic employment goals. Third, the system tends to impose a net deflationary bias upon the world economy because it places the burden of adjustment entirely upon the shoulders of the deficit country. Finally, the system encourages the adoption of restrictive policies that inhibit the flow of trade and resources. These policies promote productive inefficiency, misallocate resources and therefore reduce real income and welfare.

Given all these drawbacks, one wonders why country A's central bank does not simply stop selling gold and foreign exchange at a fixed price and, instead, simply allow the exchange rate to fluctuate.[1] There appears, indeed, to be an increasing number of economists who feel that this would be the only sensible course of action. However, before we can properly appraise the alternatives, we need to take a closer look at the theory of balance of payments adjustment under fixed exchange rates and at the effect of monetary and fiscal policies in raising the level of income under the alternatives of fixed and floating exchange rates.

---

[1] Of course it takes two to "flex." If country B wants to maintain the existing exchange rate, it can do so by engaging in exchange stabilization operations. However, with its currency undervalued it would have to continue to accumulate alphas indefinitely, and there would be little to be gained from such a policy. Meanwhile, the pressure on A is relieved since it no longer needs to supply the excess demand for betas, having placed this burden on B's monetary authority. Moreover, A is now in an optimum position because with the overvalued exchange rate it not only can sustain an import surplus, which implies that it is obtaining a subsidy from B in the form of a net balance of goods and services over and above what is paid for by exports, but it further implies that A is able to exchange its goods on far more favorable terms than would be possible were its currency not overvalued.

14–3 AUTOMATIC MECHANISMS OF ADJUSTMENT
UNDER FIXED EXCHANGE RATES

The picture, under fixed exchange rates, may not be quite as bleak as it was painted in the last section, for balance of payments disequilibrium will set off corrective forces that automatically tend to eliminate deficits and surpluses. Suppose, for example, that the balance of payments is initially in equilibrium and that a deficit is caused by a shift to the right of the demand curve for foreign exchange that occurs because of a change in consumer tastes in country A. The resulting trade imbalance will be financed by a capital movement that will have the effect of reducing the domestic money supply in A and increasing the domestic money supply in B. As a consequence, interest rates will rise in A and fall in B, and the interest rate differential will produce a reverse flow that will tend to offset the increased demand for betas by raising their supply.

However, there will be another and probably much more important mechanism at work. As B's exports rise, the level of income in B will rise, first in the export industries and then throughout the economy as a result of secondary induced effects. The increase in income will cause consumption to rise and, since part of the added goods will be bought from abroad, will cause the level of imports to rise. In country A, since consumer tastes have shifted from domestic to foreign goods, there will be a decline in domestic income and therefore in consumption and in imports from B. Thus income changes cause B to increase its imports and A to decrease its imports, and these offset a part of the initial imbalance.

Direct income effects will not, in general, produce complete offsets to balance of payments disturbances. If investment, government purchases, and taxes are constant, an autonomous increase in exports from country B of ΔX_e due to a change in tastes in country A will produce three induced effects in country B. First, the increase in income in country B will cause imports to rise by some amount ΔZ_i; second, the increase in income will cause saving to increase by some amount ΔS_i; and third, the fall in income in A due to the original diversion of expenditures from domestic production to goods produced in B will cause a fall in A's imports, and therefore in B's exports, by some quantity ΔX_i. If the level of income in country B is to reach an equilibrium level, the change in injections must be equal to the change in leakages. Consequently, it must be the case for country B that

$$\Delta X_e - \Delta X_i - \Delta Z_i = \Delta S_i \qquad (14\text{–}1)$$

where the subscripts e and i stand for exogenous and induced, respectively.

The left side of the equation is the net change in the balance of payments surplus, which must equal the change in saving if equilibrium is to be restored. Further, since B's export surplus must equal A's import surplus, it follows that saving in A must change by an equal amount (though in the opposite direction) as saving in B.

It is evident from Eq. (14–1) that if the initial increase in the exports of country B is to be offset by the induced increase in imports and reduction in exports, the net change in saving in both countries must be zero. This means that complete offset will take place only if the marginal propensity to save in one of the two countries is zero. Furthermore, since there would be no change in saving in either country, the country with the zero marginal propensity to save will undergo the entire burden of income adjustment while the income in the other country will remain unaffected. If the marginal propensity to save in country A is equal to zero, the autonomous increase in its imports (B's exports) will lower the income level in A by an amount that induces a fall in imports of exactly the same amount as the initial increase. Income in country B will therefore remain constant, and there will be no induced change in B's imports. Consequently, Eq. (14–1) reduces to

$$\Delta X_e - \Delta X_i = 0$$

On the other hand, if the marginal propensity to save in country B is zero, the autonomous increase in B's exports will increase income to the point where imports rise by exactly the amount of the original autonomous change in exports, so that income in A will remain constant. In this case Eq. (14–1) becomes

$$\Delta X_e - \Delta Z_i = 0$$

Since the marginal propensities to save cannot, in general, be expected to equal zero, we conclude that direct income effects will not yield complete adjustment of the balance of payments and that both countries will be subject to income changes as the consequence of autonomous changes in the balance of payments.

In the foregoing discussion we examined the effect of a transfer of autonomous expenditures from one country to another, and we found that this will cause income to rise in B and to fall in A. If, instead, we were to assume that total autonomous expenditure increased because of an increase in government purchases in A, we should find that both countries would enjoy an increase in income. The increased government purchases in A would raise consumer spending, which would raise the level of imports and create a balance of payments deficit. As a consequence, B's exports would rise and so therefore would its level of income. The increase in B's income would raise B's imports, which would serve to reduce somewhat the balance of payments deficit.

Even if the exchange rate between A and B is chronically out of line and A's balance of payments deficit persists, there still remains an automatic mechanism that will continue to work in the direction of adjustment. As long as A's central bank is able to sell B's currency in exchange for its own, the domestic supply of alphas will decrease continuously while the domestic supply of betas increases. Consequently, there will be a persistent tendency for interest rates to rise in A and to fall in B, and this will tend to dampen economic activity in A and to stimulate it in B. Thus, provided that these effects are not neutralized by counteracting monetary policies, there will be some continuous tendency for the balance of payments to adjust as long as it remains out of equilibrium.

Even though there are automatic mechanisms at work that tend to bring the balance of payments into equilibrium under fixed exchange rates, these automatic mechanisms produce the same kinds of undesirable effects for the economies of the respective countries as would have occurred had the adjustments been effected through the application of monetary and fiscal policies. The deficit country will tend to suffer from deflation, and the surplus country will tend to suffer from inflation. Worse still, the surplus country can use its policy weapons to counteract the expansionary tendencies that the automatic mechanisms produce, and such policies can neutralize the automatic mechanisms and inflict a higher level of unemployment on the deficit country than would have been necessary had the automatic mechanisms been allowed to work. It is therefore hard to escape the conclusion that fixed exchange rates tend to impose a rather severe cost in terms of domestic instability upon the countries of the world economy.

14–4 FIXED AND FLEXIBLE EXCHANGE RATES AND STABILIZATION POLICY

Flexible exchange rates hold particular appeal for those who prefer to use monetary rather than fiscal policy as the primary instrument of domestic economic stabilization. Flexible exchange rates tend to create economies that must rely for stabilization of income and employment primarily upon monetary policy, while fixed exchange rates imply that income and employment cannot be changed significantly except by fiscal policy.[1]

In order to draw the comparison as strictly as possible, let us assume that country A is so small relative to B (the rest of the world) that changes in the domestic money supply in A have virtually no effect on the level of interest rates elsewhere. Assume, in addition, that capital movements always operate in such a way as to equalize interest rates. Given these assumptions, we first inquire into the effects on the level of income in A of monetary and fiscal policies under conditions of fixed exchange rates. After this we shall inquire into the effects of these policies under flexible exchange rates.

If country A suffers from unemployment and its monetary authority augments the domestic money supply in order to raise domestic investment, any fall in the rate of interest that takes place will immediately cause investors to seek the relatively more profitable opportunities that now exist abroad. Consequently, investors will attempt to convert securities of country A into securities of country B. The conversion process raises the demand for betas, and, in a free foreign exchange market, this would tend to depress the price of alphas relative to betas. However, because A's monetary authority is committed to the maintenance of a fixed exchange rate, A itself must supply the added demand for betas by buying back its own currency in exchange for the excess demand for betas. This means that the attempt to increase the domestic money supply will fail. In fact, A's monetary authority will find that it has done no more than to purchase securities in exchange for betas. The stock of domestic money in A therefore remains the same as before; the interest rate and the level of income are the same; and B's rather than A's money supply is augmented.

The total world money supply is, of course, increased by A's policy and some slight increase in world income might result. However, the effects as far as country A is concerned are largely dissipated by capital mobility, and it is therefore fair to conclude, as a first approximation, that monetary policy under conditions of fixed exchange rates and perfect capital mobility will be ineffective. Moreover, expansionary monetary policy will have the added disadvantage of causing country A's foreign exchange reserves to be depleted.

An attempt by A to raise her level of domestic income and employ-

---

[1] The discussion of this section is based on Robert Mundell, "Capital Mobility and Stabilization Policy under Fixed and Flexible Exchange Rates," *Canadian Journal of Economics and Political Science*, 29:475–485, 1963.

ment by means of fiscal policy is considerably more promising. If A raises its level of government spending, this will tend to have a multiplied effect on its level of income unless, of course, the policy has the effect of raising interest rates and thereby reducing investment. However, in an "open" economy such an offset is not likely to occur because if domestic interest rates rise, there will be a capital inflow that will tend to raise the price of alphas relative to betas. Because A's monetary authority must now *buy* foreign exchange in exchange for domestic money, the money supply in A will rise. Because this process of buying foreign exchange in return for domestic money must continue as long as there is any pressure on the exchange rate, the money supply must expand by exactly enough to produce a new equilibrium at the *original* rate of interest. Since this means that the level of domestic investment will be the same as before, it follows that income will rise by the full multiplied amount of the increase in government purchases.

When the assumptions are altered and it is assumed that exchange rates are permitted to fluctuate freely, a completely opposite set of conclusions emerges. Suppose again that country A tries to raise the level of employment by increasing the domestic money supply. Because of a temporary interest rate differential, a capital outflow materializes. Because this raises the price of betas relative to alphas, A's exports become cheaper and its imports become more expensive. The effect of this is to raise A's level of exports, to reduce its imports, and these simultaneous developments raise the level of domestic income and employment. Because the rate of interest will not be restored to its original level until the added money balances are all taken up by additional transactions requirements, we conclude, as in the classical model, that the domestic level of income will rise in proportion to the increase in the money supply.

Finally, let us consider the effects of an expansionary fiscal policy under flexible exchange rates. Country A increases its level of government purchases, thereby causing interest rates in country A to rise. However, the resultant capital inflow raises the price of alphas relative to betas. This, however, makes A's exports more expensive and her imports less expensive, and this tends, in turn, to offset the expansionary effects of the increase in government purchases. Since the rate of interest must return to its original level (otherwise the exchange rate would continue to appreciate) and since the domestic money supply will be the same as before, the volume of transactions must be the same, and the increase in government purchases must, therefore, be exactly offset by a deterioration in the trade balance.

A useful way to summarize the argument is to illustrate the various alternatives by using the *IS-LM* model. Consider Figure 14–3 by means of which all four cases can be illustrated. Assume that Y_0 is the original level of income in country A and that i_w is the world interest rate. Assume first that the exchange rate is fixed and that the monetary authority in A attempts to expand the money supply in such a way as to shift the *LM* curve to LM_1 and thereby to raise the level of income. Since this action will depress the interest rate in A, a capital outflow will take place and tend to reduce the price of alphas in terms of betas. This situation will force the monetary authority to sell foreign exchange, and since this means that the domestic money supply is shrinking, the *LM* curve must be shifting back to the left. Since capital outflows will continue as long as the domestic rate of interest is below i_w, we conclude that the money supply will decline until the *LM* curve shifts back to LM_0 which means that the level of income will be the same as before.

Next assume that a fiscal policy shifts the *IS* curve to IS_1. This policy tends to raise the rate of interest above i_w. However, since this implies that there will be a capital inflow, the monetary authority must buy foreign exchange in return for domestic money. Consequently, the money supply increases, and the *LM* curve shifts to the right. Because the money supply must continue to increase as long as the domestic interest rate is in excess of i_w, we conclude that final equilibrium is established at income level Y_1 which indicates that the increase in government purchases yields a full multiplied effect on the level of income.

The same diagram can be used to illustrate the effects of monetary and fiscal policy under flexible exchange rates. A's monetary authority increases the money supply, and the *LM* curve therefore shifts to LM_1. The resultant reduction in the domestic rate of interest produces a capital outflow and causes A's exchange rate to depreciate. But since this means that exports will increase and that imports will decline, the *IS* curve must now shift to the right. Because equilibrium is not restored until i_w is reestablished, we conclude that the exchange rate must depreciate by exactly enough to shift *IS* to IS_1.

Finally, if A increases its level of government purchases and thereby shifts *IS* to IS_1, interest rates tend to rise, thereby producing a capital inflow. Since this means that A's exchange rate rises, exports become more expensive, imports become cheaper, and the *IS* curve therefore shifts back until eventually the original rightward shift is exactly offset by the deterioration in the trade balance.

This discussion has, of course, oversimplified the issues. However,

Figure 14–3   Monetary and fiscal policy under fixed and flexible exchange rates

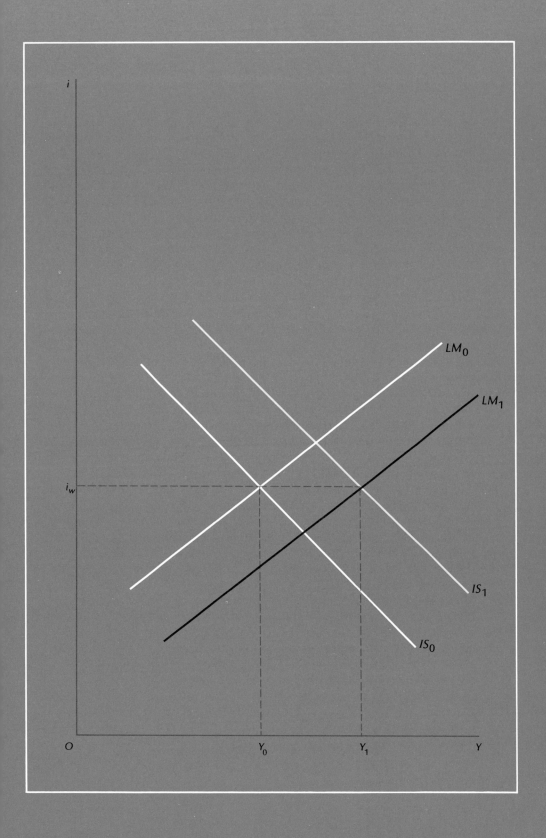

as before, we find it useful to delineate the extremes as starkly as possible in order to understand better the relevant intermediate cases. The main point of the discussion has been to suggest that the effects of various stabilization policies depend upon international as well as upon domestic conditions. In the extreme cases outlined here it appears that, in a policy sense, economies tend to be Keynesian (fiscal policy) economies under fixed exchange rates and that they tend to be classical (monetary policy) economies under flexible exchange rates. The results would have to be modified if we assume that capital mobility is less than perfect and if we considered more general cases that did not involve the assumption of a small country or a country with a large foreign sector. Nevertheless, the direction in which domestic policy tends to be biased by the nature of international monetary arrangements is clear. And it is, perhaps, useful to pause to adapt the discussion to the contemporary scene.

It has been customary to state, in appraising the American economy of the 1960s, that the direction of monetary policy has necessarily been dictated by balance of payments considerations while domestic stabilization has had to be pursued by means of fiscal policy. Given a fixed exchange rate, expansionary monetary policy would have produced capital outflows and would thereby have increased the pressure on the balance of payments. Thus it has generally been maintained that monetary policy should have been tight enough to guard against domestic and foreign interest rate differentials that would have produced an outflow of capital. If, in the face of these conditions, the economy suffers from a deflationary gap, as in fact it did, the gap should then be closed by fiscal policy, as it eventually was. Expansionary monetary policy tends to lower interest rates and produce capital outflows, while expansionary fiscal policy tends to do the opposite, and this is what accounts for the foregoing rule of thumb.

Some economists find this rule uncomfortable if not altogether objectionable. For one thing, if it is necessary to maintain excessively high interest rates, investment will be at lower than desired levels, and this may be inimical to rapid growth.[1] Other economists take a less pessimistic view and suggest that the dampening effect of high interest rates on investment may be offset by the introduction of various stimulants such as investment tax credits and accelerated depreciation.[2] Still other

[1] J. Tobin, "Europe and the Dollar," Review of Economics and Statistics, 46:123–126, 1964.

[2] W. L. Smith, "Are There Enough Policy Tools," American Economic Review, 55:208–220, 1965.

economists prefer to deal with the problem by abandoning fixed exchange rates.[1] There is, finally, a group who would probably prefer flexible exchange rates but who do not advocate this course of action because they fear that governments would not, in practice, refrain from interfering in the foreign exchange market or because they feel, given the way in which monetary policy has been conducted in the United States, that it is probably just as well that present international monetary arrangements keep monetary policy from having any real bite.

We must not lose sight of the main point. We have seen in this section that under flexible exchange rates monetary policy would become the primary and most effective means of stabilizing the level of domestic income and employment. However, we have also seen that stability, if obtained through monetary policy in conjunction with flexible exchange rates, would come at the price of severe fluctuations in the level of exports and imports. In an economy in which exports and imports are an insignificant fraction of total activity, this cost might be worth paying. However, in open economies where a large fraction of the nation's economic activity is directly linked to its foreign sector, instability of exports and imports necessarily implies overall instability, and for such economies flexible exchange rates would certainly not be an unmixed blessing.

14-5 FLEXIBLE EXCHANGE RATES

Countries A and B could abandon the whole idea of maintaining an official exchange rate, and they could effect such a decision simply by refraining from any further sales of gold and foreign exchange at fixed prices. If they decided upon this course as a permanent policy, they would find, first of all, that there would be no further balance of payments deficits or surpluses and that there would therefore be no need to deliberately destabilize their respective economies in order to stabilize the exchange rate. As an added set of advantages, they would find that there would be no further need to use valuable resources for the purpose of mining, refining, storing, guarding, and transporting such an inherently worthless commodity as gold. The gain in real income from these economies alone would be substantial. And in addition, the holders of gold, many of whom spend their time and talent engaged in the kind of speculative activities that exacerbate balance of payments

[1] One of the most forceful proponents of flexible exchange rates is Milton Friedman. See "The Case for Flexible Exchange Rates," in Friedman's *Essays in Positive Economics,* The University of Chicago Press, Chicago, 1953, pp. 157–203.

crises, might be obliged to turn their energies toward the pursuit of socially useful economic activities.

Although the abandonment of a policy of fixed exchange rates would bring about many of the happy consequences described above, enough new problems would be created by flexible exchange rates to make the desirability of their adoption considerably less than clear cut.

There is, first, the problem that the foreign exchange market may be dynamically unstable. By this we mean that if equilibrium is disturbed, the nature of the reacting forces will tend to widen the disequilibrium continuously rather than to correct it.

To illustrate this potential source of difficulty, suppose that instead of allowing the exchange rate to fluctuate freely, country A devalues her currency in order to reduce or eliminate her balance of payments deficit. The immediate effect of this policy is to increase the number of alphas that A's importers will have to pay in order to acquire goods from B. As far as the importers are concerned, the effect of the devaluation is to raise their costs. This will cause prices (in terms of alphas) to rise, and this, in turn, reduces the quantity of imported goods that the citizens of A will buy. Since this means that the overall demand for B's goods declines, the prices of these goods (evaluated in terms of betas) decline, and it therefore follows that country A will not only buy fewer units of goods from B but will also pay less in the form of betas (though more in terms of alphas) and that country A's foreign exchange expenditures will be reduced by devaluation. Or, to put the matter in terms of the demand for foreign exchange, the demand curve cannot possibly have a positive slope.[1]

Although it appears that a devaluation of A's currency will ensure that the quantity of betas demanded will decline, there is no guarantee that the supply of betas will increase. When the price of alphas declines, importers in country B find that a smaller quantity of betas than before is needed to purchase A's goods, and it therefore pays them to offer imports for sale at a lower beta price. Although this will increase the consumption of imports, there is no guarantee that the total quantity of

---

[1] If A's demand for B's goods is perfectly inelastic, the rise in the alpha price of these goods as a result of devaluation will not reduce consumption. Since producers in B will therefore observe no fall in demand, the beta price will remain the same. Consequently, in this extreme case the quantity purchased will remain the same as will the per unit beta price, and the demand curve for foreign exchange will be vertical. However, this is the most extreme case possible. Provided that a rise in the alpha price of imports reduces consumption of imports, the demand curve for betas must be negatively sloped.

betas spent on imports will increase since the increased quantity purchased comes about because the beta price of the goods falls. If the elasticity of demand for A's goods is greater than unity, the percentage fall in the beta price of the goods will be less than the percentage rise in quantity sold; the total amount of betas spent will increase, and so will the supply of foreign exchange to A. On the other hand, if B's demand for the goods of A is inelastic, total beta expenditures decline, the supply curve of foreign exchange would be negatively sloped, and A would find that it actually earns fewer betas even though it has made its goods cheaper to the citizens of B and that it is exporting a larger physical quantity of goods.

The problem is illustrated in Figure 14–4. The supply curve of foreign exchange will bend backwards if the elasticity of demand for A's exports (B's elasticity of demand for imports) is less than unity. Both π_1 and π_2 are equilibrium exchange rates. But if the official exchange rate is at π_3, there is excess demand for foreign exchange, and a devaluation by country A to π_4, which is intended to correct the situation, would merely increase the level of excess demand. Similarly, if exchange rates are flexible, any disturbance that would raise π above π_2 would create excess demand rather than excess supply, and this would cause the exchange rate to continue rising and at an even faster rate.

Many economists belittle the notion that the foreign exchange market is unstable. Others take the possibility seriously. Empirical research has been unable to settle the issue because there are simply too many variables at work to permit any accurate identification of the elasticity of demand for exports. The problem of measurement, moreover, is complicated by the fact that the measured values of the elasticities vary with the time unit chosen. It takes time for markets to adjust to changes in exchange rates, and elasticities tend therefore to be very low in the short run and to increase when sufficient time is allowed to permit adjustment to the new situation. Our own feeling about the matter is that the risk of instability is minor. Similar arguments could be made about the stability of equilibrium in any market one wishes to pick, and it seems to us that there is no decisive reason why the foreign exchange market should be singled out as a particular place in which dynamic instability is likely to be present.

Although the foreign exchange market may not be inherently unstable, there are those who believe it can be made so by the activities of speculators. We saw before that the threat of a fall in the price of alphas would cause speculators to exacerbate the situation by selling off their alphas. But now we have to be careful to distinguish between

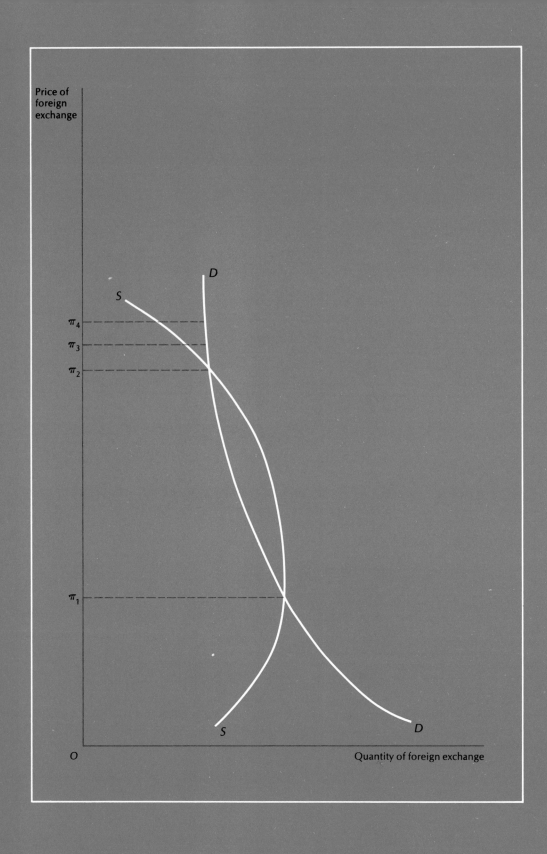

the effect of speculation under conditions of a definitive, controlled devaluation as opposed to its effect under fluctuating exchange rates.

When governments peg exchange rates and only change them under duress, they create an environment in which speculators cannot lose. Speculators who anticipate the devaluation of alphas and therefore swap their holdings of alphas for betas act to aggravate the shortage of betas, and they therefore help bring on the devaluation that otherwise might have been avoided. If then devaluation actually takes place, the speculators will make a substantial gain. The worst that can happen from the speculator's point of view is that devaluation does not take place and that he therefore merely breaks even. The dice, in short, are loaded in favor of speculators who are betting against a monetary authority that guarantees to behave in such a way as to reward them for creating a balance of payments crisis.

However, under flexible exchange rates speculators who habitually regard a price change as a signal that prices will continue to change in the same direction are eventually going to be bankrupt. Such speculators will, on balance, find themselves selling cheap and buying dear, and such a policy is a poor way to realize gains. If we therefore assume that speculators generally know what they are doing, we also have to be prepared to believe that high prices will induce selling and that low prices will induce buying and, if this is the case, that speculation is stabilizing and helps restore market equilibrium. As long as there is no assurance that the central bank will attempt to stabilize the exchange rate, speculators are left to their own devices, and if they act rationally, they will help stabilize the market. It is when the government enters the picture and allows itself to be panicked into supporting a declining exchange rate that speculation is most likely to become destabilizing.

The greatest difficulty that flexible exchange rates would create is the likelihood that the volume of exports and imports would be subject to far greater variations than under fixed exchange rates, and this, for a country with a large foreign sector, will produce serious internal instability. Earlier we saw that under flexible exchange rates an increase in the money supply would raise income because it increases the level of exports and reduces the level of imports. Similarly, an increase in government purchases would fail to raise income because the government purchase increase would be offset by an equivalent decrease in net exports (exports minus imports). To bring the point home clearly, let us consider the following examples.

Figure 14–4   Illustration of an unstable
foreign exchange market

Suppose that the United States is in the midst of a recession and that the Federal Reserve increases the money supply by purchasing government bonds on the open market. As a result of this policy, interest rates in the United States decline and capital flows abroad. This causes the dollar to depreciate relative to guilders. Because Dutch goods therefore become relatively more expensive, Dutch exports decline, and deflation and unemployment are inflicted on the Dutch economy. The net effect of the United States monetary policy is merely to export United States unemployment to Holland. Whether there is any overall net gain in world employment depends upon whether there are differences in the spending propensities of the different countries and upon whether the policy lowers interest rates throughout the world and upon whether this has any beneficial effects on investment.

As another example, imagine an economy whose agricultural sector relies heavily upon export markets and whose industrial sector is undergoing an inflationary investment boom. Suppose that the monetary authority acts to slow down the investment boom by raising interest rates. The resultant capital inflow causes the exchange rate to rise, and the agricultural sector suddenly finds itself unable to export its produce. Flexible exchange rates, as these examples suggest, can hardly be viewed as the definitive answer to all international monetary problems.

14–6 THE OPTIMUM CURRENCY AREA

The traditional case for fixed exchange rates is very similar to the case for a uniform currency within a country. Imagine trying to run a complicated manufacturing operation in Ohio when each input of materials, of labor, and of capital is valued, not in dollars, but in terms of so many chickens, pigs, and cows. And imagine further that, instead of writing checks or paying cash, we had to maintain a supply of assorted kinds of livestock, various combinations of which we shipped to Minnesota in return for iron ore, to West Virginia for coal, and to California for electronic equipment. One needs scarcely belabor the point that a uniform currency which serves as an accepted means of payment, a standard of value, and a means through which contracts for deferred payments can be made is essential if an economy is to function efficiently.

Now imagine that each state has its own monetary unit and that the monetary units of Ohio, West Virginia, and Minnesota were known, respectively, as buckeyes, W-V's, and gophers. Although the exchange of one currency for another will involve a waste of resources due to the need for added banking and brokerage services, the presence of several currencies will cause no serious difficulties for our Ohio enterprise if it can always pay its bills with buckeyes and if some kind of arrangement exists whereby the ore producers in Minnesota are paid in gophers and the West Virginia coal producers are paid in W-V's. It is, in fact, exactly this kind of situation that the international monetary system has been designed to create. And, indeed, the system will work fairly well as long as the value of the demands by Minnesota producers and consumers for goods and services from other states equals the value of the corresponding demands for Minnesota goods and services from the other states. Under such conditions there would be no net accumulation of claims by any state against any other state.

This system encounters trouble when one of the regions falls on evil days. Imagine that electric and petroleum power are developed as competitive sources of power and that the demand for coal therefore declines. West Virginia could more readily adjust to this misfortune if the price of coal were flexible and if coal miners were willing to accept lower wages. However, if prices and wages are downwardly rigid, West Virginia will be unable to maintain her exports of coal and will suffer both from a regional balance of payments deficit and from unemployment. Provided that the price of W-V's is maintained on a rigid parity with respect to the other currencies, West Virginia's economy will continue to suffer from unemployment, and it will not escape from this situation until its workers migrate to other regions, until methods are developed to make coal once again competitive, or until its government embarks on a public works program designed to put the unemployed miners to work. However, in the last case its demand for imports will remain high, and it will continue to run a balance of payments deficit. Since it will ultimately run out of its supply of buckeyes and gophers, West Virginia will either have to devalue its currency, abandon its public works policy, or impose controls designed to force West Virginia citizens to "buy at home."

Much of West Virginia's difficulty seems to be due to the fact that costs and prices are inflexible. Had coal prices fallen and had wages declined in West Virginia, its competitive position could have been maintained and unemployment could have been averted. It therefore appears that rigid exchange rates or a unified national monetary system might have worked fairly well if wages and prices had been flexible.

Suppose now that West Virginia abandons its attempt to maintain its currency on an even par with other currencies, and suppose also that the other states make no attempt to fix the price of W-V's in terms of their own currencies. The decline in the demand for coal reduces the demand for W-V's and their price falls relative to buckeyes and other state currencies. The effect of this is to make W-V's cheaper in terms of buckeyes, and this means that West Virginia coal becomes cheaper to Ohio manufacturing enterprises. This also means that the incentive to substitute other sources of power is reduced. Consequently, and this is the key circumstance to bear in mind, fluctuations in the rate of exchange between currencies serve as a substitute for cost-price flexibility.

We have now seen that fluctuating exchange rates produce the same kinds of adjustments that would occur under fixed exchange rates with flexible wages and prices. Given the fact that prices and wages are in fact rigid, it would seem to be desirable to allow exchange rates to vary. However, does this mean that each state should have its own monetary unit and that exchange rates should fluctuate between states? What is true of part of West Virginia may not be true for West Virginia as a whole. Some counties in Ohio may be as seriously affected by a decline in the demand for coal as counties in West Virginia. Within those counties the coal miners may be affected while other persons and enterprises are not. Should we then have fluctuating exchange rates between each state in the nation, between each county in each state, between each township in each county, or, indeed, between each individual economic unit?

To bring the argument to its logical end, imagine that each economic unit in the economy has the power to issue its own currency and that the currencies exchange freely, each one for all of the several million others. Assume next that a producer of horse-drawn carriages determines, in the face of competition from the automobile, to hold his ground and to maintain the price of the obsolete commodity he produces. Under a uniform currency he would quickly lose sales as the automobile made inroads, and his workers, possessed of specialized skills that are not immediately adaptable to other work, would suffer unemployment. However, if our refractory manufacturer were able to issue his own currency, the decline in his sales would produce excess supply for his currency relative to other currencies. The value of his currency would decline, and the cost of buggies would be automatically reduced to the holders of other currencies.

For the workers in the buggy industry this latter alternative is clearly preferable. The incidence of unemployment would be lower, and the transition to changing economic conditions would be more smoothly effected. However, the economy as a whole would be at a virtual standstill, for to permit each unit in the economy to issue its own currency would be to create a situation identical to a pure barter form of economic organization.

To summarize the argument: Efficiency of production and exchange benefit from the presence of a uniform currency over as wide an area as possible. On the other hand, such a system of a uniform monetary unit makes the economy less adaptable to economic change. The degree to which this is true depends upon the degree to which costs and prices are characterized by rigidity. To give small economic units the power to issue their own currencies and to let those currencies fluctuate in value relative to other currencies would minimize the impact of cost-price rigidity because exchange rate variations serve as substitutes for cost-price variations. However, the gains of such added flexibility must be weighed against the costs of forsaking the advantages of a uniform currency.

Considering the advantages and disadvantages that characterize the extremes, the economist naturally looks for an optimum somewhere in the middle. Optimum currency areas would be those areas within which uniform currencies should prevail and between which exchange rates should be permitted to fluctuate. Thus far the theorizing on the subject has failed to provide a prescription of how the world should be divided. One can, however, assert with little risk of being wrong that theoretically optimum currency areas will have small probability of coinciding with national boundaries.

PART
THREE

GROWTH AND FLUCTUATIONS IN ECONOMIC ACTIVITY

15

INTRODUCTION TO MACROECONOMIC DYNAMICS

15–1 INTRODUCTION

We are now about to embark on a discussion of problems that economists call "dynamic" in contrast to the "static" analysis of Part 2. Our first task is to inquire into the meaning of these terms. One general rule among many economists is that a "dynamic" model is a "good" model, whereas a "static" model, the kind other people invent, is a "bad" one. Unhappily, this definition will not suffice for our purposes.

A broad and rather loose notion of a dynamic model is one in which time becomes introduced as an explicit variable. Now that we are about to consider the determinants of the rate of growth of the economy, it is obvious that we have to know over what period of time the economy grows by a certain percent. Similarly, during inflation the price level, by definition, is not in equilibrium; it is, rather, changing at some rate per unit time. If we were told that the price level had risen by 10 percent, we might be bored, mildly concerned, or downright panic-stricken, depending upon whether the 10 percent increase had taken place over a period of a century, a decade, or a year. It goes without saying that the study of business cycles—the ups and downs in economic activity—is also a dynamic problem.

Except for the multiplier process of Chapter 5, the models of Part 2 are "comparative static" models. The solutions to the equation systems define equilibrium values for the variables. For example, a shift in one of the functions due to a change in the money supply or government expenditures causes the equations to give a new equilibrium point as a solution. The models did not make explicit the process by which the variables of the system move to the new equilibrium. We did, to be sure, discuss the process of adjustment from one equilibrium to the next, but the various adjustment processes were in no way implied by the equations themselves. The models would have been truly dynamic only if the equations had specified how the variables would behave when the system is out of equilibrium.

If we were reasonably sure that an increase in the money supply would lower the rate of interest and raise the level of income to a new equilibrium level, as implied by the models of Part 2, and if we were not particularly concerned about how long it took to get to the new equilibrium point, there would be no pressing reason to complicate our comparative static models by specifying exactly how adjustments to disequilibrium take place. Unfortunately, however, we cannot always be sure that the equilibrium solutions predicted by comparative static models will be correct. The equilibria may be "unstable"; i.e., if the variables of the system happen to be at the equilibrium point, they will tend to stay there. But should the equilibrium be disrupted by some disturbance, a progressive divergence from, rather than a movement toward, the equilibrium point will occur. Thus the comparative static solutions may be erroneous. For example, although an increase in the money supply leads our models of Part 2 to predict a rise in income and a fall in the rate of interest, this may not occur. The changes may, in fact, move in a direction opposite to that predicted by the static model.

As a starting point for our discussion of dynamics, let us set forth the following fundamental proposition: It is frequently impossible to determine the effect of a shift of the *IS*, the *LM*, or any other function

Figure 15–1   Product market equilibrium
(all values in real terms)

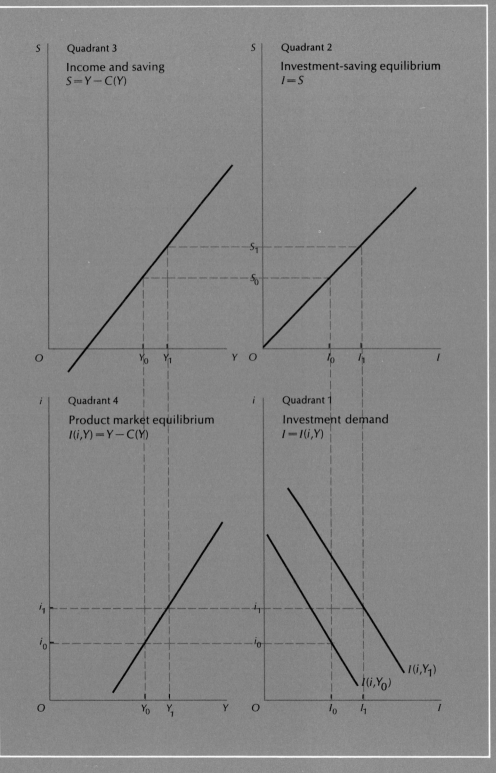

Quadrant 3

Income and saving
$S = Y - C(Y)$

Quadrant 2

Investment-saving equilibrium
$I = S$

Quadrant 4

Product market equilibrium
$I(i,Y) = Y - C(Y)$

Quadrant 1

Investment demand
$I = I(i,Y)$

$I(i,Y_1)$

$I(i,Y_0)$

for that matter, in a comparative static model without examining the underlying dynamic process of adjustment. This proposition, developed by P. A. Samuelson[1] and called the "correspondence principle," is the subject of the analysis of this chapter.

15–2 DYNAMIC ADJUSTMENT AND THE *IS-LM* MODEL

Throughout Part 2 we assumed that the investment demand equation was $I = I(i)$. However, in Chapter 7 we took note of the fact that it might be reasonable to write

$$I = I(i,Y)$$

The inclusion of the level of income as an independent variable in the investment demand equation does not at first seem like much of a change. But, as we shall see, it introduces some formidable and intriguing new problems.

With the new investment demand function the equation for the *IS* schedule becomes

$$I(i,Y) = Y - C(Y) \tag{15-1}$$

The first thing we must notice is that the *IS* schedule is no longer necessarily negatively sloped. Recall from Chapter 7 that with the new investment demand equation there will be a whole family of investment demand curves in quadrant 1. Thus in Figure 15–1 income Y_0 is associated with investment demand schedule $I(i,Y_0)$. Consequently, interest rate i_0 equates intended investment and saving at income level Y_0. Similarly, when the level of income is Y_1, the relevant investment demand schedule is $I(i,Y_1)$, so that by tracing around the four quadrants, we observe that interest rate i_1 gives product market equilibrium.

In the present example the *IS* schedule has a positive slope, although the slope may also be negative. If we define h as the "marginal propensity to invest," i.e., the increase in investment that is induced by a $1 increase in income, the *IS* curve will have a positive slope if h is greater than the marginal propensity to save and a negative slope if the reverse is the case. Let us see why this is so.

[1] P. A. Samuelson, *Foundations of Economic Analysis*, Chap. 9, Harvard University Press, Cambridge, Mass., 1947, especially pp. 276–283.

Figure 15–2 Dynamic adjustment: case 1
(all values in real terms)

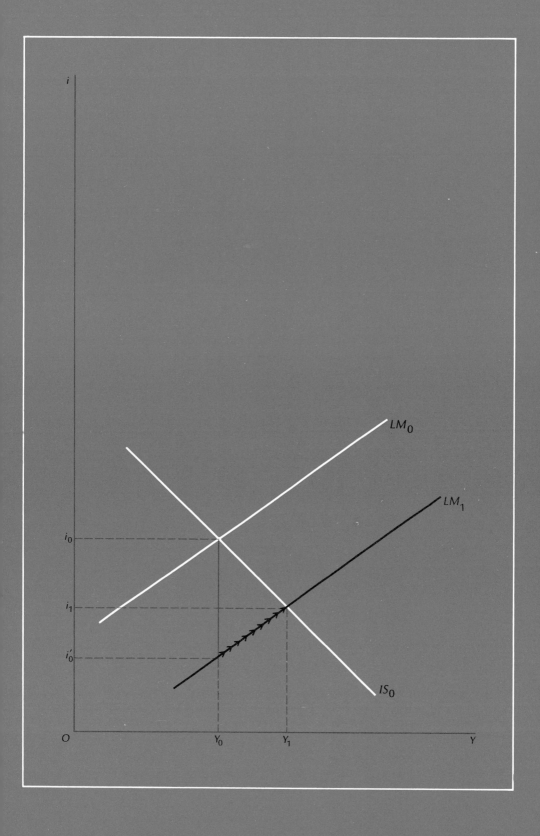

When investment increases to a new level, the level of income rises until saving has risen by an amount equal to the increase in investment. But given our present assumption about investment demand, the increase in income induces further increases in investment. If the marginal propensity to invest is greater than the marginal propensity to save, saving cannot rise fast enough to balance intended investment with saving. The level of income would therefore tend to keep rising indefinitely, and product market equilibrium would never be attained. However, equilibrium can be restored if the rate of interest rises and reduces intended investment. Consequently, when the marginal propensity to invest exceeds the marginal propensity to save, product market equilibrium implies that as the level of income rises, the rate of interest must also rise.

Let us now consider how the system adjusts to disequilibrium in this more general model. In Figure 15–2 the IS-LM curves are represented with their conventional shapes. We assume that the initial equilibrium is at i_0 and Y_0 and that the equilibrium is disturbed by a shift to the right of the LM curve.

We wish now to trace the process of adjustment to the new equilibrium point Y_1, i_1. To do this, we need to introduce some dynamic assumptions about how the system behaves when it is out of equilibrium. Accordingly, let us assume that the rate of interest adjusts instantaneously to monetary disturbances and that the speed of adjustment in the product market is equal to the difference between investment and saving (that is to say, the difference between aggregate demand and what is currently being produced). The assumption of instantaneous money market adjustment allows us to trace the path of income and the interest rate along the LM curve from which, by our assumption, we can never depart.

Referring again to Figure 15–2, we see that the shift in the LM curve together with our assumption about interest rate adjustments implies that the interest rate falls immediately to i_0'. But at i_0' with income level Y_0 intended investment exceeds saving. Consequently, income begins to rise. As the level of income rises, the quantity of money demanded for transactions purposes increases so that the interest rate also begins to rise. The adjustment now continues upward (following the arrows) along the LM curve until Y_1 and i_1 are reached. At this point intended investment again equals saving, and equilibrium is restored.

Suppose next that the IS curve has a positive slope, as shown in

Figure 15–3   Dynamic adjustment: case 2
(all values in real terms)

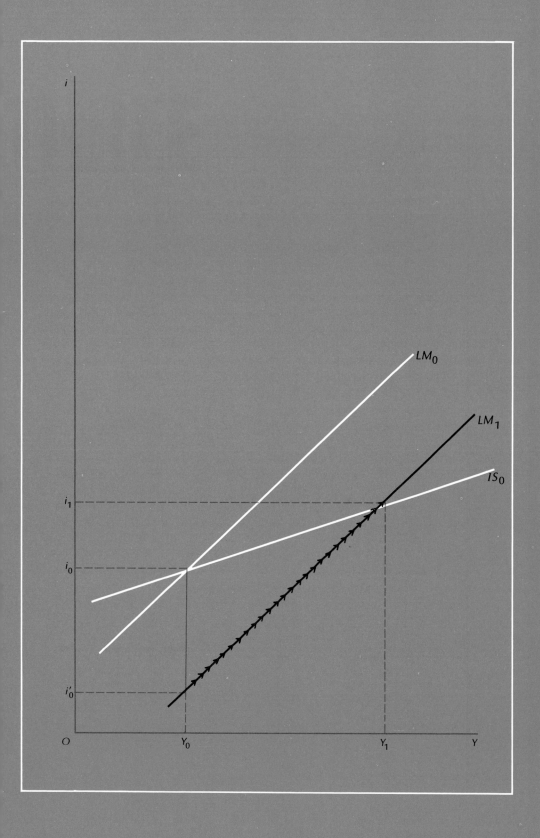

Figure 15–3. The shift in the *LM* curve causes the interest rate to fall immediately to i_0'. This again means that intended investment exceeds saving and that income must therefore rise. But the rise in income stimulates further investment because of our assumption that investment is a function of the level of profits and income. Consequently, the original monetary disturbance causes income to rise; this causes additional investment to be induced; and this, in turn, causes income to rise still further.

Will income continue to rise indefinitely, or will a new equilibrium point be found? In the present case the rise in income causes the interest rate to rise and to dampen investment more rapidly than the rise in income stimulates further investment. In other words the rate of interest that keeps the money market in equilibrium rises more rapidly than the rate of interest that keeps the product market in equilibrium. Consequently, a new stable equilibrium point will be reached at Y_1 and i_1. The path of adjustment again follows the arrows upward along the *LM* curve.

Finally, consider the third case shown in Figure 15–4. This differs from the second case in that the *IS* curve is now assumed to have a steeper slope than the *LM* curve. If we knew nothing about the adjustment process, we would assume that the shift in the *LM* curve to LM_1 would cause the equilibrium level of income to fall to Y_1 and the rate of interest to fall to i_1. Such a fall in income does not seem to be a very sensible result. And, indeed, our dynamic analysis will show that the point i_1 and Y_1 cannot be attained. The point Y_0, i_0 is also an unstable equilibrium point from which the system would tend to diverge the moment the equilibrium is disturbed.

As before, the shift in the *LM* curve causes the interest rate to fall immediately to i_0'. Consequently, investment exceeds saving, and, contrary to what the static model predicts, income, instead of moving down to Y_1, rises. The rise in income causes additional investment to be induced. In the previous case the rise in income eventually caused the transactions demand and therefore the interest rate to rise fast enough to keep income from expanding indefinitely. But in this case the actual interest rate (along the *LM* curve) rises less rapidly than it would have to rise (along the *IS* curve) in order to bring intended investment into equilibrium with saving. Thus at Y_2, for example, the interest rate that equates saving and investment i_2 is in excess of the rate of interest that gives monetary equilibrium i_2' by more than at lower income levels. Income therefore continues to rise and at an increasingly rapid rate.

Figure 15–4   Dynamic adjustment: case 3
(all values in real terms)

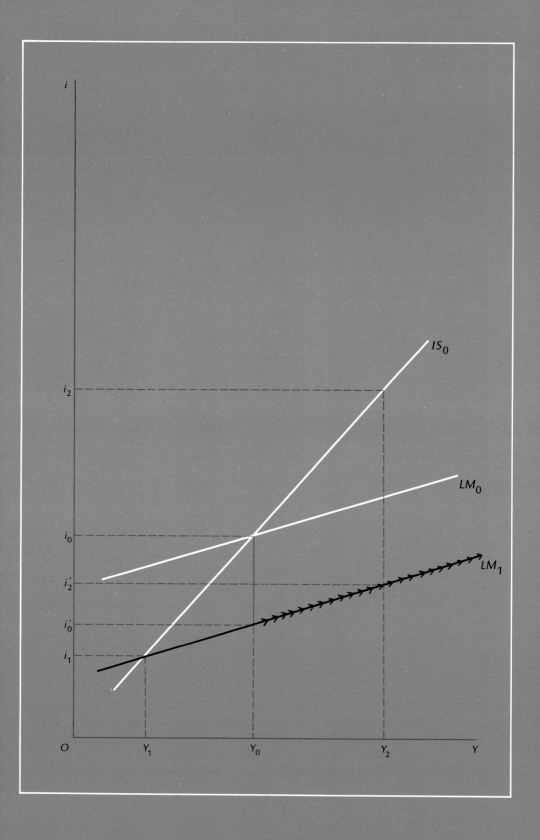

In the case just considered the system is said to be "unstable," and the intersection points of the *IS* and *LM* curves are said to be "unstable equilibrium" points. As long as we assumed that the *IS* curve was negatively sloped, we did not have to worry about this problem. Indeed, even a positively sloped *IS* curve produced an unstable system only when the slope of the *IS* curve was assumed to be greater than the slope of the *LM* curve.

15–3 IMPLICATIONS OF THE ANALYSIS

We have seen that the introduction of dynamic assumptions about how the system behaves when it is out of equilibrium is necessary to verify whether the results of comparative static analysis are correct. Thus stability analysis rules out the comparative static result in the example shown in Figure 15–4, and this means that if an increase in the money supply changes income at all, the change in income must be positive. By a similar argument we could show that a rise in government purchases or a reduction in taxes could never lower the level of income regardless of what the comparative static model may indicate. Thus stability analysis permits the analyst to eliminate erroneous results, and it thereby permits him to derive correct theorems about the direction of change of the variables of the system.

16

FUNDAMENTALS
OF GROWTH
ECONOMICS

16–1   INTRODUCTION

The models of aggregate economic behavior that we considered in Part 2 demonstrate that the maintenance of full employment requires that the leakages generated at the full-employment level of income be offset by an equivalent volume of injections. To say that a given level of investment is necessary to maintain full employment is to assume that the labor force and the productive capacity of the economy do not change. Such an assumption may well be justified when dealing with very short periods of time. For example, it is not unreasonable to assume that the increase in the productive capacity of the American economy resulting from net investment in one year is so small that it can safely be ignored within the context of the analysis of Part 2. But the cumulative effects of continued net investment over a longer period of time cannot be ignored, and therefore a certain amount of reorientation is required for the longer view.

The static models of Part 2 failed to bring out the fact that investment has a dual character. While investment expenditures are a component of aggregate demand, they are made for the purpose of increasing productive capacity. This means that they expand the potential supply of output at the same time that they increase current income. Thus a positive level of net investment means that the supply of output is capable of continued increase over time, and full utilization of this capacity will necessitate continued increases in aggregate expenditure in the future. In addition, if, as seems to be the case, the absolute volume of full-employment saving increases over time, increasing absolute amounts of investment must be forthcoming in every year if full-employment saving is to be balanced by an equivalent amount of investment expenditure. But as the absolute flow of investment increases every year, the capital stock of the economy increases by larger and larger amounts; and this means that income must increase by larger and larger amounts to maintain full employment. The economy must, in other words, run faster and faster if full employment is to be maintained.

Productive capacity not only grows as a result of net investment expenditure, but also becomes more efficient as the result of technical progress. By technical progress we mean improvements in the efficiency of the stock of capital that result from technological and organizational changes and improvements in the quality of the labor force that result from improved education, training, and health.[1] As a consequence of technical progress the productivity of capital and labor has been increasing, and this, to a large extent, is what has permitted Americans to enjoy an ever-rising standard of living.

Finally, in addition to capital growth and technical progress, population and the labor force grow with time, and this growth both creates the potential for a greater supply of output and provides some or all of the additional demand needed to ensure that the output is absorbed.

The purpose of this chapter is to explore the consequences of the dual character of investment and the effects of technical progress and population growth. We begin our study of this topic with an extension of the simple Keynesian model in which the dual character of invest-

---

[1] The most important element of technical progress in the economy of the United States appears to be the steady improvement in the quality of the working force. See T. W. Schultz, "Investment in Human Capital," *American Economic Review*, 51:1–17, 1961.

ment is highlighted but in which there is assumed to be no technical progress and in which the labor force is assumed to grow at the same rate as the capital stock. Given these assumptions, the rate of growth of income that utilizes existing capacity will also provide full employment for the growing labor force.

16–2 CAPITAL EXPANSION AND THE MAINTENANCE OF FULL EMPLOYMENT[1]

For the purpose of illustrating the ingredients of the growth process, we assume, in this section, that the level of output which the economy is capable of producing is proportional to the stock of capital. We therefore postulate the production function

$$Y = \sigma K$$

where the term σ is known as the "capital coefficient." If σ had a value of 0.25, $4 worth of capital stock would be required to produce an annual flow of output of $1.

To simplify matters, we also assume that there is no government economic activity and that there is no foreign trade. Finally, we assume, as a long-run matter, that consumption is proportional to the level of income. These assumptions imply that equilibrium income obtains when

$$I = S$$

and that the consumption function may be represented by

$$C = bY$$

Now let us consider a numerical example in which the value of the capital coefficient is assumed to be 1.0 and the value of the marginal propensity to consume is 0.5. The situation is illustrated in Figure 16–1, where it is assumed that the initial full-employment level of income is $100 billion. At this income level, the level of consumption would be $50 billion. Consequently, if full employment is to be achieved, the level of intended investment must be $50 billion.

---

[1] The simple model presented here follows the approach of E. Domar, "Capital Expansion, Rate of Growth and Employment," *Econometrica*, 14:137–147, 1946. A similar earlier approach is that of R. F. Harrod, "An Essay in Dynamic Theory," *Economic Journal*, 49:14–33, 1939. See also W. J. Baumol, *Economic Dynamics*, The Macmillan Company, New York, 1951.

Assuming that this required $50 billion of investment spending is actually forthcoming, there will be a net addition to the stock of capital of $50 billion. If our assumption that the capital coefficient has a value of 1.0 holds, it implies that in the next year the full-employment level of output will be $150 billion. Thus, as can be seen in Figure 16–1, the level of consumption will be $75 billion, and this means that investment must now rise to $75 billion if full employment is to be maintained. Assuming, again, that the required amount of investment is actually forthcoming, the full-employment output potential of the economy rises by $75 billion to $225 billion. At this income level, consumption would be $112.5 billion, and the required level of investment would be $112.5 billion.

In this example, the level of investment that maintains full employment rises in successive periods from $50 billion, to $75 billion, to $112.5 billion. The period-by-period rate of growth is therefore 50 percent. This rate of growth exactly equals the product of the capital coefficient and the marginal propensity to save; that is,

$$\sigma \, (1 - b) = 1.0(0.5) = 0.5$$

That this should be the case is no accident. Let us see why.

If full employment is to be maintained over successive periods the increase in total spending from one period to the next must exactly equal the increase in the full-employment supply of output. The increase in total spending is the increase in investment times the multiplier. Consequently, from the demand side we have

$$\Delta Y = \frac{\Delta I}{1 - b}$$

as the increase in total spending. From the production function we see that the increase in the supply of output will be

$$\Delta Y = \sigma \, \Delta K$$

However, the *change* in the stock of capital equals the *level* of investment. Consequently, we may replace the foregoing expression by

$$\Delta Y = \sigma I$$

Figure 16–1   The growth process
(all values in real terms)

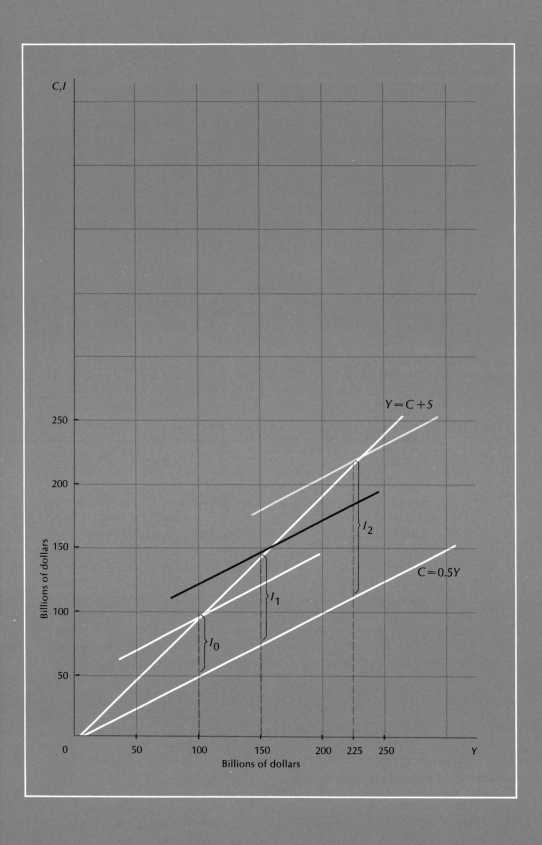

When we equate this increment to supply with the increment to demand, we obtain

$$\frac{\Delta I}{1 - b} = \sigma I$$

and when we rearrange this expression, we find that the percentage rate of growth that keeps the growth in demand and supply in balance is

$$\frac{\Delta I}{I} = \sigma(1 - b)$$

This model, which economists call the "Domar model," suggests that if we want the economy to grow more rapidly, we can attempt to make capital more productive (raise the value of σ) and/or we can increase the proportion of income that is saved. An increase in the productivity of capital implies that the output of the economy must increase at a faster rate than before because each dollar that is invested increases the full-employment level of output by more output than previously existed. Consequently, the rate of growth of aggregate expenditure that is necessary to maintain full employment must rise. Similarly, if at every level of income more is saved than previously, more will have to be invested. This means that in each period more is added to the capital stock than before, so that total spending must rise more rapidly if full employment is to be maintained.

This simple model teaches an important lesson. It is not sufficient, if we wish to maintain full employment, for the level of investment to remain constant. A constant level of investment implies a constant period-by-period level of total spending. However, as long as there is any net investment at all, the capital stock and therefore full-employment output will be growing. And this implies, finally, that investment must grow if total spending is to keep up with the ability of the system to produce. A constant level of investment would therefore imply a progressive divergence between the actual level of income and the full-employment level. The economy must, as the Red Queen in *Through the Looking Glass* would say, run faster all the time just to remain standing still.

16–3 THE RAZOR'S EDGE

The type of model that we considered in the last section has been called a "razor-edge" model because of its precarious balance and volatile behavior when there is a slight deviation from the required rate of growth. The economy appears to teeter, as if prepared to shoot off either into hyperinflation or into deep depression at any moment. While this circumstance suggests less about the real world than about the oversimplified nature of the model, it nevertheless brings to our attention the important fact that overinvestment will lead to capital scarcity, while underinvestment will lead to excess capacity. Apparently, if entrepreneurs invest too much, it will look as if they have invested too little, while if they invest too little, it will appear as if they have invested too much.

Figure 16–1 will help us understand these paradoxes. At the start there is a full-employment income of $100 billion, and the level of investment that is required for full employment is therefore $50 billion. Now suppose that businessmen underinvest in period 0; i.e., instead of investing $50 billion, they invest only $40 billion. As a result of this insufficient investment, the equilibrium level of income will be $80 billion instead of $100 billion. Thus there will be excess capacity of $20 billion because income is below the potential of period 0. In addition, the positive net investment of $40 billion, in period 0, adds another $40 billion to potential output. Consequently, at the start of period 1 entrepreneurs will discover that there is substantial excess capacity, so that investment will be further reduced, if indeed it does not collapse entirely. Underinvestment therefore leads to excess capacity. Had businessmen invested $50 billion instead of only $40 billion, they would have found that the demand for goods and services was just sufficient to employ all productive resources.

Suppose, on the other hand, that the rate of growth of money income exceeds the required rate. In this case the volume of investment goods demanded by business will exceed the supply of such goods released by saving. In the face of underproduction in the previous period, businessmen will attempt to produce more in the current period. But the increased output of the current period will induce larger investment plans in the next period, causing further underproduction. Thus the attempt to increase output too rapidly leads to renewed attempts to expand more rapidly and to continued underproduction. In Figure 16–1, if the level of intended investment in period 0 is $60 billion, aggregate demand is in excess of what can be supplied. Prices are thus bid up, and businessmen are moved to increase their investment spending even further in day 1, i.e., far in excess of the required amount of $75 billion, in order to attempt to make up the gap between the demand for goods and their productive capacity. It is, however, these very attempts to catch up that widen the gap.

16–4 NEOCLASSICAL GROWTH ECONOMICS

In recent years there has developed a body of analysis to which the name "neoclassical growth economics" has been applied.[1] The neoclassical theorist assumes that full-employment saving is automatically invested, and he attempts to analyze the properties of the full-employment growth path by making various assumptions about the rate of technical change, the rate of growth of the labor supply, and the possibility of technical substitution between the factors of production. Neoclassical theory has destroyed the simple elegance of the Domar model because it suggests that the capital coefficient cannot be treated as a parameter and that it is, instead, a variable that depends upon such factors as the rate of technical change and the relative supplies of capital and labor inputs.

Much of the analysis of neoclassical theory is quite complicated, and the mathematics is formidable. Its essential ingredients can, however, be illustrated if we assume that the production potential of the economy is represented by what is called the "Cobb-Douglas" production function

$$Y = AK^a N^{1-a} \tag{16–1}$$

where the exponent a is a positive fraction. The exponent represents the fraction of income that accrues to capital, and it also equals the elasticity of output with respect to changes in the capital stock.

The full-employment level of output in this formulation is a function of the quantity of capital K, the supply of labor N, and of a scale factor A, which we can assume grows at a steady rate and represents the effect of technical change. Implied in this formulation are the following assumptions:

1. The production function is homogeneous of degree one. In other words, if both K and N increase by some proportion, Y will increase in the same proportion.

2. Technical change is "neutral." This means that technical change (a shift in A) will raise the marginal product of both factors in the same

[1] We cannot cite all the relevant literature on the subject here. The interested student should, however, take a look at some of the fundamental contributions of Robert M. Solow, "A Contribution to the Theory of Economic Growth," *Quarterly Journal of Economics,* 70:65–94, 1956, and "Technical Change and the Aggregate Production Function," *Review of Economics and Statistics,* 39:312–320, 1957; and Edmund Phelps, "The Golden Rule of Accumulation: A Fable for Growthmen," *American Economic Review,* 51:638–643, 1961, and "The New View of Investment: A Neo-classical Analysis," *Quarterly Journal of Economics,* 76:548–567, 1962.

proportion and that the marginal rate of substitution (the ratio of the marginal products) will therefore be constant.

3. Production is subject to diminishing returns. This means that if the quantity of capital is held constant, increases in the quantity of labor will yield successively smaller increments to output.[1]

When we rearrange the production function to read

$$Y = A \left(\frac{N}{K} \right)^{1-a} K$$

and compare this with

$$Y = \sigma K$$

we see that the capital coefficient may be expressed as

$$\sigma = A \left(\frac{N}{K} \right)^{1-a} \tag{16-2}$$

and it is therefore immediately evident that the capital coefficient will rise with an improvement in technology and with a rise in the labor-capital ratio.

The presence of diminishing returns produces the important result that an increase in the fraction of income which is saved may not raise the growth rate. If the fraction of income saved increases, the required amount of investment increases and the stock of capital and the level of income initially grow more rapidly. However, as can be seen from Eq. 16-2, this implies that the labor-capital ratio falls, and this means that the increased relative supply of capital causes the capital coefficient

---

[1] A little bit of simple mathematics allows us to confirm these propositions. First, multiply K and N by a constant u. Consequently, we have

$$A(uK)^a (uN)^{1-a} = AK^a N^{1-a} u = uY$$

and we therefore see that the production function is homogeneous of degree one. To calculate the marginal products of capital and labor, we take the partial derivatives of Y with respect to K and N. This gives

$$\frac{\partial Y}{\partial K} = \frac{aY}{K} \qquad \frac{\partial Y}{\partial N} = (1-a) \frac{Y}{N}$$

and shows that the marginal products will decline as the ratios of output to capital and output to labor diminish. The ratio of the marginal products is

$$\frac{\partial Y / \partial K}{\partial Y / \partial N} = \frac{a}{1-a} \frac{N}{K}$$

which shows that the marginal rate of substitution is a function of the ratio of labor to capital and is independent of the rate of technical change.

to fall. Therefore, each dollar of investment adds less to potential output and the growth rate tends to diminish and to return to its initial level.

A constant percentage rate of growth of output implies that the capital coefficient must remain constant. As can be seen from Eq. 16–2, this implies that changes in the capital-labor ratio can be no greater than what can be just offset by technical progress. Any acceleration of the rate of capital accumulation runs into diminishing returns to capital, thereby causing the capital coefficient and the growth rate to decline.

These considerations suggest that the rate of growth may not, as in the Domar model, be a function of the fraction of income that the community is willing to save. Going back to the production function, we can calculate the rate of growth of output[1] and obtain

$$G_y = G_t + aG_k + (1 - a)G_n \qquad (16\text{–}3)$$

where G_y, G_t, G_k, and G_n are the percentage rates of growth of output, technical change, the stock of capital, and the supply of labor, respectively.

As a very long-run matter, it would be impossible for output and the stock of capital to grow at constant percentage rates that differ from each other. Investment, and therefore the stock of capital, could not perpetually grow more rapidly than income because this would mean that investment would eventually exceed the level of income, and that is obviously impossible. Consequently, if there is a constant long-run equilibrium rate of growth, it must be such that $G_y = G_k$. If this is the case, Eq. 16–3 reduces to

$$G_y = \frac{G_t + (1 - a)G_n}{1 - a} \qquad (16\text{–}4)$$

and we therefore see that the long-run equilibrium rate of growth is a function of the rate of technical progress and of the rate of growth of the labor supply.

Several important conclusions emerge from this result. First, growth

---

[1] Differentiation of the Cobb-Douglas function with respect to time yields

$$\frac{dy}{dt} = K^a N^{1-a} \frac{dA}{dt} + aK^{a-1}N^{1-a} \frac{dK}{dt} + (1 - a)K^a N^{-a} \frac{dN}{dt}$$

When both sides of this expression are divided by Y, we get the percentage rate of growth

$$\frac{1}{Y}\frac{dY}{dt} = \frac{1}{A}\frac{dA}{dt} + a\frac{1}{K}\frac{dK}{dt} + (1 - a)\frac{1}{N}\frac{dN}{dt}$$

in per capita output is not possible in the absence of technical progress. Notice that if $G_t = 0$, Eq. 16–4 reduces to

$$G_y = G_n$$

and since the rate of growth of per capita output is $G_y - G_n$, per capita output will not grow at all. In this case, aggregate output grows at a rate that is equal to, and determined by, the rate of growth of labor supply.

Second, we see that the rate of growth is not a function of the fraction of income that is saved. Returning to Eq. 16–2, we see that in the extreme case where $G_t = 0$ so that A is constant, any decrease in the ratio of N/K brought about by an increase in saving immediately reduces the capital coefficient and the rate of growth. Consequently, although the Domar result that the rate of growth is

$$\sigma(1 - b)$$

may be correct, it is not very interesting since any increase in $1 - b$ is offset by an equivalent decrease in σ.

The traditional theory of growth suggests that the well-being of the future is limited only by the willingness of the present generation to save. By foregoing present consumption, society can raise the growth rate and thereby enjoy a higher level of consumption in the future. Neoclassical theory, however, suggests that this proposition is false. The growth rate cannot be permanently raised by an increase in the fraction of income that is saved and invested because of the presence of diminishing returns to capital.

Although the equilibrium rate of growth cannot be affected by a change in the fraction of income saved, the saving ratio is an important determinant of the level of per capita consumption that society may enjoy. This can be illustrated by considering the effect of some extreme assumptions about saving behavior. A society that saves and invests nothing at all will have zero capital stock and therefore no output or consumption. At the opposite extreme, a society that is so frugal that it saves most of its output will have a large level of output, but it will have very little consumption. These extreme examples suggest that somewhere in the middle there must be some optimum saving ratio that maximizes per capita consumption. As is shown in the appendix, the optimum saving ratio is that ratio which causes society to save and invest its competitive profits and that causes it to consume its labor income.

Let us make sure, before going on, that we understand the nature of this "golden rule of accumulation." If we could raise the growth rate by saving more, per capita consumption would eventually be higher. However, neoclassical theory suggests that it is the *level* of output rather than its rate of growth that is associated with a particular saving rate. The optimum saving rate is that rate at which the reduction in per capita consumption due to the next dollar of saving is just offset by the increase in per capita consumption which the additional saving makes possible.

The model of growth that we have discussed here has been criticized on the ground that it assumes that technical change is entirely "organizational." In other words, technical change proceeds at a uniform rate and is not affected by the quantity of investment that takes place. It ought to be recognized, however, that most technological improvements enter the productive process by being *embodied* in new machinery and equipment. As Phelps has shown,[1] the assumption of embodied technical change does not affect the fundamental conclusions of neoclassical growth economics. If society A saves and invests a larger fraction of its output than society B, its stock of capital will be younger and more productive. However, this does not mean that the stock of capital is growing more rapidly. A will enjoy a higher level of output than B, but its economy will not grow any more rapidly unless its rates of embodied and disembodied technical change are greater.

In order for the growth rate to be raised by an increase in the saving rate, it would have to be the case that the *rate* of technical progress is itself a function of the quantity of investment. Frankel[2] has observed that societies that have a high capital-labor ratio tend to be the most technologically advanced. Consequently, he writes the technical change index as

$$A = B\left(\frac{K}{N}\right)^c \tag{16-5}$$

and he calls this expression the "development modifier." The idea is that although a rise in K/N will tend to cause the marginal product of capital to fall, the increased capital brings with it improved technology that offsets the tendency toward diminishing returns.

When we substitute Eq. (16–5) into the Cobb-Douglas production function, we get

$$Y = B\left(\frac{K}{N}\right)^c K^a N^{1-a} = BK^{a+c}N^{1-a-c}$$

[1] Phelps, "The New View of Investment."

[2] Marvin Frankel, "The Production Function in Allocation and Growth: A Synthesis," *American Economic Review,* 52:995–1022, 1962, and "Errata," *American Economic Review,* 53:142, 1963.

If $a + c$ just happens to equal 1, the expression collapses to

$$Y = BK$$

Thus we see that in this case diminishing returns are exactly offset by accelerated technical change and that the Domar production function once again describes the relationship between output and the stock of capital.

In conclusion: The rate of growth of output in the long run depends upon the rate of technical change and the rate of growth of the supply of labor. Changes in the fraction of income saved and invested will not affect this rate of growth, unless the effect of the increase in saving and investment is to raise the rate at which technical progress gets into the productive system. The traditional notion that more saving is always good must, apparently, be rejected even on non-Keynesian grounds.

16–5 SECULAR STAGNATION

Economic growth, by any reasonable definition, implies increasing per capita real income over time. Stagnation implies that per capita real income remains constant, declines, or grows less rapidly than it might. Stagnation may set in for two reasons. First, even though resources are fully employed, the rate of growth of output may be lower than the rate of population growth. Second, though the supply conditions for an adequate required rate of growth may be at hand, the economy nevertheless may fail to achieve its potential because of deficient aggregate demand. In the first case, society suffers from the fact that differential rates of population and capital growth reduce per capita income; in the latter case, it suffers from the fact that demand is frequently insufficient to fully utilize the resources of the economy. In either case, the per capita income situation is unsatisfactory.

The problem of predicting the path of development for a capitalist economy is one that has intrigued economists since the time of Adam Smith.[1] Smith, the father of modern economics, regarded a growing population as intimately connected with economic progress. A growing population makes possible, through widening markets, an increasing "division of labor." As the labor force expands, each individual laborer is able to become more and more of a specialist as distinct from a jack-of-all-trades. Because each worker is able to concentrate on the attainment of one or a few skills, his productiveness increases. Moreover,

[1] Adam Smith, *The Wealth of Nations,* Books I, II, and III, Modern Library, Inc., New York, 1937.

increasing specialization fosters inventiveness—the finding of more efficient ways of doing jobs—and this further increases productivity. As the per capita income level is raised by this process, conditions favorable to population growth develop, and further division of labor is rendered possible.

Smith's theory contains little reference to the role of capital in the growth process; it assumes ever-increasing returns to labor; and like the theories of most economists before the time of Marx, it concentrates its attention exclusively on the supply side of the growth process. Because he was unaware of the notion of diminishing returns, Smith was optimistic about the possibility that growth, once begun, could be a cumulative process of rising per capita income.

Smith's optimism gave way to the pessimism of his illustrious successors Robert Malthus and David Ricardo.[1] Whereas population growth was the mainspring of progress to Adam Smith, Malthus and Ricardo regarded population growth as the evil that caused a steady decline in per capita income, leading ultimately to a "stationary state" in which no economic progress takes place. Indeed, the Malthus-Ricardo analysis predicted such a bleak outlook for capitalism that Thomas Carlyle was moved to dub economics the "dismal science."

According to Malthus, population tends to grow at a geometric rate, doubling every generation, as long as there is an available supply of food. Because of limitations on the supply of land, the food supply cannot, however, be increased at the same rate. Although capital accumulation could affect the race between the expanding population and the "means of subsistence" by increasing the rate at which output increases, the rate of capital accumulation depends on profits; these profits, in turn, were, for reasons explained by Ricardo, adversely affected by the growth of population. Because of the purely biological character of population growth,[2] population inevitably outruns the means of subsistence, profits decline to zero, net investment declines to zero, and the stationary state arrives.

Why do profits decline as population grows? If a growing population is to be fed, argued Ricardo, progressively less fertile land must be

---

[1] The writings of Malthus and Ricardo are summarized in any number of standard texts on the history of economic thought, for example, F. A. Neff, *Economic Doctrines*, 2d ed., The McGraw-Hill Book Company, New York, 1950; and R. Heilbroner, *The Worldly Philosophers*, Simon and Schuster, Inc., New York, 1953.

[2] Malthus did introduce the concept of "preventive checks," but these were a later addition to the theory; and while modifying the gloomy notion of the stationary state, he did not modify his main conclusions.

taken under cultivation. If landowners are to be persuaded to bring this less efficient land into use, food prices must rise. As food prices rise, those landowners who are fortunate enough to own fertile land earn a surplus, called "rent," over and above the amount needed to induce production. At the same time, the capitalist is obliged to pay higher wages because of the rise in food prices. Thus, if we visualize a pie that represents the total national product, the pie becomes divided, more and more over time, between rents and wages. Eventually profits disappear, and when this happens, net investment falls to zero; the laboring class lives at a subsistence level; and the landowners become the only class accumulating wealth.

The stationary state could presumably be avoided if landowners were to invest their rents in real capital formation. But landowners, suggested Ricardo, are a profligate class that wastes its substance on ostentatious expenditure instead of engaging in productive investment.

In the Western world, the gloomy prognosis of Malthus and Ricardo has happily not been realized. Population has failed to grow as rapidly as predicted by Malthus, and advances in technology, despite occasional setbacks, have held the specter of diminishing returns at bay. This is not to say, however, that the classical theory of economic development is of only incidental interest to the contemporary scene.

In many developing areas, for example, population continually presses against the food supply, leaving in normal crop years such a slim margin that a moderately bad year produces widespread misery and starvation. Painfully gained increases in output are met almost instantaneously by population increases. At the same time, there exists in such countries a wealthy class that derives its income from ownership of land. By tradition and custom this class is more inclined to spend its wealth for ostentatious accumulation of material property; if it invests its wealth, these investments are likely to be made in foreign countries. Social and political turmoil in such lands frequently stems from growing awareness of the disparity of incomes and the hope that some form of public ownership of land and other resources will lead to general abundance.

The study of economics provides ample opportunity for gratifying a penchant for paradox. On the one hand rapidly expanding population is the bogey that leads to Malthus' stationary state, and advances in the productivity of capital hold out the chief hope that per capita income may rise in the long run; on the other hand it also appears to be possible that stagnation may result from too little population growth and from the fact that advances in technology are "too productive." This weird circumstance arises from the fact that although greater advances in technology relative to population growth make possible a rapidly expanding required rate of growth, these relative rates of growth of population and productivity at the same time make it difficult for the economy to generate sufficient aggregate demand to take advantage of the full-employment potential.

A. H. Hansen has most clearly and systematically expounded the view that the ingredients that make for a high required rate of growth also set up roadblocks because they tend to cause aggregate demand to be deficient.[1] Writing during the 1930s, Hansen was particularly concerned with the question of whether or not the great depression was merely an unusual adjunct of cyclical troughs or whether it foreshadowed a period of long-run stagnation for the American economy.

In the nineteenth and the early part of the twentieth centuries, America developed at an impressive rate. Population grew rapidly while physical output increased at an even faster rate, so that per capita product grew constantly. But as the twentieth century proceeded, the pace of development began to tail off. Looking for the cause of this slowdown, Hansen delineated four principal factors: a declining rate of population growth; the disappearance of the geographic frontier; the growth of the absolute volume of savings; and the tendency for new techniques of production to be capital-saving, i.e., to raise the value of σ, instead of capital-using.

Hansen saw the expanding population of nineteenth-century America as one of the mainsprings of its growth, and the geographic frontier as one of the inducements for the large increase in population. Expanding population and the settlement of new territory required tremendous investment expenditures for just about everything from houses and schools to railroads and utilities. Here indeed was the ideal outlet that channeled the tremendous volume of saving of the American economy into productive investment.

As the rate of population growth declined because of a declining birth rate and because of rigid immigration restrictions, and as the geographic frontiers became filled, the investment outlets for America's ever-growing volume of saving declined. A slowly growing population does not need many new homes, and once the railroads are built, the need for investment spending declines significantly.

Stagnation due to deficient demand might be prevented by technological developments of the capital-using type, i.e., changes in the

---

[1] A. H. Hansen, "Economic Progress and Declining Population Growth," *American Economic Review*, 29:1–15, 1939.

mode of production that would increase the average amount of capital needed to produce a particular level of output. But Hansen was not optimistic about the likelihood of such development. Indeed, he believed that advances in technology would increase rather than reduce the value of σ; this would mean that less new investment would be required to produce additional units of output. Advances in technology, for example, have replaced the railroad with the airplane, a mode of transportation that requires considerably smaller investment outlays.

Hansen's analysis came on the heels of the revolutionary work of Keynes. Accepting the Keynesian conclusion that full employment is but one of several possible equilibrium levels of employment, Hansen argued that given the level of saving that the American economy tends to generate at the full-employment level of income, it would become increasingly difficult to balance off these leakages with investment expenditures because of the gradual drying up of investment opportunities. Full employment might be attained occasionally at the peak of a cycle, but the long-run trend would be one of substantial underemployment.

Perhaps as a result of World War II and the conditions that attended its aftermath, the American economy's principal problem over the years 1940–1955 was quite the opposite of the problem that concerned Hansen. Instead of deficient aggregate demand, demand was in excess of what the economy could supply, with the result that we suffered inflationary pressures during the period. However, beginning in 1957, the economy reverted for a period of seven years to secular stagnation marked by excessive unemployment and a slow rate of growth. Hansen's analysis now appears to be not nearly as obsolete as its detractors thought it to be. Stagnation of the deficient demand variety is an ever-present danger that the economy must be ever ready to guard against.

16–6 CONCLUDING REMARKS ON GROWTH ECONOMICS

Economic growth is, of course, a great blessing. It is what enables the individuals in society to look forward to rising living standards. It is, moreover, a great social solvent. When all can look forward to rising levels of well-being, the pressure for redistribution of the existing pie is reduced. This much is axiomatic; what is unfortunate is that the growth rate has become a symbol of national prestige and is said to be regarded by uncommitted nations as the index by which the performances of the "free" and socialist economies are judged. Since force-feeding of the growth rate may be inimical to other economic and social goals, the following comments are in order.

What frightens some people is the circumstance, known to all amateur mathematicians, that if two quantities A and B grow, and if A grows at a higher percentage rate than B, then A must ultimately become larger than B regardless of how tiny it was at the start. Applied to the American-Soviet comparison, this elementary exercise in differential equations implies that if the Soviet growth rate continues to be higher than the American rate, the Soviet economy will ultimately catch up to and pass the American economy.

However, comparisons of growth rates between nations may not be particularly meaningful. The fruits of economic growth are partly quantitative but also partly qualitative and to that extent not measurable. When a "cost-saving" invention is made, it is possible to measure the effects of the invention on productivity. But when invention and innovation are directed toward product improvement, it is virtually impossible to measure the benefits that accrue. To take an extreme example, suppose that product B is introduced and that consumers switch to this product at the expense of A, which then disappears from the market. Assume next that B sells at the identical price as did A and that consumers buy the same quantity of B as they formerly bought of A. Now the national income will appear to be unaffected by the introduction of product B. But society clearly seems to be better off, as indicated by the fact that consumers prefer product B. During advanced stages of economic development, inventive and innovative activity is apt to become substantially reoriented in the direction of product improvement and away from cost reduction. When the Soviets succeed in raising agricultural output per man-hour, the effects are clearly discernible and readily measurable in the national income. When American enterprise introduces a new product or improves an existing one, the national income statistics may reflect no change whatever. Consequently, we ought to expect the Soviet economy at its present stage of development to show a more rapid growth of national income than the American economy, and we ought not to be too surprised that the rate of growth in the United States, as measured by national income data, has slowed down.

A rapid rate of economic growth enables the economy to expand its national defense, welfare, and foreign aid activities without imposing on other claims on resources. To illustrate, suppose that government expenditures are going to rise at a rate of 5 percent. If income grows at a rate of only 3 percent, either the government will have to scale down its requirements or a progressively smaller proportion of the national product will be available for consumption and investment.

Although it is true that the national income must grow at the same rate as the growth in government purchases if the ratio of government purchases to national income is to remain constant, it is not at all certain that it is better to support a growing government sector by force-feeding the growth rate, rather than by retrenching in other sectors. Accelerated economic growth is not bought at zero cost. The rate at which our natural resources are being ravaged in our present frenetic attempts to acquire consumer durable goods is frightening.

It is of course desirable to raise the actual growth rate to the rate required to achieve full employment. But if we do this, the rate at which our nonhuman resources are exploited will rise. However, not to raise the growth rate to the required rate will mean persistent unemployment and the wasting of our human resources. It is because of the belief that we are not utilizing all our human and nonhuman resources effectively that some social critics are trying to prod us into giving up some of our appliances in exchange for better schools and other forms of social capital.

17

INFLATION

17–1 INTRODUCTION

An economy that tries to grow more rapidly than the required rate of growth will suffer from inflation. Inflation may come about because the government attempts to absorb more resources than are released by the private economy at the existing price level. It may come about because various groups in the economy attempt to improve their relative income shares more rapidly than the growth of productivity. It may come about because buoyant expectations cause the demand for goods and services to rise more rapidly than the economy can expand output. And it may come about from interactions between some or all of the above factors.

For purposes of analysis it is useful to classify inflation with respect to its degree of intensity and with respect to its several causal factors.

A slowly rising price level we shall denote as "creeping" inflation, while a rapidly rising one we shall denote as "hyperinflation." With respect to causality, we may define "excess-demand" inflation as inflation resulting from the fact that aggregate demand grows more rapidly than the full-employment output potential; "bottleneck" inflation as resulting from changes in the structure of demand; and "cost push" inflation as resulting from the circumstance that many economic groups in society have the power to force up wages and prices. In this chapter we shall confine our discussion to "classical" or excess-demand inflation. The problem of cost push inflation, about which there was an enormous amount of debate during the late 1950s, can be conveniently discussed in Part 4, where current economic problems are considered.

17–2 THE CONSEQUENCES OF INFLATION

When discussing the problem of inflation, we must bear in mind that many economists do not believe the social costs of mild inflation to be very serious and that some upward creep in the price level is inevitable in a fully employed economy. The maintenance of an absolutely constant price level is very likely to require the use of excessively restrictive policies and to cause society to fall considerably short of full employment and maximum production.

While there is some debate about the seriousness of creeping inflation, there can be little doubt that hyperinflation would produce disastrous consequences. Although hyperinflation has been unknown in the United States since the Civil War,[1] a brief consideration of some elements of hyperinflation will help us to examine some of the problems that may be created by creeping inflation of the type to which we are becoming accustomed in the United States.

Hyperinflation is a phenomenon that usually accompanies war and its aftermath. It is a consequence of an attempt to finance government purchases by currency issue. At first the government deficit may be slight and the addition to the price level insignificant. However, as the price level begins to rise, the government must spend greater and greater nominal amounts of currency to obtain the same quantity of real resources. Meanwhile consumers and investors come to anticipate further price increases and intensify their bidding for real goods and services.

---

[1] For an interesting discussion of hyperinflation in the United States see E. M. Lerner, "Inflation in the Confederacy," in Milton Friedman, ed., *Studies in the Quantity Theory of Money*, The University of Chicago Press, Chicago, 1956.

Considered in terms of the *IS-LM* model, government purchases financed by currency creation mean that both the *IS* and the *LM* curves shift to the right. The resulting price increases cause a rush to exchange money balances for goods. This means that the *IS* schedule shifts again and the *LM* schedule rotates downward and to the right because the transactions velocity of circulation increases. The climax of hyperinflation appears when the flight from money is such that the velocity of circulation approaches infinity.[1]

The government cannot indefinitely acquire resources by means of currency issue. When the price level rises at such a rapid rate that the public loses faith in the stability of the monetary unit, trade will no longer be carried on with money. Such a flight from currency implies that exchanges will be made on a purely barter basis. Since the government has nothing to barter, it must resort to outright requisition.

We may well imagine how demoralizing hyperinflation would be. A merchant will not sell a good for money in the morning if he expects prices to double by the afternoon. Unless he is given a physical unit of some commodity, he will prefer to hoard his stock of goods rather than make the exchange. Exchange during hyperinflation inevitably degenerates into primitive bartering.

Production is also impaired by hyperinflation. The workers in an automobile plant cannot be paid in anything other than money. It would not do to divide a car into parts and pay workers with fenders, heaters, and radiators. Because they must be paid in money, the workers have no incentive to work, so that production breaks down except in a few areas where it is possible to make compensation in kind. If, as seems unlikely, the car actually gets produced, it is difficult to see how it can be sold because the car producer is not likely to want a car's worth of groceries or a car's worth of paperclips in return.

The social consequences of hyperinflation are no less terrifying than the economic effects. Debtors pursue creditors in order to pay back past obligations with worthless currency. The earnings of fixed-income groups are wiped out. The value of accumulated liquid savings disappears. Some groups in society are able to defend themselves against inflation while others are not. The end result can only be one in which society is set against itself and in which democratic political institutions are placed under intolerable strain.

Hyperinflation replaces industry and thrift with hoarding and specu-

---

[1] See the paper by Phillip Cagan, "The Monetary Dynamics of Hyperinflation," in Friedman, *ibid.*, for a discussion of the effect of price expectations on transactions velocity.

lation. To some extent there is danger that even creeping inflation may have similar, though less drastic, consequences. If the long-run outlook is for a rising price level, the inducement to save may be seriously impaired. Interest rates will rise drastically because of the decline in the supply of real saving and because of expected price increases. Investment and growth may therefore be retarded. Creeping inflation may also produce unfortunate consequences for small savers. Government bonds, insurance policies, savings deposits, and the other forms of fixed-interest-bearing asset holdings that appeal to small savers merely become traps through which the value of savings is eroded by a rising price level. Inflation forces everyone to become a speculator or to upgrade his propensity to consume. In either case, economic growth will be seriously inhibited.

Inflation finally is incompatible with the promotion of free international trade. A rising price level produces an excess of imports over exports and a drainage of gold. Governments that do not have the fortitude to stand firm against the rise in the price level may turn to tariffs and quota systems to avert further drains of foreign exchange. But the resultant restriction in trade reduces real income and further inhibits the growth potential of the economy.

Those economists who argue that creeping inflation is not necessarily an undesirable thing seem to feel that the alternative to creeping inflation is unemployment and a retarded rate of growth. They feel that since prices are flexible only in the upward direction in our present institutional framework, resource allocation through the price system must operate through price increases in areas of the economy that are growing rather than through price decreases in areas that are stagnating. They feel, moreover, that the monopoly power of unions and enterprises is such that price increases are inevitable and that it is better for the government not to pursue contractionary policies since this would cause unemployment rather than a fall in the price level. Finally, they feel that the goal of maximum economic growth is best served by a policy that lifts the dead hand of debt from the economy. They therefore find a policy that discriminates against creditors to the advantage of debtors a congenial one.

We move on now to an analysis of excess-demand inflation. We shall assume that it is creeping inflation rather than hyperinflation that is under consideration. This will permit us to make the assumption that confidence in the currency has not been badly damaged by price increases and that the transactions velocity of circulation (or the k ratio) remains constant. It must be borne in mind that the conclusions of subsequent sections will be valid only under these assumptions.

17-3 EXCESS-DEMAND INFLATION AND THE MONETARY SECTOR

The static analysis of Chapter 13 is a convenient starting point for considering excess-demand inflation. To simplify matters, let us suppose that the full-employment level of output in Figure 17-1 remains fixed at Y^*. General equilibrium is established at Y^* and i_0 with price level p_0. An increase in the price level may now come about as a result of an increase in aggregate demand, which shifts the IS schedule to IS_1; the resulting excess demand of $Y_1 - Y^*$ leads to a bidding up of prices so that the real value of the money supply shrinks and the LM schedule shifts to LM_{p1}, where general equilibrium is again established at the higher interest rate i_1 and higher price level p_1.[1]

Inflation is a dynamic process. It implies a steady increase in the price level over time. Thus excess-demand inflation implies that the IS and/or the LM schedules continue to shift upward over time so that excess demand for goods and services is perpetuated and general equilibrium is never established. Although an increase in the price level would normally tend to clear markets, this does not take place if demand continues to increase as fast as prices rise.

Ultimately, an excess-demand inflation that is not nurtured by an expanding money supply must come to an end. When interest rates rise to a high enough level, the demand for money will become totally inelastic with respect to the rate of interest. At this point there are no more speculative balances to be had; attempts to borrow funds either will be frustrated or, because of the resultant increase in interest rates, will come from the abandonment of other ventures. When the demand for money becomes inelastic, all funds are used for transactions purposes, and further increases in aggregate demand can then be financed only by a reduction in expenditures elsewhere in the economy or by an increase in the transactions velocity of money.

Wartime financing in the United States provides a good example of the ingredients of excess-demand inflation. Because tax receipts were insufficient to finance war expenditures, each of the war years produced a Federal budgetary deficit. It therefore became necessary for the Treasury to finance part of its expenditures via the sale of government

---

[1] Throughout this section we shall be utilizing the "money veil" model that takes no account of the effects on the IS and LM functions of an initial reduction of bond holdings by the public in consequence of open market operations. The conclusions of a more sophisticated analysis would be along the lines of Chap. 13. However, since the more sophisticated model gives the same results as the simpler model with respect to the direction of change in the price level, there is no particular need in our present line of inquiry to be formally precise.

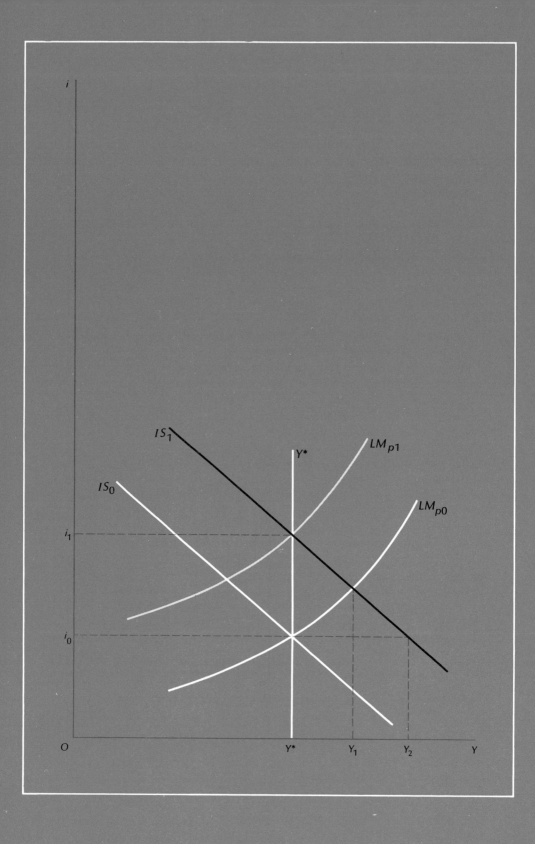

bonds. Such a steady increase in the supply of bonds would soon have driven bond prices down and interest rates up had it not been for a highly inflationary offsetting policy. All during World War II the Federal Reserve System stood ready to purchase government bonds in an amount that would stabilize bond prices and fix interest rates at a constant level. The effect of this policy was to add large amounts to the supply of money. The proceeds of the bond sales to the Federal Reserve were used by the Treasury to pay its bills, which in turn increased deposits and the reserves of the banking system.

The policy pursued by the Federal Reserve during the war, though undoubtedly the only feasible one at the time,[1] provided the means whereby a serious inflationary situation could have developed. The fact that the inflation was, in retrospect, mild is attributable to the fact that investment, prices, and consumer expenditures were all subject to direct control. Excess demand was therefore to some extent suppressed.

The postwar years of the late 1940s were marked by high levels of demand and persistent price increases. The magnitude of these increases was undoubtedly partly due to the fact that the Federal Reserve continued, until 1951, its wartime policy of supporting the government bond market. Thus each time an increase in aggregate demand impinged on the money supply and threatened to raise interest rates, the Federal Reserve, at the behest of the Treasury, would step in and purchase government bonds, thus offsetting the equilibrating effects that rising interest rates would have caused. This situation was ultimately regarded as so intolerable by Congress and by the Federal Reserve itself that the Treasury was, to the great relief of most economists, obliged to sign an accord with the Federal Reserve in 1951, in which the Federal Reserve's powers to function as a monetary stabilizing agency were partly restored.

[1] In the face of the huge annual Treasury deficit, it is difficult to see how the Federal Reserve could have pursued any other course than to stabilize the government bond market. In the absence of such stabilization, bond prices would undoubtedly have fallen drastically, and the interest burden of the debt would have risen sharply. Under normal circumstances the rise in interest rates would presumably have served to reduce the level of investment. But since investment during the war was subject to direct control, the interest rate was largely irrelevant as an economic calculator. By pursuing a bond-stabilization program, the Federal Reserve not only kept the interest burden of the debt within manageable proportions but also insured investors against capital loss. Thus government bonds became a reasonably attractive form of holding wealth; this may perhaps have helped increase the rate of saving.

Figure 17–1   Excess-demand inflation
(all values in real terms)

The inflationary process of the 1940s can be illustrated by referring again to Figure 17–1. Beginning at interest rate i_0 and income level Y^*, and again assuming, quite erroneously, that Y^* does not grow over time, we may suppose that an increase in government expenditures or the relaxation of controls on consumer and investor spending raises the *IS* schedule to IS_1. Normally this would lead to an increase in the price level and a reduction in the real value of the money supply so that interest rates would rise. In other words the *LM* schedule would shift to the left, and the rise in the interest rate to i_1 would choke off the excess demand and thus once again stabilize the price level. But if public policy is such that the prime objective is to stabilize the interest rate at i_0, the Federal Reserve must purchase the bonds that wealth holders are releasing and thereby increase the money supply and offset the shift in the *LM* schedule. Under these conditions aggregate demand (the *IS* schedule) need not even increase over time. Given a fixed full-employment level of output and a fixed level of aggregate demand, there will be a steady increase in the price level as long as the rate of interest that balances the demand for and the supply of goods and services i_1 is in excess of the rate i_0 that is pegged by policy. For example, in Figure 17–1 if the pegged rate is i_0 and the natural rate is i_1, there will be persistent excess demand of $Y_2 - Y^*$.

What is the key to the control of excess-demand inflation? If, as seems likely, the demand for money will be highly inelastic with respect to the rate of interest in a full-employment–inflationary situation, monetary control should be the primary anti-inflationary weapon. Consider Figure 17–2 in which the *LM* function is vertical at the full-employment level of income. General equilibrium is established at Y^* and i_0. In this situation an increase in aggregate demand serves only to raise the rate of interest and has no effect on the price level. This result, as we have suggested, stems from the fact that all money balances are already used for transaction purposes so that any increase in expenditures can be made only at the expense of a decrease elsewhere. In general, therefore, an increase in aggregate demand is inflationary only insofar as the increase makes it possible to sustain the same level of demand at a higher interest rate.

An increase in the money supply, on the other hand, has immediate inflationary consequences. The *LM* curve in Figure 17–2 shifts to the right, creating excess demand of $Y_1 - Y^*$ and therefore competition for the available supply of output, so that prices rise. The inflationary push

Figure 17–2 Control of excess demand (all values in real terms)

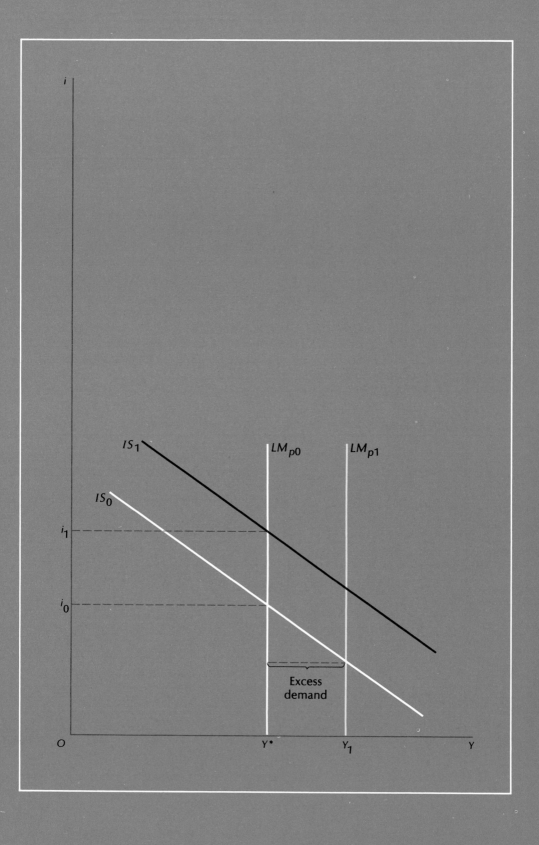

does not stop until the price level has risen by enough to reduce the real value of the money supply to its original level.

17–4 EXCESS-DEMAND INFLATION AND GAP ANALYSIS[1]

We have seen that it would be difficult, if not impossible, to sustain excess-demand inflation in the absence of increases in the money supply. A question that should be considered, however, is whether there are forces that would cause inflationary pressure to abate if the monetary authority allowed the money supply to increase in proportion to the rise in prices, or whether the absence of monetary control implies that inflation will continue indefinitely. Suppose, for example, that the monetary authority pursues a pegging policy of the kind followed during the 1940s. Whenever a rise in the price level tends to raise the rate of interest, the monetary authority frustrates the rise by engaging in expansionary open market operations.

Under the present assumption we can ignore the monetary sector and return to the simple world of Chapter 5 and undertake so-called inflationary gap analysis.

Figure 17–3 differs from other diagrams in that the magnitudes measured are "nominal" or "money" rather than real. Between a money income level of zero and p_0Y^* it is assumed that increases in aggregate money demand raise the level of real income without affecting prices. Beyond p_0Y^*, however, increases in demand leave real income unchanged but raise the level of prices. To simplify the exposition, we assume that the only components of aggregate demand are consumption and government expenditures. The consumption function is the schedule pC. It is assumed that the economy is initially in equilibrium at p_0Y^* with consumption expenditures of p_0C and government expenditures of p_0G.

Next let us suppose that the government raises its demand for real resources to G'. Nominal government expenditures henceforth will

---

[1] Of the many references that are pertinent to the discussion of this section we should at least mention A. Smithies, "The Behavior of Money National Income under Inflationary Conditions," *Quarterly Journal of Economics,* 57:113–128, 1942; J. M. Keynes, *How to Pay for the War,* Harcourt, Brace & World, Inc., New York, 1940; T. Koopmans, "The Dynamics of Inflation," *Review of Economics and Statistics,* 24:53–65, 1942; and F. D. Holzman, "Income Determination in Open Inflation," *Review of Economics and Statistics,* 32:150–158, 1950.

Figure 17–3   A convergent inflationary process

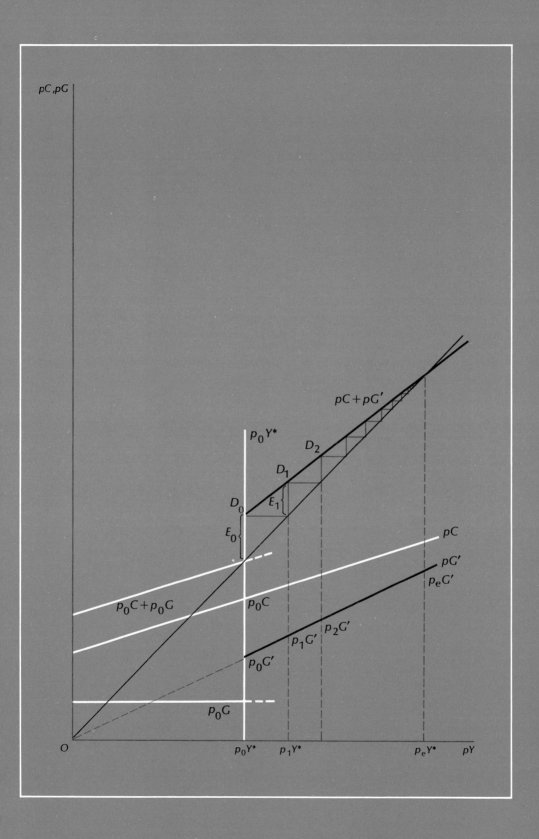

equal pG' and therefore will be given by the pG' schedule. At p_0 the government spends p_0G'. If the price level rises to p_1, the government spends p_1G'; at p_2 it will spend p_2G'; and so on. Clearly, if the government insists on obtaining the same quantity of real resources in all periods, it will have to make its nominal expenditures a constant proportion of money income.

Beginning at the initial equilibrium level, the additional government expenditure causes aggregate money demand to rise to D_0. But since the money value of the supply of output is only p_0Y^*, there is an "inflationary gap" in an amount E_0. The inflationary gap is defined as the excess of aggregate demand over the available supply of output measured at the full-employment level of money income and at the existing level of prices.

Since the level of output is fixed, the increase in aggregate demand causes the price level to rise. If consumption expenditures fail to increase, the new level of money income would be p_1Y^*. But the increase in money income that accompanies the price rise causes consumption to rise by $b'E_0$, where b' may be defined as the marginal propensity to consume out of money income. In addition, government purchases now rise to p_1G' since the price level increase means that the government can no longer obtain G' worth of real resources by an expenditure of p_0G' dollars. The consequence of the increase in consumption and government purchases is the creation of a new aggregate money demand level of D_1 and a new inflationary gap of E_1. The price level therefore increases again, and so do nominal consumption and government expenditures.

The inflationary process can be visualized as continuing in steps between the aggregate demand schedule and the 45-degree line. Observe that in the present example the gap tends to become narrower with time and ultimately to be eliminated. Thus the inflationary process comes to a halt and a new equilibrium level of money income is established at p_eY^*.

What are the characteristics of the new equilibrium point? Government expenditures at p_eY^* equal p_eG'. The government is now obtaining the real resources in amount G', whereas at the preinflation equilibrium point it obtained only G. For some reason, consumers must have been willing to release resources to the government. Observe in Figure 17–3 that the level of money consumption in the final equilibrium is a smaller proportion of money income than it was in the preinflation situation.

What have we been assuming about consumer behavior? Clearly, if consumers behave in the way outlined above, they must be subject to money illusion. Their level of real consumption has declined even though real income has remained the same. Apparently, consumers have confused an increase in money income with an increase in real income. Since an increase in real income is associated with a lower ratio of real consumption to real income, consumers end up spending a smaller proportion of their money income on consumption.

What sort of result would we obtain if we assumed that consumers attempt to maintain their level of real consumption expenditure? If at p_0Y^* (see Figure 17–4) nominal consumption expenditures are equal to p_0C^*, and if consumers insist on maintaining their level of real consumption, they would have to spend a constant proportion of any increase in money income that is not accompanied by an increase in real income. The maintenance of real consumption expenditures implies that the marginal propensity to consume out of money income must equal the ratio of consumption to income at the original full-employment level. In the present example the ratio of consumption to income at p_0Y^* is $p_0C^*/p_0Y^* = C^*/Y^*$. Consequently, an increase in money income unaccompanied by an increase in real income would require consumers to spend a proportion C^*/Y^* of the increase in money income in order to maintain a constant level of real consumption. If at p_0Y^*, for example, consumers spend 80 percent of their income on consumption, then a proportional rise in prices and money income necessitates that they spend 80 percent of any additions to money income in order to maintain their level of real consumption.

The abandonment of the money illusion assumption implies that the consumption function should be redrawn as a kinked schedule. Between income level of zero and p_0Y^*, increases in money income are assumed to be equivalent to increases in real income; p is constant while Y varies. As a consequence, increases in real and money income will be associated with a falling ratio of consumption to income. But once p_0Y^* is reached, further increases in money income result in no change in real income. There will therefore be a kink in the consumption function at p_0Y^*, beyond which money consumption expenditures remain proportional to money income. The new consumption function is shown in Figure 17–4.

If we begin at p_0Y^* and again assume that government expenditures rise to a level of p_0G', we have an inflationary gap of E_0. The bidding by the government against consumers for the available supply of output causes prices to rise to p_1 and money income to rise to p_1Y^*. Now, however, consumers attempt to maintain their real consumption expenditures and therefore spend p_1C^* dollars; and the government, in trying

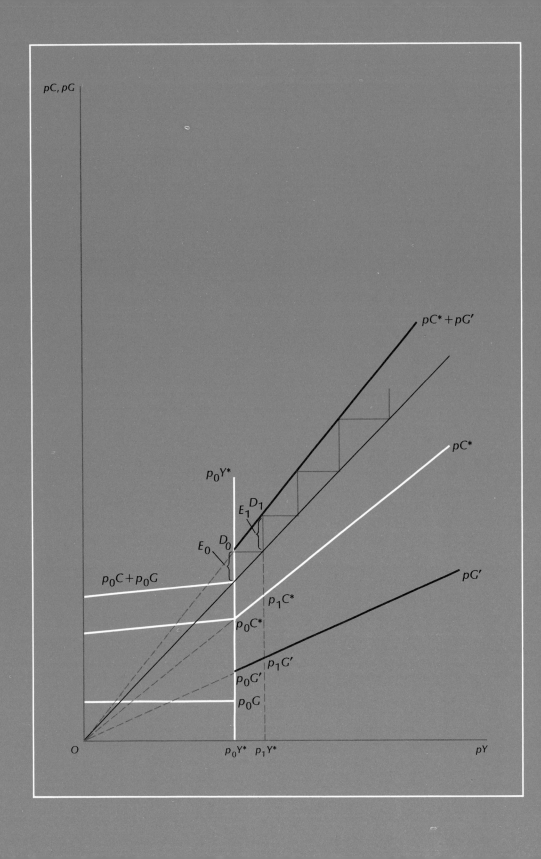

to obtain real resources in an amount G', increases its money outlays to $p_1 G'$. Thus a new gap of E_1 is created. This in turn produces a further inflationary gap.

Under present assumptions the inflationary gap gets progressively wider. Since consumers persistently try to buy a constant proportion of the available output and government persistently adjusts its expenditures to obtain G'/Y^* percent of real output, the two sectors in combination are persistently attempting to purchase more than 100 percent of the output that is available. There is therefore no end to the inflationary process.

What general conclusions can be derived from this analysis? Figures 17–3 and 17–4 indicate that the inflationary gap will become smaller and that equilibrium will be attained if the aggregate money demand schedule cuts the 45-degree line at some point to the right of the original equilibrium point $p_0 Y^*$. This implies that the slope of the aggregate money demand schedule must have a value of less than unity. But the slope of the aggregate money demand schedule is the sum of the slopes of the consumption function and the government expenditure schedules. The slope of the consumption function is the marginal propensity to consume out of money income b', and the slope of the government purchases schedule may be termed the governmental marginal propensity to spend out of money income. If we denote the latter as g', then it is clear that the condition under which inflation has a limit is

$$b' + g' < 1$$

If instead

$$b' + g' \geq 1$$

there will be persistent inflation. In the latter case the aggregate demand schedule remains above the 45-degree line at all levels of money income in excess of the original equilibrium value $p_0 Y^*$.

It is now a simple matter to broaden the analysis to include investment. Since a rise in the price level means that the same quantity of investment goods cannot be bought without an increase in money outlays, money investment expenditures will rise as money income rises in the same way as money consumption and government expenditures rise. Call the incremental money expenditures on investment goods the marginal propensity to invest out of money income, and denote this propensity by h'. Then the condition under which inflation has a limit is

$$b' + g' + h' < 1$$

Figure 17–4   A divergent inflationary process

We have seen that when we begin at p_0Y^* with aggregate money demand in excess of what can be supplied at existing prices, the three groups—consumers, investors, and the government—are together attempting to purchase more than 100 percent of the existing level of real output. Closing of the gap necessarily implies that some one or all of the groups give up this aspiration. Only if $b' + g' + h'$ is or becomes less than unity as inflation proceeds does one or more of the groups obtain a progressively smaller share of real output. What would make one or more of the three groups lose out in the struggle over real resources?

We saw earlier that consumer money illusion would cause consumers to reduce their real consumption expenditures as money income rises. Similarly, the circumstance that income taxes are progressive and geared to money income causes consumer real disposable income and therefore also consumption to decline. In the absence of our initial assumption that the monetary authority stands ready to finance inflation, interest rates would rise, and investment spending would be curtailed. Consumer installment credit would be more difficult to obtain. Thus gradual credit tightening might be viewed as a factor that reduces the marginal propensities to consume and to invest out of money income.

An effect similar to a fall in a marginal propensity to spend out of money income can be obtained by the existence of lags in the adjustment of expenditures to price level changes. As an example of the possible effect of such a lag, consider the case of government. At the existing price level p_0 the government attempts to get G' real resources, so that Congress appropriates p_0G' dollars. However, by the time the funds are spent, the price level may have risen to p_1. The appropriation subsequently rises to p_1G', but when the funds are spent, the price level may already have risen to p_2. As a consequence, the government's actual claim on real resources is not the planned level G'; instead, it is p_0G'/p_1 in the first period, p_1G'/p_2 in the second period, and $p_{n-1}G'/p_n$ in the nth period. The effective real governmental demand is therefore reduced by an amount proportional to the rate of change in the price level.

Similar lags appear elsewhere. During inflationary times wages lag behind prices, and this causes the effective marginal propensity to consume out of money income to decline. A similar effect results from the fact that the incomes of white-collar workers fail to keep pace with a rising price level and from the fact that many contracts, especially pensions and annuities, are fixed in nominal rather than in real terms.

Figure 17–5   Closing the gap by increasing output (all values in real terms)

Finally, as we saw in the last chapter, the full-employment level of real income grows over time. The inflationary push will be smaller the more rapidly Y^* can be made to increase relative to the rise in money income. One interesting aspect of this circumstance is that the less successful consumers are in the short run in maintaining their share of real consumption expenditure, the more successful they may be in the long run in attaining a higher level of real consumption. If business succeeds in bidding a share of real output away from the consumer sector and if government uses its resources to build schools, the productive potential of the economy may grow more rapidly and so also will the output of consumer goods.

Although output expansion tends to mitigate inflationary pressure, it is not true, as is sometimes supposed, that an excess of aggregate demand of E dollars over what can be supplied at current prices will be eliminated when E more units of output are produced by overtime work. Figure 17–5 shows a situation in which aggregate demand at full employment exceeds aggregate supply Y_0^* by an amount E. Can the inflationary gap of E be closed by increasing production by this amount? If output is to be expanded, workers must be induced to work overtime. Since they will want to spend b percent of any additional real income, the gap is reduced only by $E - bE = (1 - b)E$ units of real output. To close the gap fully, therefore, output needs to be increased by the multiplier value $E/(1 - b)$, namely, by enough to shift the level of production to Y_1^*, where the aggregate demand schedule cuts the 45-degree line.

18

BUSINESS CYCLES

18–1 INTRODUCTION

The picture, in Chapter 16, of an economy moving steadily along an even growth path is a useful abstraction. Its value, however, is somewhat lessened by the fact that the periodic ups and downs in economic activity play an important part in determining the long-run trend. The trend, similarly, plays an important role in determining the nature, length, and amplitude of the ups and downs.

The study of these ups and downs is called the study of business cycles or the study of industrial fluctuations. Any reasonably adequate discussion of the causes of these swings would require at least another volume as long as the present one and would take us quite far afield.

Yet because of the interrelationship between cycle and trend, it is important that we give some attention to the subject.[1]

Our approach in this chapter is to outline the bare bones of a theory of the cycle, to place the theory into the context of a growing economy, and to make such amendments and additions as seem necessary. Having accomplished this, we shall be in a position to examine the interrelationship between trend and cycle and to get a better idea of whether uninterrupted growth is possible.

18–2 A MODERN THEORY OF THE CYCLE

Judging by the volume of discussion that has appeared in books and journals during the last few years, many economists seem to be quite impressed with the notion that a significant proportion of capital investment depends on *changes* in the demand for goods and services rather than on the absolute *level* of demand. Because increases in output necessitate increases in plant and equipment, while a constant level of demand can be produced with existing plants, it is changes in demand, rather than the level of demand, that "induce" net investment. This hypothesis, known as the acceleration principle,[2] permits us to make use of the third investment demand function of Chapter 7

$$I = I(i, \Delta Y) \tag{18-1}$$

The way in which the acceleration principle generates business fluctuations can be illustrated as follows: Imagine an economy in which

[1] There are many excellent surveys of the literature of business cycles. Among the most useful are J. A. Estey, *Business Cycles*, 3d ed., Prentice-Hall, Inc., Englewood Cliffs, N.J., 1956; A. H. Hansen, *Business Cycles and National Income*, W. W. Norton & Company, Inc., New York, 1951; R. A. Gordon, *Business Fluctuations*, Harper & Row, Publishers, Incorporated, New York, 1952.

[2] Actually, the principle has been well known for quite some time. The most famous early exposition is J. M. Clark, "Business Acceleration and the Law of Demand," *Journal of Political Economy*, 25:217–235, 1917. Interest in the principle was revived when it was found that the Keynesian consumption function and the acceleration principle could be combined into a self-generating cyclical mechanism. One such attempt was P. A. Samuelson, "Interactions between the Multiplier Analysis and the Principle of Acceleration," *Review of Economics and Statistics*, 21:78–88, 1939. R. F. Harrod, *The Trade Cycle*, Oxford University Press, London, 1936, developed a theory along similar lines. More recent works on the principle include J. R. Hicks, *A Contribution to the Theory of the Trade Cycle*, Oxford University Press, London, 1950; and R. M. Goodwin, "The Non-linear Accelerator and the Persistence of Business Cycles," *Econometrica*, 19:1–17, 1951.

only one consumer good—a shmoo that satisfies all conceivable consumer needs—is produced, and assume that the production of one shmoo per day necessitates the use of one shmoo machine. Suppose further that each time a shmoo machine is built, sufficient income to purchase three shmoos is paid out; that this income is spent in the subsequent day; that the marginal propensity to consume is 2/3; that the life of one machine is 10 days; and that shmoo machines can be produced instantaneously. Given these assumptions, let us further suppose that the economy has been moving along a constant level of NNP of 20 for a number of days; that the level of current consumption during these days is 20 shmoos; and that the replacement rate of machines is even.[1] Thus, if 2 machines wear out each day, gross investment of 2 machines is required if the 20 shmoos are to be produced. Days 1 and 2 of Table 18–1 are two such constant income days.[2]

Table 18–1 should be interpreted as follows: In column 2 the level of current consumption is posted. Column 4 gives the number of machines that are available for use at the beginning of each day. Column 3 gives the number of machines required to produce the day's output. Column 5 gives gross investment, i.e., the difference between the required number of machines (column 3) and the available number (column 4).

Suppose that in day 3, consumers decide to increase consumption by 5 percent to 21 shmoos. Since only 18 machines are available at the beginning of the day, gross investment must rise by 50 percent to 3. The increase in investment of 1 machine, however, creates sufficient income to buy 3 more shmoos. Since, however, the marginal propensity to consume is 2/3, consumption in day 4 rises by 2 to a new level of 23, which means that 23 machines are now required. Gross investment must therefore rise to 4, since only 19 machines are available at the start of the day. Income therefore again rises by 3 shmoos and consumption by 2, so that in day 5, gross investment must again be equal to 4. But since this is the same level of investment as took place in day 4, no further increase in income develops. Consumption therefore remains at 25, and investment falls to 2 since it is necessary to replace only the 2 machines that are worn out. Since investment drops by 2 machines, income drops

---

[1] The assumption that the replacement rate is even is a heroic one, for it implies that investment has never fluctuated in the past and that all machines wear out in exactly the same number of years.

[2] This economy evidently is resting at the point of zero savings. Consumption expenditures are 20 shmoos, and, because net investment is zero, the level of NNP is 20 shmoos. Since gross investment of 2 shmoos takes place each year and since each machine is valued at 3 shmoos, depreciation is 6 shmoos and GNP is 26 shmoos.

Table 18–1

Time (1)	Con- sumption (2)	Required machines (3)	Available at start of day (4)	Gross in- vestment (5)
1	20	20	18	2
2	20	20	18	2
3	21	21	18	3
4	23	23	19	4
5	25	25	21	4
6	25	25	23	2
7	21	21	23	0
8	17	17	21	0
9	17	17	19	0
10	17	17	17	0
11	17	17	15	2
12	21	21	15	6
13	29	29	18	11

by 6 shmoos and consumption by 4. This means that in day 7 only 21 machines are required; since 23 are available, gross investment now drops to zero. It is now apparently not even necessary to engage in re- placement investment because there exists ample excess capacity.

The fall in gross investment to zero produces a further fall in con- sumption of 4 to a depression low of 17. At this level of consumption 17 machines are required; since 21 are available, gross investment again is zero. Since gross investment remains at zero—it cannot be negative— no further drop in income takes place. Consumption remains at 17 in day 9, and, since there are 19 available machines, there will again be no gross investment, so that consumption in day 10 again remains at 17. With just 17 machines available, gross investment still stays at zero. But in day 11 the wearing out of 2 more machines means that a situation has finally been reached in which the required number of machines (17) exceeds the available number (15). Since gross investment of 2 is therefore required, the level of consumption rises to 21; with 15 ma- chines available (day 11), gross investment rises to 6 and the cycle starts its upward course.

It is apparent from the example that durability of equipment intro- duces a strong element of instability into the economic system. An in- crease in consumption of 5 percent (day 1) causes capital goods produc- tion to rise by 50 percent. If the machines have a life of 5 days instead of 10, the level of gross investment in days 1 and 2 would be 4, so that the 5 percent increase in consumption would cause gross investment to increase by only 25 percent. If the machines lasted only 1 day, consumption of 20 would require each machine to be replaced each day so that an increase in consumption of 5 percent would necessitate an identical percentage change in shmoo-machine production. The volatility of fluctuations is apparently intimately connected with the durability of equipment.

A second consequence of a trend toward greater durability is the fact that the economy will tend to languish in depression longer than would have been the case if equipment had depreciated rapidly. In the present example, if the length of life of a machine is 5 days, 4 machines instead of 2 would wear out in each of the depression days; thus the time it takes required equipment to catch up with actual equipment would be reduced.

A third consequence of durability is that it gives rise to the phenomenon of replacement waves. A good year for a durable goods industry is apt to be followed by a good year x years later, if the average length of life of the good is x years, because buyers will be replacing more units of the good x years from the initial boom year than in the intervening years. In Table 18–1 we observe that 2 machines wear out each day up to the beginning of day 12. In day 13, however, 3 machines wear out because that is the number that was bought 10 days ago. Since 4 machines were bought on day 4, they will wear out and have to be replaced on day 14. As is obvious from the table, the backwash of the first boom serves to intensify the second boom. Once the purchase of durable goods proceeds at an uneven rate, there will be a tendency for it to continue doing so.

Replacement waves are likely to become diffused over time. All equipment, even of the same sort, does not last the same length of time. Moreover, different types of equipment have different life spans. Replacement waves tend, therefore, to wash out rather quickly for the economy as a whole. But for individual industries, in countries where a few major industries produce a significant proportion of the nation's output, and following a serious disruption such as a major war, replacement waves undoubtedly constitute a significant source of disturbance.

Returning to the acceleration principle, we may observe that since induced investment results from increases in output, an increase in investment, which is needed to keep income rising, means that consumption must not only increase but must do so at an increasing rate. Table 18–1 suggests that it is the failure of consumption to do so that causes the downturn in this model. The upturn, on the other hand, results from the fact that net investment cannot remain negative indefinitely as long as there is some positive level of consumption. When equipment wears out to the point where some replacement is required, gross investment rises, income and consumption rise, and expansion gets under way.

With some minor amendments, the type of model just described forms the basis of the most recent major cycle theory to be advanced. The theory, presented by J. R. Hicks,[1] changes the model in the following three ways:

1. Hicks points out that induced investment should depend not only on changes in consumption but on changes in output in general. In our simple model, investment was induced because increases in consumption required increases in consumer goods capacity. If, however, investment increases, there will also be a need for added investment goods capacity. Consequently, induced investment must be regarded as depending on changes in output in general, instead of merely on changes in consumption.

2. In the model above, the upper turning point resulted from the fact that consumption does not grow at a fast enough rate. While Hicks believes that such a downturn may occasionally occur—he would call such a cycle a "free" cycle—he believes that the values of the marginal propensity to consume and the acceleration coefficient[2] are such that expansion would tend to boom ahead indefinitely were it not for some outside interfering factor. This interfering factor Hicks calls the "ceiling of real resources," which is imposed by the full employment of labor and other factors of production. A cycle that hits the ceiling Hicks calls a "constrained" cycle.

3. Hicks separates investment into two components: induced investment, which depends upon changes in output, and autonomous investment, which is not geared to present profit opportunities but depends on long-run trend factors such as the growth of population and advances in technology and is assumed to grow at a constant percentage rate.

In Figure 18–1 time is measured horizontally while the logarithm of output (real income) and investment is measured vertically. The lowest

[1] Hicks, *op. cit.*

[2] The acceleration coefficient is defined as the amount of extra capacity required to produce an additional unit of output.

Figure 18–1   The Hicksian framework
(all values in real terms)

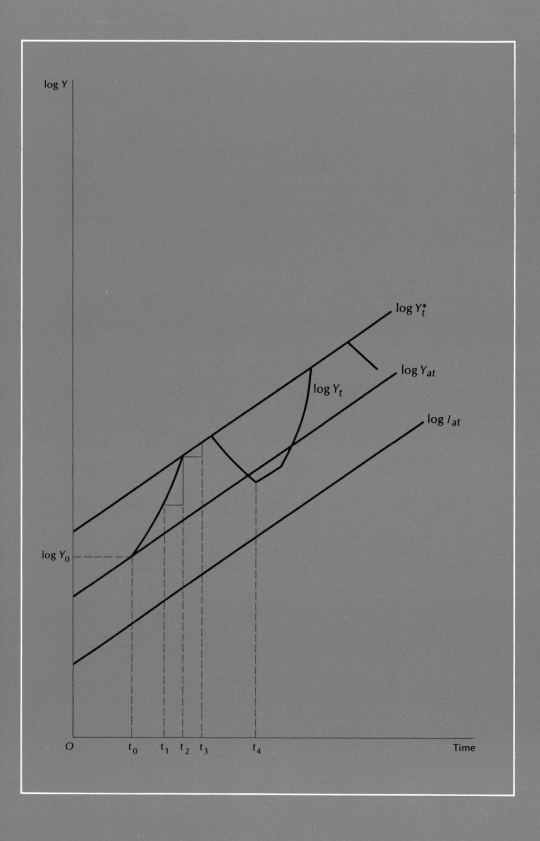

line describes the course of autonomous investment (log I_{at}). The middle line describes the log of the time path of output when only autonomous investment materializes (log Y_{at}). The highest line is the "ceiling," beyond which output cannot expand (long Y_t^*). Since the full-employment level of output presumably depends on the growth of population and the rate at which advances in technology are made, Hicks assumes the ceiling rate of growth to be the same as the rate of growth of autonomous investment.

Suppose that the economy is in the midst of depression at times t_0 with output log Y_0. Since long-run growth factors cause autonomous investment to rise, there results an automatic increase in the level of output, which, if excess capacity has been substantially reduced by depreciation and obsolescence, induces investment. But the induced investment raises the level of output still further, so that more investment is induced through additional capacity requirements. Expansion, driven by the accelerator, continues to push output upward until the ceiling is reached at time t_2. At this point output can expand only at the ceiling rate of growth. But this means that the change in output that is possible between periods t_2 and t_3 must be less than the change in the preceding period. This, however, means that an absolute fall in investment must take place. Consequently output shrinks, gross induced investment falls to zero, and the economy enters a slump. In period t_4 the bottom of recession is reached. A new expansion must now await the wearing out of the excess equipment. When growth factors again produce a positive change in output or when gross investment rises because of the necessity of replacement, expansion proceeds once more.

The Hicks model, while highly oversimplified as presented here, serves as a useful framework of analysis which, with modification, yields a fairly good picture of cyclical fluctuation within a framework of growth. It serves especially to emphasize that in a capitalist economy characterized by substantial amounts of durable equipment, a period of contraction almost inevitably follows expansion. Since the rate of expansion of output is greater than the rate at which full-employment output grows (this must be the case or full employment would never be reached), the ceiling imposes an enforced period of slowdown; because induced investment depends on changes in output, this implies that there will be an absolute fall in the level of investment.

Hicks's model also pinpoints the fact that in the absence of technical progress and other powerful growth factors, the economy will tend to languish in depression for long periods of time. There are two reasons for this: First, without technical progress, autonomous investment may not rise over time, and thus a positive change in output, needed to set the accelerator in motion, will not take place until equipment has worn out to the point where some replacement investment is necessary. Second, if there is no technical progress, the time at which this replacement is necessary will be deferred because no help is obtained from the obsolescence of existing equipment. The whole burden of starting the accelerator going is thus placed on the wearing out (depreciation) of equipment. Small wonder that depressions are more severe and long-lasting during periods when long-run growth factors seem to be in abeyance.

Before moving on, we should bring out one serious deficiency of the Hicks model. The full-employment ceiling that Hicks defines is independent of the path of output. It depends rather on the growth of population, advances in technology, etc., and is thus assumed to grow at the same rate as autonomous investment. But the full-employment level of output depends on the magnitude of the resources that are available to the economy. The capital stock is one such resource. This implies that the ceiling is raised in any period during which the capital stock is increasing. Since the rate at which output increases determines the rate at which the capital stock changes, the ceiling level of output will differ depending on the time path of output. One cannot therefore separate the long-run full-employment trend from what happens during a cycle.[1]

We move on now to supplement and amend the model by analyzing some sources of fluctuation other than changes in output.

18–3 SOURCES OF DISTURBANCE

1. Innovation and fluctuations in autonomous investment In the Hicksian scheme of things, autonomous investment—investment not geared to the current level or changes in the level of output—plays a passive role. It can, however, be argued that in a highly progressive capitalist economy the driving force may be the periodic disruptions introduced by technical progress. Indeed, there is reason to believe that the placing of primary emphasis on induced investment, while ignoring fluctuations in autonomous investment, can be compared to the tail that wags the dog.

The chief exponent of the view that business cycles are a natural outgrowth of economic progress is J. A. Schumpeter.[2] Schumpeter draws

[1] An analysis of the nature of the Hicksian full-employment ceiling is presented in T. F. Dernburg, "The Output Ceiling," *Metroeconomica*, 14:97–103, 1962.

[2] J. A. Schumpeter, *The Theory of Economic Development*, Harvard University Press, Cambridge, Mass., 1934, and "The Analysis of Economic Change," *Review of Economic Statistics*, 17:2–10, 1935. See also Estey, *op. cit.*, Chap. 8.

a sharp distinction between invention (the discovery and development of new processes, new goods, and new methods by engineers and scientists) and innovation (the process whereby entrepreneurs put the invention to commercial use). The importance of the distinction between invention and innovation lies in the fact that while invention may proceed quite smoothly, innovation tends to move in fits and starts. It is this discontinuity in the rate of innovation that, in Schumpeter's view, causes fluctuations in economic activity.

Innovation does not proceed smoothly because people are by nature conservative. They tend to stick to tried methods and to eschew new ones until the value of the new methods has been proved by others or until their deteriorating competitive position forces them to take action. There are, however, a few bold innovators who, under favorable conditions, will lead the way. Once such an innovator starts the process, others begin to follow until ultimately there is a deluge of investment spending and a full-scale boom.

Why do others imitate? For one thing, competitors cannot afford to let themselves be outstripped by an aggressive rival. The more firms that follow the lead, the greater is the pressure on the remainder. In addition, the innovation, especially if it takes place in a situation of full or near full employment, causes prices to rise because bidding for the available supply of resources is intensified. Profit opportunities appear rosier, and investment is stimulated. If there is increased investment, prices again rise and investment is once more stimulated.

We need not go into the specific details of Schumpeter's theory. We should, however, note that a boom driven by innovation is apt to have a radically different type of upper turning point than Hicks's accelerator boom. There, it will be remembered, the full-employment ceiling made it impossible for output to grow more rapidly than the long-run rate of growth, and this implied that investment would fall and income would fall because induced investment depends on changes in output. But when investment is independent of output changes, the Hicksian ceiling need pose no obstacle to the further expansion of aggregate demand. The end of the boom may come about simply because ultimately the new factories will be completed so that investment spending begins to tail off. At the same time, the new factories begin turning out large volumes of consumer goods. Coming at a time when investment is falling or increasing at a decreasing rate, the added supply of consumption goods will not all be bought, prices break, widespread disappointment with respect to profits results, and recession begins. It appears, then, that the length of an innovation boom is largely determined by the period of gestation, i.e., the length of time required for the new factories to be built.

The most significant aspect of the Schumpeterian analysis is its demonstration that the same forces that create instability are the forces that also make for economic progress. Economic progress is impossible in the absence of innovation. But since innovation does not proceed smoothly, periodic ups and downs are the inevitable consequence.

2. Capital investment, interest, and money   Most present-day writers emphasize the importance of such "real" phenomena as the acceleration principle or changes in the marginal efficiency of capital due to innovation. Most would also agree that monetary effects may be important in accentuating or moderating swings, while some would go so far as to assert that monetary disturbances are the cause of all the trouble.

Recession produces a decline in borrowing and in the volume of transactions and therefore creates excess supply of money. Insofar as this is accompanied by a fall in interest rates, recovery will be facilitated. The increased borrowing that accompanies expansion, on the other hand, tends to raise interest rates, to make borrowing progressively more difficult and costly, and thereby to help to restrain expansion. Looked at in this way, the monetary system appears as a helpful stabilizer.

Might it not be the case that in the absence of monetary disturbances there would be no fluctuations in the first place? A prominent exponent of this view is F. A. von Hayek,[1] whose theory dealing with variations in capital investment follows our present line of inquiry.

As a starting point for an examination of Hayek's theory, let us postulate a full-employment economy, let us suppose initially that banks are required to maintain a ratio of reserves to deposits of 100 percent, and let us assume that no change takes place in the money supply or in the velocity of circulation. Under such conditions, all borrowing for investment must originate with funds released through current saving. In this situation the saving habits of the community will determine the amount of current output that can be devoted to expanding the future income stream. If the community decides to consume less today in order that future consumption might be increased, savings rise, resources are released from consumption, and, because this prompts the interest rate to fall, the resources are absorbed into investment.

Those resources that are devoted to the production of current consumption goods may be said to be utilized in the higher stages of production—i.e., those closest to the consumer—while those devoted to investment goods production may be said to be devoted to the lower

[1] F. A. von Hayek, *Prices and Production*, 2d ed., Routledge & Kegan Paul, Ltd., London, 1951. See also Estey, *op. cit.*, Chap. 13.

stages of production. At full employment an increase in investment in-volves a shifting of resources from the higher to the lower stages of production. This shift is known as a lengthening of the structure of production or an increase in the "roundaboutness" of production.

As long as such a change in roundaboutness occurs as a result of the voluntary behavior of savers, no harm can come of it. The difficulty arises when cheap credit creates the illusion that it is profitable to lengthen the structure of production. Since the illusion disappears in time, a vertical maladjustment—a situation in which there are more re-sources than can be profitably employed in the production of capital goods—results. A painful recessionary period of readjustment must follow, during which the structure of production is shortened.

Under a fractional reserve banking system it is possible for entre-preneurs to obtain resources for investment over and above those that are voluntarily released by saving. The process whereby this is accom-plished is called "forced saving." Since banks are profit-making institu-tions, they will attempt to expand their loan-making operations the moment excess reserves appear. In so doing, they lower the market rate of interest below the natural rate (the rate that would maintain the proper balance in the structure of production);[1] therefore entrepreneurs are induced to use the artificially created bank credit to bid resources away from consumers. The resultant increase in consumer goods prices reduces real income and consumption and thus "forces" the community to save.

The inflationary boom that is created by this process can be sus-tained as long as the artificially low market rate of interest prevails. But as money income rises as a result of the investment expenditures, con-sumers use this added income to purchase consumption goods. Con-sumer goods prices therefore rise beyond the initial increase, and a tendency develops for resources to be bid back into consumption goods lines. As long as ample bank credit is available, this tendency can be thwarted. But as reserves grow critically low relative to deposits, lending operations are curtailed, and the market rate of interest rises. This means that many of the new projects now appear unprofitable; a vertical maladjustment develops; many of the projects are abandoned; and recession, viewed as the period during which the appropriate struc-ture of production is restored, sets in.

One of the interesting features of Hayek's theory is its attempt to

---

[1] Hayek's "natural" rate of interest may be identified with the natural rate discussed in Chap. 13, which equates the demand for goods and services with the full-employment supply.

explain the extraordinary cyclical variation in the production of capital goods. The notion of forced saving and the theory that interest rate changes may induce a lengthening of the structure of production may, in fact, help explain this.

Resort to these esoteric doctrines is necessary only if full employment prevails throughout. The typical depression is marked by unemployed resources, and this makes possible the simultaneous expansion of consumption and investment goods. The fact that in the short run the percentage of income consumed falls as income rises is all that need be said to explain why investment goods production rises in greater proportion than consumption. What the cycle would look like if unemployment existed at the outset is not discussed by Hayek, who regards any theory not starting at full-employment equilibrium to be methodologically unacceptable. Be this as it may, the fact is that interest rates will fall during recession; thus the lengthening of the structure of production, of which Hayek speaks, will, if it is brought about at all, almost invariably begin while unemployed resources are available.

Despite its rather severe limitations, Hayek's analysis serves to illustrate that once full employment is reached, a boom can be sustained by the action of the banking system. If the market rate of interest remains below the natural rate, attempts may be made to expand investment goods capacity; this necessitates forced saving. Hayek's theory also suggests that an artificially sustained boom may make the subsequent collapse all the more serious if investment has been undertaken in areas where no true long-run profit opportunities exist.

We should note in passing an interesting similarity between the theories of Hayek and Schumpeter. Both writers begin their analyses with the economy assumed to be in a state of equilibrium at full employment. This means that if there are no changes in saving habits, expansion of investment goods production must come about via forced saving. The forced saving, moreover, is made possible by the ability of banks to expand credit. But whereas the banks are the villains of the piece to Hayek, to Schumpeter they are the indispensable instruments of capitalist progress since it is they who make resources available to the innovating entrepreneur.

3. Stocks, sales, and inventory fluctuations The fluctuations in capital goods production, with which we have been concerned, are not the whole story. During some recessions—mild ones to be sure—capital investment manages to remain fairly steady while the contraction in output is primarily the result of a shrinkage in consumption and of negative inventory investment. Indeed, it is quite possible to generate a pattern of cyclical behavior, despite constant capital goods production, from the simple circumstance that merchants place orders not only to replace stocks of goods that have been sold but also to maintain inventories. These inventories are not at a constant level, but at levels that are related to current rates of sale, to the current rate of interest, and to price expectations.

A reasonable assumption to make about entrepreneurial behavior is that as long as the rate of interest is constant and price expectations are neutral, the desired level of inventory is just proportional to the level of current sales.

To illustrate the consequences of this kind of behavior, consider a model, shown in Table 18–2, in which the desired ratio of stocks to sales is 2:1 and the marginal propensity to consume is 0.5. Assume that the level of sales in day 1 is 100 shmoos. The desired level of inventory will therefore be 200 shmoos. If sales in day 2 are also 100, the desired level of inventory will remain at 200, so that orders in day 2 will be the 100 shmoos needed to replace the sales of the day.

Now suppose that in day 3 consumers decide to purchase 12 additional shmoos. Orders in day 3 must rise by the 12 shmoos needed to replace stocks at their old level plus an additional 24 because the desired level of stocks has risen to 224. Total orders in day 3 are therefore

Table 18–2

Time (1)	Sales (consumption) (2)	Desired stocks (3) = (2) × 2	Orders to adjust inventory (4)	Total orders (income) (5) = (2) + (4)
1	100.00	200.00	0.00	100.00
2	100.00	200.00	0.00	100.00
3	112.00	224.00	24.00	136.00
4	130.00	260.00	36.00	166.00
5	145.00	290.00	30.00	175.00
6	149.50	299.00	9.00	158.50
7	141.25	282.50	−16.50	124.75
8	124.38	248.75	−33.75	90.62
9	107.31	214.62	−34.12	73.19
10	98.59	197.19	−17.44	81.16
11	102.58	205.16	7.97	110.55
12	117.27	234.55	29.39	146.66

Note: Detail may not add to total because of rounding.

136. Since this represents a change in income of 36 shmoos and since the marginal propensity to consume is 0.5, sales in day 4 rise by 18 to a new level of 130. The desired level of stocks now rises to 260; therefore orders in day 4 must be

$$130 + (260 - 224) = 166$$

Again this represents an income change, and therefore consumption again rises.

The cyclical upswing advances until day 6 when, despite an increase in consumption (from 145 to 149.5), orders nevertheless fall from 175 to 158.5. Since orders fall, income and consumption subsequently fall, and the cycle starts its downward course. Eventually it reaches a point (day 11) where, despite a fall in consumption, orders nonetheless rise so that expansion begins again.

What brings about these turning points? Orders consist of two components—the amount needed to replace the day's sales and the amount needed to adjust inventory to the desired level of stocks. The first component equals the *level* of sales, while the second depends on the *change* in the level of sales. Even though the absolute level of sales rises, thereby increasing the first component of orders, overall orders may fall if the change in sales is less than it previously was. In day 5, sales are 145; since the change in sales between days 4 and 5 is 15, desired stocks rise by 30. But between days 5 and 6 sales rise by only 4.5, so that desired stocks rise by only 9. Orders to build up inventories therefore fall by 21; since this is not overcome by the positive change in sales of 4.5, there results an absolute decline in orders of 16.5.

Apparently, the fact that the marginal propensity to consume is less than unity makes it possible for the desired level of stocks to catch up to sales. Once this happens, there is no further need for upward inventory adjustment; the absolute volume of orders falls, and contraction sets in. Similarly, a marginal propensity to consume of less than unity means that sales do not fall as rapidly as orders; thus a time will come (day 11) when, despite a fall in sales, there is an absolute increase in orders because sales have fallen by less than in the preceding day. Contraction therefore is halted.

We may conclude that if entrepreneurs adapt their inventories to correspond with the level of sales in a manner similar to that postulated here, and if the marginal propensity to consume is less than unity, a self-generating inventory cycle may result. Certainly inventory fluctuations tend to intensify general cyclical swings.

The hypothesis presented above is a simplified version of the inventory-cycle analysis of L. A. Metzler.[1] In Metzler's view it is the marginal propensity to consume of less than unity that explains the turning points. If, for example, the marginal propensity to consume were equal to unity, there would be no turning point, as shown in Table 18–3. Sales would always rise by the exact amount of the change in orders; since this is always double the change in the preceding day, no downturn would result.

The eminent British economist R. G. Hawtrey[2] believed that the turning points result from the fluctuations in the desired level of stocks to sales, which are brought about by interest rate changes. In a vein similar to that of Hayek, Hawtrey believed that if it were not for faulty banking policy, fluctuations would not take place.

Our previous analysis of the transactions demand for money suggested that the average amount held idle for transactions purposes was likely to be inversely associated with the rate of interest. The higher the rate of interest relative to the cost of transactions (brokers' fees, etc.), the more profitable it would be to enter the bond market and the lower average bank balances would be.

The demand for money is but one aspect of the general inventory problem. Weighed against the desirability of holding inventories is the cost of holding inventories—a cost that is partly dependent on the rate of interest. A high rate of interest raises carrying costs and is apt to lead merchants to try to get by on a smaller margin of inventory, while a low interest rate will have the opposite effect. It is in the relationship between inventory costs and interest rates and in the behavior of the banking system that Hawtrey found the source of industrial fluctuations.

[1] L. A. Metzler, "The Nature and Stability of Inventory Cycles," *Review of Economic Statistics*, 23:113–129, 1941, and "Business Cycles and the Modern Theory of Employment," *American Economic Review*, 36:278–291, 1946.

[2] R. G. Hawtrey, *Good and Bad Trade*, Constable & Co., Ltd., London, 1913. See also Estey, *op. cit.*, Chap. 12.

Table 18–3

Time	Sales	Stocks	Orders
1	100	200	100
2	100	200	100
3	112	224	136
4	136	272	184
5	184	368	280
6	280	560	etc.

If by some means banks acquire excess reserves, they are moved to put the funds to work. The resulting fall in the rate of interest raises the desired ratio of stocks to sales; this leads entrepreneurs to borrow funds to increase inventory, and thus promotes expansion. The added income results in added consumption, which leads to further increases in orders, so that expansion billows upward as in the example of Table 18–3.

With a given volume of bank reserves, the time must come when the increased transactions impinge on the money supply. This process is aggravated, in Hawtrey's view, by the fact that during the later stages of expansion, the increased volume of transactions leads to a drain of cash from the banks. As the ratio of reserves to deposits reaches a critically low level, banks restrict credit, interest rates rise, the ratio of desired stocks to sales falls, orders decline, and contraction gets under way. As orders decline, income and consumption shrink; orders decline still further, and so on in a cumulative contraction. If the banks realized that this process of contraction ultimately causes cash to move back to the banks, they would not contract to a significant degree. But since they show no such awareness, the contraction continues until the flow of cash back into the banks again produces excess reserves; this causes a lowering of the interest rate, at which point the process starts over again.

In addition to the physical volume of sales and interest rates, we would expect investment in inventories to be highly sensitive to price expectations. The expectation of an increase in the price level causes the desired level of stocks to sales to rise, while an expected decline in the price level has the opposite effect. Since the expectation of a rise in the price level leads to an increase in orders, the expected rise is likely to materialize and thus lead to further increases in orders.

Expectations play an important role, not only with respect to inventory accumulation, but with respect to capital investment and consumption as well. No theory of the business cycle is complete without some hypothesis about expectations. Let us turn to this problem.

4. Expectations[1]   The hiatus is all the more unfortunate because all theories of the business cycle contain, explicitly or implicitly, a hypothe-

[1] Expectations are placed in a crucial role by many economists. Keynes believed that a prime cause of business fluctuations was the capricious nature of expectations. Other writers who emphasize expectations are A. C. Pigou, *Industrial Fluctuations,* The Macmillan Company, New York, 1927; O. Lange, *Price Flexibility and Full Employment,* Principia Press, Inc., Bloomington, Ind., 1944; and G. L. S. Shackle, *Expectation in Economics,* Cambridge University Press, London, 1949.

sis with respect to expectations. Hayek's divergence of the money rate of interest from the natural rate would not produce an increase in investment if no one expected the money rate to remain below the natural rate for very long. Similarly, the increased capacity needs resulting from an increase in output would not, via the accelerator hypothesis, induce investment if the increase in output was not expected to be permanent; nor would merchants adjust their inventories upward if the increase in sales was not expected to be sustained.

The difficulty of formulating a suitable hypothesis about investment behavior in a world of uncertainty can be illustrated with the acceleration principle. The equation for induced investment is often written

$$I_t = v(Y_{t-1} - Y_{t-2}) \tag{18-2}$$

where today's induced investment is some constant v times the change in output between yesterday and the day before yesterday. The constant v, known as the "acceleration coefficient," is the amount of additional capacity required to produce a unit change in output with optimum efficiency.[1] But there is a difficulty here: Suppose that there is sufficient capacity at the start of today (day t) to produce optimally the output of the day before yesterday Y_{t-2}. If this is the case, yesterday's output Y_{t-1} must, in a period of growth, have been produced inefficiently. Thus, if entrepreneurs are not constantly lagging behind in their equipment needs, we would have to assume that capacity at the beginning of day t was sufficient to produce Y_{t-1} optimally rather than Y_{t-2}. If, however, investment is to take place in day t, it will do so only if output is expected to rise above Y_{t-1}. But this means that the investment that is made is not for the purpose of producing the observed change in output $(Y_{t-1} - Y_{t-2})$; rather, the investment results because the observed change in output indicates that capacity requirements are likely to increase. The two statements obviously are entirely different hypotheses— the one being mechanical, the other depending on expectations.

Put another way, if the desired ratio of capital to output is the constant v, entrepreneurs will try to make the capital stock K_t equal to vY_t, which implies that investment, the change in the capital stock, will be

$$I_t = K_t - K_{t-1} = v(Y_t - Y_{t-1}) \tag{18-3}$$

rather than $v(Y_{t-1} - Y_{t-2})$. But Y_t is the flow of output during the current

---

[1] By optimally efficient production we mean a situation in which long-run profits are being maximized. This means that the level of output must be such that marginal revenue is equal to long-run marginal cost.

day, and this can only be guessed at at the beginning of the day. Accordingly, we should write

$$I_t = v(\text{ex } Y_t - Y_{t-1}) \tag{18-4}$$

where ex Y_t is expected output in day t, to obtain a sensible formulation of the investment equation.

How is ex Y_t to be estimated? One possibility is to suppose that the expected change in output between yesterday and today is some constant percentage n of the actual change between yesterday and the day before. In other words,

$$\text{ex } Y_t - Y_{t-1} = n(Y_{t-1} - Y_{t-2})$$

Substituting into Eq. (18–4), we now have

$$I_t = nv(Y_{t-1} - Y_{t-2}) \tag{18-5}$$

which indicates that new capacity needs are now gauged by taking the most recent observed change in output, multiplying this by the coefficient of expectations[1] to yield the expected change in output, and finally multiplying this by the acceleration coefficient.

Whereas the simple acceleration-principle hypothesis suggests that investment takes place to adjust capacity to changes in output, the more reasonable formulation above reduces the hypothesis to the much weaker statement that past observable changes in output indicate future capacity needs.

The problem is further complicated by the fact that capacity cannot be constructed instantaneously. Today's investment decisions are not translated into usable new capacity for some time. If the period involved is x days, output must be estimated x days ahead of time; thus the investment function would have to be

$$I_t = v(\text{ex } Y_{t+x} - \text{ex } Y_{t+x-1})$$

where everything clearly depends on future output expectations.

None of this would pose a serious problem if it were always possible to anticipate demand correctly. But errors in forecasting in an industrial economy are practically inevitable. The fact that it takes a long time to construct plants and equipment means that entrepreneurs must try to see a long way into the future. The farther they have to look, the greater the chance of error and the more likely that intervening circumstances will

---

[1] Metzler, "The Nature and Stability of Inventory Cycles," introduces the concept of a coefficient of expectations.

throw off the calculation. If technical progress is rapid, many investment goods may grow obsolete before they are even ready to enter into production. If the level of per capita income is high, consumer tastes will be more diversified and capricious than would be the case in a primitive economy in which expenditures are concentrated on a few basic staples. As markets expand and as the structure of production becomes more and more involved with numerous tiers of producers, processors, fabricators, and middlemen, the likelihood of errors in forecasting is compounded.

As a general rule, forecasting becomes more difficult as an economy advances to a stage of highly developed capitalism. But along with the growth of heavy industry there is a compensating factor: Competition usually declines in significant sectors of the economy. It is competition that gives rise to one of the most troublesome sources of errors in forecasting. In a competitive industry characterized by many small firms, none of the firms is likely to have a very good idea of what the others are doing. If demand increases and it appears profitable to invest, the end result may be one of disappointment because, all the others having also expanded operations, the resulting flood of goods depresses prices and inflicts losses. Since it takes time to bring the new plants and equipment into working order, the period during which expansion appears profitable is sustained; this increases the temptation to overexpand. Completion of the projects brings about the rude awakening. What would have been a correct forecast and a profitable investment for one firm, if none of the other firms had expanded, turns out to be an unprofitable move because the other firms are also busily engaged in expanding.

18–4 STEADY GROWTH: TREND AND CYCLE

Apart from random shocks and seasonal variations, it seems likely that business fluctuations would not exist in the absence of three basic features of modern industrial life: the durability of many goods, the complicated and time-consuming structure of production, and the use of money. In the absence of durability, final goods production would be exactly equal to the level of consumer demand, and changes in consumer demand would lead to proportional changes all along the structure of production. A short gestation period would eliminate most of the errors of forecast; it would eliminate the period of construction during which money income is in excess of output and thus would eliminate the stimulus to overexpansion which the rising prices of this period present. In a barter economy, finally, there could be no forced savings, no divergence of the natural rate from the money rate, no speculation resulting from changes in the overall price level, and none of the hoarding of cash balances which, as Keynes emphasized, has such damaging consequences.

But all three aspects listed above are vital and central features of industrial society. Even a highly controlled and planned socialist system is apt to suffer some dislocation from them.[1] Socialist planners must, for example, make up their minds whether they wish to introduce an innovation rapidly or slowly. If the new project is quickly built, many resources must be transferred from other areas. Completion of the project then brings about a second abrupt change and necessitates another large-scale transfer of resources. If this process is not effected smoothly and carefully—and it is difficult to see how even the most adept planners could make it so—the consequence is likely to be a temporary loss of income and production and a situation not unlike a capitalist recession. The alternative to this can only be a much slower introduction of the new method, and this implies a less rapid long-run rate of growth of output.

In the light of these considerations, and of some we have not touched upon, it seems likely that business fluctuations are an inevitable by-product of modern economic life. This being the case, it is not sufficient merely to consider steady growth economics. We must also pay attention to the interaction of trend and cycle.[2]

Let us begin by assuming that the economy grows at a constant rate at full employment with constant per capita income. There is no technical progress, so aggregate income and its components expand at the same rate as the growth of population. To facilitate the maintenance of this growth path, we suppose that the money supply also grows at the

[1] See D. McC. Wright, *The Economics of Disturbance*, The Macmillan Company, New York, 1947.

[2] W. J. Fellner, *Trends and Cycles in Economic Activity*, Holt, Rinehart and Winston, Inc., New York, 1956, makes the interaction of trend and cycle his major theme. Other attempts to analyze growth within the context of cyclical fluctuations are R. M. Goodwin, "A Model of Cyclical Growth," in Erik Lundberg, ed., *The Business Cycle in the Post-war World*, Macmillan & Co., Ltd., London, 1955; Arthur Smithies, "Economic Fluctuations and Growth," *Econometrica*, 25:1–52, 1957; and T. F. Dernburg, "Technical Progress and the Business Cycle," *Nebraska Journal of Economics and Business*, 2:23–32, 1963.

same rate as the growth of income and that the balance of international payments is in equilibrium.

Now let us suppose that an innovation is introduced and that the burst of investment spending which follows produces an innovations boom of the Schumpeterian kind. Although completion of the new projects, rising interest rates, the end of such acceleration effects as may exist, and the inevitable reversal of expectations bring an end to the boom and start the economy downward towards depression, the innovation will have raised the full-employment level of income above what it would have been in its absence. If it were possible to avert the downturn, per capita income might be considerably higher than otherwise.

The collapse can be serious or mild, depending partly upon the extent to which investment is oriented toward current profit opportunities or to long-run profit opportunities. Thus if the rate of technological change is rapid, there may be much long-range investment; if the rate of population growth is high, the demand for housing may serve to cushion the shrinkage in investment spending.

When the bottom of the slump is reached, the length of time required for recovery will again be conditioned by long-run growth factors. In the absence of any technological advance, recovery must await the wearing out of existing equipment and the time when inventories are adjusted to their desired levels. However, if innovations come on the scene, the day is hastened when desired capacity and actual capacity are again in line because the innovation renders some existing capacity and stocks of goods obsolete and because the innovation will increase the level of output. Insofar as the money supply is elastic, recovery will be hastened as borrowing for investment purposes is facilitated by low interest rates. If, furthermore, the economy responds to falling demand with a fall in the price level, investment may be stimulated both because the fall in the price level adds to the elasticity of the monetary system and because the cost of investment projects declines. The larger the percentage of the full-employment level of investment that is oriented toward the distant future, the more significant this latter factor is apt to be. The reason for this is that current output prices are likely to weigh much less heavily in long-run investment decisions than are current costs.

Expansion from depression now proceeds. Autonomous investment rises under the impulse of innovation, low costs, and interest rates. The change in output gives rise to favorable expectations and induces investment to take care of expected capacity needs. Orders exceed sales so that the ratio of stocks to sales will be maintained and even increased. All these and other factors interact to produce the boom.

The boom, however, encounters obstacles. Ultimately, if full employment is reached, output increases at a declining rate, and induced investment falls off. Other investment projects are completed so that investment expenditures slacken. In addition, interest rates rise, making borrowing progressively more costly.

If the boom is primarily an innovations boom and if it proceeds slowly, the level of output achieved at its peak will be higher than otherwise. This is so (1) because a slow boom makes available to the system in its later stages some of the new capacity that was constructed in the early stages; (2) because the innovation is labor- or capital-saving, and therefore a higher level of output per unit of capacity can be produced; and (3) because the innovation can lift the economy out of depression prior to the destruction of significant amounts of existing capacity.

It is not difficult to see that cycles condition the long-run growth path and that the long-run path conditions cycles. The key factor apparently is the rapidity with which technological advance takes place. As long as long-run growth factors are abundant, investment is less dependent on immediate profit opportunities. This implies that investment will be less sensitive to changes in demand; as a result recessions will be milder, recovery will occur more quickly, and recovery will be slower and smoother. It is not surprising that during periods of significant technical progress and growth the time spent in recession should be less than during periods of "stagnation."

Although Schumpeter emphasized that rapid growth was not possible without some instability, since such instability is a natural by-product of technical progress, it is also true that chronic instability resulting from innovation may reduce the rate at which the economy grows. For one thing, chronic instability produces a climate of uncertainty and must surely foster expectations that are not conducive to risk taking. Secondly, depressions reduce the full-employment output potential of the system because the capital stock grows less rapidly than otherwise, and in some cases (as in 1933) actually declines.

Failure to recognize the importance of this latter point—that depressions destroy productive resources—helps to explain the strange though widespread notion that recession, if not excessive, is helpful to the economy. Even a superficial glance at the statistics reveals the folly of this view. Imagine the additional output that could have been produced by the capacity that would have been accumulated had we not suffered the "mild" recessions of 1949 and 1954 and the "moderate" recession of 1958.[1]

In conclusion, although technological advance and innovation are vital to an improvement in per capita income, innovation may defeat its own purpose if it leads to such chronic instability that many of the economy's resources are destroyed or held idle for significant periods of time.

[1] The argument that "mild" recessions, which may result from the clumsiness of policy instruments, are a necessary result of attempts to halt inflationary spirals can be used to mitigate this conclusion.

FOUR

PROBLEMS IN THE CONTROL OF ECONOMIC ACTIVITY

19
THE THEORY OF MACROECONOMIC POLICY

19–1 INTRODUCTION

Most economists are confident that a recurrence of the economic disaster of the 1930s is unlikely. Among the reasons accounting for this confidence are, first, a vast array of institutional changes and reforms that now automatically provide the economy with the kind of shock-proofing that helps it stave off large-scale fluctuations in income, employment, and prices. The personal and corporate income taxes, unemployment compensation, farm price support programs, and the social security system serve to stabilize disposable income and consumption by helping offset the effects of fluctuations in national product. Another important institutional development of the past thirty-five years that fosters stability is the Federal Deposit Insurance Corporation, which insures bank deposits up to $15,000 and therefore virtually eliminates the possibility of a recurrence of banking panics. The powers over security issue and stock market speculation given to the Securities and Exchange Commission and to the Federal Reserve System, respectively, make the recurrence of a stock market collapse of the magnitude experienced between 1929 and 1933 considerably less likely.

Second, we are more confident that serious depressions can be avoided in the future because of the enormous improvement in economic knowledge that has taken place since the early 1930s. Each generation is apt to overestimate the degree to which it has advanced over the preceding generation. Nevertheless, it cannot be denied that the strides of the last thirty years have been gigantic. Had President Roosevelt heeded the prevailing economic orthodoxy of the 1930s rather than his own pragmatic political instincts, recovery would have been impeded and many of the important reforms of the New Deal would never have come about. On the other hand, the prevailing orthodoxy of the 1960s, as shown by the effect of the tax cut of 1964, has proved to be spectacularly successful.

Advances in economic knowledge and the ability to apply that knowledge to matters of practical policy making have come from several complementary sources. The first was the Keynesian theoretical breakthrough of the 1930s. The second, and perhaps equally important, was the increase in factual knowledge about the behavior of the economy. Prior to the late 1920s no systematic records of GNP and its components were published. Adequate labor force, employment, and unemployment statistics did not become available until after World War II. The third was the revolution in computer technology which has permitted economists to process vast quantities of data and to construct elaborate multisectoral "econometric" models of the economy. These models have improved forecasting and analysis to a degree undreamed of prior to World War II. It can be said without exaggeration that the last thirty years has witnessed the transition of economics from a field characterized by deductive speculation into a truly empirical policy science.

To know more about the workings of the economy is exceedingly important. It is also important to have an opportunity to apply this knowledge to policy making. There have been some startling developments in this area. By a large bipartisan majority, the Congress of the United States in 1946 passed the so-called Employment Act wherein the Federal government acknowledged its responsibility "to promote maximum employment, production, and purchasing power." In addition to accepting Federal responsibility for maintaining full employment, the act created the Council of Economic Advisers. This three-man council and its small staff are composed, in the main, of professors on leave of absence from various colleges and universities. The Council has proved to be a refreshing and forceful academic enclave within the United States government. It provides the latest in professional economic intelligence to the President, and it has been instrumental in promoting such significant legislation as the tax cut of 1964 and in designing the War on Poverty. The fact that the Council has become a vital arm of the Administration is proof that a third major development has taken place. Economic policy has emerged from academia into the world of practical affairs, where, by consensus even if not by acclamation, it has come to be regarded as indispensable.

Along with the recognition that the economy will not manage itself and that economists do, in the main, know what they are talking about, has come a certain grudging willingness to abandon some of the ancient shibboleths that hamstring rational policy making. There was a time when most businessmen believed that any expansion of government activity, except for purposes of national defense, was an unmitigated evil; that government debt was immoral and would bankrupt the country; and that economists were a group of ivory-tower crackpots who had never met a payroll and who therefore had nothing to contribute to practical affairs. Although strictures of this sort still appear at businessmen's luncheons and in conservative publications, the sound tends to be a good deal more ferocious than the substance. In fact, the retreat from fiscal orthodoxy and the advance of common sense have progressed to such an extent that President Johnson, in his State of the Union message of January, 1967, was able, for the first time in history, to forego the annual presidential promise of a balanced budget.

There seems every reason to expect that the United States economy is now in a position to avert serious depression. However, while catastrophic periods such as the 1930s are probably behind us, the experience of the recent past is a clear indication that the American economy is a long way from being able to maintain a continuously satisfactory level of economic performance. During the thirteen years that followed the Korean War, the aggregate unemployment rate for the civilian labor force was at or below 4 percent in only seven quarters. In ten quarters the unemployment rate was in excess of 6 percent. Such a performance was an extremely unsatisfactory one.

The year 1966 posed a different kind of problem brought about by the difficulty of reconciling the various economic goals. It was easy enough to say in 1961 that economic expansion was called for because it was obvious that unemployment was excessive. However, in 1966 there were those who were more alarmed about rising prices than about maintaining the momentum of the expansion. On the other hand, there were those who feared that action to halt rising prices would invite another period of high unemployment and stagnation. The members of the respective groups called for different policies. However, this did not mean that they disagreed about the policies required to achieve a particular target; it was rather a reflection of the fact that people attach different priorities to economic targets.

A further difficulty is that we still tend to confuse means with ends. It is said that a policy designed to maintain full employment will give rise to inflation because such a policy empowers unions and oligopolistic enterprises to push up wages and prices. On the other hand, it is argued that if we attempt to maintain a firm grip on the price level, we shall be slow in taking action against recession with the result that we shall not make full use of our resource potential and our long-run rate of growth will be reduced. If we try to improve our rate of economic growth by pursuing policies that stimulate investment and suppress consumption, we may magnify an unstable component of aggregate expenditure at the expense of a fairly stable and more readily predictable one. It is difficult, in short, to reconcile the three targets of full employment, price stability, and rapid growth. The problem becomes compounded when we add such irrelevant targets as the maintenance of budgetary balance, fixed interest rates, and a fixed exchange rate.

The practical problems of achieving our economic targets are the subject of this part of the book. The present chapter continues with a discussion of how economists view economic policy making as the process of manipulating certain instruments (the money supply, the budget, etc.) to achieve a set of desired targets (full employment, price stability, etc.). In Chapter 20 we shall be concerned with the targets of economic policy and how they might properly be set. And in Chapter 21, we shall review some of the problems connected with the implementation of the two most important instruments, monetary and fiscal policy.

19-2 THE THEORY OF ECONOMIC POLICY[1]

It is useful to think of economic policy making as the process of manipulating a number of policy instruments in such a way as to achieve

[1] The discussion of this section draws heavily upon the work of the famous Dutch economist Jan Tinbergen. See his *Economic Policy: Principles and Design,* North Holland Publishing Company, Amsterdam, 1956. Additional useful references are Leif Johansen, *Public Economics,* Rand McNally & Company, Chicago, 1965, Part I; and Bent Hansen, *The Economic Theory of Fiscal Policy,* Harvard University Press, Cambridge, Mass., 1958, Part I.

a set of predetermined targets. Policy economics is in the realm of normative economics and should be distinguished from the positive economics with which much of the analysis of this book has been concerned. Positive economics deals with purely analytical matters of cause and effect. For example, the question of how much the level of income will be raised by an increase in government purchases, without at the same time inquiring if the change is in some sense "good" or desirable, is a question of positive economics. Policy economics turns the question around. Beginning with some predetermined target level of income that society judges to be desirable, it asks how much of a change in government purchases will be needed to attain this target.

The first principle of economic policy is that there must, as a general rule, be at least as many policy instruments as there are targets. This principle can be illustrated as follows: The equilibrium values of the variables of the economic system may be thought of as the solutions to a set of simultaneous equations. Suppose, for example, that the target variables are the level of income and the level of prices. Suppose, further, that these variables are linear functions of the level of government purchases and of the supply of money. Such a system might be written as

$$Y = a_1 G + b_1 M$$
$$p = a_2 G + b_2 M$$

$$(19\text{--}1)$$

where, for example, the coefficient a_1 represents the change in income that, other things being equal, accompanies a change in G of $1, and it therefore represents the real income multiplier with respect to government purchases.

A question of positive economics is: Given the values of G and M, what will be the resulting values of Y and p? Or, given some change in G and M, what will be the effect of these changes upon the equilibrium values of Y and p? Policy economics reverses the questions: It adds the equations $Y = Y^*$ and $p = p^*$, where Y^* and p^* are the target values for the level of income and the price level, respectively, and it then seeks a solution for the values of G and M that cause the targets to be realized. The equations now become

$$Y^* = a_1 G + b_1 M$$
$$p^* = a_2 G + b_2 M$$

where Y^* and p^* are now treated as constants and where we now seek solutions for the appropriate values of G and M. It is evident from inspection of these equations that there is only one set of values for

G and M that will be consistent with the requirement that $Y = Y^*$ and $p = p^*$.[1]

The elimination of an instrument is akin to reducing the number of variables that appear on the right-hand side of the equations. If the quantity of money is fixed, the equations reduce to

$$Y^* = a_1 G + \text{constant}$$

$$p^* = a_2 G + \text{constant}$$

and this shows that we could have either a target income level or a target price level but that we could not, except by accident, have both. Similarly, an increase in the number of targets without an increase in the number of instruments gives us additional equations without increasing the number of right-hand-side variables. For example, if we insist upon attempting to attain a target consumption level without adding instruments, our equations would be

$$Y^* = a_1 G + b_1 M$$

$$p^* = a_2 G + b_2 M$$

$$C^* = a_3 G + b_3 M$$

Any two of the three equations could yield solutions that satisfy two targets simultaneously. However, such a solution leaves the third target unsatisfied. If an additional instrument (such as taxation T) becomes available, we have

$$Y^* = a_1 G + b_1 M + C_1 T$$

$$p^* = a_2 G + b_2 M + C_2 T$$

$$C^* = a_3 G + b_3 M + C_3 T$$

and it is evident that it would now be possible to find values for G, M, and T that satisfy all three targets.

In summary: Simple algebra teaches that there must be as many

---

[1] As can easily be calculated by simple substitution, the required values of G and M are

$$G = \frac{b_2 Y^* - b_1 p^*}{a_1 b_2 - a_2 b_1}$$

$$M = \frac{-a_2 Y^* + a_1 p^*}{a_1 b_2 - a_2 b_1}$$

Because all terms on the right side of these equations have only one value there is a unique solution for G and M.

equations as there are unknowns if a unique solution is to be found for the variables of a set of simultaneous equations. To the economist this means that there must be as many policy instruments as there are targets. It is within this context that rational discussion of economic policy begins.

Equality between the number of targets and the number of instruments is a general principle of economic policy. However, such equality is neither a necessary nor a sufficient condition for the realization of all targets. It is not a necessary condition because some targets may be realized automatically or as a by-product of the realization of other targets. In the classical theory of employment, for example, the target (full-employment) level of income obtains automatically and is independent of the level of government purchases. The money supply affects only the price level. Thus in the classical model fiscal policy is superfluous, and only the instrument of monetary policy is needed to control the price level.[1]

The condition for equality of targets and instruments is not sufficient because some targets are out of reach under any circumstances and other targets, while individually obtainable, are incompatible with each other. If we set a 10 percent growth rate as our target, we shall have to invest such a large fraction of our income in raising the rate of technical change and capital formation that it will be impossible to maintain a satisfactory level of per capita consumption. Or, if we set a 2 percent unemployment rate as our full-employment target, we may find that the labor market will be so tight that it will be impossible to keep costs and prices from rising at an excessive rate. Thus some targets are not obtainable or are incompatible with other targets, and the addition of more policy instruments may be of little use in achieving them. The mathematician would say that there are "constraints" or "boundaries" to the values that the target variables may take. The practical person would say that the targets must be realistic.

A second important principle of economic policy is that policy must be coordinated. Coordination means (1) that no single instrument should be directed solely towards the attainment of a single target

---

[1] The classical theory implies that in Eq. (19–1) the coefficients a_1, b_1, and a_2 are all zero. The model might therefore be written

$$Y = Y^*$$

$$p = p^*$$

$$p = b_2 M$$

and (2) that the value of any single instrument cannot be set without simultaneous determination of all the instrument values. To illustrate these principles, consider again the simple model

$$Y = a_1 G + b_1 M$$

$$p = a_2 G + b_2 M$$

and suppose that Y is initially below its target value but that $p = p^*$. Assume also that the Treasury has control over G and that it views its function solely as attaining the income target, while the monetary authority, which controls M, views its function as a purely price-stabilizing one. Given this situation, the Treasury uses the income equation to increase G by the amount required to make income reach its target value. However, because this raises the price level, the monetary authority reacts by reducing the money supply in an effort to lower the price level. This, in turn, reduces the level of income and provokes an expansionary fiscal response, and so on, back and forth. It is conceivable that the resultant policy-induced fluctuations in income and the price level might grow in amplitude and that the net effect of these uncoordinated stabilization measures will be to increase the amplitude of fluctuations in both the level of income and the level of prices. Had policy been fully coordinated, i.e., had a simultaneous solution by the monetary and fiscal authorities been sought, these destabilizing effects of policy could have been avoided. Notice, also, that in the present example the fiscal policy is always expansionary while the monetary response is deflationary and that lack of coordination may therefore lead to a serious distortion of the various instrument magnitudes. In the present case the level of government purchases tends to keep rising while the money supply tends to keep shrinking.

19–3 THE CHOICE OF MEANS AND ENDS

The ultimate aim of economic activity is the satisfaction of human wants. This implies that resources must be fully utilized, that production and exchange must be carried on as efficiently as possible, that income and wealth be distributed equitably, and that proper allowances be made for the growth of national product and per capita consumption. Some economic magnitudes, such as the supply of money, the rate of interest, and the magnitude of the budget, can be so manipulated as to promote or to retard these ends. At the same time the particular value or magnitude of these variables has little inherent significance. Such variables are therefore properly to be regarded as instruments of economic policy rather than as targets.

Nevertheless, correct economic policy has been, and continues to be, impeded by an ever-present tendency to confuse means with ends. A balanced Federal budget is said to be important because the "fiscal integrity" of the government must be preserved and because it is immoral not to "live within one's means." Constant interest rates are held by some to be important in order to maintain "orderly bond markets." A fixed exchange rate between dollars and other currencies is said to be necessary to maintain the "integrity of the dollar." The price level is supposed to be held constant, not because price stability promotes productive efficiency and distributional equity, but because, for some reason or other, inflation is immoral and intoxicating.

The trouble is that the value of an economic magnitude cannot be fixed without affecting the values of other magnitudes. A choice must therefore be made regarding which ends are to be considered relevant. The balanced budget fetish exacerbated the depression of the 1930s, it caused the Eisenhower administration to jeopardize national security during the 1950s,[1] and it impeded efforts to stimulate the economy during the early 1960s. The Federal Reserve's and Treasury's penchant for stable interest rates fed the inflationary trend of the late 1940s and, as we shall see subsequently, it poses a constant threat to stability of income and employment. The idea that the exchange rate between the dollar and other currencies must be maintained at all costs has impeded efforts to restore full employment to the economy, and the high interest rates that "defense of the dollar" necessitates retard investment and growth.

One of the most serious consequences of confusion of means and ends arises from the persistent notion that the Federal budget should be balanced. The damage that can be caused by setting budgetary balance as a target can be illustrated by the following example: Assume that the economy is at full employment and that the budget is balanced. Imagine next that there is an autonomous decline in the level of investment. This fall in investment will cause the level of income to decline and this, provided that taxes are a positive function of the level of income, will produce a budgetary deficit. Rational fiscal policy would ignore the deficit and attempt to restore full employment by raising

---

[1] For a documentation of this view by one of America's most eminent economists see J. Tobin, *National Economic Policy: Essays*, Chap. 6, Yale University Press, New Haven, Conn., 1966.

government purchases and/or reducing tax rates. However, the balanced budget target implies that exactly the opposite set of policies must be pursued, and this will cause the level of income to drop still further.

To make matters worse, the fact that tax collections are a function of the level of income means that a decline in government purchases will bring with it a decline in tax receipts. Consequently, the size of the required decrease in government purchases will be well in excess of the initial deficit.[1] Note that if taxes had not been a function of income, the fall in investment would not have resulted in a change in tax yield. Therefore, because no deficit would have arisen, there would have been no necessity for fiscal reaction to balance the budget. Thus, while income taxation provides an element of automatic stability, it can be converted into a destabilizer by a deflationary response to deficits.

The foregoing example is hypothetical and extreme. However, it does illustrate the importance of properly distinguishing between means and ends. Few people would argue that the Federal budget must be balanced exactly each year simply because it takes 365 1/4 days for the earth to orbit the sun. Nevertheless the United States Congress still maintains a legal limit upon the size of the Federal debt, and a substantial fraction of its membership proclaims that such limits are in the national interest. Although it has now become acceptable to run deficits, there still is enormous pressure on the national administration to keep deficits within certain limits.

If full employment is to be maintained, government must run a deficit whenever the private sector runs a surplus of saving over intended investment. Ignoring foreign trade, the equilibrium condition in the product market is

$$G - T = S - I$$

From this we can see that a government deficit implies that the private sector is generating a surplus of saving. Unless this surplus is borrowed and spent in the private sector through an increase in investment, the government must be willing to borrow and to spend the surplus. If the government refuses to borrow the surplus, spending will be less than output, and income will shrink to the point where saving is reduced to equality with investment. This consideration constitutes the relevant rationale for deficits and for compensatory fiscal policy and shows that

---

[1] Suppose that the value of the multiplier is 2 and that the marginal tax rate is 25 percent. If government purchases are reduced by $1, the level of income will fall by $2, and tax collections will fall by 50 cents. This means that the deficit is reduced by only 50 cents.

budgetary balance and full employment are probably incompatible goals.

The household portion of the private sector tends, on balance, to save more than it invests. It follows that if the budget is to be balanced at full employment, the business sector must be willing to borrow the surplus. Business corporations tend to regard borrowing to finance capital expansion as an evil, believing that investment should be limited to what can be financed internally. If there is an increasing trend of this sort, it means that the private sector will generate a relatively larger surplus of saving and that full employment will necessitate ever larger government deficits. Paradoxically, such deficits tend to be most vehemently denounced by the very businessmen whose investment decisions make the deficits inevitable.

A second illustration of confusion between means and ends is the notion, practiced and preached by the Federal Reserve System, that it is important to prevent interest rates from fluctuating beyond certain limits. During recession, interest rates should be lowered to stimulate spending, and during periods of excessive demand, they should be raised in order to dampen total spending. As a matter of course, prosperity raises the demand for money and the level of interest rates. Recession reduces the demand for money and lowers interest rates. Rational stabilization policy would attempt to accentuate these swings; i.e., during recession, it would attempt to reduce interest rates below the levels that would automatically have obtained, and during periods of excess demand, it would restrict the money supply in such a way as to raise interest rates above the levels that would have obtained in the absence of monetary policy.

In practice, monetary policy has worked in the opposite direction.[1] Historically, the Federal Reserve System has permitted the money supply to expand as the demand for money has expanded. The result has been to stabilize the level of interest rates and to destabilize the level of income and employment. Interest rates have been lower during periods of expansion than they would have been if the money supply had been kept in a constant proportion to the full-employment level of income, and they have been higher during periods of recession. Monetary policy, therefore, has had a consistently destabilizing effect.

Anyone who reads the *Federal Reserve Bulletin* will find that the justification for this kind of monetary mismanagement is that it is important to "maintain orderly bond markets" and that in order to do

---

[1] For documentation of this harsh statement see Milton Friedman, *A Program for Monetary Stability*, Chap. 1, Fordham University Press, New York, 1959.

this it is vital to "mop up excess liquidity."[1] What this means is that stable interest rates rather than stable employment becomes the target of monetary policy. If investment demand declines, the demand for money declines and this tends to lower interest rates. At the original rate of interest there would be an excess supply of loanable funds (what the Federal Reserve chooses to call "excess liquidity"), and in order to maintain "orderly" security markets, the Federal Reserve "mops up" the "excess" by selling bonds and contracting the money supply. Unfortunately, investment, and therefore national income, drop by more than they would have dropped had there been no monetary policy at all.

Irrational policy, curiously enough, can through fortuitous circumstances sometimes lead to beneficial results. Consider the *IS-LM* model depicted in Figure 19–1. Assume that the equilibrium level of income is at Y_0, that the equilibrium rate of interest is i_0, and also that Y_0 is the full-employment level of income. Given this happy situation, assume that there is an increase in liquidity preference that causes the *LM* curve to shift to LM_1. This shift of the *LM* curve tends to raise interest rates and cause the level of income to fall to Y_1. However, if the Federal Reserve reacts to this change with the aim of lowering the interest rate back to i_0, it will increase the money supply in such a way as to shift *LM* back to LM_0, and this will offset the deflationary effect of the increase in liquidity preference. The level of income, it appears, is stabilized by a policy that is directed toward the stabilization of the interest rate.

On the other hand, imagine that full-employment equilibrium is disturbed by a decline in investment demand or by some "real" disturbance that causes the *IS* curve to shift to the left. The situation is depicted in Figure 19–2. The decline in investment demand shifts the *IS* curve from IS_0 to IS_1. Along with LM_0 this implies that the level of income will fall to Y_1. However, if the Federal Reserve insists on mopping up excess liquidity, i.e., purchasing enough money in exchange for bonds to keep interest rates from falling, it will pursue a restrictive monetary policy and cause the *LM* curve to shift to LM_1. This level of income will therefore fall all the way to Y_2.

---

[1] The true reason is probably that bankers do not like to have interest rates change. The Federal Reserve System is a banking institution, and its main relationship is with banks. It is therefore probably difficult for the system to resist the temptation to pursue policies that are beneficial to the banking industry and easy for it to lose sight of the fact that these policies are harmful to the economy.

Figure 19–1   The fixed interest rate policy in response to a monetary disturbance (all values in real terms)

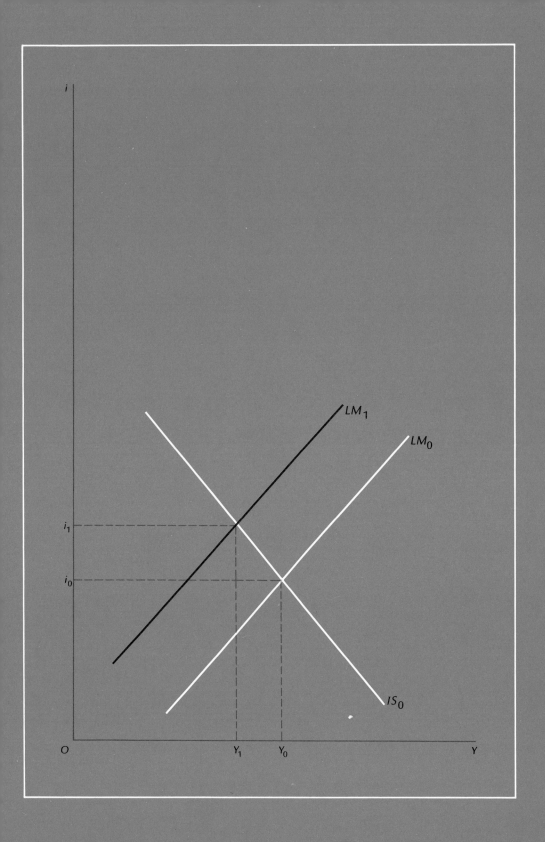

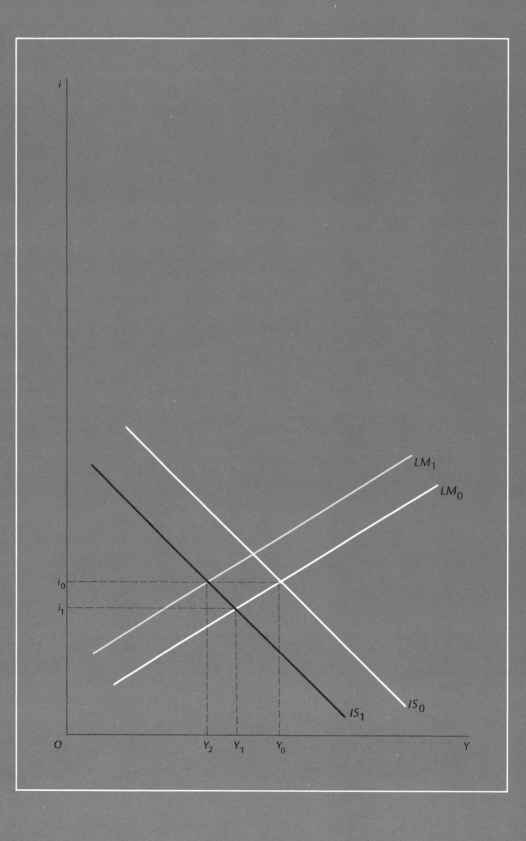

Apparently, a policy that sets a fixed interest rate as a target will be fortuitously beneficial if the disturbances that cause income to change have their origins in the monetary sector and are therefore reflected in shifts in the LM curve. However, if the disturbances are in the real sector, i.e., they shift the IS curve, the fixed interest rate policy will accentuate fluctuations in the level of income. Consequently, interest rate stabilization makes sense only if all disturbances arise in the monetary sector.

As we saw in Chapter 9 a real disturbance can be distinguished from a monetary disturbance by observing whether interest rates and the level of income change in the same or in the opposite direction. Between 1919 and 1958 J. L. Stein[1] found that 21 out of the 39 year-to-year income changes were primarily attributable to real factors. Interest rate stabilization is therefore a dangerously irrational policy. The economy, in most years, would have been better off with no monetary policy at all.

19–4   ARE THERE ENOUGH POLICY TOOLS?[2]

We have attempted, in this chapter, to provide a framework within which to begin appraising economic policies. Are there sufficient instruments? Is policy coordinated? Have means and ends been properly distinguished? Are the ends compatible? These are among the questions that policy makers must attempt to ask and to answer.

When we look at particular policies from this perspective, it becomes somewhat easier to understand the rationale for some of the policies that have been instituted and others that have been contemplated. A few quick examples will illustrate the point.

A situation such as persisted between 1957 and 1964, which finds the economy with unemployment and a balance of payments deficit, calls for an expansionist policy that raises interest rates at the same time as it expands the level of income, and this implies that expansionary

---

[1] J. L. Stein, "A Method of Identifying Disturbances Which Produce Changes in Money National Income," *Journal of Political Economy,* 68:1–16, 1960.

[2] The heading for this section, as well as the spirit of the discussion, is inspired by Warren L. Smith, "Are There Enough Policy Tools?" *American Economic Review,* 55:208–220, 1965.

Figure 19–2 The fixed interest rate policy in response to a real disturbance (all values in real terms)

fiscal, rather than monetary, policy be employed. The difficulty with expansion through fiscal policy is that the rise in interest rates may retard investment and growth. It is for this reason that additional instruments, designed to stimulate investment, are required. The 7 percent investment credit instituted in 1962 is one such device. Corporations were permitted to deduct 7 percent of the cost of any net investment expenditure from their corporate income tax liability.[1] The hoped-for effect was that this additional instrument would permit the economy to simultaneously achieve the three targets of full employment, balance of payments equilibrium, and rapid growth.[2]

A second example, which will be considered in greater detail subsequently, is the introduction, by the Council of Economic Advisers in 1962, of the "guideposts for non-inflationary wage-price behavior."[3] At the time of the announcement of the guideposts the economy appeared to be faced with the discouraging dilemma that wages and prices tended to rise even while the level of unemployment was high and at a time when aggregate demand could, by no stretch of the imagination, be regarded as excessive. It was feared, moreover, that demand expansion to reduce unemployment would tighten labor markets and that this would accelerate the rate of wage-price increase. Thus expansionary policy would raise wages and prices, while control of wages and prices by monetary-fiscal means could be achieved only through excessive unemployment. An additional instrument appeared to be needed. If business and labor could be persuaded to practice wage-price "restraint," it might be possible to raise employment without incurring inflation.

Instruments of control that rely upon exhortation and admonition tend to be inefficient and unworkable. Nevertheless, when viewed from the perspective of the theory of economic policy, the guidelines represented a reasonable attempt to provide an additional instrument of

---

[1] Since corporation profits were taxed at a rate of roughly 50 percent, the investment tax credit represented a 14 percent subsidy on invested funds over alternative uses.

[2] Policy in practice sometimes fails to appear quite so logical. During late 1966 it was decided that interest rates were too high and at the same time that the investment boom was too expansive. Because high interest rates appeared to be having an excessively restrictive effect in certain areas (in particular, the construction industry) and no discernible dampening effect elsewhere, it was hoped that a proper balance might be restored by lowering interest rates and at the same time suspending the investment credit. In 1967, when investment appeared to be lagging, the investment credit was reintroduced.

[3] *Economic Report of the President,* U.S. Government Printing Office, Washington, January, 1962, p. 189.

policy in the hope that this instrument, in conjunction with monetary and fiscal policy, might make it possible to simultaneously achieve the targets of full employment, price stability, and balance of payments equilibrium.

In his State of the Union message of January, 1967, President Johnson asked the Congress to enact a 6 percent "surtax" on personal and corporate income. The idea is for taxpayers to compute their tax liability as usual and then pay an additional 6 percent of this liability. Such a tax policy is deflationary and appeared uncalled for at a time when (in early 1967) the economic indicators began to suggest that a downturn in economic activity was likely. It made sense, however, when combined with the less restrictive monetary policy that was instituted in the fall of 1966. Some fiscal restraint, presumably, was called for if the purpose was to lower interest rates and to stimulate investment without raising aggregate demand and if, at the same time, lower interest rates were not expected to affect the balance of payments adversely. Confidence on this score was presumably enhanced by existence of the interest equalization tax and the Administration's guidelines to businessmen limiting foreign investment. New tax laws designed to encourage the repatriation of foreign profits by American parent companies must also have helped.

20
THE TARGETS OF MACROECONOMIC POLICY

20–1   INTRODUCTION

The satisfaction of human material wants in the best possible way requires that resources be fully utilized, that they be utilized efficiently, that the nation's product be distributed equitably, and that proper provision be made for the future. At the macroeconomic level it is generally believed that these targets can best be assured by promoting full production and employment, price stability, and rapid growth.[1]

---

[1] Price stability, more than full employment and rapid growth, is less an end in itself than a means to the attainment of efficient production, allocation, and equitable distribution. It is, therefore, basically a proxy or surrogate target. There is danger in the case of such proxies that their attainment becomes viewed as an end in itself rather than as a means of achieving more basic ends.

The same distinction between a primary and a surrogate target arises in connection with the goal of balance of payments equilibrium. Equilibrium in the balance of payments, like balance in the Federal budget, and price stability, deserves to be regarded as a legitimate target only insofar as the welfare of society is promoted by maintaining a fixed official exchange rate. Since the merits of fixed versus flexible exchange rates were discussed in detail in Chap. 14, we shall make only passing reference to the balance of payments in our subsequent discussion.

Although the targets may be clear and agreed upon, there are problems connected with establishing the correct values of the targets. To say that we want full production and full employment is not sufficient. We must also know what level of GNP and what level of employment actually constitute full production and full employment, respectively. Without this quantitative information it is impossible to establish appropriate targets and to determine the magnitude of the policy responses that their attainment requires.

It is the purpose of this chapter to take up some problems of measurement that arise in the attempt to establish appropriate targets. By how much must GNP be raised to bring actual output up to potential? How many additional jobs must be created in order to attain full employment?

20–2 FULL EMPLOYMENT

The extent to which labor is underutilized is usually measured by calculating the percentage of the labor force which is unemployed. The unemployment rate, as this statistic is called, is recorded for the adult civilian noninstitutional population in Table 20–1.

As can be seen from Table 20–1, the unemployment rate showed an upward trend over much of the period. The cyclical peak year of 1956 produced a higher unemployment rate than the peak of 1952, and the peak of 1959 produced a higher unemployment rate than 1956. It was not until the enactment of the tax cut of early 1964 and the subsequent stepping up of military expenditures that the economy succeeded in shaking off the stagnation which had characterized it since 1957.

Table 20–1 Unemployment as a percent of the civilian labor force

Year	Rate	Year	Rate
1949	5.9	1958	6.8
1950	5.3	1959	5.5
1951	3.3	1960	5.6
1952	3.1	1961*	6.7
1953	2.9	1962	5.6
1954	5.6	1963	5.7
1955	4.4	1964	5.2
1956	4.2	1965	4.6
1957	4.3	1966	3.9

* Beginning with 1961, the unemployment rate includes Alaska and Hawaii.
Source: *Economic Report of the President*, U.S. Government Printing Office, Washington, January, 1967, Table B–20, p. 236.

It is important to note, as the table illustrates, that even periods of high-level prosperity are characterized by the presence of some unemployment. Economists attribute some of this to the circumstance that there are, at any moment of time, workers in transit between jobs, that information as to job opportunities is imperfect, and that labor mobility is sluggish. Such factors are generally said to be responsible for "frictional" unemployment.

In any case, economists seem to be agreed that it would be virtually impossible, except under severe inflationary conditions, to lower the unemployment rate below 3 percent during peacetime. However, as is indicated by Table 20–1, 3 percent may be too ambitious a target. The unemployment rate for the year 1966 was 3.9 percent. Despite the fact that 3.9 percent is considerably short of a 3 percent target, the price level rose at a rate that began to create considerable concern. Consequently, a 4 percent unemployment rate may be about as good as we can do without having to tolerate excessive price level increases. Indeed it has become customary to speak of a 4 percent unemployment rate as the "low-full-employment" target, and a 3 percent rate as a "high-full-employment" target.

How many additional jobs would have been required to provide low full employment in 1962? The civilian labor force L consisted of 71.8 million persons; the level of employment E was 67.8 million; the level of unemployment U was 4.0 million; and the unemployment rate, $u = (L - E)/L = U/L$, was therefore 5.6 percent. If we assume that an increase in employment is not accompanied by changes in labor force participation, an unemployment rate of 4 percent would imply a level of unemployment of $0.04 \times 71.8 = 2.9$ million. Since the actual level of unemployment was 4.0 million, our estimate of additional job requirements is 1.1 million.

It is obviously important to make sure that our estimate of additional job requirements is accurate. Unfortunately, the figure of 1.1 million is considerably off the mark. The reason for this is that as employment increases, the level of labor force participation also increases, and it will therefore be necessary to raise employment by a larger amount to reduce the unemployment rate to 4 percent than would have been the case had the labor force remained constant.

Labor force, employment, and unemployment statistics are obtained by the Census Bureau through a monthly sample survey of approximately 33,000 households. Persons are asked if they were employed during the census week. If they answer in the affirmative, they are automatically recorded as employed and as labor force participants. If the answer is negative, they are asked whether or not they are actively looking for work. Only if they answer that they are actively looking for work are they classed as unemployed and as part of the labor force. If they are not actively seeking work, it is assumed that they are not labor force participants and that their unemployment is voluntary and therefore not to be counted.[1]

This method of obtaining labor force and unemployment statistics gives rise to the possibility that there might be a number of potential workers who do not seek work because they are discouraged by the lack of job opportunities but who would seek work (and therefore be part of the labor force) if business conditions were more favorable.[2]

That such a "discouraged worker" phenomenon exists has been demonstrated by a number of recent empirical studies, and the extent to which it exists is shown in Table 20–2.[3] The table is organized to show the effect of an increase in total employment of 1,000 upon employment within 14 groups, classified by age and sex, and the effect of the increase in employment on labor force participation and unemployment in each of these groups.

Table 20–2 shows, as one would expect, that labor force participation is unaffected by changes in employment among central-aged males. However, for younger males, older males, and for all female age groups, an improvement in business conditions appears to induce an increase in labor force participation. It can be seen, in summary, that an additional 1,000 jobs results in an increase in labor force participation of 454 and that unemployment declines not by the hoped-for amount of 1,000, but rather by 546. It is particularly difficult to reduce unemployment in the youngest age group. For example, for females aged fourteen

---

[1] However, any person who receives unemployment compensation payments is included as a labor force participant even if he is not looking for work.

[2] We do not mean to imply criticism of the way in which the data are obtained or the concepts of unemployment and labor force are defined. The interviewer could not very well count as part of the labor force any person who indicates that he would, under the right conditions, take a job.

[3] The estimates reported in Table 20–2 are those of T. F. Dernburg and K. Strand, "Hidden Unemployment, 1953–1962: A Quantitative Analysis by Age and Sex," *American Economic Review*, 56:71–95, 1966. Other studies of the relationship of labor force participation and the business cycle are an earlier paper by the same authors, "Cyclical Variations in Civilian Labor Force Participation," *Review of Economics and Statistics*, 46:378–391, 1964; Alfred Tella, "The Relation of Labor Force to Employment," *Industrial and Labor Relations Review*, 17:454–469, 1964, and "Labor Force Sensitivity to Employment by Age, Sex," *Industrial Relations*, 5:469–483, 1965; and W. G. Bowen and T. A. Finegan, "Labor Force Participation and Unemployment," in A. M. Ross, ed., *Employment Policy and the Labor Market*, University of California Press, Berkeley, Calif., 1965. The effect of hidden unemployment on long-range labor force projections is analyzed by T. F. Dernburg, K. Strand, and J. Dukler, "A Parametric Approach to Labor Force Projection," *Industrial Relations*, 6:46–67, 1966.

**Table 20–2 Effect of a rise in total employment of 1,000 on intragroup
employment and labor force participation (Averages for 1953–1962)**

	Change in employment (1)	Change in labor force (2)	Reduction in unemployment (3)
Male			
14–19	125	88	37
20–24	102	26	76
25–34	101	2	99
35–44	82	−3	85
45–54	72	5	67
55–64	29	−9	38
65 and over	53	39	14
Total	564	148	416
Female			
14–19	87	81	6
20–24	29	12	17
25–34	57	26	31
35–44	82	47	35
45–54	78	54	24
55–64	66	54	12
65 and over	37	32	5
Total	436	306	130
Grand total	1,000	454	546

Source: T. Dernburg and K. Strand, "Hidden Unemployment, 1953–1962: A Quantitative Analysis by Age and Sex," *American Economic Review,* 56:71–95, 1966.

through nineteen, an increase in employment of 87 leads to increased
participation of 81, and unemployment falls by only 6.[1]

Calculations of job requirements that take changes in labor force
participation into account require that estimates first be made of the
labor force that would be recorded if the economy were actually at full
employment. Dernburg and Strand calculated that if the unemployment
rate had been 4 percent in 1962, the associated "full-employment labor
force" would have been 74.2 million as compared with the actual 1962

[1] The reader will doubtless have noticed in Table 20–2 that for two of the male groups
the change in labor force participation in response to an increase in employment is
negative. In the 35–44 groups this negative change is not "statistically significant." However, for the 55–64 group, the change, though quantitatively small, is significant and
suggests the presence of an "additional worker" effect. According to the additional
worker hypothesis, a decrease in employment among primary workers causes so-called
secondary or additional workers to enter the labor force. For example, a man who has
retired and left his business to his son may be enticed out of retirement during recession if he feels the poor record of the company is due to his son's incompetence.

labor force of 71.8 million. The difference of 2.4 million represents "hidden" unemployment. Since full employment would require that 96 percent of this 74.2 million persons be employed, full employment would imply 71.2 million jobs. However, the actual level of employment was 67.8 million, and full employment would therefore have required an additional 3.4 million jobs, rather than the 1.1 million that would have been required had labor force participation been unresponsive to changes in employment.

To correct the unemployment rate for the withdrawal and entrance of discouraged workers, we should add hidden unemployment to actual unemployment and divide the resultant "manpower" gap by full-employment labor force. The resulting "gap unemployment rates" for 1962 are reported in Table 20–3, which shows that there is no significant difference between the actual and the gap rates for central-aged males. However, for young persons, old persons, and for women of all ages, the gap rates are substantially in excess of the actual rates. For the labor force as a whole the actual unemployment rate was 5.6 percent while the gap rate was 8.5 percent.

Table 20–3   Actual and gap unemployment rates for 1962

	Actual unemployment rate	Gap unemployment rate
Male		
14–19	13.4	23.4
20–24	8.9	12.7
25–34	4.5	4.8
35–44	3.6	3.5
45–54	3.9	4.2
55–64	4.6	4.7
65 and over	4.6	12.5
Female		
14–19	13.2	24.8
20–24	9.1	10.0
25–34	6.5	9.6
35–44	5.2	9.0
45–54	4.1	8.4
55–64	3.5	9.2
65 and over	4.1	18.5
Totals		
Male	5.3	7.0
Female	6.2	11.3
All	5.6	8.5

Source: See Table 20–2.

As this discussion has attempted to illustrate, naïve measurement of the full-employment target can be seriously misleading. Failure to take account of variations in labor force participation leads to an underestimation of the seriousness of unemployment (compare the gap rates for teen-agers with the actual rates) and to an underestimation of the additional jobs that are needed to achieve full employment.

20–3 FULL PRODUCTION

In the last section our concern was with underutilization of manpower and with the manpower gap. We wish now to translate this into terms of the output of goods and services and to estimate the "GNP gap." This gap will tell how much more output the economy could have produced had the economy enjoyed full employment and therefore whether we could "afford" the War on Poverty and/or a stepping-up of military expenditures, without having to sacrifice consumption.

In principle, one should attempt to estimate potential GNP by fitting an aggregative production function to past data. If properly done, this would yield estimates of the parameters of the production function. Potential GNP could then be estimated by substituting the values of the capital stock and full-employment labor force into this statistical function.

The foregoing procedure would be ideal if we knew what the proper aggregate production function actually was, if we could measure the stock of capital adequately, and if we were sure about our measure of full-employment labor force. Unhappily none of this is easy. A simpler approach is therefore useful. The most well-known such approach involves an attempt to relate potential GNP directly to the unemployment rate. The method developed by Arthur M. Okun of the Council of Economic Advisers sets a 4 percent unemployment rate as the target and relates the deviation between the actual unemployment rate and a 4 percent rate to the excess of potential over actual real GNP expressed as a percentage of actual real GNP.[1] The result, sometimes referred to as Okun's law is,

$$\frac{GNP^* - GNP}{GNP} = 3.2(u - 0.04)$$

where GNP* represents potential GNP.

[1] A. M. Okun, "Potential GNP: Its Measurement and Significance," *Proceedings of the American Statistical Association, Business and Economic Statistics Section*, 1962, pp. 98–104.

Table 20–4 Actual and potential GNP (Billions of dollars)

Year	GNP (1958 prices)	Potential GNP	GNP gap
1957	$452	$456	$ 4
1958	447	487	40
1959	476	499	23
1960	488	513	25
1961	497	540	43
1962	530	557	27
1963	551	581	30
1964	580	602	22
1965	614	626	12
Total nine-year loss	$226		
Average annual loss	$ 25		

Source: See text.

Table 20–4 shows calculations of potential GNP and the GNP gap (the difference between potential and actual GNP) for the period 1957–1965 as calculated according to Okun's formula. As can be seen from the table, the total loss in output over the nine-year period is estimated as $226 billion in 1958 prices, which amounts to an average annual loss of $25 billion. This is a truly staggering loss of output. During 1964, for example, Federal government expenditure in 1958 prices was $58 billion. Just over one-third of this cost could have been paid for merely by activating resources idle during that year.

It should be observed that Okun's equation implies a very high elasticity of GNP with respect to the unemployment rate. A one-point drop in the unemployment rate, for example from 6 to 5 percent, would imply an associated increase in GNP of 3.2 percent. This high elasticity is, as we have seen, partly due to the fact that as employment increases, labor force participation also increases. As Okun suggests, it may also be due to the fact that when production declines, employment does not drop in the same proportion because it is costly to train labor, and it is therefore better to retain the services of skilled workers during slack periods than to have to recruit and train new workers when demand again increases. And finally, it may be due to the fact that plants operate more efficiently at full capacity. An increase in demand in a situation of less than full employment would therefore produce an automatic gain in productivity.

Potential output, as calculated by Okun's formula, does not represent a ceiling in the sense of the maximum possible level of output

attainable. The implicit assumption behind the calculation is the normative proposition that a 4 percent unemployment rate is a suitable target
and that the price increases which would occur with a lower unemployment rate would be socially more costly than the gain from the additional output.

In Figure 20–1, we reproduce the line of potential output and actual
output in 1958 prices, as presented by the Council of Economic Advisers. The line of potential output plotted in Figure 20–1 should not be
interpreted as a line of optimum growth. It represents only what is
feasible at any time with the existing stock of resources. During periods
when the economy experiences high rates of unemployment, the stock
of resources does not grow as rapidly as it otherwise would. As investment spending lags, the capital stock grows less rapidly. It is possible,
moreover, that some of the workers who withdraw from the labor force
during periods of high unemployment become permanently discouraged and that the resources which industry devotes to worker training
are reduced. Periods of unsatisfactory performance may also induce
decreased immigration and increase emigration which would further
reduce the growth of the labor force. The measurement of potential
output treats such bygones as bygones and therefore does not represent the path of output growth that could have been achieved had full
employment been maintained continuously. There is, moreover, reason
to believe that the rate of growth of potential output would be greater
as the result of the favorable impact of full employment upon productivity. In any event, continuous full employment would certainly raise
the level of potential output even if it did not increase its rate of
growth.

The direct economic cost of failure to achieve potential output is
shown in Figure 20–1 by the gap between actual and potential output
that represents foregone production and by the less obvious but equally
important effect on potential output itself of high unemployment. In
its report of January, 1966, the Council of Economic Advisers raised its
estimate of the rate of growth of potential output from 3.5 to 3.75 percent per year, beginning with 1963, in recognition of the improvements
that accompanied the increase in the labor force and its productivity
as the economy moved strongly out of the substantial gap that existed
in 1961. They raised the rate again, this time to 4 percent, for the period
beginning with the fourth quarter of 1965. This increase in the rate of
growth of potential output of 0.25 percentage points per year may seem
to be relatively unimportant. However, if we begin with a GNP of $775
billion and compound this figure for ten years, a rate of 3.5 percent
gives a figure of $1,093 billion, a rate of 3.75 percent yields $1,118 bil-

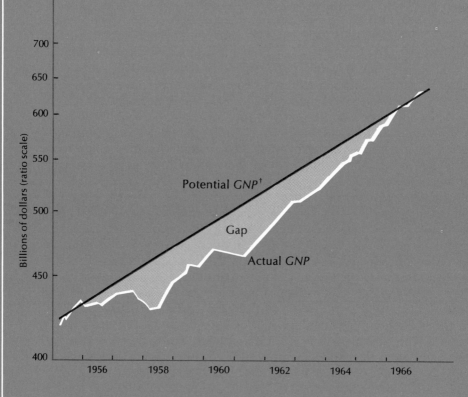

†Trend line of 3½ percent through middle of 1955 to 1962 iv, 3¾ percent from 1962 iv to 1965 iv, and 4 percent from 1965 iv to 1966 iv.

lion, and a rate of 4 percent implies a GNP in ten years of $1,147 billion. The differences between these figures may be thought of as the minimum returns from achieving full employment. They do not include the possible further increase in potential output that would result from maintaining full employment over the ten-year period of the calculation.

Figures such as those presented above are estimates made from the past behavior of the economy. They will be more or less accurate depending upon whether the responsiveness of labor force participation to changes in employment will be the same in the future as they were in the past. Their accuracy will also depend upon the composition of an increase in demand. If the distribution of the increase in demand is not in conformity with the relative distribution of slack in industrial capacity or with the relative distribution of available labor skills, the increase in real output will be less than would otherwise be the case.

It is important, too, to be aware of the problem of timing. To attempt to close the entire GNP and manpower gaps within the space of one year would undoubtedly create bottlenecks, and this closure would cause the price level to rise. Gradual expansion, on the other hand, might avert bottlenecks and permit the gaps to be closed without substantial accompanying inflation.

20–4 PRICE STABILITY

People talk about the concept of a price level so easily and so glibly that they tend to forget that in practice the concept of a price level reduces to no more than a weighted average of commodity prices. Such indexes are difficult to construct properly, they behave in the most capricious ways, and their vagaries often lead observers to the false conclusion that the price level is rising when, in fact, no such phenomenon would be noticeable in an "ideal" measure of the price level. Unfortunately, such an ideal measure of the price level does not exist.

When, as was the case during the late 1950s and early 1960s, a rise in the consumer price index (CPI) creates the erroneous impression that the economy is suffering from inflation and when this impression imposes a deflationary bias upon policy thought and action, the situation

Figure 20–1 Actual versus potential GNP (1958 prices) (*Source: Economic Report of the President, U.S. Government Printing Office, Washington, 1966, p. 43*)

becomes serious indeed. During the recession of 1958 the consumer price index continued to rise at the same time as unemployment was rising to a postwar high. It was, undoubtedly, this continuing upward creep in the CPI that partly explained the reluctance to combat unemployment aggressively and that caused the implicit target values of output and employment to be reduced to an extent that, in retrospect, seems insane. It was, in addition, this continuing upward creep in the CPI and other indexes that produced some of the most bizarre economic theorizing of the postwar generation.

The plain fact is that the CPI, or nearly any other of our present indexes of prices, contains built-in biases that make it a poor measure of price changes in a growing economy. Indeed, constancy of the CPI really ought to be interpreted as implying that the price level (in an ideal theoretical sense) is actually falling. A rise in the CPI, moreover, does not necessarily mean that the purchasing power of the dollar is being eroded. These are strong statements; let us see if they can be supported.

Part of the confusion on the score of price stability arises from a preoccupation with the relationship between wages, prices, and productivity. The marginal cost of production (MC) can be defined as

$$MC = \frac{w}{MP}$$

where w is the money wage rate and MP is the marginal product of labor, i.e., the number of units of output produced by the last worker to be hired. If this last worker produces 5 units of output per day and if his daily wage is $10, the marginal cost of producing each of the 5 last units of output is $2. If the marginal product of labor increases by 3 percent and if money wages also rise by 3 percent, the ratio w/MP will remain unchanged. Consequently, marginal costs do not rise, and prices would therefore not change unless there is a shift in the demand schedule for the industry's product.[1]

Wages can increase in proportion to productivity without raising costs. But what about cases in which the cost of the input is identical

---

[1] The reader who is uncertain about his microeconomic theory should be reminded that profits are maximized when marginal cost equals marginal revenue. Under monopolistic conditions an increase in marginal cost will cause the monopolist to reduce output and raise price. Under competitive conditions an increase in marginal cost of individual firms will shift the industry's short-run supply curve to the left, and output will therefore fall and price will rise. Thus, in either case, a rise in marginal cost will tend to raise price, while a fall in marginal cost will do the opposite.

to the value of the output? There can be no such thing as a noninflationary increase in the income of a doctor. Although his productivity may have increased greatly owing to the advance of medical technology, any increase in a doctor's compensation will show up as an increase in the CPI.

The major sources of increase in the CPI since 1950 have been increases in the cost of medical and other kinds of services. But is the increase in these costs pure inflation, or have there been productivity increases? If there have been such increases, how are the providers of this improved service to be compensated except by an increase in price? If we consider medical expenses, not in terms of the cost of an hour of medical consultation, but rather in terms of the benefits of an hour's worth of medical treatment, it is no longer quite so clear whether we are really paying more for the consultation. Similarly, it is not clear whether we are paying more for an hour's worth of classroom instruction or for an hour spent in the dentist's chair. Only if there had been no productivity increase would it have been legitimate to conclude that the increase in the nominal cost of these services implies inflation.

In general, it is true that the CPI will rise if wage increases are in excess of the rate of growth of productivity. But there is a logical fallacy in reasoning from this circumstance that any rise in the CPI implies an increase in compensation in excess of productivity gain, and therefore inflation. Doctors, teachers, lawyers, and other providers of services not unreasonably expect to be compensated for improvement in the quality of the service they perform. If we rule out the fact that such compensation can accrue indirectly through price declines elsewhere in the economy, the compensation must take the form of higher nominal returns for services. Such increases, however, quite unreasonably raise the CPI, whereas wage increases that are proportional to the rate of growth of productivity do not. Productivity increases, in combination with price stability, when that concept is used in a meaningful sense, therefore imply increases in the CPI. By the same token, stability of the CPI implies deflation.

Another way in which productivity gains accrue to the economy is in the form of improvements in the quality of the physical commodities that we buy. In a highly significant study Griliches[1] has computed the effect on automobile prices of different specifications. The effects

[1] Z. Griliches, "Hedonic Price Indexes for Automobiles: An Econometric Analysis of Quality Change," *The Price Statistics of the Federal Government,* No. 73, National Bureau of Economic Research, Inc., New York, 1961.

of changes in horsepower, weight, and length were evaluated for the "low-priced three."[1] Over the period 1954–1960 list prices of cars rose steadily. The CPI's "new automobile component" index rose from a value of 129.7 in 1954 to a value of 144.3 in 1960. However, Griliches' method of computing the index yields a fall from 128.9 to 111.3. Consequently, if quality changes are taken into account, it is by no means clear whether a rise in the price of products necessarily means that price inflation is under way.

Submit yourself to the acid test: Assume that you are given a choice of buying only the goods and services that were available in 1953 at 1953 prices or the goods and services that were available in 1968 at 1968 prices, and do not forget such items as the Salk vaccine that were not available in 1953. Only if you genuinely prefer the 1953 bundle of goods and services can you assert in any convincing way that inflation has characterized the years since the Korean War. And even if you do prefer the 1953 bundle of goods and services, you will have to admit that the price increases that have taken place since that time do not represent nearly as much "pure inflation" as is commonly supposed.

If we are concerned about the general level of prices rather than just consumer prices, we might properly be concerned with the GNP deflator rather than the CPI. But the GNP deflator suffers from the same drawbacks as the CPI and some additional ones as well. To cite one problem, the GNP deflator includes government, and the price of government services is measured at cost. Thus anytime government employees receive a pay increase, the GNP deflator records this as a price increase. This means that the GNP deflator is based on the assumption that there are never any productivity increases in the provision of public services. Although it is common to make jokes to the effect that this is not an unwarranted assumption, it is nevertheless a fact that even the postal service has done much to streamline its operations.

The inadequacy of our price indexes is very serious business. The CPI is widely regarded by economists, businessmen, and public officials as *the* measure of the price level. If it is true that we have erroneously been led to believe that the price level has risen during periods characterized by high levels of unemployment and if, because of the upward creep in the CPI, we have become so fearful of inflation that we have failed to take measures to reduce unemployment and excess capacity, then we have been paying an intolerably high price in the form of unemployment and lost production as the consequence of a faulty sta-

---

[1] Until 1961, when compacts were introduced into the CPI, the low-priced three— Chevrolet, Ford, and Plymouth—were the cars included in the CPI.

tistical construction. Writing in 1961, Ruggles estimated that "we waste through underutilization an amount equal in size to two or three times what we now spend on defense, or 20 to 25 times as much as we now are giving in foreign aid." He suggested, moreover, that "these wasted resources could rebuild our cities and automate our factories within a few short years; they could raise our rate of growth to equal or surpass that of any other nation."[1]

We have been suggesting that price stability means one thing in a context of stagnation and lack of technical progress and quite a different thing in an atmosphere of growth and productivity increase. Unhappily, many people have confused the two very badly, a confusion that has been prodigiously costly. Perhaps it will not be possible to revise our price indexes along the lines suggested by Griliches, but we ought at least to be aware that constancy of the CPI implies, if anything, a deflationary trend.

Inability to realize that rising price indexes are inevitable in a growing economy has led to attempts to explain how inflation and high levels of unemployment could coexist and to attempts to devise policies that would raise employment without accelerating the rate of price increase. Some take the view that the decline in competition and the rise in bargaining power of private economic units makes cost-price increases inevitable even when substantial unemployment exists. These are the "cost" or "wage push" inflationists. Others take the view that the unemployment rate is not an adequate measure of labor market tightness and that the rate of technical change in recent years has been so great that a high unemployment rate could easily be consistent with a very tight labor market. This is because a large overall level of unemployment does not imply that there is an available supply of workers who have the requisite skills. Those who argue in this way are called "structuralists."

If the messages preached by the structuralists and the cost-inflationists are correct, they imply that the instruments of monetary-fiscal policy will be insufficient to attain the goals of high employment and price stability simultaneously. An attempt to provide an additional instrument designed to cope with these difficulties is the Council of Economic Advisers' guideposts for noninflationary wage increases.

In the remainder of this section we shall take a quick look at those issues that bear on the problem of price stability. Can inflation arise from the cost, rather than from the demand, side? Is there anything to

[1] Richard Ruggles, "Measuring the Cost of Quality," *Challenge*, 10:6–9, 1961. Okun's law suggests that Ruggles somewhat overstates the case.

the structuralist hypothesis, and if so, what is the proper policy response? Is administrative exhortation through the invocation of guideposts a suitable solution to the problem of reconciling high-level employment with price stability?

Cost push inflation   The idea that inflation in the American economy could be caused by institutional rigidities had a pervasive influence on economic thought and policy in the 1950s, and vestiges of the idea are still in evidence. To put the argument in its crudest form, it is suggested that the market power of oligopolistic industries and labor unions has been such that acting separately or in concert, they could force continually rising prices.

To suggest that oligopolistic industries can inflict inflation on the economy whenever they please is to assume that they do not attempt to maximize profits at all times. It may be that some industries find it advantageous to concentrate price increases caused by increased demand for their output at particular points in time. But to suggest that they will attempt to raise prices continuously is to fly in the face of the theory of rational firm behavior.

To understand the behavior of labor unions, it is necessary to know whether they are attempting to maximize employment and their membership or whether they are attempting to maximize their money wages.[1] If their goal is to maximize their membership, then presumably they do not always push for higher wages for the demand for labor is not infinitely inelastic with respect to the wage rate. Only if they are indifferent to the level of union employment can they be expected to continually push for wage increases because such action would result in reduced employment in unionized occupations. While such behavior is perhaps typical of tightly controlled craft unions, it seems more reasonable to believe that unions are concerned with employment as well as wages.

There are moreover macroeconomic restraints that make a cost push inflationary spiral impossible. Wage-price increases reduce the real value of the money supply, thereby raising the rate of interest and reducing the level of investment. An increase in the price level makes the domestic market a better place in which to sell but a poorer place in which to buy. As prices and money incomes rise, the real value of tax collections increases, real disposable income declines, and consumption declines. As the price level rises, the real value of liquid assets declines,

---

[1] For a discussion of "union indifference maps" see W. J. Fellner, *Competition among the Few,* Chap. 11, Alfred A. Knopf, Inc., New York, 1949.

and the Pigou effect in reverse may be set in motion. All these circumstances mean that if unemployment is to be avoided, higher prices and wages must be "financed," i.e., offset by a proportional increase in the money supply.

It is the possibility of intervention by the monetary authorities that turns the situation into one of danger for price stability. If the money supply is increased in an attempt to reduce the unemployment caused by a wage increase, prices will rise and the real value of the wage increase will be less than expected. If the unions then force a new increase in money wages which is again countered by an increase in the money supply, a round of price inflation can be started.

The monetary authority in the United States has not behaved in such a way as to permit the kind of process described above to develop, possibly because it, itself, subscribes to the cost push theory. This, indeed, is why the cost push message is so bleak. The thesis implies that the expansionary effects of increases in the money supply will not raise output and employment but rather will be frittered away in the form of wage-price increases. It is quite likely that fear of cost push inflation is one reason why the economy was choked for many years by the noose of tight money.

Structural unemployment   An alternative attempt to explain the simultaneous presence of high levels of unemployment and wage-price increases is the "structural unemployment" thesis. People who subscribe to this view maintain that the cause of high unemployment between 1957 and 1964 lay in the speed with which technical change (automation as they like to call it) took place. The consequence of this accelerated rate of technical change is that the rate at which the skills of the labor force become obsolete has accelerated and that an increasing fraction of the labor force has joined the ranks of the hard-core unemployed. The structuralists imply that demand expansion will not raise employment because the available workers simply do not have the skills required by the newly created job opportunities. It is said that the problem is one of fitting square pegs into round holes. Demand expansion provides the round holes, but since the square pegs will not fit, the expansion of demand merely produces labor market tightness with associated increases in wages and prices, without producing much in the way of a reduction in unemployment.

The solution to the unemployment problem in the view of the structuralists is not to be found in short-term expansion of demand, but rather in intensive long-term training and relocation programs. In the absence of such programs the structurally unemployed are said to be doomed to a position similar to that of stand-by capital equipment. They would find sporadic employment during periods of excess demand. However, because price stability, along with high employment, is an important economic target, monetary and fiscal policies should, presumably, not be used to ensure the employment of these workers.

No one can deny that structural unemployment exists and that it has existed at least since the beginnings of the Industrial Revolution. The coal miner in West Virginia who has been displaced by machinery has his ancestral counterpart in the handloom weaver of eighteenth-century England. But it is quite a different thing to say that the process has been accelerating in recent years. Studies of the characteristics of the unemployed during the recent past have not supported the contention that the proportion of the labor force which is unemployed as a result of technical change has increased.[1]

The dangerous implication of the structural unemployment thesis is that it may persuade policy makers that the noninflationary unemployment target should be increased so that instead of aiming for a 4 percent unemployment rate, they aim for a 5 or 6 percent rate. The cost in foregone output of higher unemployment has already been estimated. The additional cost of a decline in the rate of growth of potential output would also be severe. In combination, these potential costs are so enormous that a powerful burden of proof rests on the shoulders of the structuralists.

A useful tool for an analysis of the problem of structural unemployment is the "Phillips curve," which is shown in Figure 20–2.[2] The percentage of change in wage rates is recorded on the vertical axis, while the percentage of the labor force that is unemployed is measured on the horizontal axis. The curve slopes downward and to the right. Periods of relatively high unemployment rates are associated with loose labor markets and small increases in wage rates. Periods of relatively low unemployment rates, on the other hand, are periods of labor market tightness and therefore of more rapidly rising prices.

The structural unemployment thesis implies that the Phillips curve has been shifting to the right. Consequently, the percentage of wage

[1] For example, see J. W. Knowles and E. D. Kalacheck, "High Unemployment Rates, 1957–1960: Structural Transformation or Inadequate Demand," *Subcommittee on Economic Statistics of the Joint Economic Committee,* U.S. Congress, U.S. Government Printing Office, Washington, 1961.

[2] A. W. Phillips, "The Relation between Unemployment and the Rate of Change of Money Wage Rates in the United Kingdom, 1862–1957," *Economica,* 25:283–299, 1958.

Figure 20–2 Phillips curve

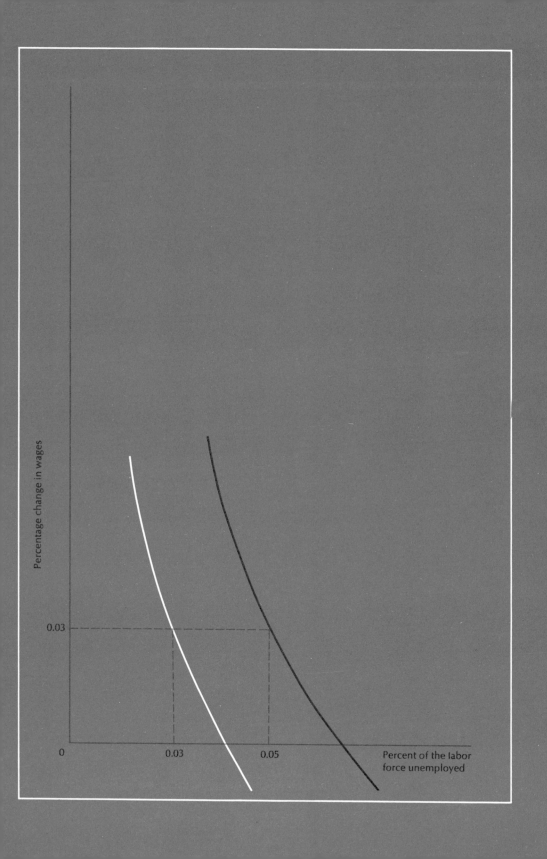

increase associated with a particular relative level of unemployment is growing larger. In Figure 20–2, for example, the shift to the right of the Phillips curve means that a 3 percent increase in wage rates is associated with 5 percent unemployment in the labor force as opposed to 3 percent prior to the shift. Therefore the implication of the structural unemployment thesis is that in order to obtain an increase in the level of unemployment, society must pay more in the form of wage and price increases than it has paid in the past.

It is important to note that even if there were some validity to the thesis, implying that demand expansion will not cure the unemployment problem, the problem still could not be solved without such demand expansion. Those who find themselves unemployed because their skills have become obsolete may have to be retrained and relocated before they can find employment again. There is, however, little to be gained from retraining people if there are no job opportunities for them. To quote Ruggles again, "Those wishing to restrict demand have labeled the unemployment 'structural,' and thereby have succeeded in removing it from their conscience. This rationalization may satisfy them, but it is not much help for the unemployed since it is obvious that the only cure for unemployment, whether structural or any other kind, is more jobs, and you don't get more jobs by restricting demand, no matter how much retraining you do."[1]

The wage-price guideposts   In the *Economic Report of the President* for 1962 the Council of Economic Advisers set forth "guideposts for non-inflationary wage and price behavior." The Council stated, "The general guide for non-inflationary wage behavior is that the rate of increase in wage rates (including fringe benefits) in each industry be equal to the trend rate of overall productivity increase." With respect to prices, the Council indicated that industries in which productivity rises faster than the national average should lower prices so that, in conjunction with rising prices in low-productivity-growth industries, the overall price level would remain roughly constant.

In affirming the necessity for such guideposts, the Council seemed to be accepting the cost-inflation argument that competition cannot be relied upon to keep wages and prices in check even in the absence of excess demand. One might also infer that the Council implicitly accepted the structuralist view that additional policy instruments were required to shift the Phillips curve back to the left.[2]

---

[1] Ruggles, *op. cit.*, p. 9.

[2] The Council, however, opposed structuralist objections and vigorously argued for demand expansion during the early 1960s.

Price stability can always be ensured by sufficiently restrictive monetary-fiscal policies. However, the cost of such stability would be excessively high levels of unemployment and retarded growth. Would it not, therefore, be desirable to find an additional policy instrument that would permit demand expansion to raise employment without raising prices? Direct controls over wages and prices are inefficient, discriminatory, and inconsistent with freedom of choice. Might it not be possible, however, to keep prices from rising by resorting to appeals to patriotism and to "industrial statesmanship" and by providing a set of guideposts for wage-price determination?

The guideposts have been widely ridiculed, and administrative interference in wage-price decisions has been regarded with displeasure and irritation by economists and by the affected parties alike. Presidential participation in collective bargaining negotiations and attempts to influence industrial price decisions have been derided as constituting "economics by admonition";[1] as interference with so-called "free collective bargaining"; and as an attempt to run the economy by resort to the "open-mouth policy."

Nevertheless there is an essential logic behind the guideposts that ought not to be obscured by the ridicule that the guideposts have evoked. To understand this logic, it is necessary to consider how wages and prices would be determined in a purely competitive economy. If there were no imperfections in labor and product markets, wages (for comparable skills and conditions of work) would tend toward equality in all industries. The general wage level, moreover, would rise at a rate equal to the national average increase in productivity. Under these competitive conditions, any industry that failed to realize the average national productivity gain would lose its relative share of the national market. This is because competition would keep wage rates at a uniform level, so that industries in which productivity did not grow at the national average would (assuming that the income elasticity of demand for all products is unitary) find marginal costs and prices rising. Resources would therefore transfer to industries where rapid productivity gains produce declining marginal costs and prices. Under such ideal conditions price increases in low-productivity areas would be offset by declining prices in high-productivity areas, and the overall level of prices would remain stable. It is the attempt to simulate competitive conditions where such conditions do not, in fact, exist that constitutes the essential logic of the guideposts.

---

[1] The phrase was coined by Ben W. Lewis. See his analysis of the guideposts and administrative exhortation, "Economics by Admonition," *American Economic Review*, 59:384–398, 1959.

One of the main difficulties with guideposts and other forms of "economics by admonition" is that they punish those who are naïve enough to comply, and they reward those who possess sufficient cleverness, gall, or public relations skill to avoid compliance. Prices, wages, the allocation of resources, and the distribution of income tend therefore to be determined by the propensity and ability of unions and business enterprises to evade administrative rules and to resist exhortations. Such a situation is bound to produce inefficiencies and inequities, and it further causes resources to be wasted by creating incentives to spend time and money on public relations campaigns designed to justify wage or price increases that violate the guideposts. Thus, means and ends become confused. Price stability is supposed to foster efficient production and distribution. Guideposts, however, tend to misallocate and waste resources. They therefore attempt to purchase price stability at the cost of forfeiting the very gains that price stability is intended to realize.

The guideposts represented an honest attempt to replace the kind of painful medicine that the restoration of competition would require with a mild sedative that would merely alleviate symptoms. Those who ridicule the guideposts and at the same time use their monopoly power to appropriate a larger share of the national income for themselves would do well to recognize this fact. They should also bear in mind that the failure of the guideposts may mean that stronger and more bitter medicine—a tough antitrust policy or direct control over wages and prices—may be the wave of the future.

The guideposts were designed to deal with a situation in which high unemployment and rising prices are simultaneously present. They were not, we assume, intended to be viable under conditions of full employment. Discretion being the better part of valor, the Council of Economic Advisers all but abandoned the guideposts in its report of January, 1967. With prices increasing at a rate close to the 3.2 percent annual rate of productivity increase,[1] one cannot very well ask labor to limit its wage demands to an increase that would barely compensate for increases in the cost of living. On the other hand, one cannot very well suggest that wages ought to increase by the rate of productivity increase *plus* the percentage increase in the cost of living, since that would accelerate the rate of increase of the price level. The guideposts, in the environment of 1966–1967, are clearly untenable.

Conclusion on prices   It is our view that the concern during the last decade over cost inflation and structural unemployment was, in large

[1] The consumer price index rose by 3.2 points from a 1965 level of 109.9 to a 1966 level of 113.1. This represents a percentage increase of 2.9 percent.

measure, harmful and exaggerated. It was harmful because it produced a deflationary bias in our national monetary and fiscal policies, and it therefore prevented the economy from realizing full employment and the growth potential of which it was capable. It was exaggerated because it was in large part based on an illusion. The illusion stemmed from the imperfection of our price indexes; from a lack of appreciation that in a growing economy increases in these indexes are inevitable; and from failure to understand that such increases do not necessarily imply that inflation is in progress.

20–5 RAPID GROWTH

Is there an objective standard of rapid economic growth? Should the target rate of growth be 4 percent a year? Should it be higher? Should it be lower? In terms of the past record of the American economy, 4 percent would be an extremely high rate of growth. The growth rate over the period from 1950 to 1964 (years of comparable unemployment rates) averaged 3.6 percent per year. On the other hand, the German economy grew at an average rate of 7 percent a year over the same period, and the Japanese economy grew at the amazing annual rate of 9.9 percent a year.

If the growth target is set on the basis of the past record of the American economy, we implicitly assume that what the economy achieved in the past is a useful standard by which to judge present and future performance. On the other hand, to say that the United States should match the growth rates of other economies is to ignore the fact that economies at different stages of development have different resource and technological bases. It also seems to suggest that countries which show more rapid growth rates possess superior wisdom and economic organization.

In examining the question of a suitable growth target in terms of the past record of the American economy, it is useful to consider an economic growth goal in two parts. First, there is the rate of growth that would be achieved if potential output could be continuously maintained. The Council of Economic Advisers estimates that this rate would initially be 4 percent and believes that it would increase over time if potential output were consistently maintained. Second, there are the additional percentage points that could be added to the growth rate if the American people were willing to make current sacrifices in the form of reduced consumption of goods and services and leisure as well.

As a minimum we want to achieve the "costless" growth rate associated with the path of potential output. To say this is to say no more than that we want full employment and price stability. The difficulty comes when the question of whether the target rate of growth at full employment should be higher is asked.

Although there is a reasonable consensus about what our full-employment and price stability targets ought to be, there is no easy standard by which to select an appropriate growth rate. The costs and benefits of a higher rate of growth are not well specified and would be difficult to measure even if they were.

Economic growth permits ever-rising living standards. It not only enables society to look forward to ever-rising living standards, but acts as a social solvent as well. When all can look forward to rising levels of well-being, the pressure for redistribution of the existing pie is reduced. Indeed there are those who believe that the ultimate solution to the problem of poverty lies in an acceleration of the rate of growth rather than in direct monetary assistance to the poor. Some would go even further and argue that a redistribution of income from rich to poor would reduce per capita income in the long run and may not be of any benefit even to the poor. According to this "trickle-down" theory, income redistribution would raise consumption, reduce investment, and therefore reduce the rate of growth.

Trickle-down arguments are a popular means of opposing "great society" programs. To be convincing, such arguments would have to show, first, that a rise in consumption will reduce investment and growth. Second, they would have to show that the resources devoted to a poverty program are less productively used than in their alternative private uses. And third, they would have to demonstrate that rapid economic growth is an effective and automatic way to eliminate poverty.

The facts do not support the trickle-down theory. As long as there is a GNP gap, consumption can be increased without reducing investment. Moreover, under conditions of less than full employment, anything that raises the one tends also to induce increases in the other. Income redistribution may therefore raise, rather than lower, the rate of growth, and it may even raise the real income and consumption of the higher-income groups who feel they are being unfairly taxed to support the poor.

Further, if the resources that go into a poverty program are used to educate, train, and rehabilitate the poor, this investment in "human capital" will raise potential output. Hence if the resources would otherwise have been spent on consumption, the result again will be to raise rather than to lower the growth rate.

Finally, the empirical evidence shows that economic growth does not automatically reduce poverty. Anderson[1] has calculated the elasticities of family income for various groups in the population with respect to overall income. He found that the incomes of families that are headed by persons sixty-five years of age or older and of families that are headed by women do not rise at all when overall per capita income rises. It appears, therefore, that such persons can only be brought above the poverty level by direct public assistance. Consequently, although it is important to have rapid economic growth, the degree to which economic growth can contribute to the solution of our economic and social problems should not be overestimated.

[1] W. H. Locke Anderson, "Trickling Down: The Relationship between Economic Growth and the Extent of Poverty among American Families," *Quarterly Journal of Economics,* 78:511–524, 1964.

21

THE INSTRUMENTS OF MACROECONOMIC POLICY

21–1 MEASURING THE IMPACT OF THE BUDGET

An essential requirement for the successful operation of countercyclical fiscal policy is that a proper method be devised for determining whether the impact of the budget is expansionary or contractionary. The presence of a budgetary surplus or deficit is not a proper indicator because the deficit (or surplus) is a function of the level of GNP. If income declines from the full-employment level, tax revenue will fall, government transfer payments will increase, and a budgetary deficit will automatically develop. Such a deficit is passively induced, and its existence should not be taken to mean that the impact of the budget is expansionary. It is in order to stress this circumstance that the Council of Economic Advisers has developed the concept of a "full-employment surplus."

Suppose that the economy is at less than full employment. If we were to make a calculation of the deficit or surplus that would result if GNP were at the full-employment level, and if that calculation showed a budgetary surplus, we should conclude that the net impact of the budget is deflationary and that this is one factor responsible for keeping the economy at less than full employment. It is the surplus or deficit that would be generated if the economy were at full employment, rather than the actual surplus or deficit, that shows whether the economic impact of the Federal budget is expansionary or deflationary.

In order to calculate the full-employment surplus, it is necessary to develop statistical relationships between revenue and expenditures and the level of GNP. From past experience the econometrician attempts to derive relationships between aggregate personal income and GNP. He then goes on to relate tax yield to personal income and in so doing obtains estimates of the elasticity of this tax yield with respect to GNP. Similar calculations can be made for other components of the tax structure such as corporate income tax yield and indirect taxes. Certain expenditures, such as the net flow of unemployment compensation funds, also vary with the level of business activity and may also, therefore, be estimated as functions of GNP. With these various calculations in hand, it becomes possible to estimate the budgetary deficit or surplus that would obtain if GNP were at the full-employment level.

Figure 21–1 shows a hypothetical relationship between the Federal government surplus or deficit, with a given fiscal program, and GNP. The surplus, which is measured on the vertical axis, is computed as a percentage of potential GNP. On the horizontal axis, similarly, actual GNP is measured as a percentage of potential GNP. The surplus function has a positive slope which shows that revenues increase relative to expenditures as the economy approaches potential output. The chart implies that when the economy is operating at 96 percent of its potential, the budget would be balanced. It must be recalled, however, that potential output represents noninflationary full employment, so that 96 percent of potential output would be associated with an unemployment rate in excess of 4 percent. At utilization rates above 96 percent, a surplus would be created, and we may therefore conclude that if the surplus function were similar to the one depicted in Figure 21–1, the net impact of the budget would be deflationary.

As the level of output falls below the full-employment level, the surplus generated by the budget program also falls or turns into a

Figure 21–1 Federal budget surplus or deficit and the level of economic activity

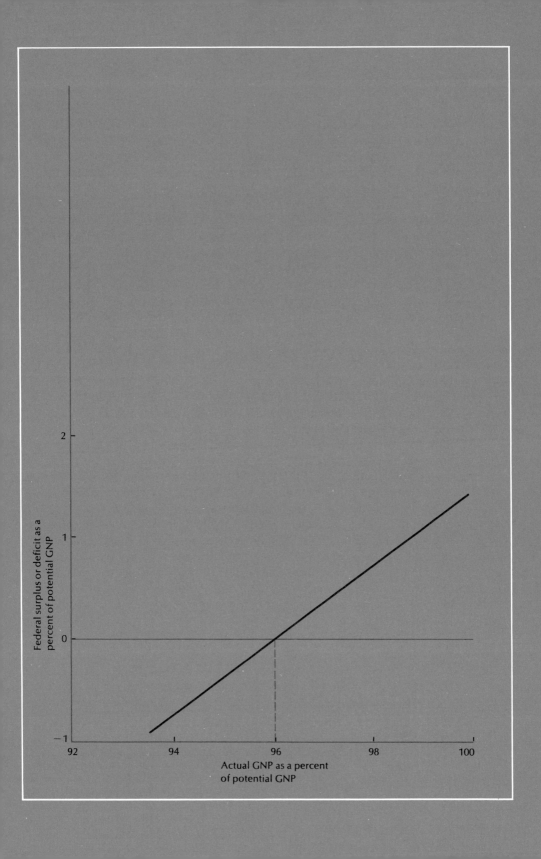

deficit. But note that the budget program has not become more expansionary. The smaller surplus (or larger deficit) arises solely because of the interaction between the level of economic activity and an unchanged fiscal program. An expansionary budget impact would arise only if discretionary policy changes were made that shifted the line in the chart downward and to the right. For example, a reduction in tax liabilities or increased government purchases would produce such a shift. Whether the line would shift in a parallel fashion or not would depend upon the effect of the discretionary policy upon the elasticity of the revenue and expenditure system with respect to GNP.

Figure 21–2 presents estimates by the Council of Economic Advisers of the full-employment budget surplus for the years 1956–1964, along with the actual budget results. The most striking thing to note is that in each of the nine years the achievement of full employment would have resulted in a substantial surplus but that there was actually a deficit in six of the years.[1] Whether a budget program providing for a surplus at full employment is appropriate or not depends upon the relationship between actual and potential output. The Federal budget should be used as a balancing device so that it can counteract movements in aggregate demand. Thus an increase in the full-employment surplus is appropriate when strong demand within the private sector is placing inflationary strains on the economy. But when actual output is below potential, a decrease in the full-employment surplus is called for.

Space does not permit a full examination of the discretionary policy changes, or lack thereof, that accounted for the movements in the full-employment surplus. However, 1960 and 1963 are of interest because of the sharp increase in the full-employment surplus in those years. In his budget message of 1960 President Eisenhower stated that appropriate budget policy would be one that "not merely balances expenditures with revenues but achieves a significant surplus for debt retirement."[2] There followed a policy of strict expenditure control together

---

[1] It would have to be assumed that full employment was achieved by an expansion of demand in the private sector and not by an increase in government purchases or a reduction in tax rates because the full-employment surplus is calculated on the basis of an existing fiscal structure. The full-employment surplus is *not* the surplus that would be recorded if full employment were attained by a changed fiscal program.

[2] *Economic Report of the President,* U.S. Government Printing Office, Washington, January, 1960, p. 54.

Figure 21–2   Federal surplus or deficit: actual and full-employment estimates (*Source: Economic Report of the President, U.S. Government Printing Office, Washington, 1964, p. 43, and 1965, p. 64)*

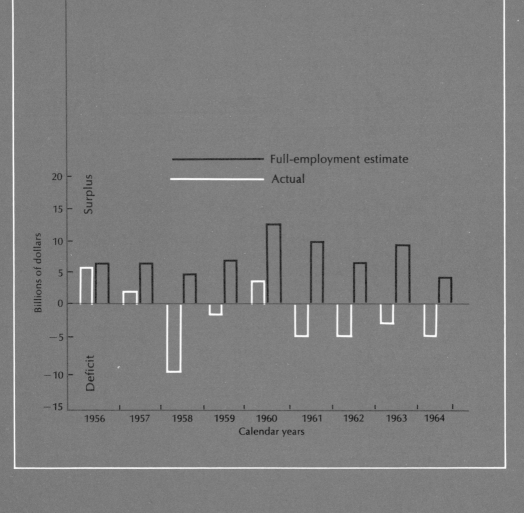

with increases in social security and excise tax rates. These policies resulted in a substantial increase in the full-employment surplus and, in view of their deflationary impact at a time of excessive unemployment, indicated that the administration was ignorant of basic economics. In the subsequent two years, increasing expenditures for defense and the space program, as well as the tax changes of 1962, more than offset the normal increase in revenues and lowered the full-employment surplus. However, the surplus was still substantial, and it became clear that further stimulation was required if the GNP gap was to be eliminated.

It was for this reason that President Kennedy called for a substantial tax reduction in his budget of 1963. Congress did not enact the reduction that year, and the full-employment surplus increased. In 1964, however, President Johnson's request for a tax reduction was heeded. The results are clearly shown in Figure 21–2. The Council of Economic Advisers in its 1965 Annual Report estimated that through 1965 the Revenue Act of 1964 would reduce tax liabilities by $11 billion and $3 billion for individuals and corporations, respectively. It was estimated that, in combination with multiplier effects, consumption expenditures would rise by a total of $22 billion. In addition it was anticipated that investment spending would rise as corporate cash flows increased and as the increase in consumer spending placed strain on existing productive facilities. These forecasts proved to be remarkably accurate. The economy, in the wake of the tax cut and the monetary expansion that this cut made possible,[1] succeeded in shaking off the pall of stagnation.

It is ironic that the American economy had to struggle through a long period of subpar performance before a tax cut finally came about in 1964. The foregone output, the direct economic waste of unemployment, can never be recovered. It is also probable that the impact on the long-run growth potential of the economy can never be fully overcome. The development of the concept of the full-employment surplus may, perhaps, be a major step forward in the search for a persuasive argument for a rational fiscal policy. In a diagrammatic form that most congress-

---

[1] Along with the tax cut came a rapid increase in the supply of money. Some economists, notably the members of the "Chicago school," argue that it was this increase in the stock of money rather than the tax reduction that brought about the expansion. To argue about whether it was the one or the other that did the trick is not terribly fruitful. Monetary expansion alone would have been impossible since this would have lowered interest rates and placed strain on the balance of payments. The effect of the tax cut, on the other hand, was to put upward pressure on interest rates, and this is what made the monetary expansion possible.

men should be able to understand, it shows clearly the impact of Federal fiscal policy and why the presence of a deficit often implies that a still greater deficit ought to be incurred.

We have seen that when revenues and some expenditures are functions of GNP, it becomes important to distinguish between the actual deficit (or surplus) and the full-employment deficit (or surplus). Another consequence of such a revenue-expenditure system is the phenomenon known as "fiscal drag." The budget program of the Federal government has a short-run elasticity of revenues with respect to GNP that is greater than 1 because of the progressive nature of the tax structure and because of the extremely high elasticity of corporate profits with respect to changes in GNP. The long-run elasticity of revenues with respect to GNP is probably smaller than the short-run elasticity because the effect of short-run fluctuations in corporate profits evens out in the long run. However, if the long-run elasticity of tax yield with respect to GNP exceeds unity, Federal revenues will increase over time more rapidly than GNP so that with an unchanged expenditure program an increasing deflationary burden will be placed on the economy in the form of ever-rising full-employment surpluses. This is what is meant by fiscal drag.

As long as the fiscal system is so designed that economic growth induces an increasing full-employment surplus, it is inevitable that continued full employment will require periodic reductions in tax rates and/or periodic increases in government spending. Otherwise fiscal drag will become progressively more burdensome to the economy, and the GNP gap will tend to widen with time. Should the problem be met by tax reduction or by expenditure increase?

If the elasticity of the revenue system with respect to GNP is greater than 1 and the government increases its expenditures in line with the increase in revenue, the government sector will come to command a larger and larger share of total output. To many people this makes tax reduction the more attractive alternative. However, among those who favor tax reduction there is considerable disagreement about the way in which the tax reduction should be undertaken. Should the corporate income tax be reduced in order to increase the cash flow of corporations and thereby the level of capital formation? Although this might raise the rate of growth of output, it would have the effect of benefiting corporate shareholders and it would produce a regressive effect on the distribution of income. Should the tax reduction be in the personal income tax? If this is the preferred alternative, should the incidence of the tax lie more heavily on the low-income groups in order to increase the saving and investment of the upper-income groups, or should the lower-income groups receive the bulk of the tax relief in order to stimulate consumption and produce a more equitable distribution of income?

The fact that Federal revenues tend to increase more rapidly than GNP as GNP grows at full employment is regarded by many citizens as a golden opportunity to expand badly needed social services. Probably the most well-known exponent of this view is John Kenneth Galbraith,[1] who argues that the major problem confronting the American economy is a chronic imbalance between the resources that are devoted to the private and to the public sectors. Galbraith, and like-minded people, argue that the marginal social benefit of the next dollar of public consumption is far greater than the marginal benefit of the next dollar of private consumption. They therefore feel that it would be in the social interest to increase the government's share of GNP. In their view the solution to the problem of fiscal drag would be to increase expenditures on slum clearance, education, medical care, transport and communications, and the control of air and water pollution, since the marginal social benefits of such expenditures exceed the benefits of the additional private consumption that tax reduction would bring about.

Another suggestion is that the Federal government maintain the long-run tightness in its fiscal system and that it transfer, with or without strings attached, increasing amounts to the states that uniformly find themselves unable to raise sufficient revenues.[2] The division of taxing power and expenditure responsibilities is a perennial source of conflict in a federal state. Canada, Australia, and Switzerland, to name but three other examples, have the same problem in this regard as the United States. Even in a unitary state there are inevitable conflicts between the central government and the various county and city governments.

In the United States, as in other advanced countries, the major expansions in expenditure demands have arisen in areas that either constitutionally or traditionally lie within the jurisdiction of the states. However, the fiscal systems of the states rely heavily on property and sales taxes whose long-run yield elasticity with respect to GNP is at best 1 and probably less than 1. State and local fiscal units, moreover, find themselves under great pressure to keep taxes low because of the threat that higher taxes will cause population and industry to move to less heavily taxed jurisdictions.

The method employed in effecting a transfer of revenues from the

---

[1] J. K. Galbraith, *The Affluent Society,* Houghton Mifflin Company, Boston, 1960.

[2] For example, see Walter Heller, *New Dimensions of Political Economy,* Chap. 3, Harvard University Press, Cambridge, Mass., 1966, especially pp. 144–172.

Federal to the state level would make an important difference in the results achieved. One method is to allocate Federal revenues on a per capita basis. However, this would mean that the most populous states, which are also the richest and therefore have the largest tax base from which to raise their own revenue, would receive the largest transfers. A more equitable system would appear to be to develop a measure of minimum social needs that should be met everywhere in the country, to calculate the tax base in each state, and from that to calculate the revenue that could be raised from within each state by an average tax effort. The difference between calculated expenditures and revenues could then be made up by transfers from the Federal government. One advantage of such a scheme is that a state would not necessarily have to tax itself as heavily as the average. However, in so doing, it would not be able to provide for the minimum social needs of its citizens, because the transfers from the Federal government would be based not on the difference between actual revenues and desired expenditures, but on the revenues that would be raised by an average tax effort. Furthermore, there would be no net advantage to a state in deliberately reducing its tax burden in order to attract industry, because by attracting industry from other states, its tax base would rise and its transfers from the Federal government would fall proportionately. The state from which the industry was attracted would find its tax base falling and its transfers rising proportionately.

To base the transfers on such a scheme would mean that the poorest states with the smallest tax bases would receive larger per capita transfers than the rich, populous states. Such a subsidy from the rich to the poor states can be easily justified, but realistically we must expect that such a concept would not automatically gain the wholehearted support of the residents of the rich states.

21–2 BUDGETARY POLICY AND STABILITY

It is obvious that the principles that govern the choice of the economy's governmental revenue and expenditure policies will play an important role in determining to what extent high and stable employment and resource utilization are maintained. Some of the principles by which it has been said budgeting ought to operate are examined in this section. To be considered are the "Swedish," or cyclically balanced budget, "formula flexibility," and the fully managed compensatory program. The principle of annual budgetary balance has already been discussed.

The "Swedish budget"   The principle of budgetary balance over the cycle was first developed in Sweden during the 1930s and has therefore come to be called the "Swedish budget."[1] A version which has been advocated by the Committee for Economic Development (CED) calls for a programming of public expenditures purely on the basis of actual government needs.[2] No public expenditure should be undertaken for the purpose of changing the level of income. Once expenditures over the period of the cycle have been determined, income tax rates would be adjusted in such a way that the surpluses during prosperous years would just balance the deficits during recession years. It is hoped that in this way the budget will achieve long-run balance, that restraint will be imposed on government spending, and that short-run stability will be fostered by the stabilization of disposable income through the operation of automatic stabilizers.

The CED proposal has found widespread approval because it combines short-run stabilizing properties with secular budgetary balance. It possesses, however, weaknesses that have led many to recommend going considerably beyond it. For one thing, it is quite unlikely that the deficits and surpluses that will occur over a cycle can be accurately predicted. Government purchases must continually be adjusted to meet various emergencies and cannot be forecast with any degree of accuracy.

There are two important drawbacks to programs that place exclusive reliance upon automatic stabilizers. First, although the budgetary policy may help stabilize the level of economic activity, it cannot guarantee that the level at which income is stabilized will be the full-employment level. Second, automatic stabilizers serve to cushion the rise and fall of economic activity, but they do nothing to promote a reversal of a deflationary or an inflationary trend. Although automatic stabilizers will produce a government deficit when income falls, the deficit must be greater than that which comes about automatically if the economy is to be turned back to full employment. To put the matter differently, a fiscal policy that results in a passive deficit induced by income shrinkage is not an expansionary policy. Should the economy turn around on its own, the stabilizers that helped dampen the decline will also operate to dampen the subsequent expansion. If full employment was the norm

[1] See G. Myrdal, "Fiscal Policy in the Business Cycle," *American Economic Review* (Supplement), 29:183–193, 1939.

[2] *Taxes and the Budget,* Committee for Economic Development, Research and Policy Committee, New York, 1947.

about which the economy tended to fluctuate, such a budgetary policy would perhaps be sufficient. Otherwise the policy might merely help stabilize the economy permanently at levels of income well below the full-employment level.

Formula flexibility   For those who value automatically operating countercyclical devices, the scheme of "formula flexibility" has considerable appeal. Under our existing system a fall in income produces a reduction in tax revenues because there is less income available to tax and because taxpayers shift into lower brackets. A more substantial effect could be obtained if tax rates on all brackets were automatically reduced at the same time as taxpayers were shifting into lower brackets. One answer would be to have an automatic reduction in tax rates when some sort of "peril point" is reached. When income shrinks, this peril point might be taken as a 5 percent fall in the Federal Reserve Board's index of industrial production or an increase in the unemployment rate to over 4.5 percent, while in the upward direction it might be taken as a 3 percent rise in the consumer price index over an arbitrary period of time.

The advantages of formula flexibility are that it goes considerably beyond the scope of the present automatic stabilization schemes and that it reduces the extent to which stabilization policy is subject to political vagaries. On the other hand, the changes in tax rates are based solely on a set of indexes that, as we have seen, is notorious for its lack of reliability. The indexes, moreover, incorporate the effects of strikes, crop failures, and other factors having little to do with whether aggregate demand is excessive or deficient. Finally, it is conceivable that the two indexes could reach their respective peril-point levels simultaneously. However, even without these technical drawbacks, it is unlikely that formula flexibility will become a part of the American scene because Congress has as yet shown little inclination to give up its role as the final fiscal authority.

Fully managed compensatory program   The policy which, in spirit, has been adopted in the United States is a fully managed compensatory policy. Such a policy recognizes the need for *ad hoc* tax and expenditure changes such as may be called for in the light of changing economic circumstances. Budgetary balance has no place as a target in such a program. The major emphasis is placed on the maintenance of full employment and a stable price level, regardless of the measures that may be required to achieve these goals. Most economists would support such a policy. It is, furthermore, the policy embodied in the Employ-ment Act of 1946 and is espoused in the platforms of our two major political parties. Neither party has, to date, made a consistent effort to implement the act although considerable progress has been made in recent years.

21–3 PROBLEMS IN THE IMPLEMENTATION OF COMPENSATORY FISCAL POLICY

The appropriate timing of changes in revenue and expenditures is the most difficult problem that practical compensatory fiscal policy has to face. The time pattern involved in making discretionary fiscal policy changes and in waiting for these changes to affect the economy can be usefully broken down into two timing lags known as the "inside" and "outside" lags. The inside lag refers to the time between a change in the economic situation and the enactment of the policy intended to offset the change, while the outside lag refers to the time between the policy change and its actual impact on the economy.

To take an example, consider the steps that would be involved in using a fiscal policy change to combat an inflationary situation. There is, first, the time interval between the beginning of the inflationary pressure and its recognition by the policy maker. The length of this lag depends upon the speed with which the data are collected and processed and upon the sensitivity of the policy makers to changes in the data. The problem of reaching a speedy decision is complicated by the circumstance that the various economic indicators rarely all move in the same direction until well after a turning point has occurred. Further-more, several policy makers will be involved, and there may be as many different interpretations of the economic indicators as there are people involved in the decision-making process. While the time taken to recog-nize the need for fiscal action to fight the inflation cannot be specified with any degree of precision, it is likely that these problems of data col-lection, processing, and interpretation are such that the lag is more ap-propriately measured in terms of months rather than days or weeks.

The next step is to coordinate the views of the administrative and legislative branches of the government in order to decide upon and en-act the most suitable policy changes. Here there are innumerable sources of delay. Some congressmen may be opposed to the change out of ignorance or misinformation while others may simply be opposed to the administration or be concerned only with the parochial needs of their constituencies. The need for legislative action may come at a time when Congress is in recess or when other legislative proposals are before it. If the request for a tax increase comes during an election year, the consideration of such an unpopular proposal will most certainly be postponed until after the election.

The outside lags of fiscal policy depend upon the time interval required to transfer the legislated change into a change in income flows. This lag need not be long, but at least a month will be required to change an increase in personal tax rates into increased tax withholding and thus a reduction in after-tax incomes. In addition, it takes time for the reduction in disposable income to affect the volume of expenditure, and still more time for this to result in a stimulation of production and employment. Depending on circumstances, a major part of the total effect will probably occur by the end of the quarter after the tax change.

The presence of these inside and outside lags, as well as the inability to predict their length, threatens to reduce the effectiveness of fiscal policy as a stabilizing device and increases the probability that ill-timed fiscal policy may have destabilizing effects. For example, a tax increase designed to fight an inflation may not have any effect until after the inflationary pressure is past, at which time it contributes to the magnitude of the subsequent deflation.

Several ways of dealing with the problem of lags in fiscal policy have been offered. First, there is the formula flexibility approach discussed above which would tie specific policy changes to various indexes of economic activity and would go into operation automatically without new legislative action. Second, the President might be empowered to reduce tax rates temporarily in response to some change in economic activity. Imagine the result if Congress gave prior authority to permit the President to suspend tax collections for a period of a month. The impact on disposable income and expectations would undoubtedly be dramatic, and recovery might well be speeded up substantially. In 1964 there was hope that some such authority might be forthcoming. At the moment, the prospect appears bleak.

Third, a reduction of the time interval of the lags might be attempted by having ready a shelf of public works projects that could be instituted by administrative action during periods of unemployment. In this way the inside lag would be reduced by prior planning and the outside lag would be reduced because production and employment could be increased immediately and would not have to await the increase in demand that results from rising consumer spending in response to a tax cut.

However even a shelf of public works is not a tool that can be turned on and off quickly.[1] Although the engineering studies may have been made, it will take time to advertise for bids, let the contracts, and get work started. Once the projects are underway, it would be difficult and wasteful to stop them. Thus they are likely to continue to have an impact even after the immediate need for them is past. However, it is possible to slow down or speed up existing projects. For example, the vast interstate highway program can be slowed down by reducing the rate at which the Federal government disburses funds from the program's trust fund. During a serious depression, moreover, the problem of timing is apt to become less important. In the year 1933 it must have seemed highly unlikely that a public works project begun at that time could not be completed in time to avert inflationary pressures, and the consideration would in any case have been dismissed as irrelevant in the face of the pressing needs of the times.

But there are numerous drawbacks to the use of public projects as a countercyclical device, even in a serious depression. First of all, it is unlikely that the resources the government wishes to obtain for its projects will be those that are in most abundant supply. If the construction materials used by the government are substantially different from those used by private industry, the effect of public construction conducted on a countercyclical basis may simply be one of creating two unstable industries where formerly there was only one. Even if the materials used for public construction are the same as those used in private construction projects, the construction industry may be overexpanded if private construction recovers while the public projects are still underway.

It is unlikely that all the resources unemployed by a fall in aggregate demand will find employment in public works projects. An advertising executive will probably not be a very good bricklayer, nor will it be possible to utilize the closed advertising agency on Madison Avenue for the purpose of making generators for a power project. If the executive is to be employed, it will be because the public expenditures produce secondary effects via the multiplier, because the government decides to go into the advertising business, or because the executive is put to work

---

[1] Problems relating to the planning, execution, and economic effects of public works are discussed by J. M. Clark, *The Economics of Public Works*, National Planning Board, Washington, 1935. Significant papers on the subject are S. Slichter, "The Economics of Public Works," *American Economic Review* (Supplement), 24:174–185, 1934; J. Margolis, "Public Works and Economic Stability," *Journal of Political Economy*, 57:293–303, 1949; S. J. Maisell, "Timing and Flexibility of a Public Works Program," *Review of Economics and Statistics*, 31:147–152, 1949.

on some project such as leaf raking that does not require a specialized talent. If the government does go into the advertising business, there will be charges that it is competing with private enterprise. Leaf raking, on the other hand, will be denounced as a boondoggle having little social utility.

21–4 THE NATIONAL DEBT

A fully managed compensatory fiscal policy that sets its sights on the targets of full employment, price stability, and rapid growth is incompatible with the notion that budgetary balance should also be viewed as a target of economic policy. If past experience is any guide, it looks as if we may be establishing a pattern of just balancing the budget or of running a small deficit during full-employment years while running substantial deficits in recession years. This means that we must expect that the national debt will continue to rise throughout the future. Let us consider, therefore, the question of how serious the presence of national debt is and whether it matters if the national debt continues to increase.

The national debt, which stood at a level of nearly $330 billion at the end of 1966, is viewed by fiscal conservatives as a horror which defiles our puritan heritage. Projected increases in the debt, moreover, are regarded as living proof that the government of the United States has become the captive of sinister and subversive forces bent on sapping our national life of its vital fluids. It is said that future generations are mortgaged by the follies of the past by an amount that averages roughly $1,700 per person.

It is often not pointed out that these follies, in part, represent efforts to combat depression, that they were incurred as the consequence of wars, and that they also represent the consequences of raising capital to make productive public investments in roads, schools, and other areas where private enterprise cannot be counted upon to perform adequately. If the future is burdened by the follies of the past, it would have to be shown that the failure of the past to "live within its means" has caused the potential per capita consumption of the future to be impaired. Finally, public investments are harmful only if the alternative private use of the resources would have yielded a greater marginal social benefit. However, since nearly all non-war-induced Federal debt is recession-induced, the resources which the government mobilizes would otherwise have been idle (i.e., their rate of return in private use is zero) and their mobilization by the government could therefore not possibly be harmful either to the present or to the future.

Public debt and private debt are fundamentally different although this fact is avidly denied by those who make budget balancing a fetish. When individuals and corporations go into debt, they receive in return a claim over real resources that they otherwise would not have had. When the time for repayment comes, real resources must be transferred back to the creditor. Hence if productive use is not made of the borrowed resources, the individual will not be able to make repayment and he will go bankrupt. The nation as a whole, however, obviously cannot borrow resources from itself in one year and pay them back in some subsequent year. Thus the idea that present debt creation comes out of the hide of future generations is pure nonsense. If some government of the future were to undertake to repay the debt, it would raise taxes and use the resultant proceeds to purchase the outstanding debt. The net effect would be to redistribute wealth. There would, however, be no net change in the real productive resources that are available to the economy and therefore in its consumption potential. It should be remembered that for every taxpayer who feels himself to be "mortgaged" by national debt, there is also a bondholder who finds himself wealthier by virtue of his ownership of such debt.

Our preceding comments should not be taken to imply that the national debt creates no problems. Indeed the effect of the national debt upon the distribution of income may be quite serious, and there is little doubt that the presence of a large national debt complicates the conduct of monetary policy. Let us consider these problems briefly.

The national debt must be serviced. This means that each year taxes must be collected in order to pay the interest that accrues to bondholders. If Federal debt is mainly held by the higher-income groups while taxes are imposed upon the public at large, growth of debt might imply that income is being continually more regressively redistributed. Thus the national debt may impose a "redistributive burden" upon the economy. The conditions under which this redistributive burden will grow or diminish with respect to time have been analyzed by Domar.[1] He defines the burden as the tax rate applied to taxable money income that is needed to service the debt, and he shows that this tax rate depends not on the absolute size of the debt but rather on its growth relative to the growth of money income.

[1] E. D. Domar, "The Burden of the Debt and the National Income," *American Economic Review*, 34:798–827, 1944.

Domar's analysis can most easily be expressed symbolically. Let us define:

pY = money net national product
i = the rate of interest
D = the debt in money terms
$U = iD + pY$, taxable money income
γ = the tax rate as a percent of taxable income needed to service the debt
α = the proportion of annual money income borrowed

The tax rate γ is the ratio of debt service to taxable money income. Consequently,

$$\gamma = \frac{iD}{U} = \frac{iD}{iD + pY}$$

Dividing numerator and denominator by iD gives

$$\gamma = \frac{1}{1 + (1/i)\,(pY/D)}$$

from which it can easily be seen that the tax rate, given a constant rate of interest, depends entirely upon the ratio of money income to the debt. Notice also that the tax rate can never exceed 100 percent. This is because the interest on the debt is itself taxable income, and it would therefore not be possible for the debt to be so large that there is insufficient income available for debt service.

It is clear from the foregoing expression that if the debt grows while money income fails to grow at all, γ will approach 100 percent. As shown in the appendix to this chapter, γ will also approach 100 percent even if money income grows at some absolute amount each year while borrowing continues at a constant percentage of money income. But if money income grows at a constant percentage rate, while α percent of money income is borrowed, γ approaches the constant rate,

$$\gamma = \frac{1}{1 + (1/i)\,(r/\alpha)}$$

In this case, the burden will rise as the interest rate rises and as the annual percentage borrowed rises. Should the rate of growth of money income rise, the burden would fall. Even if real income were to remain constant, an increase in the price level would reduce the burden of the debt, while hyperinflation would wipe out the public as well as all private debt. Future governments could default on the debt by resorting to the printing press as surely as if they had repudiated the debt by fiat.

In the United States the ratio of debt to income, and therefore the tax burden of the debt, has fallen from its 1946 all-time high. The relevant data are given in Table 21–1, where column 2 gives the total gross Federal debt; column 3 gives the debt in per capita terms; column 4 gives the interest payments on the debt; and column 5 gives the interest payments as a percentage of net national product. Although column 5 is not exactly comparable to Domar's γ, it is close enough to be suggestive. Observe that while the debt increased from $269.4 billion in 1946 to $317.3 billion in 1965, interest payments as a percentage of net national product fell from 2.4 to 1.8 percent.

The problem of income stabilization is complicated by the presence of the national debt both because the debt contains some inherent de-stabilizing features and because the effective pursuit of anti-inflationary monetary policy may conflict with the attempts of the Treasury to man-

Table 21–1 The "burden" of the total gross Federal
debt for the United States, selected years, 1929–1965

Year (1)	Total gross debt (billions) (2)	Total gross debt per capita (3)	Interest payments on the total gross debt (billions) (4)	Interest payments as a percentage of net national product (5)
1929	$ 16.9	$ 139	$ 0.7	0.7
1933	22.5	179	0.7	1.4
1938	37.2	286	0.9	1.2
1944	201.0	1,456	2.6	1.3
1946	269.4	1,905	4.7	2.4
1949	252.8	1,695	5.3	2.2
1953	266.1	1,667	6.5	1.9
1958	276.3	1,588	7.6	1.9
1961	289.0	1,573	9.0	1.9
1963	305.9	1,615	9.9	1.8
1965	317.3	1,631	11.3	1.8

Sources: Columns 2 and 3, 1929–1957: U.S. Department of Commerce, *Historical Statistics of the United States, Colonial Times to 1957,* U.S. Government Printing Office, Washington, 1960, Series Y 368–369, p. 720; 1958–1965: U.S. Department of Commerce, *Statistical Abstract of the United States, 1966,* U.S. Government Printing Office, Washington, 1966, Table 557, p. 405. Column 4, 1929–1957: U.S. Department of Commerce, *Historical Statistics,* Series Y 354, p. 718, U.S. Department of Commerce, *Statistical Abstract, 1966,* Table 557, p. 405. Column 5: Column 4 as a percent of net national product. See Figure 1–1 for source of net national product.

age the debt. During the inflationary era of the 1940s and early 1950s no subject occupied economists more intensively than the problem of debt management and monetary policy. Today the issues that were raised at that time are less pressing. There is, however, the possibility that the future will bring about a similar era and that we may then look back to our past experience with profit.

On balance, the debt probably has an inflationary impact in that it constitutes a stock of liquid wealth for its owners, and liquid asset holdings are positively correlated with consumption expenditures. One of the fears held by economists during the late 1940s was that the public might at a moment's notice attempt to convert its large stock of liquid assets into physical assets, thereby creating inflationary pressure. Without a large accumulation of debt, it is doubtful whether consumers would have been able to increase their spending by as much as they did at the start of the Korean War.

There may also be stabilizing benefits to be derived from the existence of the national debt. When prices and incomes shrink, the Pigou effect is strengthened by the existence of a large stock of government obligations. When the price level rises, it is possible that the reverse effect may take place. These effects may be reversed by price expectations that are likely, in an inflationary period, to lead to attempted conversion of liquid into physical assets, while the reverse can be expected to occur during a period of falling prices. Both of these destabilizing movements are facilitated by the existence of public debt.

One of the more unfortunate aspects of having to live with the national debt was that an inflationary bias became built into policy during the 1940s. There was an ever-present temptation to lower interest rates below the natural rate in order to make debt management easier.[1] As we have suggested before, this can be accomplished by forcing the Federal Reserve System to peg the market rate of interest by buying up such quantities of bonds as are necessary to maintain their prices. The effect of such an operation is inflationary and therefore serves the added purpose of reducing the real value of the government debt.

This last point is worthy of special emphasis because it was rarely mentioned during the days, prior to 1951, when Secretary of the

---

[1] Recalling the discussion of Chap. 7, if a long-term bond issued for a par value of $1,000 pays 5 percent interest on the par value, a rise in the market rate of interest to 10 percent will reduce the market value of the bond to approximately $500. At the maturity date the Treasury must pay the par value on the old issue, and, if it refinances (i.e., issues new long-term bonds to replace the old ones), it must offer 10 percent per $1,000 if it is to sell the issue. The service charge therefore doubles from $50 to $100 per $1,000 borrowed.

Treasury Snyder proclaimed himself the champion of an "orderly" bond market and the defender of widows, orphans, educational institutions, and other conspicuous holders of the Federal debt. Whether widows and orphans are protected by pegging operations is open to doubt. At any one time there will be some natural rate of interest that equates the demand for goods and services with the full-employment supply. At full employment, any attempt to lower the market rate below the natural rate by monetary expansion will produce increases in the price level. The bondholder thus has two unpleasant alternatives: (1) policy makers may allow the market rate to rise to the natural rate, in which case bondholders take an immediate capital loss; (2) policy makers may peg the rate so that bondholders take their capital loss in the form of a reduction in the real value of their bonds caused by a rising price level. In practice, the latter alternative is likely to be chosen since it creates the illusion of easing the day-to-day problem of Treasury financing and because wealth holders are apt to be more conscious of a quick and sharp capital loss than of the long-term attrition that results from a rising price level. Although there is no net benefit for bondholders inherent in this process, except in the short run, the pegged-interest-rate gospel was preached with a high degree of success during the years following World War II. By 1952 about all we had to show for the policy was a badly inflated price level and the expectation of further price increases.

The pegging policy of the postwar years went considerably beyond such Federal Reserve bond purchases as were required to maintain stable interest rates. On several occasions the Federal Reserve lowered member bank reserve requirements. Such action, during an inflationary period, might have been taken as prima facie evidence of insanity had it not been for the pressing need to find a resting place for Federal debt. A reduction in reserve requirements makes it possible for banks to substitute part of the public debt in place of the required reserves otherwise held idle in their reserve accounts. While this policy of subsidizing commercial banks helped to place the debt, it also presented banks with "secondary reserves" that they could convert into other forms of earning assets by simply allowing their short-term government obligations to mature. A reduction in reserve requirements at a time of full employment is obviously inflationary and can have no justification in terms of economic stability.

What can be done to reduce the conflict of interest between credit control and Treasury financing?[1] Most of the suggestions that were made

---

[1] R. V. Roosa, "Integrating Debt Management and Open Market Operations," *American Economic Review* (Supplement), 42:214–235, 1952, provides a comprehensive survey of the issues.

were in the form of gimmicks designed either to isolate portions of the debt from market fluctuations or to lengthen the average maturity of the debt so as to reduce the number of refunding operations in which the Treasury would have to engage. Proposals of the former sort involved recommendations that the commercial banking system be forced to hold a certain portion of required reserves in the form of short-term government debt and that part of the debt be converted into nonmarketable bonds such as the familiar Series E bond, which could only be sold back to the Treasury. The proposal to freeze part of the debt in the hands of the banks was criticized on the ground that it would not affect the marginal holdings that banks switch into alternative uses when the opportunity arises. However, if such a freeze had involved an addition to required reserves rather than a mere substitution of debt for required money reserves, the policy would clearly have had a deflationary impact and would have served to quarantine a portion of the debt.

The proposal to convert marketable debt into nonmarketable bonds of the Series E variety appears to have some merit. But if interest rates were to rise significantly under the impact of Federal Reserve credit restraint, these bonds would be sold back to the Treasury, and a drain of cash from the Treasury would take place. The tight money policy would thus be thwarted, and the Treasury would lose funds at the very time when added borrowing would prove to be most expensive. It is, moreover, unlikely that large investors in government obligations could be persuaded to hold nonmarketable bonds without an extremely high yield inducement. This is not to say that some progress might not be made with nonmarketable debt. It is possible, for example, to program a redemption schedule that puts a high penalty on early redemption and makes it more and more attractive to hold the bonds as maturity is approached. The fact remains, however, that as long as the debt is marketable at the Treasury, a rise in interest rates will lead to redemption and a drain of Treasury cash at a time when the Treasury's borrowing prospects from the public are the poorest. The Treasury may then be driven to borrow from the Federal Reserve System and thereby to negate the System's attempts at credit restraint.

The second type of proposal called for a concerted attempt on the part of the Treasury to lengthen the maturity of the debt. This was recommended in the hope that the number of times the debt had to be refinanced would be reduced and that more time would be left between funding operations during which credit restraint might be applied. The ideal situation would be achieved if all the debt were funded into consols since this would remove the necessity, once and for all, of refinancing maturing debt. On the other hand, there is some advantage in debt of varying maturities. Long-term debt presumably competes with other long-term uses of funds, whereas short-term debt competes with other short-term uses. Thus some economists argue that during recession the debt should be funded into short-term debt, in the hope that the long-term funds thus released will be driven into capital formation. During an inflationary period, on the other hand, the debt should be lengthened so that holding long-term debt becomes an attractive alternative to capital formation.

21–5 SOME ISSUES OF MONETARY POLICY

There is considerable agreement that monetary policy on several occasions in the past has operated in a manner that was blatantly inconsistent with the targets of full employment and price stability. Between 1929 and 1933 the Federal Reserve allowed the money supply to shrink when it should have done everything in its power to increase the money supply. In the late 1940s and into the 1950s it allowed the money supply to expand at an inflationary rate in order to keep interest rates pegged below natural rate levels. It pursued a tight money policy during the last half of the 1950s when unemployment and retarded growth were crying for monetary expansion.

An issue which economists debate at great length is whether monetary policy can be improved within the existing framework by improving forecasting techniques and raising the economic sophistication of those who make monetary policy decisions, or whether substantial progress is impossible without far-reaching institutional reform.

There is, first, the question of whether some of the instruments of monetary policy should be abolished or reformed. Control over the supply of money is exercised by changes in the rediscount rate (the rate at which the Federal Reserve System lends to member banks), by changes in legal minimum reserve requirements, and by the open market purchase and sale of government securities. Are these three instruments necessary for monetary control, or would it be better to find the single best instrument and abolish the rest? The Federal Reserve System likes to talk about coordination of its instruments. In practice, however, attempts to tighten credit by means of open market sales of government securities can be frustrated if banks are permitted to replenish their reserves by borrowing from the System at an unchanged rediscount rate.

Not only can rediscounting be used as a means to offset the intended effects of open market operations, but the presence of the rediscount privilege adds to the likelihood that monetary policy will be destabilizing. During prosperous periods, market interest rates tend to rise while during periods of recession they tend to fall. It has been argued that the authorities deceive themselves into believing that if the rediscount rate over the course of the business cycle is held constant, this means that they are pursuing a neutral monetary policy. In fact, however, such a constant rediscount rate is destabilizing. It implies that during recession banks can borrow at the discount window on less favorable terms than from the market at a time when the Federal Reserve System ought to be making borrowing easier. Conversely, during prosperity, the rediscount rate is below the market rate, and banks can therefore borrow on more favorable terms from the discount window than from the market at a time when the authorities ought to be restraining the ability of banks to borrow.

In addition, a rise in the rediscount rate does not necessarily imply that a tight money policy is being pursued. If the market rate of interest rises from 3 to 5 percent and the rediscount rate is raised from 3 to 4 percent, the policy is still inflationary since it is still easier to borrow from the discount window than from the market. Proper stabilization policy requires that during inflationary periods it should be more difficult to borrow from the Federal Reserve System than from the market, and during deflationary periods the opposite should be the case. Thus the rediscount rate should be higher than market rates during inflationary periods and lower than market rates during recession. However, the rediscount rate, in practice, has not been adjusted in this manner and the mere fact that it is raised during expansionary periods and lowered during recession does not in any way imply that monetary policy is stabilizing.

Changes in the rediscount rate are newsworthy, and they therefore create "announcement" effects of a kind that may be destabilizing. To illustrate, consider again the preceding example. When an increase in the rediscount rate from 3 to 4 percent is announced, it creates the belief that credit will become tighter. However, no such thing is, in fact, happening. It is still possible for banks to borrow at the discount window on more favorable terms than on the market and the Federal Reserve System is therefore still pursuing an expansionary policy. If, however, businesses believe that the change in the rediscount rate signals a change in the direction of monetary policy, they may change their plans with respect to production, inventory accumulation, and investment on the basis of a wholly erroneous signal.

Considerations of the foregoing sort have led some economists[1] to

[1] Notably, Milton Friedman; see his A Program for Monetary Stability, Chap. 2, Fordham University Press, New York, 1959.

take the view that the rediscount privilege should be abolished. It is possible to control the supply of money by open market operations and such operations create no announcement effects. Rediscounting, on the other hand, creates announcement effects; it reduces the degree to which the money supply can be controlled by open market policy; it may be destabilizing; and finally, it provides a wholly unjustifiable means of subsidizing commercial banks at the expense of a public institution and therefore, ultimately, of the taxpayer.

Complaints similar to those that have been lodged against rediscounting have also been made against the changing of legal minimum reserve requirements. Changes in reserve requirements are abrupt; they occur only upon occasion; and they are newsworthy. They therefore tend to create announcement effects. These effects may be quite misleading and therefore unsettling to business activity. For example, if banks hold an average of reserves to deposits of 25 percent, while the legal minimum reserve requirement is 20 percent, and if the Federal Reserve raises the legal minimum requirement to 22 percent, this action does nothing whatsoever to force contraction of the money supply and it is therefore not a tight-money policy. The increase in reserve requirements may, however, foster the belief that monetary tightness is underway or is imminent and produce responses that, as in the case of the rise in the rediscount rate, are based upon a misleading signal. Business may respond to the news by accelerating its rate of borrowing and increasing investment in order to obtain credit before it becomes more costly, or it may scale down its investment plans because it believes that credit will be harder and more expensive to get. The outcome is unpredictable and that, basically, is the trouble with announcement effects.

Economic stability and productive efficiency are benefited by the creation of an economic environment that minimizes uncertainty and confusion, and that facilitates, rather than obstructs, rational production and investment planning. The rediscounting and reserve requirement instruments are not conducive to the creation of such an environment. At the same time they add nothing to the ability of the Federal Reserve System to control the supply of money. It is for these reasons that consideration should be given to their abolition.

The presence of inside and outside lags is every bit as serious a problem for monetary policy as it is for fiscal policy. Indeed, some economists believe that the problems of timing are so formidable that any given discretionary monetary policy has no more than a fifty-fifty chance of being stabilizing. If, in addition, the cost of raising the unemployment rate from 4 to 5 percent through ill-timed policy is greater than the benefit gained from lowering the rate to 3 percent by correct policy, it might be better to abandon discretionary policy altogether and to adopt, instead, a set of fixed monetary policy rules that would operate independently of the current economic situation.

The most well-known such rule is Professor Friedman's proposal that the supply of money be increased at an annual rate of 4 percent and that this rate be maintained, without fail, under all conditions. The presumption is that this would at least prevent monetary policy from being destabilizing, and that it would have the added advantage that business enterprise would always know exactly what monetary policy was up to and therefore not be led into the planning mistakes that may occur from the false signals which discretionary policy may produce.

Reliance upon rigid rules is not a popular alternative except to members of the Chicago school of economics. Even among those who agree that the economy would have been better off in the past had the Friedman rule been followed, there are many who believe that reliance upon such rules implies an excessively optimistic view of the ability of the economy automatically to recover from autonomous shocks. They feel, moreover, that submission to a fixed rule for all future time represents an admission of defeat and a surrender to the notion that further progress in the development and improvement of economic analysis cannot materially improve the performance of economic policy.

The question of whether monetary policy is a more or less effective stabilization instrument than fiscal policy still obsesses some economists. This question is, or ought to be, a question of the past. The issues of the present and the future will be how to improve forecasting, how to measure and control lags, how to prevent monetary policy from having periodic destabilizing effects, and how to bring about better coordination between monetary and fiscal policies in an attempt to bring about a truly integrated and carefully planned program for economic stability and growth.

MATHEMATICAL
APPENDIXES

These appendixes are presented for the benefit of the reader who has an interest in the quantification and mathematical analysis of economic theories, and who may find it interesting and useful to have the verbal and diagrammatic exposition of the text supplemented by mathematical methods. The contents of these appendixes simply represent mathematical verification of what was said in the text, and the reader who is unfamiliar with mathematical methods should not feel excessively deprived.

APPENDIX TO CHAPTER 6: ALGEBRAIC ANALYSIS
OF TAX AND EXPENDITURE POLICIES

1. Lump-sum taxation   In linear form the basic model from which the conclusions of Chapter 6 were derived is

$$Y = C + I + G \qquad (6\text{--}1)$$

$$C = a + bY_d = a + b(Y - T) \qquad (6\text{--}2)$$

where the levels of intended investment and government purchases are assumed to be autonomous. Combining (6–1) and (6–2) and solving for Y yields

$$Y = \frac{a + I + G - bT}{1 - b} \qquad (6\text{--}3)$$

as the equilibrium level of income. When Eq. (6–3) is differentiated with respect to I, G, and T, respectively, we obtain the multipliers

$$\frac{dY}{dI} = \frac{1}{1 - b} \qquad \frac{dY}{dG} = \frac{1}{1 - b} \qquad \frac{dY}{dT} = \frac{-b}{1 - b} \qquad (6\text{--}4)$$

When the government purchase and tax multipliers are added together, the result is the balanced budget multiplier,

$$\frac{dY}{dG} + \frac{dY}{dT} = \frac{1}{1 - b} - \frac{b}{1 - b} = \frac{1 - b}{1 - b} = 1$$

2. Income taxation   Assume that taxes are a linear function of the level of income, and let the tax function be

$$T = u + tY \qquad (6\text{--}5)$$

where T is the level of net tax yield and t is the marginal tax rate. Substitution of the tax function into Eq. (6–2) gives the consumption function

$$C = a - bu + b(1 - t)Y \qquad (6\text{--}6)$$

where the slope of the function $b(1 - t)$ is the marginal propensity to consume real NNP (Y), and b is the marginal propensity to consume disposable income. When Eq. (6–6) is substituted into Eq. (6–1) and we solve for Y, we have

$$Y = \frac{a - bu + I + G}{1 - b(1 - t)} \qquad (6\text{--}7)$$

The multipliers for I and G are obtained by differentiating Eq. (6–7) with respect to these variables. The result is

$$\frac{dY}{dI} = \frac{dY}{dG} = \frac{1}{1 - b(1 - t)} \tag{6–8}$$

and since $1 - b(1 - t) > 1 - b$, we see immediately that income taxation reduces the value of the multiplier and therefore provides the system with "automatic" or "built-in" stability.

The effects of a change in tax legislation depend upon whether the entire tax structure is shifted, as when the value of u is changed, or whether the changes are at the margin and therefore involve a change in t. In the former case,

$$\frac{dY}{du} = \frac{-b}{1 - b(1 - t)} \tag{6–9}$$

and in the latter case,

$$\frac{dY}{dt} = \frac{-bY}{1 - b(1 - t)} \tag{6–10}$$

From Eq. (6–10) we see that the effect of a change in t depends upon the value of Y prior to the change in the marginal tax rate. The lower the level of income, the less the effect a given change in t will have on tax yield and disposable income, and therefore on consumption and on the equilibrium level of income.

When the government purchase multiplier and the multiplier that results from a shift in the tax structure are added together, the result is

$$\frac{dY}{dG} + \frac{dY}{du} = \frac{1 - b}{1 - b(1 - t)} \tag{6–11}$$

which does not equal unity and suggests that the balanced budget multiplier does not hold under income taxation. However, this conclusion is incorrect. From the tax function it can be seen that

$$dT = du + t(dY) \tag{6–12}$$

and this implies that if there is some induced income change that results from the change in the tax structure, the shift in the structure will differ from the change in total tax yield. To put it differently: du is the change in tax yield that would occur if the level of income did not change.

From Eq. (6–12) it can be seen that the value of du that would make $dT = dY$ is

$$du = (1 - t)\, dT$$

When this result is substituted into Eq. (6–9), we obtain the multiplier with respect to the change in tax yield

$$\frac{dY}{dT} = \frac{-b(1 - t)}{1 - b(1 - t)}$$

and when this is added to the government purchase multiplier, we have the balanced budget result

$$\frac{dY}{dG} + \frac{dY}{dT} = 1$$

We conclude that the balanced budget multiplier holds provided that the tax multiplier is defined as the ratio of the change in income to the total change in tax yield.

A similar analysis can be performed with a change in the marginal tax rate. In this case we have

$$dT = t(dY) + Y(dt)$$

as the change in tax yield. The change in the tax rate that would just make $dT = dY$ is

$$dt = \frac{(1 - t)(dT)}{Y}$$

and when this change is substituted into Eq. (6–10), we again obtain

$$\frac{dY}{dT} = \frac{-b(1 - t)}{1 - b(1 - t)} \tag{6–13}$$

Finally, when Eq. (6–13) is added to the government purchase multiplier, the result again is to yield a balanced budget multiplier of unity.

We conclude that the balanced budget multiplier holds provided that the tax change is defined, not as the shift in the tax structure or change in the tax rate at a given level of income, but rather as the change in tax yield taking induced effects into account. This means that it is always possible to find some change in the tax structure or in the marginal tax rate that will yield additional revenue equal to a change in government purchases and that if this budget-balancing change is effected, the result will be to change the level of income by an amount equal to the change in the balanced budget.

APPENDIX TO CHAPTER 10: MONETARY AND FISCAL POLICY

The policy analysis of Chapter 10 may be derived mathematically. To simplify matters, we confine ourselves to the model of Section 10–2. Ignoring taxes, but including government purchases, product market equilibrium is given by

$$I(i) + G = Y - C(Y)$$

which for convenience may be rewritten as

$$G = Y - C(Y) - I(i) \tag{10-1}$$

Monetary equilibrium is given by

$$m = kY + L(i) \tag{10-2}$$

The effect of an increase in the money supply can be observed by differentiating the equations totally with respect to m. This yields

$$0 = (1 - C_y)\left(\frac{dY}{dm}\right) - I_i\left(\frac{di}{dm}\right) \tag{10-3}$$

$$1 = k\left(\frac{dY}{dm}\right) + L_i\left(\frac{di}{dm}\right) \tag{10-4}$$

where C_y is the partial derivative of consumption with respect to income (the marginal propensity to consume); I_i is the partial derivative of investment with respect to the interest rate (the reciprocal of the slope of the investment demand schedule); and L_i is the partial derivative of the speculative demand for money with respect to the interest rate (the reciprocal of the slope of the speculative demand function). Evidently

$$\frac{dY}{dm} = \frac{I_i}{L_i(1 - C_y) + kI_i}$$

and

$$\frac{di}{dm} = \frac{(1 - C_y)}{L_i(1 - C_y) + kI_i}$$

In the Keynesian case, L_i is infinite, so that

$$\frac{dY}{dm} = 0$$

and

$$\frac{di}{dm} = 0$$

In the classical case $L_i = 0$, so that

$$\frac{dY}{dm} = \frac{1}{k}$$

and

$$\frac{di}{dm} = \frac{1 - C_y}{kI_i}$$

The change in the rate of interest therefore depends on the slope of the saving function, the transactions demand for money function, and the investment demand schedule.

The effect of an increase in government purchases can be observed by differentiating Eqs. (10–1) and (10–2) totally with respect to G. This gives

$$1 = (1 - C_y)\left(\frac{dY}{dG}\right) - I_i\left(\frac{di}{dG}\right) \tag{10–5}$$

$$0 = k\left(\frac{dY}{dG}\right) + L_i\left(\frac{di}{dG}\right) \tag{10–6}$$

so that

$$\frac{dY}{dG} = \frac{L_i}{L_i(1 - C_y) + kI_i}$$

and

$$\frac{di}{dG} = \frac{-k}{L_i(1 - C_y) + kI_i}$$

In the Keynesian case L_i is infinite so that

$$\frac{dY}{dG} = \frac{L_i}{L_i(1 - C_y) + kI_i} = \frac{1}{(1 - C_y) + (kI_i/L_i)} = \frac{1}{(1 - C_y)}$$

i.e., the ratio of the change in income to the change in G equals one divided by the marginal propensity to save. Again, since L_i is infinite,

$$\frac{di}{dG} = 0$$

In the classical case $L_i = 0$, so that

$$\frac{dY}{dG} = 0$$

and

$$\frac{di}{dG} = \frac{-1}{I_i}$$

which implies that the change in the interest rate depends on the slope of the investment demand schedule. As we saw before, the rate of interest must rise by enough to just choke off investment in an amount equal to the change in government purchases. The amount of the rise in the interest rate needed to reduce investment by exactly this amount must obviously depend upon the slope of the investment demand schedule.

APPENDIX TO CHAPTER 11: MONEY WAGE RATES AND EMPLOYMENT

In this appendix we attempt to analyze the effect of a cut in money wage rates on the level of employment. Including government expenditures, but excluding taxes, the model of Chapter 11 can be written

$$G = Y - C(Y) - I(i) \tag{11-1}$$

$$\frac{M}{p} = kY + L(i) \tag{11-2}$$

$$Y = X(N,K^*) \tag{11-3}$$

$$\frac{w_0}{p} = X_n \tag{11-4}$$

To simplify matters, write Eq. (11–3) as $Y = X(N)$ and substitute Eqs. (11–3) and (11–4) in Eqs. (11–1) and (11–2). This gives

$$G = X(N) - C[X(N)] - I(i) \tag{11-5}$$

$$\frac{MX_n}{w_0} = kX(N) + L(i) \tag{11-6}$$

To observe the effect of a money wage cut, we differentiate the last two equations with respect to w_0. This gives

$$0 = (X_n - C_y X_n)\left(\frac{dN}{dw_0}\right) - I_i\left(\frac{di}{dw_0}\right) \tag{11-7}$$

$$\frac{-MX_n}{w_0^2} = \left(kX_n - \frac{M}{w_0}X_{nn}\right)\left(\frac{dN}{dw_0}\right) + L_i\left(\frac{di}{dw_0}\right) \tag{11-8}$$

from which it follows that

$$\frac{dN}{dw_0} = \frac{-(1/w_0^2)(MI_iX_n)}{X_n(1 - C_y)L_i + I_i\left[kX_n - (M/w_0)X_{nn}\right]} \tag{11-9}$$

and

$$\frac{di}{dw_0} = \frac{-(1/w_0^2)MX_n^2\,1 - C_y)}{X_n(1 - C_y)L_i + I_i\,[kX_n - (M/w_0)X_{nn}]} \tag{11-10}$$

The Keynesian case is the simplest. Here L_i is infinite so that

$$\frac{di}{dw_0} = 0$$

and

$$\frac{dN}{dw_0} = 0$$

Notice also that an infinitely inelastic investment demand schedule, that is, $I_i = 0$, will make

$$\frac{dN}{dw_0} = 0$$

and

$$\frac{di}{dw_0} = \frac{-MX_n}{L_i w_0^2} \tag{11-11}$$

By writing Eq. (11–4) as

$$p = \frac{w_0}{X_n}$$

and differentiating with respect to w_0, we have

$$\frac{dp}{dw_0} = \frac{X_n - w_0 X_{nn}\,(dN/dw_0)}{X_n^2} \tag{11-12}$$

In the Keynesian case, $dN/dw_0 = 0$, so that

$$\frac{dp}{dw_0} = \frac{1}{X_n} = \frac{p}{w_0}$$

which means that the price level falls in proportion to the wage cut so that no change in real wages materializes.

The classical case is more complicated. Here $L_i = 0$ so that

$$\frac{dN}{dw_0} = \frac{-MX_n}{w_0^2[kX_n - (M/w_0)X_{nn}]} < 0 \tag{11-13}$$

and

$$\frac{di}{dw_0} = \frac{-M(X_n)^2(1 - C_y)}{w_0^2 I_i[kX_n - (M/w_0)X_{nn}]} > 0 \tag{11-14}$$

An understanding of this can be obtained by noting that Eq. (11–14) may be substituted in Eq. (11–13). This yields

$$\frac{dN}{dw_0} = \frac{I_i}{X_n(1 - C_y)}\left(\frac{di}{dw_0}\right) < 0 \qquad (11\text{–}15)$$

Notice that $I_i/(1 - C_y)$ is the simple multiplier that translates a change in investment into a change in income. Multiplying the denominator by the marginal product of labor converts this into an employment multiplier. Notice also that no change in employment can take place unless the wage cut stimulates an investment expenditure increase via a change in the rate of interest. Observe finally that since $X_{nn} < 0$, the denominator of Eq. (11–13) is necessarily positive so that $dN/dw_0 < 0$; since $I_i < 0$, the denominator of Eq. (11–14) is negative so that $di/dw_0 > 0$.

Referring back to Eq. (11–12) and rewriting the expression as

$$\frac{dp}{dw_0} = \frac{p}{w_0} - \frac{w_0 X_{nn}}{X_n^2}\left(\frac{dN}{dw_0}\right)$$

we note that, since $dN/dw_0 < 0$,

$$\frac{dp}{dw_0} < \frac{w_0}{p}$$

which means that the real wage will change in the same direction as the money wage.

APPENDIX TO CHAPTER 13: EFFECTS OF MONETARY POLICY AT FULL EMPLOYMENT

1. The neutral money case   The model of Section 13–3 can be represented by the equations

$$I(i) = Y^* - C(Y^*) \qquad (13\text{–}1)$$

$$\frac{M}{p} = L(i,Y^*) \qquad (13\text{–}2)$$

When we differentiate the equations with respect to M, we obtain

$$I_i\left(\frac{di}{dM}\right) = 0 \qquad (13\text{–}3)$$

$$\frac{1}{p} - \left(\frac{M}{p^2}\right)\left(\frac{dp}{dM}\right) = L_i\left(\frac{di}{dM}\right) \qquad (13\text{–}4)$$

From Eq. (13–3) it is apparent that the equilibrium interest rate does not change. Consequently, Eq. (13–4) becomes

$$\frac{1}{p} = \left(\frac{M}{p^2}\right)\left(\frac{dp}{dM}\right)$$

or

$$\frac{dp}{p} = \frac{dM}{M}$$

The percentage change in the price level is therefore equal to the percentage change in the money supply.

2. Consumption depends on the level of wealth When consumption becomes a function of the real value of privately held wealth, we have

$$I(i) = Y^* - C(Y^*, W) \tag{13-5}$$

$$\frac{M}{p} = L(i, Y^*) \tag{13-2}$$

$$W = \frac{aY^*}{i} + \frac{M}{p} \tag{13-6}$$

Let us assume first that the money supply is increased by gold production or that money is simply dropped out of airplanes. We assume also that this miracle somehow comes to pass without increasing the level of disposable income. Differentiating the three equations with respect to M gives the set of simultaneous linear equations

$$0 = I_i\left(\frac{di}{dM}\right) + C_w\left(\frac{dW}{dM}\right) + 0 \tag{13-7}$$

$$\frac{1}{p} = L_i\left(\frac{di}{dM}\right) + 0 + \left(\frac{M}{p^2}\right)\left(\frac{dp}{dM}\right) \tag{13-8}$$

$$\frac{1}{p} = \left(\frac{aY^*}{i^2}\right)\left(\frac{di}{dM}\right) + \left(\frac{dW}{dM}\right) + \left(\frac{M}{p^2}\right)\left(\frac{dp}{dM}\right) \tag{13-9}$$

When we use these equations to solve for a change in the rate of interest, we obtain

$$\left(\frac{di}{dM}\right)\Delta = \begin{vmatrix} 0 & C_w & 0 \\ 1/p & 0 & M/p^2 \\ 1/p & 1 & M/p^2 \end{vmatrix} = 0 \tag{13-10}$$

where

$$\Delta = \left(\frac{M}{p^2}\right)\left(\frac{C_w aY^*}{i^2} - I_i - C_w L_i\right) \tag{13-11}$$

Notice, first, that since I_i and L_i are both negative while C_w is positive, Δ must be positive. Second, when we evaluate the determinant in Eq. (13–10) we find that it has a value of zero. Consequently, if $di/dM = 0$, it follows immediately from Eq. (13–8) that

$$\frac{1}{p} = \left(\frac{M}{p^2}\right)\left(\frac{dp}{dM}\right)$$

so that

$$\frac{dp}{p} = \left(\frac{dM}{M}\right)$$

and from Eq. (13–9) that $dW/dM = 0$.

Apparently, then, an increase in the money supply that is brought about in the way specified above yields the classical conclusions. The rate of interest does not change; the price level rises in proportion to the increase in the money supply; and the level of wealth remains constant.

The foregoing analysis suggests that the results obtained by Metzler are independent of the amount of money that is pumped into the system. They depend, rather, upon changes in the value of privately held securities. Consequently, we may ignore the money supply and see what happens when the quantity of securities held by the public declines. The constant a has been assumed to be the proportion of Y^* that is in the form of corporate profits. An open market operation that transfers private security holdings to the monetary authority will reduce the proportion of total profits accruing to private individuals. Consequently, the effect of the open market operation can be analyzed by examining the consequences of a change in a.

Differentiating Eqs. (13–5), (13–2), and (13–6) with respect to a yields the set of simultaneous linear equations

$$0 = I_i\left(\frac{di}{da}\right) + C_w\left(\frac{dW}{da}\right) + 0$$

$$0 = L_i\left(\frac{di}{da}\right) + 0 + \left(\frac{M}{p^2}\right)\left(\frac{dp}{da}\right)$$

$$\frac{Y^*}{i} = \left(\frac{aY^*}{i^2}\right)\left(\frac{di}{da}\right) + \left(\frac{dW}{da}\right) + \left(\frac{M}{p^2}\right)\left(\frac{dp}{da}\right)$$

In this case,

$$\frac{di}{da} = \frac{(M/p^2)C_w(Y^*/i)}{\Delta} \tag{13–12}$$

where Δ has exactly the same value as before. Since we know that $\Delta > 0$

and since the denominator of the above expression is positive, di/da must be positive. A fall in a therefore causes the rate of interest to fall.

Similarly,

$$\frac{dW}{da} = \frac{-(M/p^2)I_i(Y^*/i)}{\Delta} \tag{13-13}$$

Since $I_i < 0$, dW/da is positive, and this means that a fall in a reduces the value of privately held wealth.

Finally,

$$\frac{dp}{da} = \frac{C_w L_i(Y^*/i)}{\Delta} \tag{13-14}$$

Since $C_w > 0$ and $L_i < 0$, $dp/da < 0$, which means that the price level rises as a falls. Observe from Eqs. (13–12) and (13–14) that the interest rate and price level would not change if C_w were zero.

In conclusion, in a sense money is still neutral. An increase in the money supply, in and of itself, does not affect the rate of interest. But if the method of increasing M results in a transfer of earning assets from the public to the monetary authority, the rate of interest will decline.

APPENDIX TO CHAPTER 15: STABILITY ANALYSIS

To follow the argument of this appendix, the reader should be familiar with the concepts of a differential equation and its solution and with the concept of Taylor's expansion.

The static model that underlies the analysis of Chapter 15 consists of the two equations

$$I(i,Y) = Y - C(Y) \tag{15-1}$$

$$m = L(i,Y) \tag{15-2}$$

It will be useful for future reference to know the equations for the slopes of these functions. Differentiation with respect to i and Y gives

$$\left(\frac{di}{dY}\right)_{IS} = \frac{1 - C_y - I_y}{I_i} \tag{15-3}$$

$$\left(\frac{di}{dY}\right)_{LM} = \frac{-L_y}{L_i} \tag{15-4}$$

All the symbols except I_y, the marginal propensity to invest, are familiar. We assume that $I_y > 0$, although beyond this we know very little about it. Since $L_i < 0$ and $L_y > 0$, the slope of the LM function is definitely positive. Since $I_i < 0$, the slope of IS will be negative if $(1 - C_y) > I_y$, i.e., if the marginal propensity to save is greater than the marginal propensity to invest, and it will be positive if the reverse is the case.

If we increase the money supply, we obtain the familiar set of simultaneous linear equations

$$0 = (1 - C_y - I_y)\left(\frac{dY}{dm}\right) - I_i\left(\frac{di}{dm}\right)$$

$$1 = L_y\left(\frac{dY}{dm}\right) + L_i\left(\frac{di}{dm}\right)$$

From these equations it follows that

$$\frac{dY}{dm} = \frac{\begin{vmatrix} 0 & -I_i \\ 1 & L_i \end{vmatrix}}{\Delta} = \frac{I_i}{\Delta}$$

and

$$\frac{di}{dm} = \frac{\begin{vmatrix} (1 - C_y - I_y) & 0 \\ L_y & 1 \end{vmatrix}}{\Delta} = \frac{(1 - C_y - I_y)}{\Delta}$$

where

$$\Delta = \begin{vmatrix} (1 - C_y - I_y) & -I_i \\ L_y & L_i \end{vmatrix} = L_i(1 - C_y - I_y) + I_iL_y \tag{15-5}$$

Observe that the sign of Δ is ambiguous. $L_i < 0$, but $(1 - C_y - I_y)$ may be either positive or negative depending upon whether the marginal propensity to invest is greater or less than the marginal propensity to save. Consequently, we cannot tell whether the increase in the money supply will raise or lower the level of income and the rate of interest. Notice also that if we had retained our assumption of Part 2 that investment is not a function of the level of income, $I_y = 0$, we would have

$$\Delta' = L_i(1 - C_y) + I_iL_y \tag{15-6}$$

which is definitely negative. Thus an increase in the money supply would unambiguously raise the level of income and lower the rate of interest. But when $I_y > 0$, our comparative static analysis no longer gives unambiguous results, especially since we know very little about the value of I_y.

In this situation dynamic analysis can help us out. Let us assume, as we did in the text, that the rate of change of income is equal to the difference between intended investment and saving and that money market adjustments are instantaneous. This permits us to write the dynamic model

$$\frac{dY}{dt} = I(i,Y) - Y + C(Y) \tag{15-7}$$

$$m = L(i,Y) \tag{15-8}$$

where dY/dt is the rate of change of income.

To make further headway, we need to find linear approximations to these equations. What we can do is to assume that in the neighborhood of equilibrium the functions are linear. Accordingly, we apply Taylor's expansion and retain only linear terms. Equations (15–7) and (15–8) are therefore rewritten as

$$\frac{dY}{dt} = -(1 - C_y - I_y)(Y - Y_0) + I_i(i - i_0) \tag{15-9}$$

$$0 = L_y(Y - Y_0) + L_i(i - i_0) \tag{15-10}$$

where $Y - Y_0$ and $i - i_0$ are the deviations of income and the rate of interest from the equilibrium values Y_0 and i_0, respectively.

By substituting Eq. (15–10) into (15–9), we can reduce Eq. (15–9) to a linear first-order differential equation in Y. Such an equation has a solution of the form

$$Y = Y_0 + ae^{qt} \tag{15-11}$$

where a and q are constants and e is the base of the natural logarithmic system. If the term ae^{qt} is to disappear and Y is to return to Y_0, the root q must be negative.

By differentiating Eq. (15–11) with respect to time, we obtain

$$\frac{dY}{dt} = q(Y - Y_0) \tag{15-12}$$

Using this expression to replace dY/dt in Eq. (15–9) allows us to rewrite Eqs. (15–9) and (15–10) as

$$0 = -(1 - C_y - I_y + q)(Y - Y_0) + I_i(i - i_0) \tag{15-13}$$

$$0 = L_y(Y - Y_0) + L_i(i - i_0) \tag{15-14}$$

If these equations are to be valid for all values of the variables, the determinant formed by the coefficients must be zero. Accordingly,

$$0 = \begin{vmatrix} -(1 - C_y - I_y + q) & I_i \\ L_y & L_i \end{vmatrix} = [L_i(1 - C_y - I_y) + I_iL_y] + L_iq$$

Now observe that the term in square brackets is nothing other than Δ. Hence

$$\Delta + L_i q = 0$$

or

$$q = \frac{-\Delta}{L_i}$$

Since stability, i.e., a return of Y to Y_0 after a disturbance, requires that $q < 0$ and since we know definitely that $L_i < 0$, it follows that Δ must be negative.

Since we now know definitely that Δ must be negative if the system is stable, the logical step is to examine the properties of Δ and see what the stability condition implies. We know that

$$\Delta = L_i(1 - C_y - I_y) + I_i L_y < 0 \qquad (15\text{–}15)$$

This expression can easily be rearranged to read

$$\frac{(1 - C_y - I_y)}{I_i} + \frac{L_y}{L_i} < 0$$

From Eqs. (15–3) and (15–4) it is apparent that this is equivalent to

$$\left(\frac{di}{dY}\right)_{IS} - \left(\frac{di}{dY}\right)_{LM} < 0$$

In other words, the slope of the IS curve plus the slope of the LM curve with its sign changed must be negative. Recalling the three cases of the text, the first case, in which IS had a negative slope, clearly meets the stability condition. IS has a negative slope and LM has a positive slope. When we add the slope of the IS curve to the slope of the LM curve with its sign changed, the sum must be negative.

In the second case IS had a positive slope, but we still found the equilibrium to be stable. According to our condition for stability, this would imply that the positive value of the slope of IS must be absolutely less than the value of the slope of the LM curve. If we check back again to Figure 15–3, we can see that this is indeed the case.

In the third case the slope of the IS curve was greater than the slope of the LM curve. We found this situation to be unstable, a result that is confirmed by the mathematical analysis. In this case the sum of the slope of the IS curve and the slope of the LM curve with its sign changed will be positive. This means that Δ is positive; q will therefore also be positive; and the term ae^{qt} of Eq. (15–11) will grow progressively larger. The static equilibrium values Y_0 and i_0 are therefore irrelevant. Although the system may lodge at this point for a time, any disturbance will make the variables of the system deviate progressively from the equilibrium levels.

In summary: Stability analysis makes it possible to identify cases in which the results of comparative static analysis are erroneous. The present analysis, for example, has shown that if an increase in the money supply changes income at all, the change in income must be positive. This conclusion could not have been derived from comparative static analysis, and it is therefore evident that an examination of the underlying dynamics of the system is an important step which the careful analyst must take.

APPENDIX TO CHAPTER 16: THE GOLDEN RULE OF ACCUMULATION

Although a sophisticated analysis of the long-run growth process would employ a more general production function, our purpose here can be served by confining ourselves to the Cobb-Douglas function

$$Y = AK^aN^{1-a} \tag{16-1}$$

where K and N are the stock of capital and the labor supply, respectively, and A is an index of technical change. When we differentiate Eq. (16-1) with respect to time, we obtain

$$\frac{dY}{dt} = K^aN^{1-a}\frac{dA}{dt} + aAK^{a-1}N^{1-a}\frac{dK}{dt} + (1-a)AK^aN^{-a}\frac{dN}{dt}$$

which, via Eq. (16-1), can be written

$$\frac{dY}{dt} = \frac{Y}{A}\frac{dA}{dt} + a\frac{Y}{K}\frac{dK}{dt} + (1-a)\frac{Y}{N}\frac{dN}{dt}$$

Dividing both sides of this expression by Y gives the percentage rate of growth of output

$$\frac{1}{Y}\frac{dY}{dt} = \frac{1}{A}\frac{dA}{dt} + a\frac{1}{K}\frac{dK}{dt} + (1-a)\frac{1}{N}\frac{dN}{dt} \tag{16-2}$$

In the short run it would be possible for capital and output to grow at different rates. However, as a very long-run matter the two quantities, if they are both growing at a constant percentage (exponential) rate, must grow at the same rate. If this were not the case, investment would either be becoming a steadily larger or steadily smaller fraction of national income. Since investment is a component of national income, such differential growth rates are not permanently possible. Therefore since we have to assume that

$$\frac{1}{Y}\frac{dY}{dt} = \frac{1}{K}\frac{dK}{dt}$$

it follows from Eq. (16–2) that as a long-run matter

$$\frac{1}{Y}\frac{dY}{dt} = \frac{(1/A)\,(dA/dt)}{1-a} + \frac{1}{N}\frac{dN}{dt} \tag{16–3}$$

which confirms the result of the text that the rate of income growth depends on the rate of technical change and the rate of growth of the labor force, and that if technical change is absent no growth in per capita output is possible.

Under competitive equilibrium conditions the share of capital in the nation's output must equal the marginal product of capital times the quantity of capital. Returning to the production function, we see that

$$\frac{\partial Y}{\partial K} = aAK^{a-1}N^{1-a} = a\frac{Y}{K} \tag{16–4}$$

which means that the share of capital is

$$K\frac{\partial Y}{\partial K} = aY \tag{16–5}$$

and the share of labor, of course, must be

$$N\frac{\partial Y}{\partial N} = (1-a)Y \tag{16–6}$$

Notice also that

$$\frac{K}{Y}\frac{\partial Y}{\partial K} = a \quad \text{and} \quad \frac{N}{Y}\frac{\partial Y}{\partial N} = 1-a \tag{16–7}$$

These quantities are ratios of percentage changes and therefore elasticities. We denote a as the "capital elasticity of output" and $1-a$ as the "labor elasticity of output."

Now notice that the production function could just as well be written

$$Y^{1/(1-a)} = A^{1/(1-a)}\,K^{a/(1-a)}\,N$$

Let $B = A^{1/(1-a)}$ and divide both sides by N. This yields

$$\frac{Y}{N}\,Y^{a/(1-a)} = BK^{a/(1-a)}$$

Next divide both sides of this expression by $Y^{a/(1-a)}$ to obtain

$$\frac{Y}{N} = B\left(\frac{K}{Y}\right)^{a/(1-a)}$$

and observe that the level of per capita output is a function of the state of the arts B and the capital output ratio. To simplify the notation let Y/N be denoted by z and K/Y by x. We then have

$$z = Bx^{a/(1-a)} \tag{16–8}$$

which defines the level of per capita output.

Our problem is to find that saving ratio which maximizes per capita consumption through time. Let c stand for per capita consumption and note from Eq. (16–8) that

$$c = bz = bBx^{a/(1-a)} \tag{16–9}$$

Differentiation of Eq. (16–9) with respect to b and x yields

$$dc = Bx^{a/(1-a)} \, db + \frac{a}{1-a} bBx^{a/(1-a)\,-1} \, dx$$

Dividing through by c to obtain the percentage change in c and using Eq. (16–9), we obtain

$$\frac{dc}{c} = \frac{db}{b} + \frac{a}{1-a}\frac{dx}{x} \tag{16–10}$$

When c is a maximum, dc/c is zero so that Eq. (16–10) becomes

$$\frac{db}{b} = -\frac{a}{1-a}\frac{dx}{x} \tag{16–11}$$

One of the assumptions of neoclassical growth economics is that investment equals the full-employment level of saving. Consequently,

$$\frac{dK}{dt} = (1-b)Y$$

and from this it follows that

$$\frac{1}{K}\frac{dk}{dt} = (1-b)\frac{Y}{K} = (1-b)\frac{1}{x} \tag{16–12}$$

However, if the rate of technical change and the rate of growth of the labor force are constant, it is evident from Eq. (16–3) that the rate of growth of the capital stock must be constant, and this means that if we differentiate Eq. (16–12) with respect to b and x, we get

$$\frac{dx}{x} = \frac{-db}{1-b} \tag{16–13}$$

Using this result to substitute in Eq. (16–11), we obtain

$$\frac{db}{b} = \frac{a}{1-a}\frac{db}{1-b}$$

whence it follows that

$$a = 1 - b$$

Long-run maximization of per capita consumption is therefore attained if society saves and invests a fraction of income equal to the capital elasticity of output. To put the conclusion somewhat differently: Society should always consume its labor income and invest its competitive profits if it wishes to maximize per capita consumption over time.

APPENDIX TO CHAPTER 21: THE BURDEN OF THE DEBT

Domar performs his mathematical analysis of the burden of the debt with the help of differential equations. His results can also be obtained with the simple mathematics employed in Chapters 5 and 7 if we assume that magnitudes remain the same during a time period but change between time periods. Let the symbols used in the analysis be the same as in the text. The burden then will be

$$\gamma = \frac{iD_t}{iD_t + p_t Y_t} = \frac{1}{1 + (1/i)(p_t Y_t/D_t)} \tag{21-1}$$

from which it can easily be seen that the tax rate, given a constant rate of interest, depends uniquely on the ratio of money income to the debt. Assuming that α is the proportion of each year's income borrowed, the debt at the beginning of year t will be

$$D_t = D_0 + \alpha(p_0 Y_0 + p_1 Y_1 + p_2 Y_2 + \cdots + p_{t-1} Y_{t-1}) \tag{21-2}$$

One possibility considered by Domar is the case in which money income fails to grow at all. In this case Eq. (21–2) becomes

$$D_t = D_0 + \alpha p_0 Y_0 t$$

so that the ratio of debt to income,

$$\frac{D_t}{p_t Y_t} = \frac{D_0}{p_0 Y_0} + \alpha t$$

approaches infinity as time goes on. If money income fails to grow while the debt mounts, the tax rate needed to service the debt will ultimately approach 100 percent.

If the level of money income grows at a constant absolute amount β each year, income in year t will be

$$p_t Y_t = p_0 Y_0 + \beta t$$

so that, substituting in Eq. (21–2), we have for the debt

$$D_t = D_0 + \alpha p_0 Y_0 + \alpha\{[(p_0 Y_0 + \beta) + (p_0 Y_0 + 2\beta) \\ + \cdots + ([p_0 Y_0 + (t-1)\beta])]\}$$

or

$$D_t = D_0 + \alpha p_0 Y_0 t + \alpha\beta[1 + 2 + 3 + \cdots + (t-1)] \tag{21–3}$$

The term in the brackets is an arithmetic series which has the sum $t(t-1)/2$. Consequently, Eq. (21–3) becomes

$$D_t = D_0 + \alpha p_0 Y_0 t + \frac{\alpha\beta t(t-1)}{2} = D_0 + \alpha t\left(p_0 Y_0 - \frac{\beta}{2}\right) + \frac{\alpha\beta t^2}{2}$$

and the ratio of debt to income becomes

$$\frac{D_t}{p_t Y_t} = \frac{D_0 + \alpha t \,[p_0 Y_0 - (\beta/2)] + \alpha\beta t^2/2}{p_0 Y_0 + \beta t}$$

Because the square term dominates, the ratio of debt to income approaches infinity, and the tax rate approaches 100 percent of taxable income.

Finally, if income grows at a constant percentage rate r,

$$p_t Y_t = p_0 Y_0 (1 + r)^t$$

Substituting in Eq. (21–2), we have

$$D_t = D_0 + \alpha p_0 Y_0 [1 + (1 + r) + (1 + r)^2 + \cdots + (1 + r)^{t-1}]$$

The term in the brackets is a geometric series that has the sum $[(1 + r)^t - 1]/r$ so that

$$D_t = D_0 + \frac{\alpha p_0 Y_0 (1 + r)^t}{r} - \frac{\alpha p_0 Y_0}{r}$$

and the ratio of debt to money income becomes

$$\frac{D_t}{p_t Y_t} = D_0 + \frac{\{[\alpha p_0 Y_0 (1 + r)^t]/r\} - (\alpha p_0 Y_0/r)}{p_0 Y_0 (1 + r)^t}$$

As t grows larger and larger, this expression approaches the constant term α/r, so that the tax burden becomes

$$\gamma = \frac{1}{1 + r/i\alpha}$$

which increases as i, the rate of interest, increases and as α, the percentage of annual money income borrowed, increases and decreases as r, the rate of growth of money income, increases.

INDEX